The Chronicle of
Jean de Venette

NUMBER L OF THE RECORDS OF
CIVILIZATION, SOURCES AND STUDIES

Austin P. Evans, EDITOR

The Chronicle of Jean de Venette

Translated by

JEAN BIRDSALL

LATE ASSOCIATE PROFESSOR OF HISTORY
VASSAR COLLEGE

*Edited, with an Introduction
and Notes, by*

RICHARD A. NEWHALL

BROWN PROFESSOR OF EUROPEAN HISTORY
WILLIAMS COLLEGE

NEW YORK

Columbia University Press

1953

RECORDS OF CIVILIZATION, SOURCES AND STUDIES

EDITED UNDER THE AUSPICES OF THE
DEPARTMENT OF HISTORY, COLUMBIA UNIVERSITY

Editor

AUSTIN P. EVANS, Ph.D.
PROFESSOR EMERITUS OF HISTORY

Advisory Board

Preface

THE IDEA OF A TRANSLATION OF JEAN DE VENETTE'S CHRONICLE, BASED UPON THE MANUSCRIPT COPY IN the British Museum which previous editors have ignored, originated with Miss Birdsall more than twenty years ago. Working from a photostat, she completed her translation before her untimely death in 1935. It remained to provide explanatory notes for her text and to write an introduction discussing the author and describing the manuscript. This has been done by myself. During the checking of the translation with Géraud's published text of the chronicle it became clear that the translation seemed to vary in so many places from that text that it would be advisable to indicate how the manuscript text differed from the published text. This has required a large number of notes giving Latin phrases and passages. These serve not only to justify the translation, but they also help to explain wherein the manuscript may be regarded as a more complete and correct copy of Jean de Venette's original work.

Since the translation is Miss Birdsall's we are fortunate to have her comment on Jean de Venette's style.

His Latin is the Latin of a French peasant become a churchman—Latin which must often be turned back into the French in which he is thinking to be made comprehensible. He writes *per totum*—he is thinking *partout;* he writes *nam isti plus petebant, alii minus reddere volebant*—he is thinking *plus les uns, moins les autres;* he writes *ecce quod subito*—he is thinking *voilà que tout à coup*. In general, his style is at once incorrect and turgid. Vicious constructions are his common coin—interminable periods in which the most attentive reader loses the main idea in a throng of subordinate ideas. But passion serves as his substitute for style.

I am glad to express my thanks to Edith, Lady Payne-Gallwey, for her gracious permission to quote a long passage from the volume, *The Crossbow,* written by her husband, the late Sir Ralph Payne-Gallwey. Similar thanks are due to James MacLehose and Son, Publishers, of Glasgow, for permission to make quotation from *The Scalacronica of Sir Thomas Gray,* translated by Sir Henry Maxwell.

R. A. N.

Williamstown, Massachusetts
January 15, 1953

Contents

Introduction

Introduction

I. THE AUTHOR AND HIS WORK

Because a fifteenth-century copyist included the chronicle here translated at the end of his manuscript of the Latin chronicle of Guillaume de Nangis and his continuators, it was published as the final continuation (1340–68) of that chronicle. Consequently, for a long time our chronicler was referred to as the second continuator, or the final continuator, of Guillaume de Nangis. In actual fact he was neither. Since it has been shown that the continuation of Guillaume's chronicle from 1301 to 1340 has a double authorship, the term "second continuator" really belongs to the unknown writer of the later part of this section, who is also the final continuator, since it is now clear that there is no connection whatever between Guillaume de Nangis's work and the chronicle before us. But for more than two centuries publications and scholarly references to this work have treated it as a continuation; consequently this connection with Guillaume de Nangis has gained some sort of status by prescription.

The identification of the author rests upon internal evidence. As early as 1735 J.-B. de La Curne de Sainte-Palaye demonstrated [1] that he was the Carmelite friar, Jean de Venette, called "Fillons," author or translator of a long poem on the three Marys, which was written about 1357. Carmelite records show Jean de Venette to have been prior of the Paris convent from 1339 to 1342, becoming in the latter year head of the order's French province. In this capacity his name appears among those present at chapter general meetings until 1366. When the next of these meetings was held in May, 1369, a new provincial prior for France is listed.

Jean de Venette was reputed to have been particularly interested in promoting study among the younger brethren, and to have been active in gathering information on the antiquities of the Carmelite order. His concern with ignorance as the partner of sin appears in his comment on the effects of the Black Death upon elementary education.[2] It is not hard to see how a peasant boy who had become a master in theology at the University of Paris might have a lively interest in education. About 1360 he wrote a short history of the order for the instruction of *fratres juniores,* telling the story from the days of Elijah, the original Carmelite, until 1240, when two English barons first brought some Carmelite hermits to western Europe from the Holy Land.[3] The editors of this short chronicle mention the author as a master in theology and remark, "valde clarus in Ordine fuit Joannes de Vineta, Armoricus Brito, Prior Parisiensis, et Provincialis Franciae per plures annos." Since it is certain that this Jean de Venette must also be the author of our chronicle, the designation of him as a Breton is an error. Our author, by his own assertion,[4] was a native of Venette, a small village on the right bank of the river Oise, about two kilometers west from Compiègne in the modern department of the Oise.

It is always important to know as much as possible about a chronicler in order to evaluate his report, but in the case of Jean de Venette we could wish that we knew much more than we do, because his story has qualities of individuality and independence which are almost unique. For a long time scholars familiar with the usual forms of the monastic chronicle have been impressed with the notable difference in character which Jean de Venette has given to his work. "He writes," says his most recent editor, Géraud, "in a spirit diametrically opposed to that which generally animated medieval chroniclers, and particularly Guillaume de Nangis and his first continuators. This sort of revolt against the method and the ideas universally adopted, especially by ecclesiastical writers, gives our chronicler a character of marked originality." According to this same scholar, Jean de Venette compensates for the crudity of his style by a superiority in his manner of understanding and writing history.

Up until his time history was little more than a report. The facts were set forth in all their simplicity with no bond between them except chronology, no criticism, no comment, leaving the reader to disentangle cause and effect, to pass judgment upon men and events and institutions, while the historian, avoiding everything of that sort, made himself oblivious. But Jean de Venette follows a very different method. His bold and independent pen not only outlines the events which he observed or reported, but also includes his own impressions. He discusses, blames, and approves with complete freedom the acts of power, the excesses of the nobles, popular resistance. Participating at heart, and perhaps in action, in the civil struggles of his times, which drenched France in blood, he carries into his story of events all the independence of his point of view, all the warmth of his convictions. Feeling takes the place of talent and style, and for the first time, under the heavy burden of medieval Latin, history comes alive, takes on color and becomes dramatic in a way hitherto unknown.[5]

According to A. Molinier, Jean de Venette "has the spirit and the energy of a popular preacher" who was temporarily a partisan of Marcel and Charles of Navarre, but who soon rallied to the Valois side, although "without ever giving up his disposition to oppose and criticize." [6] Joseph Calmette calls him "a sincere interpreter from the lower classes" and credits him with an *esprit frondeur* entitling him somewhat to the standing of a democratic historian.[7] Patriotic admiration can be noted in all these comments.

Careful and thoughtful reading of this chronicle makes it somewhat hard to accept all of these exuberant characterizations of its author. That he was a democrat, a *frondeur,* a partisan, or indeed a participant in any real sense in the events of his time seems very doubtful. He was an interested but cautious observer, sharing in the current moods of public opinion, but he gives no sign of action. His sympathies with the peasants, who are the miserable victims of war, plague, and plunderers, are very real, but they are as much the feelings of a humane Christian as of a man from peasant stock. No doubt his peasant background enabled him to realize vividly the sufferings of the country people, and he takes pride in their legitimate success. But he certainly does not entertain any democratic sentiments, and his indifference to the Estates General is notable. The indignation which he shows towards the nobles is not a class antagonism, for it is due to his belief that they are not performing their proper function in society. It is their duty to protect the people from the ravages of war. But they are not doing this, either from cowardice or from love of ease. Yet at the same time, they continue to collect from the people the dues which are supposed to pay for such protection, or, even worse, they plunder the people themselves.

A passage dealing with the events of 1356 contains most of the items in his indictment. The nobles are blamed for the discord in the Estates General, which defeated the latter's efforts to provide effective rule for France.

From that time on all went ill with the kingdom and the state was undone. Thieves and robbers rose up everywhere in the land. The nobles despised and hated all others and took no thought for the mutual usefulness and profit of lord and men. They subjected and despoiled the peasants and the men of the villages. In no wise did they defend their country from its enemies. Rather did they trample it under foot, robbing and pillaging the peasants' goods.[8]

As an officer of the Carmelite monastery on the Place Maubert he would come in close touch with the refugees, both peasant and religious, driven to seek protection within the walls of Paris. As provincial of his order he would travel about from one monastery to another, and this would bring home to him the dangers of the road and would enable him to see over and over again the destruction of war and the devastation of the countryside. Repeatedly he records the appalling state of affairs and his own indignation at the failure of the ruling class to find a remedy.[9] "There was none to defend the people [against plunderers] nor to meet these dangers and perils [to travelers]. Rather did the burdens which bore so heavily upon the people seem to please the lords and princes whose duty it was to oppose and remedy these evils with a strong hand." [10] And here, like a good preacher, Jean de Venette illustrates his point with the fable of the dog and the wolf,[11] adding later the final repetition of his complaint. "Furthermore, the friends whose duty it was to protect our peasants and wayfarers were themselves, alas! all basely intent upon plundering and robbing travelers indiscriminately as if they were foes."

Probably Jean is giving expression to opinions widely held after the battle of Poitiers. Both his ideas and his words suggest such contemporary tracts as the *Tragicum argumentum de miserabili statu regni Francie* [12] and the "Complainte sur la bataille de Poitiers." [13] No doubt he shared the views which these set forth and in so doing reflected the popular feeling of the time. In recognizing the independent quality of Jean de Venette's history, a quality which gives it much of its unique value, we must recognize also the limitations under which he suffered as to his sources of information. Anything which was generally known he would know. Much of what he presents is clearly common report. At times he seems to be writing down facts or opinions drawn from the public speeches made by Marcel, the dauphin, and the king of Navarre in explanation and justification of their actions. At one point our author testifies that he was present in the crowd when Marcel reported to the people the murder of the marshals.[14] This passage is the chief ground for presenting Jean de Venette as a participant in the revolutionary activities of the year 1358. Here as elsewhere in his text, however, he seems to be writing of something he has seen and heard rather than of something which he has done.

When thinking of Jean de Venette as the champion of the common man, as some historians do, we should note that, while understanding the desperate fury of the peasants during the Jacquerie, nevertheless he condemns them for presuming to act without proper authority and for perpetrating atrocities upon the nobles, nor does he give any hint of censure on the treacherous way in which the peasant leaders were seized and killed. The peasant exploit which truly delights him, the defense of Longueil, was accomplished after the people had asked and received permission to fortify their strong house, both from the regent and from their local lord the abbot of Saint-Corneille. Their victory also, be it noted, was over the foreign enemy. Clearly obedience to legitimate authority is a virtue ranking high in the mind of a monastic official. It was "unnatural" for the Flemings to expel their count. It was improper for them to resume the interdicted church services before receiving papal permission. God protected the faithful clergy who obeyed the interdict even at their peril. The Flagellants were a fatuous and reprehensible sect because they were unauthorized, but they were praised for promptly obeying the papal order to disperse. This is an attitude of mind quite compatible with our author's condemnation of the ruling class for failure to do its duty.

However much Jean de Venette may display an approach to events different from that of the ordinary monastic chronicler, he is before all else a churchman, repeatedly expressing pious attitudes, voicing concern for the prevailing wickedness, hoping prayerfully that God in His goodness will mitigate the suffering of his people, and not unmindful of the practical, worldly interests of the Church. For him it is clearly a matter for satisfaction that so many plague victims died in grace, enjoying absolution and leaving "many inheritances and temporal goods to churches and monastic orders." [15] In addition he was a good Frenchman, much concerned with the tribulations of the kingdom of France. He is probably giving us unconsciously a glimpse of himself when he characterizes Marcel as "a man very solicitous for the commonweal." Yet it would be a mistake to consider him a partisan of Marcel or of Navarre. It is true that he reflects, rather vaguely, some of the temporary popularity of the latter, and on occasion he echoes the king of Navarre's speeches, to which he may have listened. His account does not sound like the official pro-Valois chronicles, which serve as striking illustration of how the victors write the history of events which future generations accept. But Jean de Venette knew nothing of the distinction between the Valois John "the Good" and the Navarrese Charles "the Bad." For him both of them were guilty of violent, brutal actions which he deplores. He seems to avoid an opinion on the strength of the latter's pretensions to the French crown or his claims to the Burgundian inheritance. Does he, in this connection, reflect a current phase of public opinion? With our knowledge of the six following centuries of French history we tend to forget that the Valois dynasty in the mid-fourteenth century, like the English Tudors at a later date, was struggling to hold the crown it had seized. It was a collateral line, not an upstart family, but there were other collateral lines asserting claims, which may well have appeared more valid to many in Jean de Venette's generation than they did in modern times to later royalist or patriotic French historians. Our chronicler shows that there was need for explaining that the disasters suffered by the Valois kings were due to God's displeasure with something other than the validity of their claims to the throne.

If Jean de Venette is anywhere a partisan, it is in the dispute between the prelates and the mendicant orders. Even here, however, he avoids polemics, being willing that God and the pope should defend the right. The account which he offers of this controversy is one of the unique items in his chronicle, but he himself recognizes that it is a digression from his main theme. Perhaps there is the partisan satisfaction of a regular in his recording of the election of a Benedictine abbot instead of a cardinal as pope, but he is very cautious in registering his approval. Possibly he is guilty of *Schadenfreude* with respect to high churchmen impoverished by the war, but he covers it with a moral cloak.

Instead of being a partisan or a *frondeur,* our author seems in fact to have been very careful in his observations. While having opinions of his own as to what is just and right, he shows himself a man who is on his guard against accepting every common report. He understands clearly how improbable are the charges against the Jews at the time of the Black Death. He also shows that he recognizes the propaganda of the Spanish pretender, Henry of Trastamare, for what it is, although he has no other source of information on Spanish affairs. There is even a touch of pathos in his patriotic skepticism regarding the report that the Burgundians had come to terms with the enemy, followed sadly by the admission that it was really true. At times he gives the impression of a man looking on both sides of a question, or of one who is neutral on the matters at issue, or of a cautious person protecting himself from censure by expressions of obedience. John of Montfort is called a rebel and the cause of his rival is labeled just, but Jean de Venette rejoices when the former's victory at Auray brings a peace which he hopes will last. This attitude of partial aloofness does not extend to enemies of the Church, and Lewis the Bavarian is never mentioned without being stigmatized as a usurper. But when Jean was writing Lewis had been dead for some years, and his usurpation was no longer part of an active controversy.

Should we attempt to determine some leading purpose behind the writing of this chronicle, it would seem to lie in Jean de Venette's interest in the validity and interpretation of astrological portents and of prophecies. Alongside of this we can see the good Frenchman and the good churchman much concerned about the long continued success enjoyed by the enemies of the king and the Church. There also appears the mind of a man who realizes that he himself has witnessed a series of extraordinary and calamitous events, famines, wars, and pestilence, such as had not "been heard of or seen or read of in times past," and which were worthy to be recorded. Jean de Venette shared with his contemporaries the interest in portents and prophecies. For a long time these had been a matter of special interest in certain circles among the mendicants, but there is nothing but this chronicle to connect Jean de Venette with such circles. He begins and ends his story with a comet, and prefaces his history with a couple of prophecies and a promise of more to come. While carefully refusing to commit himself "whether [these prophecies] speak truth or not," he makes a point of recording events which seem to him to be the fulfillment of prophecy, and he promises to note any similar fulfillments which may occur at later dates. Apparently he regarded the prophecy of 1356 as applying so clearly to the events which followed that it was unnecessary to indicate the specific connection. Possibly his statement relative to the election of a Benedictine abbot as Pope Urban V, "But I firmly believe that the cause is not hidden from the Holy Spirit," may be an extremely cautious indication that he connects this unexpected choice of a monastic pope with the prophecy that "after tribulations and dangers in Christendom, the mercy of the Lord shall come to his desolate people and an angelic vicar of Christ shall be sent from the heart of Christ to make all wills His and to bring back all ecclesiastics to Christ's and the Apostles' way of life." [16] But when he refers to Edward III as a "second Antiochus" he is showing clearly that he associates the events of 1359–60, which were taking place while he was writing, with the prophecies of Jean de la Roche-Taillade.[17] Jean de Venette protects himself from censure by writing, "One must not put trust in [these prophecies], since the Church does not approve," but he promises that "if any of it shall come to pass hereafter, in whole or in part, it will be so stated in the following pages." [18] He is much impressed with the saintly, sober and honest life of Jean de la Roche-Taillade, whose books he had read: "Though I put no trust in them, yet have I seen many of the events which they prognosticate come to pass. Nor do I think it impossible that God may have revealed much to him as He has aforetime to the holy fathers, for example, in interpretations of the sacred prophecies."

Since the chief interest in Jean de Venette's story arises from its contemporary character, it is important to determine as best we can the time when it was written. Molinier states that "it was certainly written from day to day for the years 1358–1359," [19] but a careful study of the internal evidence does not support this assertion. From his own statement we know that Jean was writing about the English invasion when news reached Paris of the agreement made by the Burgundians with King Edward on March 10, 1360.[20] A few paragraphs later he wrote, "I have thought fit to write down on these pages as clearly as I could the events which I know to have occurred up to this time in March of this year." [21] This could mean that much, perhaps all, of his history up to that date was completed. But must we assume that he wrote the chronicle from the beginning in 1340 continuously to that date? The disjointed, annalistic character of the narrative requires no such assumption. It could easily have been written piecemeal in the preliminary stages of composition, and it would seem reasonable to suppose that the parts dealing with affairs more nearly contemporary with March, 1360, were jotted down first, while the author's recollections were fresh in his mind. At the same time he could be gathering information and could write the earlier part as a sort of necessary introduction to the narrative of the really important events of the later 1350s.

Internal evidence provides considerable data for formulating a theory on the date of composition. Reference to the peace of Pontoise in the part dealing with the events of 1358 shows that that section must have been written after King John and King Charles came to terms on August 21, 1359.[22] But the section on 1359 prior to the English invasion was written before the French recovered Creil, an event which probably occurred in late November, 1359.[23] Were we to assume from this that Jean de Venette wrote most of his story during the fall, winter, and spring of 1359–60 it would be compatible with the other internal evidence. In his section on 1347 he refers to the marriage of Philip de Rouvre, duke of Burgundy, in a way which shows that he must have been writing after 1357, the year of the marriage, and before November, 1361, when the young duke died.[24] In the section on 1349 there is allusion to the marriage of a French princess to the duke of Milan. The betrothal in this case was in May, 1360, and the marriage in September. But this is a place where Jean de Venette makes a serious error of fact by naming the wrong man as bridegroom.[25] It is suggested that this would not have happened had the wedding actually taken place when the account was being written, but might have happened if Jean were writing while marriage negotiations with Milan were in progress, which would be in the period just preceding the betrothal. The comment at the end of the section on 1356 about the construction of extra defenses for Paris, which were also "diligently pursued the next year and thereafter," [26] is phrased to suggest a time of writing later than 1358. And when recounting an episode of December, 1357, Jean's aside indicates that the ditches around Saint-Germain-des-Prés had been dug between that date and the time when he was writing.[27] This digging could have been done in the spring of 1358, or in the early part of 1360.[28] It is hard to believe that the story about the prelates and the mendicants in the last part of 1357 could have been written after the death of the archbishop of Armagh (November 16, 1360), without making mention of that occurrence.[29] In the whole history of the period 1340–60 all other references to subsequent events, of which there are about a dozen,[30] apply to happenings between 1354 and 1360. Looking for some particular reason why Jean de Venette should be moved to write history late in 1359, we discover that it was then that the English destroyed his native village.[31] In this connection he wrote a literary description of the desolated countryside, indicating how keenly he felt the devastation caused by the war. He also recounted the story of Grandferré and the defense of Longueil, explaining that this took place near his home and remarking upon the pleasure which he felt in telling this tale of peasant valor.[32]

An analysis of the whole chronicle for the period 1340–60 leaves the impression that the really important part of the story begins with 1354. If this is correct, then Jean de Venette agreed with the author of the *Chronique du Mont-Saint-Michel,* who regarded the murder of Charles of Spain as the beginning of a series of disasters for France.[33] But the events of 1354 and 1355 seem to have been regarded by our author as a unit,[34] a sort of preface to the "still more noteworthy events" which he introduces with the prophecies of Jean de la Roche-Taillade. Were we to assume that Jean de Venette originally planned to begin with these prophecies and intended to show how events were their fulfillment, it would not be hard to imagine that soon he found it necessary to write about earlier events in order to explain the feud between the kings of France and Navarre. This, however, can never be more than a matter for speculation.

A curious problem, difficult to solve, appears in this connection.

The story of 1354 opens with a statement about an earthquake which destroyed the city of Basel. One of the interesting variants of the Arundel manuscript, on which this translation is based, is the addition of a phrase showing that the author himself was at Reims when the earthquake was felt there. An earthquake in western Europe is sufficiently unusual so that we might expect one to make quite an impression on any observer. This particular earthquake excited considerable attention because of its violence, and it is widely mentioned in the chronicles.[35] Nevertheless our author, although accurate as to the day of the month, makes an error of two years in his date. The earthquake actually occurred in 1356. Did he make an extremely careless mistake or is he resorting to a deliberate literary device? Modern scholars are so devoted to high standards of chronological exactitude, and are so accustomed to calendars, almanacs, and other aids for securing such exactitude, that they find it hard to imagine Jean de Venette's situation and probable point of view. He has a sufficiently large number of chronological errors to permit us to suspect him of a somewhat nonchalant attitude towards exactitude. While this may scandalize the scholar it will probably be condoned, even today, by the popular preacher who, like our Carmelite chronicler, is chiefly interested in drawing a lesson and pointing a moral. Can we believe seriously that after only four years, he could not remember when he was at Reims, or that this earthquake occurred a month after the battle of Poitiers? But in addition the rest of his story for 1354 excites question. He only includes events which happened between January 8 and March 4 of that year. These, since they were before Easter, would ordinarily have been put by the author in the latter part of 1353.[36] May we assume that Jean, despite his nonchalance towards correct dating, felt obliged as an annalist to record something for each year, and that he distributed his data accordingly when he found himself without interesting items for particular years?[37] May we also assume that he liked to begin a story with some unusual natural phenomenon and used the earthquake in the absence of a convenient comet? Again, it is impossible to do more than speculate.

In connection with this attempt to ascertain the probable time of composition, there are certain other matters on the precise dating of events which merit consideration. For that part of the chronicle dealing with the thirteen years before 1354 there are only five indications of time other than the year, two for the month only and three for the day as well.[38] One of these, August, 1348, when a strange star appeared in the evening, cannot be verified as to its accuracy. Two of the others, the dates for the battle of Crécy and for King John's coronation, are wrong by a day. But when we come to the years 1354–58 there are nine indications of time, five of them precise dates.[39] Of these the first one, the Basel earthquake, is correct as to day but, as previously discussed, wrong by two years. Three others are correct and are for such outstanding events as the murder of the marshals, the massacre of the Paris militia at Saint-Cloud, and the death of Marcel. The fifth one, referring to the Rouen funeral of Navarre's friends, is put incorrectly on Innocents' Day (December 28, 1357), when in fact it was nearly two weeks later.[40] The probable explanation for this is that burial was in the chapel of the Innocents in Rouen cathedral. Two of the more general efforts at dating are not particularly accurate. To mention the escape of Charles of Navarre, which was in November, 1357, as being "a little before" February 22, 1358 [41] is certainly not very precise, nor would events of August ordinarily be described as before Christmas.[42] It may be significant, however, that in this portion of his work Jean de Venette shows that he is carefully dating his years from Easter. King John's arrest of Charles of Navarre (April 5, 1356) is put in Lent, 1355, i.e., before Easter (April 24), 1356. When referring to the murder of the marshals (February 22, 1358) he explicitly states "these things were done in the year 1357, according to the reckoning of France, on the feast of the Chair of Saint Peter." [43]

Precise and correct dates become numerous in that part of the chronicle dealing with late 1359 and particularly with the spring of 1360. There are as many dated statements for this period as for all the preceding years, and there are no good reasons for doubting their accuracy. Clearly history is here being written as events took place, or shortly afterwards, as the chronicler indicated when he mentioned the Burgundian treaty with the English. Here also is found a definite statement about his dating when he writes, "Towards the end of the year 1359, beginning the year with Easter as one should in all piety." [44] His first reference to the weather is also in this section.[45] This is a subject which interests him, but we recognize it as a form of information more likely to be recorded contemporaneously than to be set down from memory after any considerable lapse of time.

That our author, in first instance, wrote his chronicle continuously from the beginning is not a necessary assumption. It is suggested that his impulse to write came when he learned of the burning of Venette and of the peasant success at Longueil. He then wrote about that episode, including the literary passage describing the desolation of his native village. Becoming aware that this was merely part of a series of great events, which he himself had seen and which might be the fulfillment of prophecies, he wrote down the prophecy of Jean de la Roche-Taillade and proceeded to tell the story of its fulfillment. But this made it clear that the beginning of this story consisted of those "misfortunes and noteworthy events [which] took place in the years 1354 and 1355," [46] so he wrote them as a prelude. He also realized that the English war was another important part of the story requiring explanation, so he wrote his introduction,[47] properly provided with prophecies, and followed it with a summary of events through 1345. One of the chief peculiarities of this early part of the chronicle is its chronological confusion. Jean de Venette's methods of research are unknown, but this section might have been written by a man with a retentive memory who had read another contemporary chronicle without taking notes. That Jean sometimes thought his history backward appears from his chapter on 1357, which begins with an event of February 22, 1358 (N.S.) and then tells what went before.

Turning to the chapters covering the years 1346 through 1353, we note the first of those great events which Jean de Venette saw with his own eyes, the English invasion and the enemy army burning villages up to the very walls of Paris. It is possible to see in his narrative of this a vague allusion to the more formidable invasion of 1360.[48] This is followed by the story of Calais siege (1347), which he may well have heard from a refugee friar in his own monastery.[49] The Black Death (1348) was something he could easily write from his own memory even after ten years. The Flagellants, the Jubilee, and the first part of the controversy between the prelates and the mendicants would be topics of special interest to a religious, and the last of these would have been brought to his mind when he wrote about the more recent phase of the dispute under the year 1357. For the last three years of this period our author seems to be running short of material. Most of what he offers would be of interest to a churchman but is not particularly germane to his subject. Where it might have had some appropriate bearing upon his topic of the wars afflicting the French kingdom, such as the local warfare against the English in 1353, he is without information. This may indicate that he is writing quite a while afterwards, when stories of local activities, numerous enough in the sections for 1359 and the following years when they were items of current interest, were not easily available. Possibly at this point Jean de Venette was chiefly interested in linking the early part of his chronicle with the really important section.

If we assume some sort of preliminary composition, the narrative in its final form appears to have been put together or recast with the plan of the whole period from 1340 to 1360 clearly in mind. When presenting the introductory prophecy the author shows that he already plans the insertion of "another and clearer prophecy in its proper place below." He repeatedly indicates his intention to describe the events which develop from some episode in such way as to imply not only that he knew what had happened, but also that he had planned what he would write. The affairs of Brittany in 1341, for instance, "did not remain peaceably settled. . . . On the contrary, many ills and great wars very soon grew out of it, as shall be described below." When he concluded his prelude, his promise to describe the extraordinary events and misfortunes which befell France, and which he himself had seen and heard, would indicate a plan about to be carried out. When first referring to King Charles of Navarre he adds, "Of him I shall speak hereafter"; and when he comes to the reconciliation in 1354 of King Charles and King John his comment is, "Alas, it did not last nor endure long, as shall be told afterward." Other phrases of this sort indicating clear knowledge of what will appear later in the text are to be found at several other points in the sections preceding 1360.[50] This gives added support to the theory that this portion of the chronicle was planned and written in the fall, winter, and spring of 1359–60. That the earlier part was complete when the section on 1356 was being written appears from the reference to the previous comment on the shocking dress of the nobility.[51]

It is in this preliminary part that we find considerable confusion, not only as to chronology, but also with regard to some of the royal and noble persons about whom Jean de Venette was writing. His information about the dukes of Brittany is garbled.[52] He persists in calling the father of Philip de Rouvre a duke of Burgundy,[53] although he never succeeded to the duchy because he predeceased Duke Eudes IV by several years. He is badly confused as to the Valois princesses.[54] Probably these inaccuracies indicate an indifference to inconsequential detail similar to his nonchalance toward over-exact chronology. When this first part was completed can only be surmised. Jean himself indicates that it was finished by 1365,[55] but his statement does not show how long it had been finished at that time. It seems probable that it had been complete for several years, since it is hard to believe that the section on the Black Death (1348) could have been written after the recurrence of the plague in 1363 without some allusion to the later epidemic. It is even possible to argue that the epidemic of 1361 in England would have been noticed in some way if this earlier section had not already been completed by that year. As things stand, it is a reasonable assumption that the whole chronicle through 1360 had been written by the end of that year.

For the period following 1360 the narrative takes on characteristics which are in considerable contrast with the earlier parts. There is more miscellaneous information. There are many more indications of time, both precise and general. There are more frequent references to the weather and the crops, and to interesting stars. All this suggests that the author, having completed his history of events from 1340 to 1360, is jotting down memorable occurrences in preparation for writing additional sections of his original work. At intervals he seems to have taken these notes and written up his annals from them.

The first section of continuation seems to cover 1361–63, and it is suggested that Jean wrote up his notes for those years during the spring of 1364, beginning in March and finishing some time in May. His comment on the winter of 1361–62 could not have been written as it stands until the latter part of 1363 at the earliest.[56] His section on King John's visit to Avignon was written after the king's return to Paris in the summer of 1363, but it was also written in the same year in which he made the journey since the author uses the phrase, "this present year." [57] Such a phrase, however, could have been used accurately as late as March 23, 1364. From his own statement we know that he was writing the section on 1363 after King John's death (April, 1364), and the ejaculation of sorrow relative to the king's death suggests that he was writing that particular paragraph soon after the sad news arrived.[58] The description of the very cold winter of 1363–64, which follows this, was written before the year was far enough advanced to show what bad effects came of it. "With God's favor I shall describe what sort of season for vines and fruit ensued when I treat and write of the events of the next year." [59] This could have been written in April or May. If he were writing his story currently, or writing up each year by itself, it is hard to see how he would make the chronological errors which he does make in the short sections on 1361 and 1362. In three instances, the deaths of the duke of Burgundy and the duke of Lancaster, and the royal proclamation of good money, he puts the item in the wrong year.[60] The error of a month in the death of Pope Innocent is perhaps to be explained by the way news would travel from Avignon to Paris, so that an event at the Curia of mid-September might not be known in Paris until October.[61]

Considerable time must have elapsed before he again sat down to write, because the promise quoted above, to tell how the harvest was affected by the very cold winter, is completely forgotten. When he did make the record of 1364 he had so much to write about that he found no place for agricultural items. The long section covering 1364 and 1365 was apparently being written up in the summer of 1365. The part on 1364 was being written after the prisoners captured at Auray had been ransomed,[62] and it seems probable that one of the most prominent, Bertrand du Guesclin, was held until some time in 1365, perhaps as late as August. It is possible that the comment on Du Guesclin's appointment as count of Longueville actually applies to a promise made by him in August, 1365.[63] It is clear that the account of the troubles at Tournai, which forms the last part of the story of 1364, was written after the royal letters of March 14, 1365, had been issued, but before the pacifying influence of those letters had declined and affairs in the city had again become disturbed.[64] But why Jean should have begun his account of 1364 with the story of the controversy between the citizens of Reims and their archbishop, an affair which happened a year before, is completely baffling.[65] He tells us himself that he was writing the history of 1365 when news reached Paris which must have been in a papal letter written in Avignon on June 9, 1365,[66] and the following portion for this year could well have been written in July, immediately following the successful peace negotiations in June. It must have seemed to Jean that these really marked the end of his story. The English war had ended in 1360, and now in 1364 and 1365 the Breton [67] and Navarrese wars were also concluded. When he wrote "Amen" [68] we may believe he felt that he was ending the chapter, although he knew some pessimists doubted the permanence of peace in Brittany. Jean himself is beginning to have doubts as to how much longer he may be spared to write history. He promises to tell his readers whether or not the pessimists proved to be correct "if I live," [69] and he injects a cautious "perhaps" into his promise to report later what might come of the crusade.[70]

The story of 1366 is devoted entirely to the Spanish campaign and must have been written after the battle of Nájera (April 3, 1367), but before it could be known in Paris how extensively that victory had effected the situation in Spain. Any time in the late spring would meet this requirement. As for the last two years, 1367–68, they appear to have been written up about the middle of April, 1368. The section on 1367 covers only three topics. Of these the papal move from Avignon to Rome would be known to Jean de Venette only by hearsay. The other two, the great storm at Boulogne and the student affray in Paris, were within his personal experience. The first topic concludes with the statement that the pope and the Curia journeyed to Rome where they remained "to this day." [71] This could have been written only after their arrival in Rome on October 16, 1367, and it implies that some time had elapsed since that date. The other two episodes both took place in December, 1367. The story of the storm is so long and circumstantial that it scarcely requires the words "as I myself saw" [72] to indicate that the author himself was in Boulogne at the time, and that fact offers an easy explanation for the space which he

devotes to it. The account of the row between the students and the
police was written after the burial from the Carmelite church of the
student victim. This took place "after the lapse of some time," [73] when
the body had been recovered from the river. But clearly Jean de
Venette did not know that the release of the police sergeants had been
ordered on April 13, 1368. The following section shows that he was at
Reims at that time. But the passage on the comet, which he saw at
Reims, provides the evidence indicating that the concluding part of
the chronicle was written before April 22, 1368.[74] Indeed, the reference to "Easter Day" [75] in the final paragraph gives ground for thinking that the work was finished on April 9.[76] This recurrence of a
comet provided our author with the same sort of event with which he
started his story. The wheel had come full circle. He seems to have
welcomed the occasion to write his conclusion.

2. THE MANUSCRIPT

In 1878 Léopold Delisle called attention to the existence at the
British Museum of a manuscript copy of the chronicle of Jean de
Venette.[1] He ascribed this to the late fourteenth or early fifteenth
century, and said it deserved to be collated with Géraud's published
text because it seemed to promise useful emendations. The very first
sentence, he remarked, contained the additional word "Parisius," not
found in the other manuscripts, and indicating more explicitly the
author's locale.[2] Twenty years later Eugène Déprez, in an article
"Une Tentative de réforme du calendrier sous Clément VI: Jean
de Murs et la chronique de Jean de Venette," [3] stated that he was preparing a new edition of this chronicle based upon this British Museum
text, which would appear in the *Collection des textes pour servir à
l'enseignement de l'histoire.* More recently this title was included in
the announcement for the series "Les Classiques de l'histoire de France
au moyen âge," to be published under the auspices of the Association
Guillaume Budé. Géraud, when editing the chronicle of Guillaume
de Nangis and his continuators for the Société de l'histoire de France
in the early 1840s, might have utilized this text, since the printed
Catalogue of Manuscripts in the British Museum, which indicates its
existence, was published in 1834, but he took no notice of it, and
presumably confined his work to Paris. Roland Delachenal, in con-

ducting the researches for the first three volumes of his *Histoire de Charles V,* which were published in 1909–16, consulted this manuscript for whatever new information it might offer. Miss Birdsall made the present translation from a photostat of it and from Géraud's published text. This Arundel manuscript unquestionably offers an independent version, unrelated, except through the original, to the manuscripts used by Géraud and the earlier editors, and there are very good reasons for thinking that it is an earlier and superior text, following the original more closely than the others.

The two earliest editions of the chronicle of Guillaume de Nangis and his continuators, including Jean de Venette, made by the Benedictine editors at Saint-Maur, were based upon a single manuscript described by Géraud as written in a bad fifteenth-century hand. It had been part of the library at the monastery of Saint-Germain-des-Prés. It is still in the Bibliothèque Nationale (fonds Saint-Germain, No. 435; regroupé: Lat. 11729) Dom Luc d'Achery, the first editor, also had available some variant readings from a manuscript in the Dijon library, which had formerly belonged to the abbey of Citeaux and was written in the last quarter of the fifteenth century. Apparently Géraud, in preparing his edition, did not consult this manuscript directly but contented himself with the variants which D'Achery had published in Volume XIII of *Spicilegium.* He did compare his basic text with two other manuscripts. One of these (Bib. Nat., fonds Saint-Germain, No. 999; regroupé: Lat. 13704) he describes as written in an equally bad fifteenth-century hand as No. 435, on which he concluded it was based. The variant readings he ascribed to a Renaissance copyist, who sought to improve on the medieval Latin of his original. The second manuscript, which confines itself to the continuators, is much later, and the handwriting seems to be that of two distinguished seventeenth-century scholars, André Duchesne and Etienne Baluze.[4] Géraud thinks it is based upon a text different from either of the other two.

When we turn from these to the Arundel manuscript we find we are dealing with a very different text from those previously studied and published. This manuscript consists of twenty-five parchment folios, with forty-seven full pages and one half page of writing. This means that, as far as the text of our chronicle is concerned, the last

folio is blank. At the bottom of the first page of this folio there is a
note in a good fifteenth-century hand stating that this chronicle recounts the events of sixty-eight years, that is, from 1301 to 1368, and
that it belongs to someone with the monogram AA. Clearly then we
have only the last half of a manuscript which originally included the
whole continuation of the chronicle of Guillaume de Nangis, but was
not itself connected with that chronicle when it came into AA's possession. Each page has been carefully ruled with lines for the copyist,
forty-three lines to the page, except folio 15, which has forty-four on
both sides, making a total of 2,050 lines of text. The writing is in a very
good book hand, highly abbreviated but very legible. It has been
carefully corrected,[5] and the corrector made note of the completion
of his work at the bottom of the last page. The margins are wide, and
spaces were left for ornamental initial letters, but these were never
filled in. The first third of the manuscript, through folio 9r, has been
marked with certain words in red indicating the subject matter. None
of these have been included in the translation. The capital letters at
the beginnings of sentences have been touched with red, and frequently the dates have been underlined in red. Occasionally such items
as the titles of Jean de la Rochetaillade's writings or the name of a
popular song are also underlined in the same way. Once or twice a
whole word is in red. But from folio 9v on, except for folio 17v and
two words (*Sepulto rege*) on folio 19v, this rubrication is lacking.
This also seems to indicate that the copyist stopped before his work
was finished. Presumably this was a work of calligraphy intended for
some book collector and probably made to order.

The chief differences between this Arundel text and that of the
other manuscripts are those of length and style. More than five
hundred readings different from Géraud's published text will be
found noted in the pages which follow. These do not include mere
variation in word order. Nearly three hundred of them are additional
words and passages. Thirteen of the latter are of some notable length,
the shortest of eleven words, the longest of one hundred and forty-
two. The remainder are phrases where the Latin of the Arundel text
differs in form but not, generally speaking, in meaning from that
of the other texts. Consideration of these differences leads quickly
to the conclusion that the Arundel text is very probably much more

closely related to Jean de Venette's original than the other copies. It is easy to see how a copyist would omit words which he thought were superfluous and passages which seemed to him uninteresting, but it is incredible that he would go in for interpolation on a large scale and without apparent pattern or purpose. The outstanding example is a long passage describing the rural devastation prevailing in 1359.[6] Here we can see Jean de Venette struggling to give literary expression to his personal feelings, and we can also see some copyist, better schooled in classical Latin, saving time and space by omitting a paragraph for which he felt contempt and which added nothing to the story. Again our peasant author, when referring to Grandferré's heavy ax,[7] could add quite naturally *seu guysarmiam,* and the copyist could, with equal naturalness, omit this unnecessary and barbaric phrase. In general, it may be admitted that most of the additional phrases and words could be omitted without injury to the sense, and often with improvement to the style. Two of the additions, however, refer to the author himself, one in the first sentence placing him in Paris, and the other indicating that he himself was at Reims when the earthquake was felt there. These could hardly be interpolations, and the second of them is in the first person. Another peculiarity of the Arundel text is its greater accuracy as to proper names and their correct spelling. This too suggests close relationship to the original. The final item is in the last section, the blank space left in the text for the period during which the comet was visible.[8] If this was in the original, as it might well have been, a careful copyist would include it in his copy, but he certainly would not have inserted a blank had the original read *per plures dies.*

It would be possible to offer further data in support of the superiority and completeness of the Arundel text, but to do so would be laboring the obvious. The form of writing indicates that it is much earlier than any of the other manuscripts, and it is not impossible to think that it was made directly from the original within a relatively short time after Jean de Venette's death, while enthusiasm for Bertrand du Guesclin was strong.[9] In all probability there is no relationship between this copy and any of the other existing manuscripts. There are more than fifty places where the Arundel text lacks words and phrases which are to be found in the manuscripts used by Géraud.

Since, in general, the latter agree among themselves on these varia-
tions, and since they also agree in omitting the passages peculiar to
the Arundel manuscript, we may reasonably conclude that they are
all derived from a copy made from the original but now lost; and that
such copy would be the one in which all the words and passages now
found only in the Arundel text were deliberately omitted in the
interest of style and space. It is suggested therefore that D'Achery's
original manuscript, the Citeaux manuscript, and the Duchesne-
Baluze copy were all derived from this lost copy, and that Géraud's
second manuscript was derived from D'Achery's original.

The history of the Arundel manuscript can only be a matter of
speculation based upon limited information, most of which is to be
found in the markings on the manuscript itself. In the British Museum
it forms part of the Arundel collection, which takes its name from
Thomas Howard, earl of Arundel (1592–1646), a friend of Cotton,
Selden, and Camden, and a collector of books and manuscripts. But
this particular manuscript has at the top of the first page the name
of William Howard, the date 1590, and, at the bottom, a drawing
of a lion rampant on an ermine cap of maintenance, which may be
recognized as a Howard crest. This must refer to Earl Thomas's
uncle, Lord William Howard of Naworth, and is presumed to be
in his handwriting. This same William Howard owned a manuscript
copy of Walsingham's *Historia Anglicana,* which he marked in the
margins.[10] His markings of Jean de Venette's text seem to be confined to the first folio. In the second line he underlined the words
"quam ego frater quidam" and wrote in the margin "Quare quis
author." A few lines below in the first of Jean's prophecies he underlined "genus sancti Petri vituperabatur," a phrase not without interest
to one who had experienced the Elizabethan phases of the English
Reformation. Two lines below this he underlined "vidi dum eram"
and wrote "Author" in the margin. None of the later references in
the chronicle to its author have any similar markings. Fifteen lines below the last mark Howard underlined the name in the text and wrote
"Johannes de Muris" in the margin. Lower on this same margin but
without underlining in the text he wrote "Phillippus Valesius rex
francia filius Caroli fratris Philippi regis Pulchri," and in the margin
opposite the last line "Robertus de Artois Guliel comes Flannonia."

In the text he underlined "Guilli" here, but that is to be associated with a correction which he made at the top of the next page, where by mistake the copyist wrote *"Johannes"* and Howard underlined it and wrote in the margin "Gulielmus in pagina precedente." Somewhat farther down on this margin is a sketch of the English coat of arms with the French lilies, which looks as if it were made with the same pen as Howard's marginal notes. After that there is nothing more except the marginal note on folio 6*v*,[11] which may be in Howard's hand, jeering at an earlier annotation respecting the pope's defense of the friars.

But on the back of the last folio there are more of Howard's markings. The man who copied Jean de Venette's chronicle left this page blank but sometime in the late fifteenth century someone covered this last page with a series of brief statements relating to the events in England in 1471. William Howard underlined the names of the battle of Barnet and the mention of Lord John Howard, baron, a member of King Edward's party. Possibly it was this page rather than Jean de Venette's chronicle which excited William Howard's interest in this manuscript. These "Yorkist Notes" for 1471 have been published by C. L. Kingsford in his *English Historical Literature in the Fifteenth Century*.[12] He thinks they were all written at the same time, shortly after September 22, 1471. For our purpose these are interesting because they indicate that our manuscript was in England at that time. On the margins of the chronicle of Jean de Venette there are ten annotations in a hand very similar to that in which the notes are written, although it cannot be stated for certain that it is the same hand. With one exception, these notes are confined to the early pages of the chronicle. The exception is a *Notus* beside the story of the transfer of Dauphiné to the Valois dynasty (folio 20*v*). Of the others the last is opposite Jean de la Roche-Taillade's prophecy (folio 17*v*). This last one thanks God that John's prediction of clerical spoliation had proved false, the one preceding it calls attention to the pope's defense of the mendicants.

There are several other sets of marginal markings, but when they were made and who made them is hard even to surmise. We have already remarked upon the note at the bottom of folio 25. This reads, "Memorandum quae hec cronica contenet gesta tantum lxviii annos viz ab anno domino ~~130~~ 1301 usque ad annum 1368 Et pertenet ad me AA." This is in a clear, large fifteenth-century hand, which could be earlier than 1471. On the pages of the chronicle there are four (perhaps five) annotations in letters similar to this, only smaller, suggesting that these may be AA's notes. The first is a marginal note reading, "Benedictus papa XII ordinis cisterciensis" (folio 12). Since no similar notice is taken later of any other popes, and the text here merely mentions this pope's death without reference to his order, this suggests the possibility of a special Cistercian interest. This gains plausibility from the fact that two of the other marginal notes in this group are notes calling attention to the paragraphs on extravagant styles (folios 8, 23). The fourth (folio 7*v*) does the same for Jean de la Roche-Taillade, "fratre ordinis minorum." It will be recalled that one other copy of Jean de Venette's chronicle was made at the order of the abbot of Citeaux.

The other markings are not very enlightening. They consist of fifteen or twenty items in rather large Gothic letters, different in style from the book hand of the text. They could be as late as the sixteenth century. It is not clear whether there are two or three different hands, but since they tell us nothing, it does not matter. For the most part they are place names or merely *Nota bene* or *Nota*. They too, like the others, are more numerous on the earlier folios. To all appearances, the medieval readers of Jean de Venette found little of note in those parts of his story which have the greatest interest for us.

Only one series of marginal notes really goes through the chronicle from beginning to end. There are more than a hundred topical headings indicating in considerable detail the subject matter of the text. Most, but not all, of these are surrounded by some sort of line or a set of brackets, but there seems nothing significant to distinguish the ones outlined from those not so marked. Nor can I see any good reason for thinking that the ones outlined are a different series from the others. They all seem to be in the same hand. The most probable theory is that these were made by the man who corrected the text as he went through the copy and compared it with the original. The marginal notes seem to be in the same hand as the corrections, although somewhat larger. This theory gains considerable support from the fact that on folios 21 and 22, on both sides, the marginal notes are written in another, much smaller, but contemporary, hand. Only one of them is outlined. The corrections on these pages are unquestionably in this same new hand. But on folio 23 the previous hand appears again and continues to the end. When this correcting and writing was done cannot be guessed from anything in the marginal notes. The only item of possible interest is on folio 8, where the heading opposite the story of the battle of Poitiers refers to the capture of King John and his son Philip and refers to the latter as "le hardi." Presumably this nickname was applied to Philip of Burgundy in popular speech. Contemporary writers, with the exception of Jean le Bel, do not use it. Possibly this is one of the earliest written appearances of this name, which has become one of the common marks of distinction in history for this particular prince, but how early it was written is still obscure.

Any attempt to formulate an hypothesis on the origin and early history of our manuscript is merely to speculate. But even the scholar may take note of facts which could be relevant and which offer the opportunity to say, "Perhaps; it could have been so." It is true, for instance, that Queen Jeanne of Evreux, widow of King Charles IV of France, was a special patron of the Carmelite monastery in Paris. In such circumstances she would probably have known an official of Jean de Venette's rank, and she might have known about his historical writing. The events which he described included episodes in which she participated. She was also a collector of books, and at least nine volumes from her collection found their way into the library of King Charles V.[13] The Arundel manuscript appears to have been a first-class job of copying, which suggests a well-to-do patron. But only the text was finished. The decorative initials remain blank. Did something happen to the patron for whom it was intended, which prevented completion and delivery? We do not know. But Queen Jeanne died March 4, 1371, three years after Jean de Venette wrote his last paragraph. How the manuscript got to England is also obscure, but we may recall that the English occupation of Paris in the 1420s and 1430s provided opportunities for collectors like Duke John

of Bedford and Duke Humphrey of Gloucester to add to their libraries
from the spoils of war.[14] No one will pretend that these facts provide a history of the Arundel manuscript. They merely make possible
a plausible theory, which is in accord with the meagre information
at our disposal. It is only in that modest guise that they are offered to
the reader's attention.

The Chronicle of
Jean de Venette

px/6

The Chronicle of Jean de Venette

I 340 LET ANYONE WHO WISHES TO BE REMINDED OF MOST OF THE NOTEWORTHY EVENTS which happened in the kingdom of France [1] from 1340 on read this present work in which I, a friar at Paris,[2] have written them down briefly, in great measure as I have seen and heard them. I shall begin with some [3] hitherto unknown prognostications [4] or prophecies which have come to hand.[5] What they mean is not altogether known. Whether they speak truth or not I do not say but leave to the decision of the reader. This is one such.[6] A priest of the diocese of Tours, freed in A.D. 1309 from the hands of the Saracens, who had held him captive for the space of thirteen years and three months, was saying mass in Bethlehem where the Lord was born. While he was praying for all Christian people in the Secret of the Mass,[7] there appeared to him letters of gold written in this wise:

In the year of the Lord [8] 1315, on the fifteenth day of the month of March, shall begin so great a famine on earth that the people of low degree shall strive and struggle against the mighty and rich of this world. Also the wreath of the mightiest boxer shall fall to the ground very quickly afterwards. Also its flowers and its branches shall be broken and crushed. Also a noble and free city shall be seized and taken by slaves. Also strangers shall dwell there. Also the Church shall totter and the line of Saint Peter shall be execrated.[9] Also the blood of many shall be poured out on the ground. Also a red cross shall appear and shall be lifted up. Therefore, good Christians, watch.

These are the words of this vision, but what they mean is not known.[10]

Yet you must know that I, at the age of seven or eight, saw this great and mighty famine begin in the very year foretold, 1315.[11] It was so [12] severe in France that most of the population died of hunger and want. And this famine lasted two years and more, for it began in 1315 and ceased in 1318. Then, suddenly, by God's providence, crops became as abundant as they had been scarce and the famine ceased. Furthermore, women began to conceive more abundantly than before and gave birth to fair offspring. If any other items of the vision come to pass they will be noted hereafter.

Another prophecy is even more obscure.

The son reigning in the better part of the world shall be moved against the seed of the lion and shall stand in the field amid the thorns of the region. Then the son of man shall come, carrying wild beasts on his arm, whose kingdom is in the land of the moon, and with a great army he shall cross over the waters [13] and enter the land of the lion who is in need of aid, since the beasts of his region have torn his hide.[14] In that year shall come an eagle from the east, its wings extended in guile, with a great multitude of its eaglets, to the aid of the son of man. In that year castles shall be destroyed, a great terror shall be upon the people, and in the region of the lion there shall be a lily. Among many kings in that day there shall be a deluge of blood, and the lily shall lose its crown, wherewith afterward the son of man [15] shall be crowned. For four years following, wars shall be waged in the world among the faithful; the greater part of the world shall be destroyed; the head of the world shall be brought down to the ground, but the son of man with the eagle shall prevail. Then there shall be peace and plenty throughout the world; then, wonderful sign, the son of man shall cross over to the land of promise, since all things promised of the first cause shall then be fulfilled.

These are the words of this prophecy which, it is said, Master Jean de Murs,[16] a great astronomer in his time, composed. What it means I do not know, and many others share my ignorance. I shall insert another and clearer prophecy in its proper place below.[17] Now, as I promised, I come to some of the noteworthy events, though not to all, which took place in the kingdom of France, and to a few which took place elsewhere, about A.D. 1340 and thereafter. I shall narrate them truthfully, as I saw them or heard about them.

About A.D. 1340, a comet appeared in Gaul between the south and the west.[18] Its tail and rays extended toward the east and north. It is thought that this star was a presage of tribulations and wars to come in the kingdom. For about this time, in the twelfth year of the reign of Philip of Valois, son of Charles of Valois, count of Anjou, who was the brother of King Philip the Fair, Edward, king of England, became convinced that he and none other should reign in France, by reason of his mother Isabelle, daughter of King Philip the Fair.[19]

According to him there was no male heir to the French throne closer than he. For this reason he had before renounced his allegiance to Philip of Valois, king of France, although he had long before done homage for the lands which he had held and continued to hold in France.[20] At this time he determined to make war on the kingdom of France and to cross over to France; this on the advice of Robert of Artois [21] and of William, count of Hainaut, whose daughter King Edward had married. So at that time the king of England made alliances with John, duke of Brabant, with William,[22] count of Hainaut, with many Germans, and also with the people of Flanders,[23] who had driven their count, Louis, from the country and had unnaturally set up a certain burgess of Ghent, Jacques van Artevelde by name, a very eloquent man, to rule over them.[24] Philip, king of the French, on learning that King Edward, with a large number of armed men, had embarked for France, sent [Nicholas] Behuchet,[25] a burgess of Tours or Le Mans, with a great multitude of ships and fighting men to meet him at sea and to prevent his making port. At a naval battle begun before Sluys in Flanders near Cadzand, Behuchet, who bore himself bravely, was conquered with his men by the English and put to death.[26] The Flemings who were helping the king of England, English nobles, and others were slain in large numbers by the French.[27] Then the king of England came to Sluys and then, by further seafaring, to Antwerp in the duchy of Brabant.[28]

At this time Philip, king of the French, seeing the Flemings in rebellion against their count and against the kingdom of France,[29] begged the Church to lay an interdict on Flanders. And the Church did so. This interdict was very [30] faithfully and obediently observed by all the clergy—to their great peril, because that Jacques, who was tyrannically ruling over all Flanders, endeavored to kill the clergy who obeyed the interdict. But God, the protector of the obedient, did not permit this.[31]

The king of England with his army traversed Brabant, reached Thiérache,[32] and headed [33] for Guise, plundering, burning,[34] and devastating French territory.[35] Philip, king of the French, with a very large multitude of men-at-arms from Aquitaine, Brittany, and other parts of the kingdom, marched out to meet him as far as Buironfosse in Thiérache near Guise. There was no battle. On the contrary, a truce was arranged, and the king of England returned through Flanders to his own country and the king of France returned [36] to Paris.

Shortly after this, Edward crossed the sea again and was again received by the Flemings. By their counsel, he took the title of king of France and of England and quartered the arms of England with those of France on his shield and elsewhere, to designate his new domain.[37] While he was sojourning in Ghent, his wife, who had come [38] pregnant from England, gave birth to a son, who, by his command, was baptized Lionel.[39] His usurpation of the title of the king of France and of the arms of France was a source of no slight scandal and roused the indignation of the king of France and of many others, churchmen and laymen alike.[40]

The king of England then asked Lewis, duke of Bavaria, at that time excommunicate and schismatic because of his usurpation of the Empire against the will of the Church,[41] to make him his vicar in Hainaut and Cambrai.[42] When he had obtained his request, he marched through Hainaut with the purpose of attacking Cambrai, whose bishop and citizens were bringing aid and comfort to the French king.[43] The men of Cambrai sustained [44] many injuries from the king of England and from the men of Hainaut, but they offered manful resistance.[45] Then the cardinals sent by the pope into France to make peace imposed a truce upon the kings.[46] So the king of England went back to Flanders, where he remained a long time, planning the invasion of France, which he carried out afterward, as shall be told. But first let us speak of some happenings at this time in various places.

Men were now beginning to wear disfiguring costumes.[47] This was especially true of noblemen: knights, squires, and their followers, but it was true in some measure of burgesses and of almost all servants. Garments were short to the point of indecency, which was surprising in a people who had up to this time conducted themselves becomingly. Everyone also began to grow long beards. This fashion which nearly everyone in France, except those of royal blood, adopted gave rise to no little mockery on the part of the common people. Men thus tricked out were more likely to flee in the face of the enemy, as the event afterwards [48] many times proved.[49]

In the same year [50] Philip of Valois detained his sister, the wife of Robert of Artois, and her children in prison on her husband's account. He had been banished from France and had fled to England, where he remained, assisting the king of England in all the undertakings of his war against the king of the French.[51]

I34I IN THE FOLLOWING YEAR, 1341, AN ILLUSTRIOUS PRINCE DIED, JOHN II,[1] DUKE OF BRITtany, son of Duke Arthur and husband to Jeanne of Savoy. He was buried at Ploërmel in Brittany, in the monastery of the friars of Blessed Mary of Carmel,[2] next to his grandfather, Duke John, called Mauclerc,[3] founder of the monastery and father of Arthur. A grievous and dolorous war for the possession of the duchy of Brittany arose from the fact that Duke John II died without male heirs. More than thirty thousand men were killed and every conceivable ill befell Brittany as a result of it. The duke had a brother, John, count of Montfort in France, who desired to be duke in his brother's stead, and a niece, Jeanne, daughter of a third brother who was older than the count of Montfort and who had died before the duke. Charles, son of the count of Blois, had married Jeanne and had claimed the duchy in his wife's name, saying that though her father was dead, she took his place [and enjoyed the right of succession which he would have enjoyed had he lived].[4]

Out of this controversy, dissension grew. At length both claimants sought the judgment of Philip, king of France, in the Parlement at Paris. After the arguments and claims of both sides had been heard and the customs of Brittany consulted, the duchy was adjudged to Jeanne and her husband, Charles, and not to the count of Montfort.[5] The latter [6] did not accept this decision, but left Paris secretly and set out for Nantes. There he made agreements with the citizens and with the citizens of other towns in that part of Brittany, and made ready to rebel, thinking to take the land by force of arms. He sent his wife Jeanne, sister of Louis, count of Flanders, and his only son John to England, that they might have the protection of the English king, the enemy of the king of France. When Philip, king of France, learned of the count's rebellion, he sent into Brittany against him his eldest son John, duke of Normandy, with a great multitude of men-at-arms. The duke attacked Champtoceaux, a strongly fortified place on the river Loire, at the entrance to Brittany, took the castle by force of arms, and destroyed the whole town by fire. Proceeding thence,[7] he drew near to Nantes. So great was the fear of the citizens that they surrendered their city and brought the keys [8] to the duke of Normandy, promising obedience for the future [9] to Charles of Blois and his wife as their rightful rulers. The count of Montfort had withdrawn to Lower [10] Brittany, and on learning this he followed his wife to England. He desired the help of the king of England against Charles of Blois and his wife in recovering Brittany. He had a large part of Breton Brittany [11] on his side and some of the Breton barons, though not all, for Charles of Blois had won many over to his side. After the surrender of Nantes, the duke of Normandy entered the city peacefully and peacefully withdrew. The citizens with one accord received Charles of Blois, with his wife, as their lord and duke. But the matter did not remain [12] peaceably settled thereafter. On the contrary, many ills and great wars very soon grew out of it, as shall be described below, perchance.[13]

At that time William, count of Hainaut, died.[14] He was the father of the English queen and father-in-law of Lewis, duke of Bavaria, who was wrongfully [15] conducting himself as emperor. William had been hostile to the king and kingdom of France and had taken the part of the king of England, for the sake of the queen of England, his daughter. Yet his wife [16] was the sister of the king of France [17] and a saintly lady and devout. After her husband's death, seeing that war and misery were becoming inveterate and that her son William, the young count, like his father before him, was hostile to her brother the king of France, and grieved by her powerlessness to apply any remedy, she became a nun in the abbey of Fontenelles of the Cistercian order, near Valenciennes. The sisters there know best how her saintliness and devotion abounded. At this time, Pope Benedict XII, of the Cistercian order, was ruling the holy Mother Church. Now we must speak of the deeds of the kings of France and of England and of the war between them.

In the same year, 1341, Edward, king of England, in alliance with John, duke of Brabant, with Jacques van Artevelde, who, as I have said, was tyrannically and unnaturally ruling over the Flemings, and with many Germans, laid siege to the city of Tournai [18] with a great company of men-at-arms. At this siege the men of Flanders attacked from the side of Tournai toward Flanders; the duke of Brabant and his men, from the side toward Brabant; William, count of Hainaut, from the side toward Hainaut; the king of England with the English and the Germans, from the side toward Lille and Saint-Omer. During this siege [19] the country round Tournai suffered grievously from the devastations of the enemy. The count of Hainaut with the men of Valenciennes took the town with its abbey of Saint-Amand,[20] three leagues from Valenciennes, and many towns in the neighborhood and plundered and burned them all. Philip, king of France, on learning of the siege [21] of Tournai and of the wasting of this district, sent his eldest son John, duke [22] of Normandy, to defend the land of France from its adversaries.[23] He devastated Hainaut as the men of Hainaut had devastated the parts of France near Hainaut. He burned Haspres and many other towns on the border, right up to the gates of Valenciennes, and then returned to his father the king. Then King Philip set out for Tournai. He halted at Arras with a great company and there held many parleys with the king of England and the men of Flanders. It was agreed that the king of France should have the interdict which he had had laid upon Flanders lifted, and that the enemy should withdraw from the siege of Tournai. The king of France, so far as it lay within his power, had the interdict lifted, and there was great joy in Flanders. The Flemish, the king of England, and the rest abandoned the siege; and thus Tournai, which was already beginning to feel [24] a shortage of supplies, was delivered from danger.[25]

The Flemings resumed with joy [26] ecclesiastical music, both song and organ, but quite without consulting the Roman Church, the source of all penance, grace, and remission.[27] Consequently, holy Mother Church did not sanction the relaxation [28] of the interdict until the time of Pope Innocent VI. He heard the humble petition of the Flemish and totally relaxed the interdict, mercifully ordaining that all those liable to punishment be absolved,[29] now that their captain Jacques van Artevelde was dead, slain by his own followers who had long supported him in rebellion against the count.[30]

1342 IN 1342 POPE BENEDICT XII DIED AND PIERRE ROGER, CARDINAL AND BLACK [1] MONK, WAS consecrated pope as Clement VI. He was a doctor of sacred theology, a native of Limoges, and a kind man, much loved. Before his cardinalate he had been archbishop of Rouen.[2]

In the same year the count of Montfort asked Edward, king of England, to assist him in recovering his land of Brittany. The king consented and sailed to Brittany.[3] There he took a large part of Brittany [4] by force of arms, namely, the city of Vannes and many other castles as far as Malestroit inclusive. The king of France,[5] on hearing this, quickly made preparations for the defense of Brittany against him. He reached Ploërmel, where Duke John was buried, and there prepared to fight the king of England, but two cardinals sent by the pope intervened,[6] and with the consent of both kings [7] imposed a truce of two or three [8] years on them. The agreement was that Vannes should remain in the hands of the Church until a good peace had been finally concluded,[9] and that the king of England should continue to hold the other places which he had taken until it was decided to whom the land belonged. Then each king returned to his own place.[10] The king of England dispatched Thomas Dagworth, a brave and noble knight,[11] to guard his share, while the king of France sent Charles of Blois as the man to whom the whole land was subject in his wife's right. At this same time, the count of Montfort, for whom the king of England had fought in Brittany, died. His only son John was in England.[12] Thus his party was greatly weakened.

1343—1345 IN THE YEARS A.D. 1343 AND 1344 THE EARTH WAS VERY QUIET, but in the year 1345 Charles of Blois, duke of Brittany, gave battle at La Roche-Derrien in Lower Brittany to Thomas Dagworth, stationed in Brittany in the interests of the king of England, who was taking the part of the count of Montfort, or rather of the count's [1] son, a young boy, then in England with his mother. In this conflict many were slain on both sides, especially a large number of Breton barons and knights. At last [2] Duke Charles was defeated and captured by the

English and was taken, a prisoner and a captive, to England.[3] After a heavy ransom had been agreed to, he returned to Brittany and to his wife,[4] leaving his children as hostages in England until he should fully have satisfied the king of England by payment of the ransom.[5] Meantime, all Brittany suffered great desolation and injury, for the English recovered Vannes[6] and took and burned many other towns and castles. They laid waste Blain[7] and Ploërmel and many other places which I omit for the present. There were many local wars between the French sent to guard Brittany by King Philip, on the one hand, and the English and their supporters among the Bretons, on the other.[8] The English sometimes lost, as in the conflict at Redon, where Thomas Dagworth was killed with his men,[9] or at Ploërmel, where by agreement thirty Frenchmen fought thirty Englishmen and the English were defeated.[10] Then, on the other hand, there were battles like that at Mauron, where Guy de Nesle and d'Offémont, marshal of France, an upright and brave knight, fell, together with Robert Mulet, seneschal of Anjou, and many Frenchmen, Bretons and Normans.[11]

In the same year, William, the young count of Hainaut, with a great multitude of men-at-arms,[12] barons, and knights from Hainaut, went by sea to make war on the Frisians. He wished to subjugate and dominate them completely, but the affair did not fall out as he had planned. For when he disembarked, before all his men had been brought over, he found the Frisians armed and ready for him on the shore. He and many of the knights and men with him fell speedily in the battle that followed. When the rest of his men who were on the ship behind came up and saw what had happened, they gathered up the bodies of their count and his men and sailed back at once to their own land. This count, like his father before him, had opposed the French king and had sided with the English king in their war, although the French king was his uncle. Yet it is said that he was beginning to return to the party of his uncle. Wherefore good King Philip mourned his death very greatly, knowing him to have been noble and high-spirited, and so he would have been had he lived longer.[13]

What has been told was the prelude to extraordinary events and misfortunes which thereafter came to pass in France[14] and in various other parts of the world, but especially in France. For those who wish to know about them, I shall describe the greater part of them as I saw and heard them, leaving to others who wish to undertake it a fuller description and a more prolix statement. I am unwilling to do more than touch in a general way upon most of the matters which follow, but I wish to record and note down more exactly the years [15] and dates of events which I saw in my own lifetime.

1346 IN THE YEAR OF THE LORD 1346, IN THE MONTH OF JULY, EDWARD, KING OF ENG-land, he who called himself king of France and had quartered [1] the French lilies with the English leopards, and who had sided with the count of Montfort in Brittany against Philip of Valois, the king of France, and against Charles of Blois, duke of Brittany, as mentioned previously—the count of Montfort had been dead a long time now, and likewise Robert of Artois,[2] on whose advice Edward had entered upon the French war—set sail from England with a great multitude of armed men.[3] He made for Normandy, in Neustria, for he wished to [4] assault and take Caen, which he did. When the king of France [5] heard of his approach, he sent against him a man mighty in arms, the count of Eu, constable of France,[6] and the chamberlain of Tancarville [7] and many men, himself following as far as Rouen.[8] The king of England encamped near the town of Caen, which at that time had neither walls nor any enclosure.[9] The English, under the leadership of Geoffrey of Harcourt,[10] a knight brave in arms and astute, who had been banished from France, entered Caen by a surprise attack, with the intention of taking [11] it and plundering it. They met with stout resistance on the part of the townspeople and of the constable and the chamberlain [12] and many other nobles with them. The fighting took place in the center of the town, by the bridge, and higher up, in front of the church of Saint Pierre. A fine *châtelet* or castle has now been built, for the first time,[13] on this bridge.[14] Many from both sides fell in the combat. At length the English prevailed because of the fresh reenforcements which kept coming up from the fields near the abbey of nuns where the English king had encamped. The men of Caen were defeated, and the constable of France [15] and the chamberlain were taken prisoner and were carried off to England.[16] The king of England [17] took the town and plundered it, burning and laying waste the greater part of it. Then he withdrew, taking many men and women with him as captives.[18] Yet he did not take the castle, which is very strong, because he could not.[19] He then turned his steps toward Rouen,[20] burning and wasting the countryside and such places as Trouchart [21] and many other towns. The English [22] journeying with their king stayed at the monastery of Bec-Hellouin,[23] where the only damage they did was to take food supplies. And so they reached the neighborhood of Rouen, where King Philip of France then was, at the beginning [24] of the month of August.[25] They set fire to some little houses in that part of Rouen which is near the monastery of Notre-Dame-du-Pré,[26] and then, retreating toward France, they came to Pont-de-l'Arche, where they burned the suburbs and the wood on the banks of the Seine.[27] They did the same thing at Vernon.[28] In this way they continued through the country beyond the Seine in the direction of Chartres, burning and wasting [29] and meeting with no resistance, except from good towns like Vernon and Meulan,[30] until they came to Poissy.[31] King Philip of France left Rouen, followed after them quickly on the other side of the Seine,[32] and reached Paris while the king of England and his men were in Poissy.[33] Then the king of England marched to Saint-Germain-en-Laye, plundered it, and burned the royal palace there. The English also burned many villages nearby, as Nanterre, La Chaussée, Rueil,[34] and others, right up to the gate of Neuilly. They [35] burned even the tower of Montjoye, which the king of France had had magnificently rebuilt not long before.[36] I who have written this saw all these [37] deeds, for they [38] could be seen from Paris by anyone who would ascend a turret.[39] These fires and the close approach of the English to Paris overwhelmed everyone in the city with stupefied amazement, for no one had thought ever to see such a thing.[40] And yet these events were but trivial in comparison with what the future was to bring forth.[41] In the English army at Poissy [42] was Geoffrey of Harcourt, an astute [43] Norman knight. No one interfered with what the English were doing, and King Philip of France passively awaited [44] their withdrawal. When, on the vigil of the Assumption,[45] he was told that the king of England and his men were making all preparations to move on in the direction of Chartres,[46] he believed the news to be true and immediately planned to offer stout resistance. He left Paris

and went to Antony, beyond Bourg-la-Reine, and there pitched camp.
But while he was waiting there for the king of England to come by,
that same king was having the bridge at Poissy, which had been
broken down against his approach, repaired. He then crossed the
bridge with his men and took the road to [47] Beauvais. Thus the king
of France was tricked and waited two days at Antony.[48] After the
bridge of Poissy, the king of England came to the county of Amiens,[49]
where he encountered many good men [50] who bore themselves
bravely in the face of the English attack. But the English, being much
more numerous and defending themselves with arrows, prevailed
and slew all of them.[51] Then they proceeded toward Picardy, laying
waste the countryside with fire and sword as they went. They passed
near Beauvais but did not enter it, since it was a walled city. They
burned Saint-Lucien, a stately monastery of black monks, at this
time situated outside the walls,[52] and its church as well. Pressing on,
they took Poix and the castle. Coming to the river Somme near the
town of Abbeville, they headed for a ford where the water was very
low, in the place which is called Albataque, Blanchetaque in French,
and there they crossed with their horses and baggage, unhindered and
without danger, though Sir Godemar with many armed men was
waiting on the other side to oppose them. For when Godemar, a Burgundian knight, saw them cross bravely in huge numbers, he did
not wait on the bank but turned and fled with his men.[53] The
English [54] thus crossed the river Somme freely and came to the town
called Le Crotoy, which they burned. Then, near Crécy in Ponthieu,
which they burned, they pitched their tents and took up their lodg-
ing and station in all safety on the edge of a wood and waited to
see if anyone would attack them. When Philip of France, who was
awaiting the English king at Antony, heard that he had withdrawn
from Poissy and that he had repaired the bridge, a feat which the
French had thought impossible, and had crossed over it, Philip
realized that he had been duped and tricked and was sorrowful
therefore. He again gathered an army of nobles and foot soldiers
and many of the best Genoese crossbowmen, in greater numbers than
could be believed possible, and swiftly followed the king of England
to Crécy.[55] He had with him in his company and army the king of
Bohemia, very brave and skilled in arms. His prowess in arms and

the greatness of his heart attest his bravery, for he was blind in both eyes and old and yet had not therefore relinquished arms.[56] He had a son, Charles, who afterwards became Roman emperor, who was also present there. He also had a daughter named Bonne, whom John, duke of Normandy, King Philip's first-born son who is now reigning, had married.[57]

Then when the king of France and his men came near Crécy, where the king of England was, he boldly attacked the English drawn up facing them and their great multitude of archers in battle array, on the battlefield near Crécy, on Saint Louis's Day, 1346, at the end of the ninth hour.[58] While our Frenchmen were disposing themselves for battle, lo! suddenly rain descended from heaven. All the atmosphere, which before had been clear, darkened. The strings on the cross bows of the Genoese crossbowmen who had come to aid the French [59] were soaked by the rain and shrank, so that when it was time for them to be drawn against the English, they were, woe is me! useless. It was not so with the bows and arrows of the English, for when the rain began as they were awaiting battle, they had quickly protected their bows by putting the bow strings on their heads under their helmets. When the French lines attacked [60] in some disorder and confusion, on account, it is said, of undue haste on the part of the French king, and the crossbowmen were told to draw against the English, they tried in vain and could not, in spite of all their efforts, stretch the cords to the bows,[61] so shrunken were they. And so the Genoese crossbowmen could not shoot a single bolt, though in an attack they should have been first, according to the custom of war. Our Frenchmen, seeing this and not knowing the cause or impediment,[62] supposed that they were feigning treacherously and were making no attempt to shoot because they had received money from the other side to that end. They accordingly began to kill and massacre them, refusing to accept their excuses though all the while the crossbowmen were excusing themselves with great cries.[63] The enemy, who had been terrified, regained their daring on seeing this, and bravely attacked our ill-ordered French lines, wounding the French soldiers with bows and arrows and swords, until they could not stand against them in the conflict. They fell in battle in numbers that cannot be believed and those who could escape speedily turned

and fled. And so the French lost the field, and a great number of
our Frenchmen—nobles, knights and footsoldiers—lay there dead,
and with them the blind king of Bohemia, of whom I spoke before.
He had had himself led to battle and, unable to see, had struck as
many allies as foes, or more,[64] with his sword. There also [65] fell the
count of Alençon, the king's brother, the count of Blois, his nephew,
Count Louis of Flanders, who had been cast out [66] of Flanders by his
Flemings under Jacques van Artevelde, the count of Bar, the count
of Harcourt (who was the first count of that county, since before
him the title had been baron, not count), the count of Sancerre, the
duke of Lorraine—and I think there was another duke [67] whose name
I cannot recall—and incredibly many others.[68] Many of the English
perished, but not so many as of our men. King Philip, grief-stricken,
retreated that night to Amiens and afterwards to Paris.[69] The victorious king of England withdrew with his spoils, many horses and
other riches. He passed close to Montreuil and burned Etaples. Proceeding further, he came up before Calais and there pitched his tents
in the fields near the church of Saint Pierre, which was then in the
fields outside the town. He occupied and devastated the whole countryside, wishing to take Calais by force of arms or otherwise; and
this he did later.

In the same year, 1346, John, duke of Normandy, eldest son of
King Philip, with a multitude of armed men laid siege to the town
and castle of Aiguillon in Gascony, but he accomplished little. There
the noble and illustrious prince, Philip, duke of Burgundy, died, not
in battle but of natural infirmity.[70] When the duke of Normandy
heard that the king of England had crossed over and had come to
France, he abandoned the siege, and in the garb of a hospitaler returned with his men to France.[71]

At this time and even before, tailles, gabelles on salt, and pecuniary
impositions on merchandise [72] had begun to flourish in France. But
none of these bore so heavily on the people as the changes in currency
which were made repeatedly.[73] At this time and thereafter, as well
as before, florins were clipped, on account of new coins which were
newly made. And if any coins other than those which had just been
issued were found in anyone's possession, these older coins were without mercy clipped. Thus they who had the coins involuntarily paid

wages to the clippers for their labor. Then it was necessary to turn these coins over to the money changers, to the considerable loss of the possessor.[74] At that time and later,[75] the changes in the coinage were so great and so frequent that the common people mourned and lamented the losses which they thus incurred. At the same time the king, with the consent of our lord the pope and of the Roman church, levied tithes on the churches.[76] Thus unlimited sums of money were raised at frequent intervals by various devices. But in truth, the more money was extorted in such ways in France, the poorer the king became. No prosperity in the kingdom ensued, but on the contrary, woe is me! every misfortune. Officials were being enriched, the king impoverished. Money was contributed to many nobles and knights that they might aid and defend their land and kingdom, but it was all spent for the useless practices of pleasure, such as dice and other unseemly games.

1347 IN A.D. 1347, KING EDWARD WAS BEFORE CALAIS AND MADE MANY ATTACKS ON THE town, but the burgesses defended themselves extraordinarily well from within with machines and other sorts of ballista, and they made sorties in which they slew many of the English and triumphed over them.[1] King Philip sent them food supplies by land and sea to strengthen them. If they had only received these supplies in sufficient quantities they would never have had to hesitate with regard to the English. But those entrusted with the provisions for the men of Calais, so it is said, converted them to their own uses. The king and his council, however, knew nothing of it.[2] When the king of France saw that the king of England was not relaxing the siege of Calais, he went thither with a great multitude[3] of armed men, for he was told that the burgesses had no more food.[4] They were, in fact, eating their horses, and mice and rats, and many were dying[5] miserably of hunger.[6] When the king of France came near Calais and those within the city saw him,[7] they were filled with a great joy not to be wondered at, for they thought that he would lift the siege and relieve them of all their dangers. They signaled to him at a distance, by means of fires displayed[8] on the turrets, that they could hold out three

or four days provided that the king came vigorously to their assistance.[9] This he meant to do and would have done had he been wisely
counseled. When the English heard of his arrival, they sent ambassadors to him, who said guilefully that King Edward would gladly
treat [10] of peace and withdrawal with him if he would grant him a
truce and armistice of three days. The king of France, ill advised,
granted the truce thus guilefully sought and entreated, without the
knowledge of the men of Calais. In the interval, the English speedily
and energetically dug such a great ditch across the fields and marshes
between the town of Calais and the army of the king of France that
it became impossible for the king of France and his men to cross over
to Calais.[11] Furthermore, the English surrounded themselves so effectively with ditches and towers and carts that no one could approach
them against their will. On the Flanders side they had friends among
the Flemings who constantly supplied them with food and other
necessaries [12] from Ypres and other towns in that region, to use
against the French. When the ditches had been dug and communi-
cations blocked, the king of France saw that he had been deceived
and that he could in no wise [13] draw near to Calais.[14] So, very sorrowful that he could not [15] succor the men of Calais nor attack [16] their
enemies, he returned to France without delay. When the men of
Calais saw his retreat from afar and perceived that he had withdrawn
in confusion without having given them aid or being about to give
them any, they were overwhelmed with fear and dismay, because of
their lack of reenforcements and of food. Wherefore, not long after,
they were forced to surrender themselves and the whole town to
the king of England, on condition that their lives should be spared
and as many of their goods as they could carry themselves. And thus
the king of England took the town of Calais. He expelled all the
inhabitants and all the friars of the order of Saint Mary of Carmel
who resided there and put others from England in their places. He
populated the whole town with English. Many of the men whom he
expelled, impoverished and stripped of their possessions, were forced
with their wives and children to beg their bread throughout the
world.[17] All this was true of the adjacent countryside as well as of
the town, for the English shortly took the castle of Guînes [18] and
devastated the countryside. Thus they hold and occupy fortresses and

towns in that district to this day, to the no small detriment of that district and of the kingdom.

About the same time, in the year 1347, Charles of Bohemia, son of the blind king of Bohemia who had died in the battle of Crécy, was elected Roman emperor, confirmed by the church, and crowned in Bonn near Aix-la-Chapelle.[19] Up to this time, Lewis of Bavaria had usurped the empire.

In the same year or thereabouts, while the king of England and his men were besieging Calais, David, king of Scotland, came with many men to besiege the town of London in England, but he was captured and made prisoner by the English in the battle which ensued between him and the English who had remained in England to guard the land.[20] This capture completed the joy of the English.

In the same year, Lewis of Bavaria, who had called himself emperor for many years and who had usurped the empire against the will of the church, died a bad death. For as he was setting out for the hunt on horseback, he fell from his horse and died of a fractured skull when excommunicate. He had been repeatedly excommunicated with the gravest imprecations on account of his contumacy. Then King Charles of Bohemia, who had already been elected emperor, was peacefully crowned at Aix-la-Chapelle. Afterwards he went to Rome for another crown, and elsewhere, as emperors are wont to do.[21]

At that time, Louis, the young count of Flanders whose father had died with other nobles at the battle of Crécy, was detained in Flanders by the Flemings against his own and his mother's will. She was the daughter of Philip the Long, king of France of pious memory. He was brought to the court of the king of England, who was in the neighborhood at the time. Overpersuaded by the king of England and constrained by some Flemings who were adherents of the king, he promised that he would marry a daughter of the king's, who was in England. As long as the betrothal endured, the young man was sorrowful and never assented cordially to the marriage. He kept wondering how he could remain with a quiet mind in the midst of those who had slain his father, even though it were in battle. He decided that he would never enter into marriage, since his promise was forced, not voluntary. Wherefore he decided to flee from the

king's court even though he was very carefully watched.[22] And so
he did one day when he got permission to go hawking. When he
found himself in the fields [23] with a few companions and mounted
on a fast horse, he drove the spurs into his horse's sides, took the road
to France, and did not slacken speed until he had shaken off his
guards and had escaped. He went directly to King Philip, then in
Paris or nearby,[24] who received the young count,[25] his cousin-german,
with the greatest joy, praising God. The king of England and the
Flemings who had arranged the marriage, Jacques van Artevelde and
others,[26] saw that they had been tricked and were filled with the
greatest sadness. So was also the daughter of the king of England.
Wherefore, a song was written in her name which was sung everywhere in France in French: *J'ay failli à celui à qui je estoie donnée
par amour*—I have lost him whose love I was given to be.[27] In the
course of time, when the king of England had gone away to his own
country, the young count returned to Flanders and was received by
his subjects peacefully and with honor. He married the daughter of
the duke of Brabant [28] and had one daughter who, though immature
and under age, is now married to the duke of Burgundy, who is also
young.[29]

1348 IN A.D. 1348, THE PEOPLE OF FRANCE AND OF
ALMOST THE WHOLE WORLD WERE STRUCK
by a blow other than war. For in addition to the famine which I
described in the beginning and to the wars which I described in the
course of this narrative, pestilence and its attendant tribulations appeared again in various parts of the world. In the month of August,
1348, after Vespers when the sun was beginning to set, a big and very
bright star appeared above Paris, toward the west. It did not seem,
as stars usually do, to be very [1] high above our hemisphere but rather
very near. As the sun set and night came on, this star did not seem to
me or to many other friars who were watching it to move from one
place. At length, when night had come, this big star, to the amazement of all of us who were watching, broke into many different rays
and, as it shed these rays over Paris toward the east, totally disappeared
and was completely annihilated. Whether it was a comet or not,

whether it was composed of airy[2] exhalations and was finally resolved into vapor, I leave[3] to the decision of astronomers. It is, however, possible that it was a presage of the amazing pestilence to come, which, in fact, followed very shortly in Paris and throughout France and elsewhere, as I shall tell.[4] All this year and the next, the mortality of men and women, of the young even more than of the old, in Paris and in the kingdom of France, and also, it is said, in other parts of the world, was so great that it was almost impossible to bury the dead. People lay ill little more than two or three days and died[5] suddenly, as it were in full health. He who was well one day was dead the next and being carried to his grave.[6] Swellings appeared suddenly in the armpit or in the groin—in many cases both[7]—and they were infallible signs of death. This sickness or pestilence was called an epidemic by the doctors. Nothing like the great numbers who died in the years 1348 and 1349 has been heard of or seen[8] or read of in times past. This plague and disease came from *ymaginatione* or association and contagion, for if a well man visited the sick he only rarely evaded the risk of death.[9] Wherefore in many towns timid priests withdrew, leaving the exercise of their ministry to such of the religious as were more daring.[10] In many places not two out of twenty remained alive. So high was the mortality at the Hôtel-Dieu in Paris that for a long time, more than five hundred dead were carried daily with great devotion[11] in carts to the cemetery of the Holy Innocents in Paris for burial.[12] A very great number of the saintly sisters of the Hôtel-Dieu who, not fearing to die, nursed the sick[13] in all sweetness and humility, with no thought of honor, a number too often renewed by death, rest in peace with Christ, as we may piously believe.[14]

This plague, it is said, began among the unbelievers, came to Italy, and then crossing the Alps reached Avignon, where it attacked several cardinals and took from them their whole household.[15] Then it spread, unforeseen, to France, through Gascony and Spain, little by little, from town to town, from village to village, from house to house, and finally from person to person. It even crossed over to Germany, though it was not so bad there as with us. During the epidemic, God of His accustomed goodness deigned to grant this grace, that however suddenly men died, almost all awaited death joyfully. Nor was there anyone who died without confessing his sins and receiving the holy viaticum. To the even greater benefit of the dying, Pope Clement VI through their confessors mercifully gave and granted absolution from penalty to the dying in many cities and fortified towns.[16] Men died [17] the more willingly for this and left many inheritances and temporal goods to churches and monastic orders, for in many cases they had seen their close heirs and children [18] die before them.

Some [19] said that this pestilence was caused by infection of the air and waters, since there was at this time no famine nor lack of food supplies, but on the contrary great abundance. As a result of this theory of infected water and air as the source of the plague the Jews were suddenly and violently [20] charged with infecting wells and water and corrupting the air. The whole world rose up against them cruelly on this account. In Germany and other parts of the world where Jews lived, they were massacred and slaughtered by Christians, and many thousands were burned everywhere, indiscriminately. The unshaken,[21] if fatuous, constancy of the men and their wives was remarkable. For mothers hurled their children first into the fire that they might not be baptized and then leaped in after them to burn with their husbands and children. It is said that many bad Christians were found who in a like manner put poison into wells.[22] But in truth, such poisonings, granted that they actually were perpetrated, could not have caused so great a plague nor have infected so many people.[23] There were other causes; for example, the will of God and the corrupt humors and evil inherent in air and earth.[24] Perhaps the poisonings, if they actually took place in some localities, reenforced these causes. The plague lasted in France for the greater part of the years 1348 and 1349 and then ceased. Many country villages and many houses in good towns remained empty and deserted.[25] Many houses, including some splendid dwellings, very soon fell into ruins. Even in Paris several houses were thus ruined, though fewer here than elsewhere.

After the cessation of the epidemic, pestilence, or plague, the men and women who survived married each other.[26] There was no sterility among the women, but on the contrary fertility beyond the ordinary.[27] Pregnant women were seen on every side. Many twins [28] were born and even three children at once. But the most surprising fact is that children born after the plague, when they became of an age for teeth, had only twenty or twenty-two teeth, though before that time men commonly had thirty-two in their upper and lower jaws together. What this diminution [29] in the number of teeth signified I wonder greatly, unless it be a new era resulting from the destruction of one human generation by the plague and its replacement by another.[30] But woe is me! the world was not changed for the better but for the worse [31] by this renewal of population. For men were more avaricious and grasping than before, even though they had far greater possessions. They were more covetous and disturbed each other more frequently [32] with suits, brawls, disputes, and pleas.[33] Nor by the mortality resulting from this terrible plague inflicted by God was peace between kings and lords established. On the contrary, the enemies of the king of France and of the Church were stronger and wickeder than before and stirred up wars on sea and on land. Greater evils than before pullulated everywhere in the world. And this fact was very [34] remarkable. Although there was an abundance of all goods, yet everything was twice as dear, whether it were utensils, victuals, or merchandise,[35] hired helpers or peasants and serfs,[36] except for some hereditary domains which remained abundantly stocked with everything. Charity began to cool, and iniquity with ignorance and sin to abound, for few could be found in the good towns and castles who knew how or were willing to instruct children in the rudiments of grammar.[37]

In the same year, 1348, Blessed Yves [38] Hellory of Brittany, priest and confessor of wonderful virtue and grace, was canonized by the Church and Pope Clement VI. The following year his body was raised from the ground by the prelates and the clergy of Brittany, and many signs and wonders were then wrought through him and by God on his account.[39] At that time also the church under his invocation in the street of Saint Jacques of Paris was first begun and the foundations laid. How his virtues and sanctity flourished is clearly declared in the church at Tréguier in Brittany, where his body rests.[40]

1349   IN THE YEAR 1349, WHILE THE PLAGUE WAS
        STILL ACTIVE AND SPREADING FROM TOWN
to town, men in Germany, Flanders, Hainaut, and Lorraine uprose
and began a new sect on their own authority. Stripped to the waist,
they gathered in large groups and bands and marched in procession
through the crossroads and squares of cities and good towns. There
they formed circles and beat upon their backs with weighted scourges,
rejoicing as they did so in loud voices and singing hymns suitable to
their rite and newly composed for it. Thus for thirty-three days they
marched through many towns doing their penance and affording a
great spectacle to the wondering people. They flogged their shoulders
and arms with scourges tipped with iron points so zealously as to draw
blood.[1] But they did not come to Paris nor to any part of France, for
they were forbidden to do so by the king of France, who did not want
them. He acted on the advice of the masters of theology of the University of Paris, who said that this new sect had been formed contrary
to the will of God, to the rites of Holy Mother Church, and to the
salvation of all their souls.[2] That indeed this was and is true appeared
shortly. For Pope Clement VI was fully informed concerning this
fatuous new rite by the masters of Paris through emissaries reverently
sent to him and, on the grounds that it had been damnably formed,
contrary to law, he forbade the Flagellants under threat of anathema
to practise in the future the public penance which they had so pre-
sumptuously undertaken.[3] His prohibition was just, for the Flagellants, supported by certain fatuous priests and monks, were enunciat-
ing doctrines and opinions which were beyond measure evil, erroneous, and fallacious. For example, they said that their blood thus
drawn by the scourge and poured out was mingled with the blood of
Christ. Their many errors showed how little they knew of the Catholic faith.[4] Wherefore, as they had begun fatuously of themselves and
not of God, so in a short time they were reduced to nothing. On being
warned, they desisted and humbly received absolution and penance
at the hands of their prelates as the pope's representatives. Many
honorable women and devout matrons, it must be added, had done
this penance with scourges, marching and singing through towns and
churches like the men, but after a little like the others they desisted.[5]

In the same year, 1349, Jeanne, queen of Navarre, daughter of Louis called Hutin, quondam king of France, died. She had inherited the kingdom of Navarre from her parents [6] and had married Philip,[7] count of Evreux, a noble and upright man who as long as he lived was called king of Navarre as his wife's representative. He had died before this in Prussia or Granada, whither he had gone to fight against the infidel for the Faith and the Church.[8] Jeanne had borne him three noble sons, Charles, the eldest,[9] Philip, and Louis, and two daughters, the eldest of whom, Blanche, was married to Philip of Valois, king of France.[10] After the death of the queen of Navarre her son Charles was count of Evreux in his father's place and king of Navarre in his mother's. Of him I shall speak hereafter.[11]

In the same year, 1349, the lady [12] Bonne, wife of John of France, the eldest son of Philip of Valois, king of the French, died.[13] John was duke of Normandy and Aquitaine. He had four sons, the eldest of whom was Charles, and two daughters. In the same year died the lady Jeanne of Burgundy,[14] queen of France, wife of Philip of Valois, then reigning.[15] She had borne the king two sons, John, duke of Normandy, and the duke of Orléans; a daughter who was married when very young to Charles of Evreux, king of Navarre; another daughter who was married afterwards to Bernabo, lord [16] of Milan; and a third who was married to the duke of Bar.[17] Philip of Valois, king of France, then took for his wife the lady Blanche,[18] daughter of the late queen of Navarre and sister of Charles, the new king of Navarre. Philip had a daughter by her that year and died very soon after, as shall be told.

1350

IN THE YEAR A.D. 1350 POPE CLEMENT VI, DE-SIRING TO PROCURE THE SALVATION OF THE souls of men, decided to reduce to fifty years the interval between the plenary indulgences which are granted in the holy city of Rome every hundred years after the Lord's Incarnation.[1] For the life of men is perishable and transitory and the wickedness of men [2] abounds in the world, woe is me! and increases. Therefore in the year 1350 he granted plenary indulgence to all who, truly penitent, would journey to visit the places sacred to the apostles Peter and Paul and to the other saints in the city of Rome. Great numbers of both sexes went on this pilgrimage throughout the year in spite of the recent plague, which was still active in certain parts of the world.[3]

In the same year died the illustrious prince, Philip of Valois, king of France,[4] while the hard war between him and Edward, king of England, was still going on. Lord John, duke of Normandy, his eldest son, reigned in France. He was peacefully crowned in the same year at Reims, with great solemnity, on September 25, which fell on Sunday that year.[5]

When King Philip knew that he was dying he sent for his two sons, the first-born, John, and Philip, duke of Orleans, and showed them formal documents in which the doctors of theology and the doctors of both laws [6] had set forth their decision and the conclusive reasons wherefore the inheritance and the crown of France belonged by hereditary right to him and his children after him and not to the king of England, who was unjustly stirring up war for that inheritance and that crown.[7] He showed them, too, refutations of the arguments to the contrary advanced by the English, and he urged them, especially his first-born who would succeed him, to defend their rights and to fight courageously for their kingdom against the English. He said that although a just cause always requires defense and those who strive to defend it sometimes fail in part, yet in the end they always prevail. With the help of God and the return of fortune, they finally succeed, though not so quickly as they would like, and bravely overcome and beat down their enemies. "So," he said,[8] "it will be with you if you strive hard, fear God, and govern the state with zeal and love." Then he strongly urged them to love one another and to dwell in perpetual peace and concord. He said that it was his wish that John have the kingdom and the crown, as was just, and that Philip have the county of Valois whence he himself derived his cognomen.[9] To this John willingly agreed. Then King Philip of Valois gave up the ghost, and departed to God, leaving the two sons aforementioned and a daughter by his second wife, Blanche, the sister of Charles, king of Navarre. He was buried with the other French kings in the abbey of Saint Denis in France, with honor and devotion.[10] King John came to Paris very soon after his coronation [11] and had the count of Guînes, who was constable of France, taken and beheaded at night in the Hôtel de Nesle at Paris, next to the house of the Augustinian friars.[12]

1351

IN A.D. 1351, CERTAIN CARDINALS, MANY PREL-ATES, AND A HOST OF CURATES ATTACKED the mendicant orders in the Roman Curia at Avignon [1] and besought Pope Clement VI to annul them and suppress them utterly. They maintained stoutly in consistory [2] that the mendicants were not called and chosen of the Church and that it was not incumbent upon them to preach to the faithful, to hear confessions, or to take burials belonging to others. Wherefore the prelates and curates demanded that the mendicants be suppressed or that they cease from the practices aforementioned or that, at least, all the profit, and not merely the fourth part, of alien burials go to the curates. For the mendicants had greatly enriched themselves by such burials, according to the prelates and the curates. These and other like allegations were brought against the mendicants.[3] A cardinal made a long speech, but the mendicants there present made no answer, for they reflected upon what is written: "Our Lord will fight for you and you shall hold your peace." [4] This straightway came to pass, for when the charges against them had come to an end the pope straightway took up the word for the mendi-cants. He argued judiciously in their favor, proving by many laws and documents that they should not be spurned and destroyed, as their enemies urged, and showing that they had been called by God and the Church, even though it were at a later date than many, to assist in the rule of the Church, and that they must rightly be reck-oned among those so called. He proved this, among other arguments, by blessed Paul, the apostle, who, although he had not been from the first of the number of the twelve apostles but, on the contrary, had been a great persecutor of the Church, had yet been afterwards inspired by Christ, called and made a vessel of election, and approved as one of the more excellent of the apostles. The pope then asked the prelates and the curates of what they would preach to the people if the mendicants were silenced. "Of humility? But you," said the pope, "above all the estates in the world, are mighty, proud, puffed-up, and pompous, and in the matter of mounts and other luxuries very sumptuous.[5] Of poverty? But you are so grasping, avaricious and covetous [6] that all the prebends and benefices in the world are not sufficient for you. Of chastity? Concerning this we keep silence, for God knows how each of you conducts himself and to what degree you give your bodies over to luxury." The pope added that these were the reasons why many prelates and curates hated the mendicants and that they closed their doors to them lest their lives be seen by the mendicants. Wherefore also they provided pimps and tricksters with temporal goods more often than they did the mendicants. He told them again that they ought not to complain if the mendicants had received some temporal goods at the time of the recent plague in the course of their visitation of the dying,[7] since they had undertaken the cure of souls when many curates had fled. "If with these temporalities they have constructed buildings, you have no cause for complaint, for all this wealth spent on their fine [8] buildings is spent for the adornment of the entire Holy Catholic Church of God and not for pleasures and immodest acts," [9] the Pope said. "You do not conduct yourselves like them, nor have you in the past, and yet you complain that you have not everything to spend at your pleasure. Therefore you vehemently accuse the mendicants. Yet to speak the truth of many of you, you have leisure only for vain things and zeal only for corruptible things.[10] And now you have come hither against the mendicants like a herd of bulls among cows, to separate off those who have been tried like silver." Finally, he showed [11] them how many and what great ills would arise in the Church if they were to have their way against the mendicants.[12] Nevertheless he told them that they might put in writing anything they had against the friars, and the friars their response, and that he would give them the best auditors. So the prelates and the curates went empty away, grieving and put to confusion, but the friars rejoiced and praised the true God. What was done after that I do not know.

1352 IN A.D. 1352, POPE CLEMENT VI DEPARTED FROM THIS WORLD, WHICH WAS AT THAT time involved in many wars and tribulations. He was a native of Limoges, a doctor [1] of theology, a great and distinguished preacher.

Before he was raised to the papacy [2] he had been a monk called Pierre Roger. He desired to be buried in the monastery of Chaise Dieu in the diocese of Saint Flore in Auvergne, where he had been a monk.[3] Innocent VI, also of Limoges, was elected and consecrated [4] to the papacy after him. His name had been Etienne Aubert. He was a cardinal priest, a doctor of both laws, and a good man, simple and just.[5]

1353

IN THE YEAR A.D. 1353, THERE WAS MUCH LOCAL WARFARE BETWEEN THE ENGLISH and the French in Brittany, Normandy, and Picardy. The English burned and destroyed many castles and towns throughout Brittany and Normandy, in the dioceses of Coutances and Bayeux and even in the dioceses of Le Mans and Chartres. They took the castle of Domfront and inflicted many other losses upon the French.[1]

1354

IN A.D. 1354, ON SAINT LUKE'S EVE AND ON SAINT LUKE'S DAY THERE WAS AN EARTH-quake so violent that many castles and cities in different parts of the world were ruined, especially in Germany. There the city of Basel was utterly ruined, even to the cathedral. The falling houses crushed large numbers of people. After the collapse of the houses fire broke out and reduced everything to ashes. This earthquake was felt at Reims where I was at the time and at Paris and elsewhere, it is said.[1]

In the same year [2] Charles of Spain, constable of France, who was of the blood of the French kings and who was much beloved by John, king of France, and very intimate with him,[3] was murdered in the town Laigle in the county of Alençon by the command and order of the king of Navarre and in his presence. The murder was the result of bitter words exchanged by the two men and other causes unknown to us. It was a brutal deed, done at night when Charles of Spain, stripped of arms and clothing, was in bed and as he implored mercy and pity with tears.[4] There were present at the time the then count of Harcourt, Philip of Navarre, brother of the king of Navarre previously mentioned, the seigneur de Graville, another knight named Maubue, Nicholas Doublel, a squire, and many others.[5] King John was very sorrowful when he heard of it, as were many others throughout the world and in the kingdom, holding in horror the way it was done. Thus the king of Navarre incurred the indignation of King John in no slight degree.[6] He wished to correct and punish this great crime through judicial procedure even though the king of Navarre had his daughter to wife,[7] and he would have done so but for Guy of Boulogne, cardinal, who had been sent by the pope to make peace between the kings of France and England.[8] He, with Queen Jeanne of Evreux, widow of the late King Charles of France and aunt of the king of Navarre, and with Blanche, widow of Philip of Valois, king of France, but recently dead, and with many barons and prelates interceded with King John for the king of Navarre and obtained his pardon by their earnest entreaties, on certain terms and conditions.[9] Especially was it stipulated that the king of Navarre should endow many chapels and chantries in which many priests should celebrate masses for the soul of the dead man for the rest of time. So King John spared him and took him back into favor, together with all those who had been present at the murder.[10] This reconciliation greatly pleased the whole kingdom, because the king of Navarre was at that time loved and cherished by everyone. But alas! it did not last nor endure long, as shall be told afterward.[11]

1355 IN A.D. 1355 EDWARD, KING OF ENGLAND, CROSSED OVER TO CALAIS AND THENCE with a great army proceeded to Hesdin, laying waste many villages on the way. There on the frontier he stayed several days. John, king of France, on hearing of his arrival, immediately set out with many armed men in his direction. When he reached Amiens he sent messengers to the king of England to arrange a pitched battle between the two kings and their armies. The king of England saw that a battle would not be expedient for him and therefore answered that he had waited long enough and that since he had found no one to fight with him, he would wait no longer, and then returned speedily to Calais. The king of France returned to Paris.[1]

In the same year, 1355, during Lent, a lamentable deed was done in the castle of Rouen. Charles, duke of Normandy, the eldest son of John, king of France, held a solemn feast in the castle of Rouen and he bade to the banquet Charles of Evreux, king of Navarre, son-in-law to the king of France, of whom we have spoken before. He invited also the count of Harcourt, the seigneur de Graville, a knight powerful in his own district, and many other different [2] knights and nobles. It is believed that something sinister reported to King John concerning the king of Navarre, the count of Harcourt and the other banqueters was the cause [3] of that which straightway befell. For while [4] the guests were feasting at table [5] with the duke, sitting behind [6] closed and barred doors, lo! suddenly and unexpectedly, King John, armed and with many followers, broke in upon them. He had dined not far from the city and had come unnoticed through the little door of the castle that gives on to the fields. Everyone was overwhelmed with amazement at his appearance. He laid hands on the king of Navarre and ordered him to be swiftly seized and incarcerated there. Then without delay he ordered the count of Harcourt, the seigneur de Graville, the knight Maubue, and Nicholas [Colin] Doublel, squire to the king of Navarre, to be arrested. [7] All the other guests at the banquet fled, climbing over walls in their terror. The king had the count of Harcourt, the seigneur de Graville, Maubue, and Doublel put into carts which stood ready and taken through the postern gate the shortest way to the gibbet. Halfway to the gibbet, however, the king ordered them to be beheaded in the field below, in his presence and that of the duke, his son. Then he had their bodies dragged the rest of the way, firmly bound about the shoulders with iron chains and suspended from the gibbets, and their heads, affixed to lanceheads, placed above. The men of the city knew nothing of all this until toward the end of the captures they were roused by the reports of the fugitives. This deed caused the greatest wonder and amazement everywhere in France and elsewhere. [8] The king of Navarre was thrust into prison and harshly treated. He was moved about in a pitiable manner, now sent to Château Gaillard, afterward to the Châtelet at Paris, and then to various castles here and there, now in Pontoise, now in Picardy. [9] He was charged with certain machinations against Charles, duke of

Normandy, the king's eldest son, but what they were and whether the charge was true I do not know.[10] He sustained many severities and shocking experiences while he was in prison. For sometimes men were sent to him who announced falsely that he certainly [11] was going to be beheaded and then others arrived who forbade it. It is said that he endured everything with patience, since he was aware of no evil deed on his own part. He remained in various prisons, chained and harshly treated, for a year and a half and more, in peril of his life.[12] After King John had thus thrust the king of Navarre into prison he divided up and gave away his lands and those of the men who were taken with him and killed.[13] But he could not easily get possession of them nor dispose of them at his pleasure very soon, for the men of the king of Navarre who had not come to Rouen but had remained in Evreux, of which the king of Navarre was count, withdrew to the castle and fortress in the city of Evreux. Many armed men came from France to Evreux and vigorously attacked the town and the castle.[14] The Navarrese in the castle perceived [15] that they could defend it no longer and therefore set fire to the city. The cathedral with the houses of the canons, a large part of the city, the house of the Friars Minor, so it is said, and the monastery of Saint-Taurin—there is also an abbey of black nuns there—were all burned.[16] The Navarrese then betook themselves to Pont-Audemer and established themselves in the very strong castle there. This they held against the king of France and the duke of Normandy in spite of many vigorous assaults delivered by the French.[17] Thus in that part of Normandy, as well as in France, tribulations and griefs increased many fold. For afterward the men of Navarre joined the side [18] of the English, and thus the English seemed much stronger than before to the French. Philip of Navarre, brother of the imprisoned king, revolted from the king of France and leagued with the king of England.[19] With English support he held castles in Normandy, in person and by his friends, and thus inflicted many injuries upon the land in those days.[20] A younger brother, Louis, went to Navarre and governed the kingdom vigorously in his brother's stead.[21] These misfortunes and noteworthy events [22] took place in the years 1354 and 1355, and many others as well in other places, in the course of the private warfare in France,

Picardy, Brittany and Normandy. Now let us turn to still more noteworthy events.

1356

IN A.D. 1356 A FRIAR MINOR WAS BEING AND HAD LONG BEEN [1] DETAINED, HONORABLY, however, in the papal prisons at Avignon, because he foretold future events as if by a spirit of prophecy.[2] Many questioned whether he were not mistaken or were not telling falsehoods or were not speaking [3] by some pythonic or evil spirit. Yet he led a saintly life, sober and honest. That he was a clerk well read in the writings and texts of the Sacred Canon and in prophetic books is apparent [4] in the works and pamphlets concerning future happenings and events which he dictated. I have seen two of these, one entitled the *Ostensor,* the other, *Vade mecum in tribulatione,*[5] and though I put no trust in them, yet I have seen many of the events which they prognosticate come to pass. Nor do I think it impossible that God may have revealed much to him as He has aforetime to the holy fathers, for example, in interpretations of the sacred prophecies. To this friar minor incarcerated in 1356 this question in writing was put by the archbishop of Toulouse,[6] at Avignon: "How long will the wars which have been and still are in France endure?" The answer made by the friar on the same piece of paper follows.[7]

You sent me this question, saving your honor, to the very great blasphemy of God, for only God knows what is herein contained. I am a vile and abominable sinner and no prophet, and I say what I say not out of my own head but from my understanding of the prophecies. Why do you keep asking me, or indeed any man, that which is only in the power of God? Now, you ask me whether the wars will endure. I say that they will endure and will increase until they reach the heavens. What we see now is nothing, for the whole state of the world must be changed. Soon tyranny shall reign everywhere. Many mighty and noble men shall fall and be cruelly slain by the commons [8] and be cast down from their dignities. Infidels shall invade the kingdoms of the Latins, and the severity of the English scourge shall increase until every part of the kingdom has been smitten. More than twenty years before the present wars began I publicly foretold them and was on that account reputed senseless and mad. Mark you that all the rents of the church shall shortly be lost, because the people in all lands [9] shall so despoil ecclesiastics of their temporalities that they shall hardly have their daily bread.[10] The Roman Curia shall flee from the sinful city of Avignon and it shall cease to be where it now is before six years from the present year of 1356 are completed.[11] All the haughtiness of clergy and magnates alike shall be closed up in mire, and all the depravity of the world shall be destroyed. Every man shall lament for horror of the misfortunes close to him. Robbers shall prevail, but afterward they shall themselves be robbed. The haughtiness and luxury of women shall wither. Many shall be defiled and left widowed in utter sadness. The delights of the city shall be turned to dust, and the avarice of the world shall consume itself. But after tribulations and dangers in Christendom the mercy of the Lord shall come to His desolate people, and an angelic vicar of Christ shall be sent from the heart of Christ to make [12] all wills His and to bring back all ecclesiastics to Christ's and the Apostle's way of life. He shall scrutinize and root out every crime and he shall sow every ecclesiastical virtue in the world. He shall convert the Jews, he shall destroy many Saracens, he shall convert Tartars and Turks, but first he shall destroy all who refuse to be converted to Christ.[13] The whole world shall be at peace under him and the peace [14] shall last almost a thousand years. Therefore from this time forward misfortunes shall increase in the world. A great prince shall lament and a king shall be clothed in mourning. The hosts of the people shall be destroyed until such time as that vicar of Christ shall be sent to reform the whole world in the midst of its destruction.[15] Happy he who will pray that He come quickly if he who prays does penance meantime. They shall be saved who flee from the midst of evil to Mount Carmel,[16] for the judgment of the Lord is general and particular upon all. Happy, therefore, all those named above in this list if they soon die a good death in peace, for they shall not see many disasters. They need take no thought as to who shall inherit [17] their lands, since he who acquires shall not possess and he who possesses shall not retain, for the wheel of fortune has now made full turn.

This is the interpretation or prophecy of that Friar Minor concerning future events from that year 1356 on. Although one must not put trust in it, since the Church does not approve it, yet if any of it shall come to pass hereafter in whole or in part, it will be so stated in the following pages.[18]

In the same year, 1356, the luxury and dissoluteness of many of the nobles and the knights became still more deeply rooted. I have described above the far too brief and scanty garments which they had already adopted. Now they began to disfigure themselves in a still more extravagant way.[19] They wore pearls on their hoods or on their gilded and silver girdles and elaborately adorned themselves from head to foot with gems and precious stones. So assiduously did all men, from the least to the greatest,[20] cover themselves with these luxuries that pearls and other precious stones were sold for high prices and could hardly be found at all in Paris. I myself remember seeing two small[21] pearls which had been bought long before for 8 denarii and which sold at this time for 10 librae. Men also began to wear the plumes of birds fastened on their hats.[22] By night they devoted themselves immoderately to the pleasures of the flesh or to games of dice; by day, to ball or tennis.[23] Wherefore the common people had reason to lament, and did lament greatly, that the taxes levied on them for the war were uselessly spent on such sports and converted to such uses. It was at this time that the nobles in derision called peasants and simple folk Jacques Bonhomme. That year men sent[24] to the wars who bore arms in rustic fashion of peasants were given the name Jacques Bonhomme by those who mocked and despised them, and thus lost the name of peasant. Both French and English[25] called peasants this for a long time afterward.[26] But, woe is me! many who then derided peasants with this name were later made mortal sport of by them.[27] For many nobles, as shall be told, perished miserably at the hands of peasants and many peasants in turn were cruelly[28] slain by the nobles and their villages burned in revenge. Let us leave these matters for the present and turn to still more remarkable and terrible events.

In the same year, 1356, the prince of Wales, eldest son of Edward, king of England, was sent by his father to France with a great multitude of men-at-arms, English and Gascon and German mercenaries.[29] While his father remained in England he rode along through the kingdom, burning and destroying until he came to the borders of Poitou.[30] John, king of France, heard of his approach and, after defeating and ejecting enemies who had established themselves in the castle of Breteuil and the castle of Verneuil in the neighborhood of Chartres, he straightway assembled a very large and mighty army.[31] With Charles, duke of Normandy, his eldest son, two other sons,

and Philip, his youngest, he soon drew near to Poitou against the
English prince and his army.[32] In the French army were the duke of
Bourbon, a great noble, the duke of Athens, constable of France, and
many marshals, barons, counts, knights, and nobles.[33] There were
also two prelates in arms, William of Melun, archbishop of Sens, and
the bishop of Châlons,[34] and a very large number of foot soldiers.[35]
There came there also two cardinals sent by the Church to arrange a
peace. When both armies had come within about two leagues of
Poitiers the cardinals went back and forth between the lines, solic-
itously interposing their good offices. But impeded by that enemy
of human kind, Belial, and some of his sons, they failed to bring
peace to the discordant parties. On the contrary, pride reigned, confidence in the might and multitude of armed men persisted, and as a
result a pitched battle was agreed upon.[36] King John came to battle
in high spirits. He desired to fight on foot with his men,[37] and this
he did. After he had sent away his horses, he entered the conflict and
attacked the enemy boldly and bravely.[38] He slew several and
wounded many mortally. Had all the nobles and knights borne themselves as bravely as the king they would have triumphed gloriously
over all [39] their enemies. But many, become pusillanimous and
sluggish, were loath to attack their adversaries.[40] The English, em-
boldened by this, made a spirited attack on King John. Though he
defended himself manfully and slew many, he could not withstand
so overwhelming an attack. Many of the French nobility were killed,
for example the duke of Bourbon and all his men, and the duke of
Athens, the constable, with his,[41] and, by the will of God and the
opposition of Fortune who makes the outcome of wars uncertain,
King John with his youngest son Philip was taken by the English
and made prisoner.[42] When his eldest son Charles, duke of Normandy, saw this, he and his men [43] abandoned the battle and retreated, and his brothers the duke of Anjou and the count of Poitou
did likewise. All who could escape fled from the battle. The English
pursued the fugitives, slew many, and took and plundered many
knights and foot soldiers. Some unable to flee surrendered themselves indiscriminately [44] to varlets and servants without offering any
defense; others who did not know how to yield to the fury and the
swords of their foes were slain.[45]

In this way, then, the king was captured and held a prisoner, some of the people slain, others put to flight and scattered, and others captured and held for ransom, including many knights and barons and the archbishop of Sens.[46] The bishop of Châlons was killed.[47] King John, his younger son Philip, and many other prisoners were taken by the English and the Gascons, who had come to the aid of the English, by the direct route to Bordeaux.[48] The king, though a prisoner, was treated with great honor by the prince of Wales and the English.[49] As soon as they came to Bordeaux they drew up a treaty of peace, which, however, was never put into effect; for the king of England was unwilling to approve the treaty and commanded that John be taken a prisoner to England.[50] And this was done very soon. He was taken overseas [51] to the city of London in England.[52]

Charles, duke of Normandy, John's eldest son, first took refuge with his men, after fleeing the battle, in the city of Poitiers.[53] Thence he came to Paris, where all the people,[54] grief-stricken by the capture of his father the king, received him with honor.[55] The people were confident that through him and his aid his father would return and the whole country of France [56] would be saved. On his arrival in Paris the citizens of all the good towns and the prelates and the knights assembled in his presence in order to see [57] to the recovery of the king and the governance of the state and the kingdom.[58] Then Charles, eldest son of the king and duke of Normandy, was appointed regent and defender of the realm.[59] It was decreed [60] unanimously, with his consent, that the three estates, or rather wise representatives chosen from the three estates—that is, prelates chosen to represent the clergy, nobles to represent the nobility, and citizens to represent the communes of the people—should conduct under the authority of the prince the business of government. Representatives of the three estates, thus chosen, conducted many matters of business and reform and punishment. They offered to supply the regent with thirty thousand [61] armed men at the expense of the communes [62] of the realm, and to continue to support that number if he wished to cross over to England to recover his father.[63] This duty he neglected utterly and went very soon to visit his uncle, Charles of Bohemia, who was at that time Roman emperor, at Metz. He made the journey at great cost and expense and then returned to Paris.[64]

Queen Jeanne, daughter of the former count of Boulogne and wife of King John, then in England, withdrew to Burgundy and to her son the duke of Burgundy, who had inherited the duchy from Philip, duke of Burgundy, dead at Aiguillon in Gascony ten years before.[65]

The three estates were still the rulers of the state when the regent returned, but they did not retain [66] that office much longer. For the nobles utterly refused to settle certain matters as the other two estates, the clergy and the burgesses, wished.[67] Thus discord arose and all three estates abandoned the task they had begun.[68] From that time on all went ill with the kingdom, and the state was undone. Thieves [69] and robbers rose up everywhere in the land. The nobles despised and hated all others and took no thought for the mutual usefulness and profit of lord and men. They subjected and despoiled the peasants and the men of the villages. In no wise did they defend their country from its enemies. Rather did they trample it underfoot, robbing and pillaging the peasants' goods. The regent, it appeared clearly, gave no thought to their plight. At that time the country and whole land of France began to put on confusion and mourning like a garment, because it had no defender or guardian. For this land, which before all the kingdoms and parts of the world had been secure in glory and honor and the blessings of peace and renown, and opulent in the affluence of every good thing, came more and more to be held by [70] the other nations in derision [71] and opprobrium, woe is me! Highways and roads were almost everywhere uncertain and dangerous on account of freebooters [72] and robbers. What more can I say? Thenceforward infinite harm, misfortune, and danger befell the French people for lack of good government and adequate defense.[73]

In the same year, 1356, the citizens of Paris, fearing the enemy and putting little trust in the nobility, placed iron chains across the streets and crossways of Paris. They dug a ditch round the walls on the west and round the suburbs on the east where no walls had been before, and they built new walls with gates and bastilles like the others, in addition to digging a ditch. They fortified the towers with ballista, garrots, cannons, machines, and other instruments of war. They destroyed all the houses which adjoined the wall either within or without. At that time many handsome and splendid dwellings both within and without the walls were condemned to complete demolition and ruin so that ditches might take their way [74] over the ground on which these dwellings and manors [75] stood. I myself saw the destruction of houses and the construction of ditches and walls, diligently pursued the next year and thereafter, and I shall speak of the matter again in the following pages.[76]

1357 IN A.D. 1357, WHILE KING JOHN WAS IN ENG-LAND, MISFORTUNE WAS ADDED TO MISFORtune, as I have said, in France and about Paris. For enemies multiplied throughout the land, and robbers increased to such a degree that they despoiled the inhabitants [1] of country villages in their own houses. Yet Charles, duke of Normandy, the king's eldest son, who was bound by hereditary right to defend the realm and to rule the state, applied no remedy. Wherefore a large proportion of the rural population, unable to stay longer in their villages, began at this time to hasten for protection to Paris with their wives and children and other goods. The enemy seized many castles and fortresses and captured the men who dwelt round about. Some they held for ransom; some they slaughtered miserably.[2] Nor did they spare the religious. Therefore monks and nuns abandoned their monasteries and took refuge as best they could with their friends in Paris and elsewhere. Thus the sisters of Poissy and Longchamps, the nuns of Maubuisson and Saint-Antoine, the Minoresses of Saint-Marcel near Paris, and other nuns, and monks as well, dwelling outside walled towns, were compelled by fear to leave their houses and finally to enter strongholds.[3] Though this situation aroused no slight wonder and amazement among the people, nothing was done to remedy it.[4]

The prévôt of the merchants of Paris and the citizens wondered and grieved that the regent and the nobles about him did nothing, though they went to him many times, urging and imploring him to provide a suitable remedy for all these ills. He kept promising to do so, but without the slightest result. The nobles seemed actually, both then and afterward, to take pleasure in the misfortune and afflictions besetting the people.[5] Taking all this into consideration, the prévôt of the merchants of Paris, who was at that time Etienne Marcel, a man very solicitous for the commonweal,[6] and the other magistrates of the city took counsel with the citizens. Would that their counsel had never actually taken effect! This was their decision, as the prévôt himself [7] with his men publicly [8] confessed in my hearing and that of many others.[9] For since the regent frequently promised at the requests of the citizens and the prévôt to apply a remedy to the aforesaid dangers, and yet never fulfilled by performance what he said with his lips, the prévôt and his following thought that he neglected them on the advice of those about him who, in the opinion of the prévôt, kept dissuading the regent from trusting them in anything. Therefore, the prévôt and the citizens of Paris decided among themselves that it would be a good plan to remove some of the regent's councilors. They ordered that all should wear caps which were half blue and half red, in token of this league for the defense of the state.[10] All the men wearing these congregated in great numbers with their prévôt and then proceeded to the royal palace where the regent was. They ascended to the chamber of the regent, where he and those with him wondered what they sought or what they willed. Approaching the regent, the prévôt said to him,[11] "Fear not, my lord duke, we have something to accomplish, here in this place." Then he turned to the wearers of the caps and said, "Eya, beloved, do quickly [12] what you came to do." Then they all [13] with drawn swords rushed against two peerless knights [14] who were standing by the regent and who were both of his council, Robert of Clermont, marshal of France,[15] a man greatly skilled in arms but at that moment unarmed, and the marshal of Champagne,[16] a man upright and devout and very noble. They pierced them through in the presence of the duke and slew them. Then, with the duke still looking on and lamenting the murders, they dragged [17] the dead bodies down the palace steps to the courtyard near the marble stair, where, bloodstained as they were, they afforded a horrible spectacle.[18] Many of the duke's council, on learning of the murders, quickly took to flight. Among the number was a distinguished and eloquent lawyer of Paris, Reginald d'Acy. As he was escaping in rapid flight, he was pursued and cruelly slain in a street near his house.[19] Alas! why did they perpetrate these crimes? It is not possible to describe the misfortunes that resulted from these excesses, the men that were slain and the villages that were devastated.

This execrable deed did not remain unpunished, as you will see in part hereafter. These things were done in the year 1357, according to the reckoning of France, on the feast [20] of the Chair of Saint Peter.[21]

In the same year, 1357, a little before the events just narrated,[22] Charles, king of Navarre, who had long been held captive in prison [23] by King John, was freed from prison through the industry and diligence of certain Picard nobles, among others Jean de Picquigny, and burgesses.[24] He went first to Amiens, where he was received by citizens and people with great joy. Then, after he had accepted gifts from them and had declared to them the miseries which he had endured in prison,[25] he went on to Paris.[26] There he accepted the hospitality of the monastery of Saint-Germain-des-Prés, for the sake of the quiet.[27] He watched for an opportunity, and when a large number of people had been summoned and had gathered in the Pré-aux-Clercs (the ditches round the monastery had not yet been dug), he stood upon the walls and began to preach to the people in a loud voice. Taking as his text these words in very good Latin, "Because our Lord is just and hath loved justice: his countenance hath seen equity," he expounded them to suit his purpose. He showed at great length in the presence of all how he had been captured and imprisoned, as he said, without cause, and he set forth the anxieties, griefs, and fears [28] which he had endured in prison to such good effect that he provoked the people to tears and lamentations.[29] At length, through the intercession of many magnates, especially of that most noble and devout lady, Queen Jeanne of Evreux, the aunt of Charles of Evreux and former wife of the late King Charles of France, and of Queen Blanche, the king of Navarre's sister and the relict of the late King Philip of Valois, peace and concord were restored between the duke of Normandy, regent of the kingdom [30] for the time being, and the aforesaid king of Navarre.[31] For they had not been the best of friends before, by reason of the arrest made formerly in Rouen Castle in the duke's presence. Peace was restored between them on these terms: that the duke of Normandy take back the king of Navarre and all his men into his friendship and favor, condoning all misdeeds, if such there had been, and restoring to the king of Navarre his lands in Normandy and elsewhere which had been confiscated, and also to their children [32] the lands of the nobles who at the time of his arrest in Rouen had been killed and affixed to the gibbet. Permission was granted to the king of Navarre to take down the bodies from the gibbet, if he wished, and to give them Christian burial.[33] Thus peace was restored between these lords amid general rejoicing. Then the king of Navarre, after receiving many gifts and much money from the citizens of Paris,[34] left the duke in Paris and went off rejoicing to Rouen.[35] There he was received with honor and there he expounded his sufferings eloquently as he had at Paris. This done, he had the bodies which were affixed to the gibbet, that is, those of the count of Harcourt and his two companions, of whom mention is made in the section dealing with the year 1355, taken down on Innocents' Day and borne in procession with great lighted [36] candles and a great multitude of people to the cathedral of Saint Mary at Rouen. There, after the bells had been rung and masses solemnly celebrated and a sermon delivered by the king on the text, "The innocent and righteous have cleaved to me: because I have expected thee," the bodies were buried honorably in the chapel of the Innocents to the no small wonder of all the people.[37]

The king of Navarre, much as he wished to, could not recover all his lands, for several who had held and were still holding [38] his castles were unwilling to give them up. They declared and maintained that since it was King John of France, now in England, who had entrusted them with the castles, it was to him only and not to the king of Navarre nor to the duke that they were bound to deliver them up. Their refusal was a source of grief to the king of Navarre.[39] Since he supposed that it was made by the orders of the duke of Normandy, he was again provoked to enmity and discord with the duke. Thus the peace so recently made did not hold and was without effect, and at this time there began between the king and the duke war and discord from which the whole country of France, near Paris [40] and elsewhere, afterward suffered,[41] woe is me! as shall be told. All these deeds of the king of Navarre were done shortly before the knights were struck down by the swords of the citizens of Paris in the presence of the duke-regent, and their cruel death took place very shortly afterward.

In the same year, 1357, the archbishop of Armagh, primate of Ireland, crossed over to the Roman Curia to preach against the mendicant orders.⁴² He composed pamphlets and treatises against them in which he urged very strongly that they ought not to be supported by the Church.⁴³ One of these arguments was that Christ and the apostles, though poor men, had none the less never been mendicants. He cited many laws and writings to prove that the Church should abolish the orders or should at least deprive them of its support in their privileges of preaching, confessing, and burying and in other ⁴⁴ exemptions, and should no longer grant them immunity.⁴⁵ The friars, in making their defense, pointed out many heretical statements in his argument and contested them.⁴⁶ Which side will prevail in the end will be clearly apparent.⁴⁷ Therefore let us leave this subject and return to our main theme.

1358 IN THE YEAR A.D. 1358 NEW WONDERS WERE ADDED TO OLD.¹ FOR CHARLES, DUKE OF Normandy, eldest son of King John of France, then in England, regent,² as we have said, of the kingdom of France in his father's place, felt such indignation against the citizens of Paris, especially those who were chiefly ³ responsible for the violent and insolent murder of two knights in his presence and for the death of the lawyer, that he withdrew from the city of Paris in consternation of spirit and departed with the intention of not returning until he should have avenged these deaths. He hastened quickly to Compiègne, where he remained for some time.⁴ He summoned many nobles thither to advise him how he might take vengeance on the prévôt of the merchants of Paris and his accomplices for the deeds which they had dared to attempt ⁵ in his palace and in his presence. All the nobles, especially the friends of the murdered men, were of one heart and one mind with him,⁶ and counseled him either to have the principals killed ⁷ or, if the number of their supporters made this impossible, to besiege the city of Paris bravely and to harry it by armed attacks and by obstruction of its food supply,⁸ until the citizens themselves should help him to realize fully his purpose of putting the prévôt of merchants, his accomplices, and other magistrates to death. On learning this, the prévôt and the others who had taken upon themselves ⁹ the governance of the city after the duke's withdrawal entreated the University of Paris to go to the duke, on their behalf and that of the whole city, and to entreat him to put his wrath against the citizens of Paris mercifully out of his heart, and to promise him condign amends, saving the lives of all, and fitting honor and respect. The University accordingly, for the good of the city,[10] willingly sent a distinguished deputation to make this entreaty. The deputies were received with all courtesy by the duke and the other lords, and brought back word that if the citizens would deliver to the duke a very small number of men, ten or twelve, or at least five or six, of those chiefly suspected of the crime done in Paris—and the duke did not purpose their death—he would gladly resume his previous friendship with the citizens of Paris.[11] But the prévôt and his followers, not believing that,[12] once in the hands of their opponents, they could escape a terrible death, were with reason afraid and unwilling to expose themselves to such formidable danger. Wherefore, they adopted a policy of boldness and formed a league in order to involve all the citizens with them. They sent to the regent both at Compiègne and at Meaux, whither he sometimes removed, many other deputations like the first, but they received no other amicable reply, only hard words, severe and threatening. Therefore, fearing the destruction of the city, which, it appeared, the regent and the nobles with him were eagerly striving for, and desiring to protect the city completely from any danger that might arise, they began to fortify themselves. The citizens promptly took the castle of the Louvre near the old walls of Paris into their own hands, after expelling the garrison who held it for the duke.[13] They blocked up the gates on the water side and made an entrance from the side of the city. This action provoked the duke to still greater indignation. At that time all began to secure themselves strongly with arms,[14] and to repair walls, to deepen carefully ditches already begun, to construct new,[15] small walls over the ditches on the eastern side, and to erect bastilles [16] by all the gateways.

In the same year, 1358, many gates were permanently closed and ditches dug in front of them. This was the case with the Porte d'Enfer [17] which gave on the Carthusians between the Jacobins and the Minorites, with the gate of Saint Victor (its faubourg had been destroyed), with the gate which gave on the Pré-aux-Clercs, and with several others of whose names we are ignorant.[18] The same year, the dwellings and houses which the Jacobins and the Minorites had built outside the walls of Paris were destroyed. The Jacobins had infirmaries, vaulted chapels,[19] halls and other honorable, regal, and splendid buildings: the Minorites had a refectory with walls of stone and wooden flooring, kitchens, storehouses, and other useful and seemly buildings. Both orders were in the habit of reaching their houses and their very spacious and pleasant gardens outside the walls through the houses of the city,[20] by the courtesy of the owners. Not only did they lose their [21] houses which they had built outside the walls but also those inside which adjoined the walls,[22] in order that a path and way might be made between their dwelling and the walls. All the buildings along the city wall on the west were cleared away in like manner.[23] The men digging ditches in front of the house of the Jacobins next the wall on the outside, uncovered there, about in the center of the ditches, to their great wonderment, the foundations of towers and castles of great strength, perhaps the work of Saracens. The masonry was composed of blocks of limestone and burned bricks so closely bound together [24] that even mallets and iron tools could only partially destroy them and break them asunder. This was done that the ditches might be dug deeper. It is said that there had once been here a palace or castle called by men of old, in lays which are still extant, Hautefeuille, of which traces yet remain.[25]

By such activities was Paris set in order and made ready for defense. In all the country round about, however, misfortunes and losses due to certain nobles and freebooters were increasing more and more. Foulques de Laval [26] with many Bretons plundered the Beauce and set fire to many villages. He pillaged Etampes, which had already been taken and burned once by freebooters like him, for the second time.[27] The robbers came as far as Orléans and beyond, so that no one dared take the direct route from Paris to Orléans. Neither was the road to Compiègne or anywhere else safe or secure.[28]

At this time, the duke of Normandy, then regent, with his wife, the duchess, and a very great throng of nobles, left Compiègne [29] for the city of Meaux. They were all planning how to weaken Paris, whether by arms or by preventing food supplies from being brought across the Seine. They fortified the castle or fortress at Meaux, seizing their food supplies in the city and the neighboring countryside,[30] and shut themselves up there.

The prévôt of merchants and the citizens of Paris, seeing that the regent was opposed to them, held a council concerning the government of the city. They felt the lack of a captain and therefore sent to Charles of Evreux, then in Normandy, whom they knew to be in fresh discord and dissension with the duke, and asked him to come to Paris with a good supply of men-at-arms, to be their captain and defender against all their adversaries whomsoever, saving only King John of France, who was still detained in England. He accepted gladly and came to Paris, bringing with him many Navarrese and many stout English mercenaries. The citizens of Paris gave them a splendid reception, for they thought that the king and his men would be their best possible defense against the regent and the nobles.[31] Their invitation to the king, however, provoked the duke and his men and, in truth, many others to still greater indignation. Wherefore, the nobles began to approach Paris and to show themselves in the fields, fully armed and mounted on horses gay with trappings, prepared for battle if perchance the citizens should issue from the city to give them battle. The Parisians, however, remained firmly inside their walls and refused to go out, for they said that they would not fight against their lord but that they would certainly resist and defend themselves against those who desired to harm them.[32]

On one occasion, they were told that their enemies had established themselves in Corbeil in order to cut off the supply of bread which usually came from Corbeil to Paris along the Seine. The nobles had built a bridge over the Seine, to the great inconvenience of the Parisians. Wherefore, the prévôt of merchants and the citizens went with a goodly number of armed men to Corbeil, cast out the nobles, destroyed the bridge which was so injurious to them, and returned with joy to Paris, safe and blithe.[33] The duke was at this time residing at Melun and elsewhere, but chiefly at Meaux.[34] At another time, I have been told, it happened that the nobles and the duke came armed to the place where the bridge had been, near the bridge of Charenton, to attack the king of Navarre and the men of Paris. The king of Navarre, captain of the men of Paris, went out [35] armed with his men to meet them. He spoke to them at great length and then returned to Paris without giving battle. The men of Paris, seeing this, suspected that since he was a noble he had been plotting some secret harm to them with the other nobles. Therefore they spurned the king of Navarre and removed him from his office.[36] He then, with his men, left Paris in great indignation. His men, especially the English whom he had brought with him, did everything in their power to irk and insult the men of Paris as they retreated, but, in truth, many of them were atrociously slain by the swords of the Parisians before they could leave the city. Then the king of Navarre went to the monastery of Saint Denis in France and remained there several days. Meantime, his following did much harm in the neighborhood of Paris. Both the English who had escaped from Paris and the Navarrese overran the fields and vineyards, slaying or taking captive anyone they found in the fields and burning several villages, among others La Chapelle-Saint-Lazare, the town of Saint-Laurent near Paris, the granary of Lendit, Saint-Cloud, and some others nearby. The men of Paris remained shut up in their city, carefully guarding the gates with armed men by day and keeping many watchmen on the walls by night. Many citizens who issued from Paris [37] on Magdalen's Day against the English at Saint-Cloud were all killed there and did not return. Every part of the countryside [38] that lay outside of fortifications was totally devastated at this time, and the common people were plundered. No one knew by whom this was done unless it were by the king of Navarre.[39] Losses and injuries were inflicted by friend and foe alike upon the rural population and upon monasteries standing in the open country. Everyone robbed them of their goods and there was no one to defend them. For this reason many men and women, both lay and religious, were compelled to leave their abode on all sides and to seek out the city. This was true of the ladies of Montmartre. To speak briefly, there was not a monastery in the neighborhood [40] of Paris, however near, that was not driven by fear of freebooters to come into Paris or some other fortification, abandoning their buildings and, woe is me! leaving the divine offices unsung. This tribulation increased [41] in volume, not only round Paris but also in the neighborhood of Orléans, Tours, Nantes in Brittany, Chartres, and Le Mans, in an amazing way. Villages were burned and their population plundered. Men hastened to the cities, with their carts and their goods, their wives and their children, in lamentable fashion. At this time the town of Meun, near Orléans, and Beaugency were captured by the English on the feast of Saint John the Baptist, and Beaugency, outside the castle, was wasted by fire. At that time, also, the city of Luçon in Poitou was burned and the church where the people had taken refuge attacked fiercely, though not taken, thanks to the brave defense made by the town. These and the like outrages were perpetrated throughout the land, and there was no one to meet them with the proper remedy.[42]

 While, then, these cities and the city of Paris were being ill treated and little defended, there befell near Paris something hitherto unheard of. In the summer of the same year, 1358, the peasants living near Saint-Leu-d'Essérent and Clermont in the diocese of Beauvais, seeing the wrongs and oppression inflicted on them on every side and seeing that the nobles gave them no protection but rather oppressed them as heavily as the enemy, rose and took arms against the nobles of France.[43] They combined in great numbers and appointed Guillaume Cale, an astute peasant of the town of Mello,[44] their captain. Then, going forth with their arms and standards, they overran the countryside. They killed, slaughtered and massacred without mercy all the nobles whom they could find, even their own lords. Not only this:[45] they leveled the houses and fortresses of the nobles to the ground, and, what is still more lamentable, they delivered the noble ladies and their little children upon whom they came to an atrocious death. Thus, they destroyed the castle of Ermenonville,[46] then the strongest in France, and slew many noble men and women who were in hiding there.[47] This tribulation increased in strength until it reached even to Paris. A noble hardly dared appear outside his stronghold, for if he had been seen by the peasants or had fallen into their hands,[48] he would either have been killed or would have escaped only after rough handling. The number of peasants eager to extirpate the nobles and their wives and children and to destroy their manor houses[49] grew until it was estimated at five thousand. Therefore the nobles kept themselves in seclusion and did not appear abroad as they had before. But this monstrous business did not long endure. For, since the peasants had begun it entirely of themselves, not of God nor of due authority such as that of an overlord, all their desire suddenly [50] failed and came to an end. Those who had begun with a zeal for justice, as it had seemed to them, since their lords were not defending them but rather oppressing them, turned themselves to base and execrable deeds. It is said that they subjected noble ladies to their vile lust, slew their innocent little children, as I have said, and carried off such property as they found, wherewith they clothed themselves and their peasant wives luxuriously.[51] What was so ill done could not long endure, nor was it fitting that it should.[52] The nobles, perceiving this, began little by little to unite against the peasants with the caution of men skilled in arms. Thus the king of Navarre summoned some of the unsuspecting peasant captains to him with smooth words and slew them. After they had been killed, the king and his men with the count of Saint-Pol, near Montdidier, rushed upon many peasants who were in disarray [53] and slew and destroyed them with the sword.[54] Thus their whole fatuous faction and unjust stewardship vanished like smoke and ceased.[55] Nor did this fatuous business remain unpunished. For the knights and nobles recovered their strength and, eager to avenge themselves, united in force. Overrunning many country villages, they set most of them on fire and slew miserably all the peasants, not merely those whom they believed to have done them harm, but all they found, whether in their houses or digging in the vineyards or in the fields. Verberie, La Croix-Saint-Ouen near Compiègne, Ressons, and many other country towns lying in the open fields which I have not seen and do not note here, mourned their destruction by fire.[56]

In the same year, 1358, the duke of Normandy, regent of the kingdom, still retained his indignation against the citizens of Paris, and the strength and numbers of the nobles at Meaux increased. While the duchess and the nobles were residing in the fortress of Meaux and the duke was away [57] at some distance, a conflict broke out between the nobles shut up in the fortress and the mayor and citizens of Meaux. It was said at Paris that the citizens of Meaux hated the nobles because of their exactions and would gladly make war on them, if they were to receive any substantial aid from the Parisians. Therefore, some armed men came from Paris to Meaux and, in point of fact, the citizens attacked the nobles and the duchess in the fortress, and there was fighting in the gateway on the bridge.[58] The nobles, skilled in arms as they were, overcame the citizens with their swords and were victorious.[59] The nobles then issued from the fortress and overran the city like madmen, killing all the people indiscriminately, except those who were able to escape, and plundering the whole town. They seized men and women and shut them up in the fortress and left nothing portable in the churches and houses. Then they gave the whole town to flames and destroyed all that they could of it except the fortress. Afterwards they went raging over the adjacent country-side, killing all the men they found and setting fire to various villages. The misery caused by the nobles in the vicinity of Meaux reached such a pitch at that time that there was no need for the enemy English to come to complete the destruction of the countryside. For in truth the English, who had been the chief enemies of the realm before,[60] could not have done what the nobles of France did.[61]

Nor did this destruction suffice them. They marched from Meaux with great numbers of armed men to take Senlis.[62] The citizens of Senlis, forewarned, made the best possible preparations for their reception.[63] They put wagons at the top of the main street, which ascended a fairly steep hill, and detailed some strong men to push the wagons violently down upon the enemy as they climbed up the street. They stationed armed men inside houses, hidden so that the enemy could not see them and so that they could burst upon them. Women were placed at the windows who were to pour great quantities of boiling water down upon the enemy. All these preparations had been sagaciously made by the time that the nobles came up and clamored at the Paris gate, demanding in the regent's name that the gates be opened and the keys and the city delivered speedily into their hands. It was not true that the regent had commanded them to take Senlis. They were obeying only their own temerity and insensate presumption. The citizens, who were armed and had of their company some nobles whom they had called in, opened their gates and allowed them to enter freely. The nobles, supposing that all was theirs from the start,[64] entered arrogantly and proudly. They walked with drawn swords up the middle of the street and, when they saw no one prepared to resist them, they raised the shout customary at the attack of a city.

At this, the men stationed by the wagons on the hill released them, with a tremendous push, against the enemy. The nobles, part way up the slope, could neither ward them off nor hold their own against them and were rolled over and over in the most humiliating way. Thereupon, the men hidden in houses issued forth and struck the foe, now prostrate on the ground, with their swords. The rest of the nobles' party who were still passing through the gate received a bath [65] of boiling water and speedily turned and fled. Thus many of the nobles were killed and those who escaped were forced to flee in confusion. When they got back to Meaux and related their misadventure, they were a laughing stock to all their friends. Those of them at least who lay dead at Senlis harmed the men of Senlis no more.

Now we must return briefly to the citizens of Paris. In the aforementioned year, 1358, while the indignation of the regent still endured, a still more surprising event occurred in Paris. The prévôt of merchants and many of the leading citizens of Paris, by whom the whole city of Paris seemed to be governed, were of the opinion that the duke's indignation, roused by the murders committed in his palace, in his presence, on the feast of the Chair of Saint Peter last, was steadily increasing, and they were afraid lest something worse, even death, might befall them as a result of it.[66] Therefore they planned secretly how [67] to make sure of their safety. They sent,[68] so it was charged against them afterward, to Charles of Evreux, king of Navarre, whom they had once before called to be their captain and then had repulsed and insulted, and arranged to summon him secretly to rule over them again and to defend them against the duke.[69] They agreed further that, since he was of the royal race and lineage, he should succeed to the royal scepter and reign over the kingdom of France. It is said [70] that this is what the king of Navarre was striving for with all his might. So, then, it was secretly arranged by the prévôt and several burgesses who were his adherents that, on the appointed day, the king of Navarre with a large supply of armed men should stealthily approach Paris and remain in hiding nearby until it was time; that the prévôt of merchants should possess himself of the keys of the city gates and have the gates watched by his men and, at a moment when the citizens were off guard, should speedily introduce the king of Navarre and all his men into the city; and that the king should then kill without mercy [71] his opponents in the city whose doors he would find marked. Thus, when he had triumphed, the people remaining in ignorance the while, and held the whole city at his pleasure, he would, after the defeat and dethronement of the duke and of the king who was a prisoner in England and who had deeply injured the king of Navarre, attain to the dignity of royalty, to the headship of the kingdom and to the crown, and would at last reign. Both he and the Parisians thought that he could easily win over other cities and towns to his party, once he controlled Paris.[72] They thought also that those who brought this about would be wholly delivered from all danger of death by his support. Man proposes, God disposes. They dug a ditch for others and [73] themselves fell into it. Matters went otherwise than they had planned.

On the eve of the feast of Saint Peter's Chains,[74] which is the first day of the month [75] of August, in the same year, 1358, the prévôt and a few burgesses who were privy to his plans [76] and schemes for the city of Paris, met at the city gates at break of day and set about relieving certain men of their watch and sending them to their own houses, saying that fewer men would suffice to keep watch. They also, in their capacity of rulers of the city, took from them the keys of the gates and gave them to men of their own choice. At length [77] they came to the new gate or the bastille Saint-Antoine [78] and there tried to do the same thing, but the distinguished burgesses who for a long time had had that gate and its keys in their keeping wondered why the prévôt of merchants and those with him should suddenly wish to deprive them of the keys and the custody of the gate and give them to men who, it seemed clear to them, were inadequate. Immediately there arose in their minds a strong suspicion of bad faith and treachery on the part of the prévôt and of the men who had just come there with him. They declared they were adequate and quite as capable as the men to whom the prévôt was trying to entrust the watch. The prévôt and his men asserted the contrary. Thus arose an altercation and a dispute about the custody of the gates and also about proclamations made with the trumpet. The custodians of the gate wished all proclamations to be made in the name of the duke, then regent, and the prévôt wished the duke's name to be suppressed and the king's name proclaimed. There were those who wondered which

king he meant.[79] In the midst of the altercation, one of the custodians said with a loud voice, "In truth we are betrayed by that prévôt and his following.[80] What is this?" Others said the like, and the
dispute went on until [81] one of the custodians lifted his sword or ax [82]
with great force, struck the prévôt of merchants a mighty blow, and
killed him cruelly. Then the supporters of him who struck the blow [83]
assailed the prévôt's companions, four in all,[84] wounded them with
their swords, and finally killed them all. They dragged their bodies
to the square in front of the church of the friars of Val-des-Ecoliers,[85]
stripped them, and left them there unburied for several days, ignominiously exposed to the public view. They would not permit the
bodies to be removed from the square until the duke should arrive and
should see that he had at last been avenged upon his enemies, who
lay there dead. At the news of the death of the prévôt of merchants
and his allies, a great uproar broke out in Paris and the greatest wonder prevailed. Popular opinion changed, and the hatred in which
the duke had been held turned into the reverse. Those who in the
morning had taken arms against the duke were all, with one mind,
ready in the evening to take his side and to receive him and to be
reconciled with him. Joy and gladness resounded through the city.
Friendly shouts acclaimed the duke. Those red caps which had been
worn so ostentatiously were now hidden away and laid aside. Early
in the morning of the next day, proclamation was made that if anyone knew any members of the prévôt's party, he was to seize them and
conduct them to the Châtelet, but that he was not to touch their property nor molest their wives and children. Several were seized and put
to the torture [86] and, then, on the third [87] day led to the market place
and there beheaded according to judicial procedure. They were the
men who had governed the city with the prévôt and by whose counsel
everything had been done. Among the number were some very distinguished, eloquent, and learned burgesses. One of them, it is said,
as he was being led along, broke into words like these: "Woe is me!
O king of Navarre, would that I had never heard thee nor ever seen
thee." [88] The duke heard all that had been done and came to Paris
within five days or less of these events.[89] He was received with honor
by everyone and, on learning of the punishments that had been meted
out, he put aside his former indignation and became reconciled and

at peace with the city.[90] The citizens then agreed in the choice of a
new prévôt.[91]

When the king of Navarre saw that he was not to have his desire through Paris, he considered whether he might accomplish elsewhere his purpose of obtaining the kingdom. Wherefore he went to
Amiens [92] with a large number of armed men. He won over, by
smooth words and promises, the mayor [93] of the city and the abbot
of a neighboring monastery, and they consented to help him with all
their might to take the city.[94] One night the king of Navarre, with
the cognizance of the mayor, stationed his men within the city in
order to take it and rule over it. The citizens suspected nothing. The
king of Navarre and his men, who were housed in the faubourgs
between the old and the new walls, attacked suddenly, killing and
slaying the people and setting fire to the houses. The citizens dwelling in the heart of the city then ran to arms, rang the bell of the commune, and called upon the mayor, who as their captain and defender
should have been first in the fray, to help them meet the danger and
without delay to succor them in their need. He dissimulated and de-
ferred his assistance so long that, had it not been for the count of
Saint-Pol on the Ternoise,[95] who was at that time, by God's will, in
Amiens with a large force, the city would have been completely conquered [96] and taken that day by the Navarrese. For while the mayor
lingered designedly, the count of Saint-Pol and his men opposed
the Navarrese bravely and furiously. When the Navarrese encountered this opposition and heard the bell ringing and the people hurrying [97] to arms, they were forced to turn and flee from the burning
city. The citizens of Amiens were deeply grieved by the wasting and
burning of their faubourgs.[98] They seized their mayor, whom they
suspected of treacherous participation in the disaster, and the distinguished abbot near the city and put them both to torture. After
they had finally confessed their wrongdoing and treachery, they received condign punishment and were publicly put to death. A new
mayor afterward succeeded the old. The citizens realized that the
ruins of their large and extensive faubourgs which had been destroyed by the voracious [99] flames would do them more harm than
good and therefore destroyed them utterly, together with the buildings of the Preaching Friars and Minorites, which had been very fine,

and the house of the Augustinian Friars, and levelled them with the ground. Manor houses within the walls were temporarily assigned to the friars.[100]

Charles, king of Navarre, and his men returned in confusion to Normandy.[101] Thenceforth, as a result of these misdeeds, the deadly hatred and immeasurable discord between the regent and the king grew steadily.[102] A very great war began, in the course of which the king of Navarre inflicted many losses and unheard-of injuries upon the people of France. He and his brother, Philip, allied themselves with the king of England against the duke and the French.[103] At this time he inflicted no slight damage throughout Normandy on land not his own.[104] He fortified Vernon, Mantes, and Meulan [105] and thus closed the river Seine to the west so completely that nothing from Rouen nor from the sea could be brought by boat to the duke in Paris. In the same year, he rode about France, laying waste country and town, burning, plundering, and taking miserable captives. And what is more, he went to Melun. This had formed part of the dowry of his sister, Queen [106] Blanche, and had been restored to her. She was residing there at this time, before the Lord's Nativity, in the year 1358. He entered with many armed men, took the fortress with the lady's consent, and fortified it, in spite of the captains and soldiers who were holding another part of the town for the duke, the regent, and guarding it against the king of Navarre and his supporters.[107] The occupation and fortification of Melun by the king of Navarre was damaging to Paris and its vicinity, for the Navarrese closed navigation so that neither wood nor wine could be brought from Burgundy to Paris. The king of Navarre and his men, so long as they stayed there, seriously injured all the adjacent countryside, plundering and burning many houses and towns. A great shortage of supplies, wood and everything else, troubled the people of Paris, since they could not go up [108] and down the Seine, as they were wont, either [109] from Rouen or in the opposite direction. They cut down trees in the vineyards and along the highways. Fagots which formerly sold for two solidi now sold for a florin.[110] Wherefore, the regent and the people of Paris were finally compelled to lay siege to Melun, but though they assailed it vigorously with siege engines, they could not conquer it nor take it.[111] The stronghold remained in the hands of the king of Navarre and his men until, by God's will, his heart was changed for the better, and peace was restored between the two lords.[112] Of this I shall speak under the year following. So, then, while this went on, the country of France was multiply afflicted and pierced by the sword of two wars. The nobles did little to help at that time.[113]

In the same year, 1358, the English took many castles by force, to the great detriment of the country of France. They took, for example, the famous [114] castle called Mauconseil, near the city of Noyon, where the bishop of the city and many other nobles were taken prisoner by the English in the conflict; [115] they now hold the very strong castle called, in French, Creil, on the Oise, near Pont-Sainte-Maxence, in the diocese of Beauvais; [116] the castle of Remy [117] near Compiègne; and La Hérelle. In the territory of Senlis they took Chaversy [118] and Juilly [119] and many others whose names I do not know. Near Orléans they took Châteauneuf,[120] a fair and splendid dwelling, and Fay-aux-Loges [121] nearby. They took other fortresses and castles here and there in various parts of France and had already, long before now, taken others elsewhere. Wherefore the whole population and the very roads and highways had reason to mourn and grieve, for by reason of seizures and depredations the highways were closed. Neither merchants nor anyone else could travel and journey, except timidly. And not only had the grass-grown roads reason to mourn and grieve but also the churches [122] and monasteries which stood outside walls and fortresses. For example, the monastery of Saint Barthélemy of regular canons at Noyon, and of Saint Euverte of the same order at Orléans, and of Saint Aignan, an illustrious college of secular canons, were all in this year leveled to the ground by the citizens for fear lest the enemy establish themselves therein to work harm to the surrounding country.[123] The like destruction of churches standing outside walls, by the inhabitants and the people living nearby, occurred in many different places and cities. In the Ile de France, Poitou, Anjou, Amienois and Tournaisis and elsewhere, many monasteries whose names I cannot [124] mention were destroyed. Their restoration is reserved by the Divine Will for Its own good time.

In the same year the English attacked the city of Orléans. They

laid waste the faubourgs and set fire to them in their retreat. No one
offered any resistance or defense.[125]

In the same year, 1358, all the churches in Paris, including the
collegiate churches, were forbidden to ring their bells between Vespers and daybreak the next morning, in order that the sentinels and
the men on the walls [126] who kept a lookout for the enemy might
not be confused. Curfew was, however, still rung at Notre Dame,
though at an early [127] hour. The canons now sang their matins quickly
after Compline instead of devoutly concluding the office at midnight
to the solemn ringing [128] of bells.

In the same year the English entered Lagny,[129] took the town,
pillaged it, killed many men,[130] took others as prisoners to [131] their
fortress of La Ferté-sous-Jouarre,[132] set fire to the town, and retreated
unharmed, having encountered no opposition.

In this same year, in the Ile de France and elsewhere, the peasants
dwelling in open villages with no fortifications of their own [133] made
fortresses of their churches by surrounding them with good ditches,
protecting the towers and belfries with planks as one does castles,
and stocking them with stones and crossbows. Thus they could defend themselves if perchance [134] enemies should attack them as, I
have heard, they did fairly frequently. At night the peasants and their
wives and children slept in these strongholds in comparative safety.
By day [135] they kept lookouts on top of the church towers, and little
boys stood there and kept watch. When they saw the enemy coming
in the distance, they blew a horn or rang bells. Then the peasants
who were at work in the fields or busy with other tasks in their
houses ran with all speed to the churches which they had fortified
and took refuge in them.[136] The men in certain districts along the
Loire betook themselves to islands or to boats, well drawn out from
the banks, as their nightly sleeping places, building cabins and huts
on boat or island for the safekeeping of themselves and of their
families and flocks.[137]

In the same year, 1358, the English entered the city of Auxerre,
took it,[138] sacked it, despoiling it of untold wealth, and then left
it.[139] Other English soldiers took Epernay [140] in the diocese of Reims,
and Vailly-sur-Aisne,[141] killing the inhabitants and carrying off un-

counted wealth. They took several other towns as well. They rode over the country round Reims as far as Châlons and Soissons without encountering any resistance. They came, after this, to Soissons, and fighting vigorously, entered the city and took it. But there was an unnamed knight there who with his men withstood them so manfully that he drove them out.[142]

At this time the English tried to storm Troyes and take it by force of arms in the same way, but the bishop of the city and the count of Vaudemont, sire de Joinville, opposed them manfully and, going out to meet them in a pitched battle, attacked them vigorously. After fighting a long time, the men of Troyes triumphed[143] over the English and overcame and vanquished them. There fell in that battle two hundred sixty[144] English, over and above the prisoners and fugitives.[145] The bishop and his men and the count accomplished these and the like remarkable feats in this war.

In the same year the English in Creil took the town of Montmorency near Saint-Denis in the Ile de France, pillaged it, and then burned it.[146] They took many prisoners and led the wretched men back[147] to Creil, heaping insults upon them, in order that they should ransom themselves. They continually overran the highways and roads between Paris and Compiègne and Senlis, and whomever they found on the roads or in the villages they either captured and took back to Creil or killed. Few dared go abroad, for none was safe from them who had not obtained letters of safe-conduct.[148]

In those days, the insensate pomp of many bishops throughout France was first brought low and greatly diminished. They could no longer rejoice in their rich rents and gains, as they had been wont, for their[149] noble manors, monasteries and abbeys, in various places, where once divine service had been offered up, were, woe is me! in different ways ignominiously seized by the enemy or destroyed and overthrown by friends lest the enemy should perchance take comfort from them. Thus many impoverished abbots, monks and abbesses were forced by the diminution of their wealth to seek new homes in Paris and elsewhere. Now, those who had been wont to travel with a great number of horses and squires were content to proceed in sober state, accompanied by only one servant or monk on foot. For, as we have said, their houses and monasteries had been, in whole or in part, demolished and plundered of their wealth and food supplies.

1359 IN THE YEAR A.D. 1359, RECKONING THE BEGINNING OF THE YEAR FROM EASTER AS BEfore,[1] the following events took place. The constable of France, at that time the sire de Fiennes,[2] with many men-at-arms from Picardy, besieged the English in the fortress of Saint-Valery by the sea in Picardy. They had completely destroyed by fire the monastery which stood there. Our men could have defeated the English conclusively and have taken them but they permitted them to withdraw freely and without hindrance with the booty which they had taken from the town and the district round it.[3] Some who were grieved by this attacked many of them, took their spoils from them and killed them. In the same way, they drove out from various fortresses others who were doing harm in Picardy.

The men of Noyon, in the same year, seeing that they could not drive the English out of the castle of Mauconseil near them and realizing the calamities and perils with which it threatened them, bought the castle from the English. The moment the English had left it, after they had taken their money and gone away, the men of Noyon destroyed the castle utterly, and especially the tower which was very strong and fine.[4] Thus the whole region and the roads became more secure.[5] The monastery of Ourscamp of the Cistercian order which stood opposite the castle had received irreparable injuries at the hands of the English and had been almost entirely destroyed by fire. It could tell in lamentable fashion from its experience what a bad neighbor Mauconseil had been and why maledictions had been heaped upon it. What the strength and beauty of the castle of Mauconseil had been of old, its ruins and remains still make clearly [6] manifest to all who pass it by.

In the same year Philip of Navarre, the king of Navarre's brother, who sided with the English and was much opposed to the French, came with a large force of armed men to Vermandois, wishing to injure the very rich city of Saint-Quentin and the countryside adjacent. He took up his position in Fervacques,[7] the stronghold of some nuns, well situated in the midst of streams and swamps. Yet it was not so strong a place that it could not be easily taken in war by one who acted wisely. The constable of France, sire de Fiennes, heard this and therefore went thither with speed with a very strong and powerful following of men from the district.[8] As soon as they had arrived, the men of the district were very eager to make an immediate and spirited and vigorous attack on the Navarrese and the English, for they saw that they could not escape them if they were to attack very suddenly.[9] Their numbers were much smaller, and already, so it seemed to the men of the district,[10] they despaired of their strength and of their powers of resistance. But after a council, of which nothing is known, the constable restrained [11] his men from attacking for the present, saying that it would be better and more convenient to wait until the next day, since then they could take them at their pleasure. Therefore, at the command of the constable, the men of the district withdrew, though unwillingly, looking forward to the booty, both the bodies and the possessions of their enemies,[12] which they would take the next day. During the intervening night, while they were planning to enrich themselves on the morrow, the enemy withdrew undisturbed and all unknown to them. Thus frustrated in their hope and put to confusion, the men of the district went home, grieving that they had let the others go unharmed. No slight suspicion was felt about the constable and no slight blame was attached to him by people both near and far, perhaps groundlessly.[13]

In the same year, 1359, the citizens of Paris and the regent, Charles, duke of Normandy, saw that the king of Navarre was sorely inconveniencing Paris by blocking navigation on the Seine in both directions and that the vigorous attacks which the regent in person and his men had made repeatedly on Melun, and were continuing to make, accomplished nothing.[14] They accordingly decided that a peace between the two lords should be amicably discussed by nobles [15] representing each. This plan was carried out with the assent and agreement of both parties.[16] But after the peaceful arrival of both lords at Pontoise, and after many discussions of ways peace could be obtained, it became clear that agreement between the representatives was difficult. On the king of Navarre's behalf, many requests for towns, money and castles were made which the spokesmen for the other side refused,[17] setting forth their terms more and more strongly. Though the negotiators persisted long [18] in their discussions, they could not find a plan for peace which would satisfy the honor of either side, for the more the one asked, the less the other was willing to grant. Yet it is true that the duke or regent made generous offers to the king: many castles and towns in Normandy, the county of French Champagne, and sufficiently large sums of money.[19] At length, since the councilors were carrying on the discussions at cross purposes and could find no way of peace, they were preparing, sadly enough, to go home after a banquet when lo! the king of Navarre, as if inspired by the Holy Spirit,[20] said suddenly to his followers, "I wish to speak to my brother, the regent." (He was the duke's brother-in-law, having married his sister.) When the rest of his council were told what he had said, they rejoiced with exceeding great joy. And so it came about that the two lords came together and that the king of Navarre, very courteously and modestly, spoke these words, or their like.[21] "Lo! my lord duke and brother, I would have you know that I regard and consider you as my direct overlord; and though I have long waged war against you and the land of France, I would have you know that I will not continue or foment this war further, but that I will be a good Frenchman henceforth, your subject and friend and close supporter and defender against the English and all others, and I beg you to pardon wholly me and mine for whatever I have hitherto done to your disadvantage. I want no lands or towns offered or promised to me, but if I do well and you find me faithful hereafter, give me and do for me whatever my merits require and demand." When the duke heard these words, he rose up to give him abundant, courteous, and heartfelt thanks. Then they joyfully partook together of wine and spices in token of peace. All those standing by [22] who had been trying to negotiate a peace exulted and rejoiced immeasurably [23] at what they saw and heard, giving thanks to God Who blows where He lists and accomplishes in a moment what men, relying on their own strength, cannot accomplish over long periods of time.[24] From that moment Melun was returned to the duke and the river was reopened to free navigation in both its upper and its lower reaches. At Paris and throughout the countryside there was great joy and jubilation at these tidings. When peace between these lords had been effected and declared, as has been told and even better than has been told, they went their ways.

The English grieved at this peace and tried to harass the land still more grievously. They did not succeed in all their enterprises and sometimes, by God's will, had the worst of it in single engagements. I will recount on this page such an instance for the pleasure it gives me, as I heard it at first hand, for it took place near the village where I was born. This affair was valiantly conducted by the peasants, by Jacques Bonhomme.[25] In a little village called Longueil,[26] near Compiègne, in the diocese of Beauvais, not far from Verberie but on the other side of the Oise,[27] there is a farmhouse, strong and well built, which belongs to the monastery of Saint-Corneille at Compiègne. The peasants dwelling round it realized that it would be dangerous for them if perchance [28] the enemy were to occupy this stronghold. Wherefore, they sought the permission of the regent and the abbot of the monastery and established themselves in it, after they had stocked it suitably with arms and food, and appointed one of their number their captain. All this they did with the permission of the duke, promising him to defend it stoutly,[29] even at the risk of their lives. With the same permission, many peasants from the neighboring villages took refuge there. They made Guillaume l'Aloue, a tall handsome man, their captain. He had with him his servant, another peasant who took the place of a squire, an incredibly strong and powerful man, exceptionally tall and broad-shouldered and well proportioned, and, in addition, full of energy and daring. This giant, as humble and modest as he was strong, was named Grandferré. There came to the stronghold about two hundred men, all laborers who supported their humble existence by the work of their hands. The English in Creil castle, on hearing that it was men of this sort who were preparing to resist men of their quality, despised them and regarded them as nothing worth. They made ready to attack them, saying, "Let us drive out these peasants and make this well-stocked and well-built fortress our own." Two hundred of them came up before Longueil and, finding the peasants off their guard and the doors open, boldly pushed into the courtyard. The peasants, who were on the second story of the manor house by the windows, caught sight of all these fully armed men and were at first stunned by the unexpectedness of the attack. Their captain, however, descended with a few of his men and began to lay about him on all sides. His courage availed him little, for he was surrounded by the English and was mortally wounded. Perceiving this, those of his companions who were still in the upper room, Grandferré among them, said, "Let us go down and sell ourselves dearly. Otherwise they will slay us without mercy." They descended cautiously in small groups and issued from different doors. They struck at the English as if they were engaged in their wonted task of flailing wheat in a barn. They lifted their arms so high and brought them down upon the English with such force that no blow failed to inflict a mortal wound. Grandferré groaned deeply for the grief he felt on seeing his master, the captain, lying close to death. He attacked the English, over whom as well as over his companions he towered head and shoulders, brandishing his ax and redoubling heavy, mortal blows upon them. He struck to such purpose that he emptied the court in front of him. One of his blows, aimed straight, never failed to cleave a man's helmet and to leave him prostrate, his brain pouring out of his skull. Thus he broke the head of one, the arms of another and dashed a third to the ground. He bore himself so surpassingly well that in a scant hour he had, in this first encounter, killed with his own hands eighteen, in addition to those he had wounded. His companions, too, watching his prowess, struck at the English with good courage.

What more need I say? The English fell in such numbers, especially before Grandferré, that the survivors were forced to turn and flee. Some leaped into [30] the moat and were drowned; some thought to escape by the door and reeled under the blows of the peasants holding the farmhouse. Grandferré went to the center of the court where the English had fixed their banner, slew the standard bearer, pulled up the banner, and told one of his companions to carry it to the moat through an opening there was in the walls. (The wall had never been completed.) The man shook his head and said that he could not do it because there were too many Englishmen between them and the moat. Grandferré then said to him, "Follow me with the banner." He went ahead and, lifting his ax with both hands, struck furiously to the right and to the left. Thus, by his courage, he opened a path to the moat,[31] killing and overwhelming most of the men in his way, and his follower was able to throw the banner into the moat without hindrance. Grandferré [32] returned to the conflict after a moment's rest and attacked those who remained in such a way that all who could quickly fled. On that day almost all the Englishmen who came to that fight were slain or drowned, or disabled by the aid of God and by Grandferré. It is said that he wounded sorely or slew more than sixty [33] men in that conflict. The captain, Guillaume l'Aloue, who had been, as I said, mortally wounded in the first assault,[34] was still breathing at the battle's close. He summoned all his men to his bed and in their presence made another captain in his stead, and then, forthwith succumbed to his grievous wounds and departed this life. They buried him with many tears, for he had been wise and kind.

The other Englishmen in France mourned the death and destruction of their men deeply, saying that it was too much that so many of their good fighters had been killed by mere peasants. Wherefore, all the English from the fortresses in the neighborhood assembled and marched against the peasants at Longueil. They were taken by surprise, for they feared nothing more from the English for the present. Yet when the English assailed their farmhouse stoutly, they came forth to battle with good courage. In the front rank was Grandferré, of whom the English had been told, and of whose crushing blows they had heard.[35] No sooner had they seen him and felt the weight of his ax and the force [36] of his arms than they heartily wished that they had not come to that battle on that day.[37] For, to be brief, all of them were put to flight or mortally wounded or slain. The peasants captured some English noblemen of high rank for whom they would have received all the money they wanted had they been willing to hold them for ransom. But they refused and said that these men should have no chance to do them further harm. So it was that the English were defeated twice because Grandferré struck so hard and bore himself so well that they could not defend themselves against him.

When the English had been defeated and the battle was over, Grandferré, heated by the excessive warmth of the day and by his violent exertion, drew up and drank off great quantities of cold water and was forthwith seized with a burning fever. He took leave of his companions and returned with his wife [38] to his cottage in a nearby village called Rivecourt. He went to bed, ill, but not without his ax, which was so heavy that an ordinary man could only with great difficulty lift it from the ground to his shoulders. When the English heard that Grandferré was ill, they rejoiced greatly, for no one had dared attack Longueil so long as he was there. They were afraid that he might recover and, accordingly, sent secretly twelve of their companions to strangle him in his house. His wife saw them coming in the distance, ran to her husband lying on his pallet [39] and said, "Alas! dearest Ferré, the English are here, looking for you, I verily believe. What can you do?" Unmindful of his fever, he armed himself swiftly and, taking up his heavy ax or gisarme [40] with which he had already overwhelmed so many [41] enemies, went forth from his house. As he came out into his little yard, he saw the Englishmen and cried out, "Robbers, you have come to take me in my bed but you have not yet taken me." He stood with his back to the wall so that he could not be surrounded and assailed them violently, wielding his ax with all his old spirit. They pressed him cruelly for they desired with all their hearts to take him or kill him. On seeing himself so extraordinarily hard pressed, he hurled himself mightily [42] upon them with such an access of fury that no one whom he struck escaped an ill death. The mere sight of his blows took from the English almost all desire to defend themselves. In a moment, he had laid five of them prostrate on the ground with mortal wounds. The other seven then left him and turned and fled in confusion.[43] Thus triumphant over them, he went back to bed, and heated by the blows he had delivered, drank abundantly of cold water and so relapsed into a still more violent fever. He grew worse [44] and within a few days he had received the last sacraments and had departed this world. He is buried in the cemetery of his village. That village and the whole countryside lamented Grandferré's death, for as long as he lived the English dared not come near.

After his death the English destroyed, burned, and plundered many little towns and villages in this part of the diocese of Beauvais, capturing or even killing the inhabitants. The loss by fire of the village where I was born, Venette near Compiègne, is to be lamented, together with that of many others near by. The vines in this region, which supply that most pleasant and desirable liquor which maketh glad the heart of man, were not pruned [45] or kept from rotting [46] by the labors of men's hands. The fields were not sown or ploughed. There were no cattle or fowl [47] in the fields. [No cock crowed [48] in the depths of the night to tell the hours. No hen called to her chicks. It was of no use for the kite to lie in wait for chickens in March of this year nor for children to hunt for eggs in secret hiding places. No lambs or calves bleated after their mothers in this region. The wolf might seek its prey elsewhere and here fill his capacious gullet with green grass instead of rams. At this time rabbits and hares played freely about in the deserted fields with no fear of hunting dogs, for no one dared go coursing through the pleasant woods and fields. Larks soared safely through the air and lifted their unending songs with no thought of the whistling attacks of eyas or falcon. No wayfarers went along the roads, carrying their best cheese and dairy produce to market. Throughout the parishes and villages, alas! went forth no mendicants to hear confessions and to preach in Lent but rather robbers and thieves to carry off openly whatever they could find.] Houses and churches no longer presented a smiling appearance with newly repaired roofs but rather the lamentable spectacle of scattered, smoking ruins to which they had been reduced by devouring flames.[49] The eye of man was no longer rejoiced by the accustomed [50] sight of green pastures and fields charmingly colored by the growing grain, but rather saddened by the looks of the nettles and thistles springing up on every side. The pleasant sound of bells was heard indeed, not as a summons to divine worship, but as a warning of hostile incursions, in order that men might seek out hiding places while the enemy were yet on the way. What more can I say? Every misery increased on every hand, especially among the rural population, the peasants, for their lords bore hard upon them, extorting from them all their substance and poor means of livelihood. Though there were few flocks or herds, those who owned any were forced to pay their [51] lords for each animal; 10 solidi for an ox, 4 or 5 for a sheep. Yet, their lords did not, in return, repel their enemies or attempt to attack them, except occasionally.

In the same year the enemy [52] took the castle of Roucy near Laon,[53] and the count in it; but when a ransom had been paid for him, they cast him out and kept the castle for themselves. Afterwards, however, the men of Reims bought it back from them and after their withdrawal destroyed it utterly.[54] Similarly, in the same year, the men of Paris and of other good towns such as Senlis and Compiègne bought back the fortress of Creil [55] from the English for a large sum.[56] The English took the money and retreated and then immediately entered the town of Pont-Sainte-Maxence hard by, fortified it, and held it at their pleasure.[57] Very soon afterward they took the very strong castle of Clermont, also hard by in the Beauvaisis, from our men dishonestly. They burned the greater part of the city after they had pillaged it and captured or killed or put to flight the population.[58] Thus the sufferings of that region and of France increased.

During this same time many abbeys and monasteries in Anjou, Poitou, Touraine, and the Orléanais were utterly destroyed. For example, four establishments belonging to four orders of mendicant friars at Orléans were torn down because they were outside the walls; the monastery of La Madeleine, where there were more than sixty nuns, the priory of Saint Laurent outside the walls, and the church of Saint Aignan were all destroyed by the people living in their vicinity, in order that the enemy should not entrench themselves in them. The monastery of Saint Euverte and many churches had already been destroyed.[59] At this same time many country villages in France, Poitou, Touraine, Anjou, and Brittany which received no protection from their proper lords against the ravages and depredations of the enemy and which were continually goaded by the English, made themselves tributary to them. Only thus did the English permit them to live in peace and to cultivate their fields and vineyards.[60] When the natural lords of the villages heard this, they wished to force them to pay tribute to them as well as to the English; in truth, the only desire of the nobles was to ruin the peasants and to work them to death and to give them no protection against their adversaries. Thus the wretched peasants were oppressed on all sides, by friend and foe alike, and could cultivate their vineyards and fields only by paying tribute to both sides.

In the same year, 1359, about the feast of All Saints,[61] Edward, king of England, the prince of Wales, the duke of Lancaster,[62] and a great multitude of men-at-arms [63] again invaded [64] France. One detachment of the English attacked several little towns and castles, notably Bray-sur-Somme, to which they crossed over. The men holding it offered such a brave defense and a stout resistance that the English could not take it by storm. On the contrary, many of them were killed, and the survivors retired.[65] The king of England traversed Hainaut and Thiérache with a very large army and sat down before Reims.[66] It is said that he planned to take the city in order to be crowned king of France there, and then to reign, a second Antiochus,[67] over two kingdoms. But when he saw that the city was rich and almost impregnable and that its inhabitants were prepared for strong and wholehearted resistance,[68] he went to Châlons. During the time which he spent around [69] Reims, he accomplished nothing but the devastation of the countryside.[70] When he saw that Châlons likewise was well fortified, he abandoned the siege at once and proceeded towards Burgundy.[71] The Burgundians, on learning of his approach, entered into an agreement with him to this effect: on condition that he promise to inflict no injury upon them, they promised to give him large sums of money, to allow him and his army to enter and leave Burgundy unmolested, to furnish him with food supplies at their own expense and sell them to him as long as he was in France and did them no harm.[72] So it was reported at Paris, where I was as I wrote these words.[73] Whether it is true or not will perhaps appear later. I do not wish to believe easily that this noble and faithful people with whom the queen of France, the wife of John, king though captive, was residing at this time, would be willing to do anything [74] to the hurt of his kingdom and to the comfort of its enemies. If they did this, which I do not believe, they will be held in everlasting scorn and derision—and rightly, unless they can offer our lord the king and the regent some legitimate excuse. I have heard that it is true that they bought themselves off as I have said.

In the same year the Normans fought a battle with the English near Pont-Audemer. Though the Normans bore themselves bravely, they were defeated by a surprise attack made from ambush after the usual English fashion. Many were killed and many were captured. Guillaume Martel, a valiant and brave knight, fell mortally wounded and the noble knight, Louis of Harcourt, was taken prisoner, and Le Baudrain de la Heuse and many others as well.[75]

Toward the end of the same year, 1359, beginning the year with Easter [76] as one should in all piety, many nobles, foot soldiers, and burgesses of Picardy, together with large numbers of men-at-arms and ships from that region and from Normandy and Flanders as well, took ship and sailed across the Channel with the intention of invading England in full force and, if God granted them the good fortune, of bringing back King John from his captivity in triumph after a glorious victory. They hoped that those who had not been able, by reason of God's disfavor [77] or perchance of their own demerits, to defend themselves on their own ground from the enemy might with humility and diligence recover on foreign soil the fame and wealth lost at home and return with honor and renown by God's aid. They put to sea [78] on the fourteenth day of March, crossed to England, and took the town of Winchelsea by force of arms. They sacked it and burned it, slew the inhabitants, and after two days returned immediately to their own land.[79]

I have thought fit to write down on these pages as clearly as I could the events which I know to have occurred up to this time in March of this year. I shall now record that at this time in Paris the currency was so weak that [80] the silver gros of Saint Louis was reckoned generally at 20 Parisian solidi or less, and the florin of Florence was reckoned by the money-changers at 13 Parisian librae.[81] The like had never been seen before, at least not by men now living. Therefore all food supplies were dear. A setier of wheat which could once have been bought for 10 [82] solidi now sold for 30 Parisian librae or more. A quartant of good wine could be shared with good companions only by paying 24 Parisian solidi for it.[83]

In the same month and year the English took a place called L'Ile-Adam between Pontoise and Beaumont on the Oise.[84] They strengthened the fortress still more and held it so effectively that all that Lent the fish and other food supplies which are usually brought to Paris from the sea could not be transported by the direct route. As a result of this culpable interference with trade on the part of these and other [85] Englishmen, the city of Paris was almost entirely without sea fish, herrings, sardines, and anchovies. Nevertheless, the men of Paris remained inactive and took no prompt action to prevent this interference. Both the citizens and the greater and lesser nobles endured the deprivation for no reason at all, for a long time.[86] Finally, however, the English were killed and the fortress was destroyed by the nobles and others.

The spring of this year must not be passed over in silence.[87] The weather in March throughout Lent was as fair, mild, pleasant and warm as anyone could ever remember having seen it.[88] The peasants were sick at heart that so fine [89] a spring should slip by without vines and fields being properly cultivated, and they very much feared a serious shortage of food the next year throughout France, as a result of their inability to work the land then.

Toward the end of this year, that is, before Easter, the value of the currency dropped at Paris on the eve of the Annunciation to a point where a royal [90] florin or a florin of Florence, worth 13 [91] librae before, was worth only 32 solidi, and the white denarius, which had been worth 2 solidi, was worth only 12 [sic] [92] Paris denarii. What had sold before for 2 white pennies worth 4 solidi now sold for 4 silver pennies worth only 8 denarii of stronger money.[93] These and many other noteworthy things happened that year.

1360 IN A.D. 1360, EDWARD, KING OF ENGLAND, HIS ELDEST SON, THE PRINCE OF WALES, AND the Duke of Lancaster left Burgundy for France.[1] They passed through [2] the Nivernais and burned and wasted the whole district. At length, at Eastertide they reached Châtres and Montlhéry,[3] within six leagues of Paris. The king spent Easter at a fine and very pleasant manor called Chanteloup, near Châtres.[4] He stayed on there for six days longer while his troops,[5] dispersed throughout the vicinity, wasted and burned everything so thoroughly that not a man nor a woman was left in one of the villages near Paris, from the Seine to Etampes. Everyone fled in terror and took refuge in Paris or elsewhere. The residents of three faubourgs of Paris, Saint-Germain-des-Prés, Notre-Dame-des-Champs, and Saint-Marceau left their houses empty and came into the city. On Holy Saturday the famous butchery of Saint-Marceau was moved to the Place Maubert near the Carmelite friars, and the butchery of Saint-Germain was also moved within the walls.[6]

The English took and utterly destroyed all the church towers which had been fortified in the country villages around Paris. Among these was a church and its tower in a village near Paris called Orly,[7] which had been fortified by the men [8] of the village. They had fitted it for a strong defense as well as possible and had stocked it with crossbows and other means of defense and with food in abundance. About two hundred men from the village occupied it. But those who trusted their strength and their fortress were in the end undeceived. The English came up on Good Friday [9] and stormed it. While the men inside were defending themselves manfully, with no thought of what was to come, and were fighting a hand to hand conflict with one group of the English, another group was breaking down the wall on the other side of the church. Thus the invaders took the besieged in the rear,[10] slew about a hundred of them, and took the rest captive. All who could fled. Then the English laid the stronghold waste, seized the supplies, and returned to their headquarters near Châtres and Montlhéry. On that Good Friday and Holy Saturday the English set fire to Montlhéry in the bourg and to Longjumeau and to many other towns round about. The smoke and flames rising from the towns to the heavens were visible at Paris in innumerable places. Thither a great part [11] of the rural population had fled. It was lamentable to see men, women, and children desolate. On Easter Day, I myself saw priests of ten country parishes communicating their people and keeping Easter in various chapels or any spot they could find in the monastery of the Carmelite friars at Paris. On the following day, the nobles and burgesses of Paris ordered the faubourgs of Saint-Germain, Notre-Dame-des-Champs, and Saint-Marceau to be burned. Permission was given, so it is said, to everyone to carry off anything he could from the houses: wood, iron, tiles, or any other materials; and to go openly and pillage. There were found many to do this, who ran swiftly to execute the edict. Then you might have seen some rejoicing over their gains and others groaning and moaning over their losses.

On that day several fine mansions and some very beautiful and

sumptuous manor houses were destroyed and burned by the inhabitants to prevent the enemy's establishing themselves in them and
doing mischief. Many houses, however, remained untouched. In
Easter week the men of the village of Châtres, which is near the
place of Chanteloup,[12] fortified their church. It was at that time a
fine handsome building with a stone bell tower roofed over with lead.
They put in it a large supply of food and all their possessions, household goods and utensils and tools, and prepared for a strong defense
by stocking it as completely as possible with crossbows, lead, stones,
and other instruments of war. They blocked the windows and doors
with stones and surrounded the church with a very wide and deep
ditch. Then on the arrival of the English[13] they shut themselves up
in it with their wives and children, confident that with their captain
they could successfully withstand the enemy. The English stationed
themselves above them on the hill, on whose slope the church and
the whole village were situated, and speedily prepared engines for
hurling stones down upon them. Thereupon the captain and some of
the more important men, in fear of the siege machines, abandoned the
common people in the church and in the turrets round the tower and
shut themselves up in another smaller[14] and stronger tower which
was less likely to be harmed.[15] When the common people realized
that they had been left in danger while the others had found safety,
they began to murmur against their leaders, saying that they had done
ill to leave them alone and helpless, and that as for themselves, they
would certainly surrender at discretion to the English. The captain
and those with him feared that their own capture would result from
the common people's surrender, and to prevent it, ordered their servants or hirelings[16] to set fire to the church from within. The moment
the fire was set the flames leaped up, began to burn the church within
and without, and thence spread swiftly to the tower in which the captain and his companions were hiding. So great was the violence of the
flames that the whole church, the tower and the bells were consumed.
Still more lamentable, alas! is the fact that of twelve hundred men,
women and children there did not remain three hundred who were
not pitiably burned to death by the voracious flames. For all the
doors and windows of the church were walled up, as I have said.
What is more, those who did get out by jumping or by letting them-

selves down [17] by ropes found in their path the English, who were attentively watching the disaster and deriding them because they and not the English had inflicted this damage upon themselves, and they were all brutally slaughtered. The captain alone, since he was a noble man, escaped and surrendered to the English. Thus that church, which was very fine, was utterly destroyed with all that was in it. Besides the parish church of this good and rich town, there was a priory there and a cloister of monks [18] belonging to the monastery of Saint-Maur-des-Fossés. The population was almost entirely [19] wiped out. I heard this lamentable story, as I have told it here, in Paris from a man who had been shut up in the church and had escaped alive by the grace of our Lord Jesus Christ, Whom he justly [20] extolled for his salvation.[21]

At the same time similar and equally lamentable events were occurring in Thoury in Beauce. Thoury was a village situated on the plain on the road between Etampes and Orléans and contained fine, handsome buildings, the residences, in many instances, of great princes and barons as well as of the people. In the center of the town was a castle which the inhabitants had fortified with ditches and watch towers for a strong defense and were now holding. When the English came to this district, the men of the town with their goods, wives, and children took refuge in this fortress. They built [22] huts and cabins within the fortifications and hid in them for the time being. For they had set fire to their houses as a measure against the English, as the English would have set fire to the same houses later [23] as a measure against them. It happened that when the English were already close at hand, the captain who was the keeper of the castle noticed a little house standing near the castle which had escaped the flames and commanded that it be set on fire like the others.[24] Eyewitnesses have told a dolorous tale of the disaster that ensued, alas! As soon as the house was fired, a sudden, strong gust of wind arose and carried burning coals glowing with devouring flames to the castle and into the courtyard. The flames pitiably consumed all the huts and the multitude of their inhabitants, except for a few who managed to escape by leaping from the walls.[25] It is fitting that I remain silent as to the amounts of wine, money, grain, vessels, and household goods which perished there, since the destruction of human life is a source of much greater concern. Thus that country town, once distinguished for its population and its mansions, was pitiably reduced to nothing by its own inhabitants.

In the octave of Easter [26] the English decided [27] to abandon the siege which they were maintaining before Paris. A great multitude of their men-at-arms drew near the city at this time, overran the vineyards and fields, and showed themselves near Notre-Dame-des-Champs and the monastery of the Carthusians. [28] When the French saw them, those who had been ordered to do so manned the walls, and others, especially the nobles who were present in the city in large numbers with the regent at this time, armed themselves and took up their station outside the walls. They did not go far from the walls, for the English drew back when they saw them prepared for battle, and thus there was no fighting that day. [29] It is said that some of the English made this demonstration in order that the rest might retreat safely with their carts, wagons, and other impedimenta. The French were engaged to prevent their offering any hindrance to the retreat to the Chartrain which the English were making. The next day, however, that is, the second feria, [30] it rained and hailed so abundantly all day long that the strength of the horses failed. They could not pull their loads, and the wagons, soaked with rain, remained stationary on the roads and highways. Many horses and their drivers were pitiably drowned by the hail and the torrential rains. It is said that the English incurred very heavy losses both of baggage and of men on that day. [31]

In this fashion the English made their retreat from Paris to the Chartrain. On the way, they seized or destroyed many fortresses and plundered and burned many towns. An incident which occurred at Compiègne [32] between the town and the wood may serve as an example of the harm they did in many places. In a conflict there between the townsmen and the English, who were hiding in the wood, many of the townsmen were wounded, slain, or captured as a result of unwise leadership. The truth is that several of the townsmen had issued forth bravely to conquer the English in the wood, whom they had supposed to be far less numerous than they were, and that the nobles of the region, who had resorted to the town in large numbers to save their skins, gave them no help in the battle. The present narrative now turns from the consideration of further misfortunes and disasters to treat briefly of an occasion of joy and gladness, the peace between two kings.[33]

As the time drew near at which our Lord Jesus Christ, after reconciling in wondrous wise God the Father and humankind, ascended with rejoicing into Heaven according to the reckoning of His church, that is, the feast of the Ascension of our Lord and Savior,[34] the Lord, beholding the afflictions of the unfortunate and hearing the groans of the poor captives, willed to suffer no longer the anguish of the French people, who had borne for twenty-four years and more the burdens and disasters of the wars waged by the English and their other enemies, and willed to have mercy on a people so afflicted. Hence it was, the Savior thus disposing, that on the Sunday on which *Cantate* is sung in the church,[35] there came to Chartres, in the region where the king of England and his men were attacking France, ambassadors and councilors of distinction from the regent to negotiate a peace between the two kings.[36] The king of England, being desirous of peace, likewise designated ambassadors of distinction, provided with safe-conducts, to represent him in the negotiations.[37] The representatives of each side conferred and finally agreed upon the terms of a peace,[38] by the inspiration of the Holy Spirit and to the joy of the angels, as we believe. When the peace had been sworn to by both sides, many of the English nobles with joyful devotion made a pilgrimage barefoot to the cathedral of Saint Mary of Chartres, which was at some distance from their tents. The French ambassadors who had negotiated the peace returned at once to Paris. With them went the English [39] ambassadors who were to swear to the peace on behalf of the king of England and his son [40] in the presence of the regent and to receive his oath, as was proper. Both the English and the French ambassadors on their arrival at Paris were received with all honor by the duke and the citizens on every hand.[41] And it came to pass on the Sunday before the Ascension of the Lord Jesus,[42] on which *Vocem jocunditatis* [43] is sung, the regent with his ambassadors and the English ambassadors went to the cathedral of Notre Dame [44] of Paris to hear the treaty read out and to swear to it.[45] Such was the pleasure of the regent and his council and the citizens. After hearing the treaty, the regent for himself and for his subjects took

solemn [46] oaths on the holy relics to keep the treaty of peace, which
had been placed on the altar, and steadfastly to observe it, and the
English did likewise. The ratification of the treaty brought ineffable
joy to all the populace. Straightway the cathedral bells broke into loud
pealing and devout melody and all the canons and clergy joyfully
and devoutly sang *Te Deum laudamus,* praising God and giving Him,
as was meet, thanks for the peace. The same things were done in
all the churches and collegiate churches of the city.[47] On that day
throughout the city there was heard the voice of joy and of glad
exultation in the tabernacles of the just and of the afflicted.[48] All men
rejoiced, and rightly, save perchance those who in time of war make
great gains from the deeds of war through which other men suffer
loss; the armorers, for example, and those who, having set aside the
fear of God, are eager to carry on illicit robbery and other nefarious
works and to fill their purses dishonestly with what is not theirs,
of which they will have to render a strict account on the Day of
Judgment. False traitors and notorious thieves lamented the peace
because they now feared that they would be accused of all their crimes
and misdeeds, be brought to trial, and finally [49] be hanged on a gibbet.
But enough of this.

Peace, so long desired, was by God's will established on these terms:
that John, king of France, who was being detained in England,
should without delay be restored, well and active, to the government
of his kingdom; that the king of England should remain in undisturbed possession of the duchy of Guyenne or Aquitaine, the counties
of Saintes, Angoulême, Poitou, Bigorre, Périgord, Ponthieu, Guînes,[50]
and the towns of La Rochelle and Calais; and that he should receive,
within a limited space of time, for his expenses and the ransom of
the king of France, three million florins d'écu of good gold and
weight, and other moneys for the return of the fortresses around
Paris held by the English.[51] Observe that a million florins are equivalent to ten times a hundred thousand florins and that the total was
thirty times a hundred thousand florins d'écu.[52] Such [53] were the
famous terms of this peace as they were made public. A truce to
permit the fulfillment of the peace terms was declared from the
feast of Saint Michael next to the feast of Saint Michael thereafter.[54]
Proclamation was made that no one was to insult or molest the Eng-

lish in any way and that they were to be permitted to go and come and buy and sell in peace; and that whosoever desired was to trade with them peacefully and quietly. The king of England, moreover, could and should [55] go to Calais without let or hindrance, and cause King John to be escorted thither and there confirm and swear to the peace treaty with him.[56] This done, King John would be free to return joyfully to Paris.

Although, by God's will, peace had been declared, misfortune and suffering did not on that account cease. It is true that the English ceased to oppress and rob the common people, but many Frenchmen did not refrain from doing so. Robbers and thieves grew in power along the highways and roads and in the woods. They attacked wayfarers more fiercely than ever before, not only robbing them, but even cutting their throats without mercy, as they had not been wont to do before. Many of these thieves and murderers were afterward taken, brought to justice, and hanged. Indeed, the English who were still occupying fortresses captured some robbers of this sort, judged them, and hanged them from trees, thus showing themselves kinder to the peasants in the villages than were their own natural lords.

At this time, after peace had been made, there arose a violent dispute between John of Artois, who had called himself count of Eu,[57] and the town of Péronne in the diocese of Noyon concerning the fortification of the castle of the town. Since the controversy continued, Jean laid siege to Péronne, a good town, strong, walled, and populous. He called to his aid many nobles from France, the duke of Orléans, brother of King John, among others, and many English mercenaries. After many assaults upon the town, he finally took it. He then pillaged and burned it, slaying many of the inhabitants, and he burned many neighboring towns as well.[58] The nobles of France at that time [59] withdrew their protection from many of the good towns and the cities, and inflicted injuries upon the burgesses, to both their bodies and their possessions, if they chanced to venture forth.[60] These nobles destroyed the good town of Chauny-sur-Oise, among others. Thus those who were most bound to defend their country troubled it most at this time. Wherefore the citizens of Paris, for the distrust they felt of the nobles, kept watchmen on duty at night and sentries at the gates by day [61] as diligently as if they were expecting an English attack. They longed for the return of King John, that at his coming the wicked noblemen who were molesting the land and all other robbers might be brought to justice, the whole land be made safe, and the roads and woods be cleared of the robbers who were lurking in them on every hand in untold numbers. The highways and roads were actually less safe at this time than they had been when the English were waging war on France, except that houses were not set on fire nor men taken captive. The fair of Lendit [62] was held [63] as usual near Saint-Denis in the Ile de France this year but according to reports few merchants came to buy merchandise, so great was their fear of being robbed or of being killed for their money by the robbers who infested the woods and the roads.

In the same year, 1360, about the time of the feast of Saint John the Baptist, King John of France returned in peace from England to France.[64] He disembarked at Calais and stayed there some time, until the first payment of his ransom had been made to the king of England and hostages had been exchanged as pledges of the ultimate fulfillment of the conditions of peace.[65] This done, at the time of our Lord's Advent, King John of France came to Paris, where he was received with the greatest distinction and honor by all the citizens, clergy and laity alike.[66] At this time the robbers in the highways and woods of Champagne and Picardy began to abate a little, but no road beyond Orléans was safe on account of the English who refused to withdraw at once from the fortresses which they had held.

That same year arose those sons of Belial and men of iniquity, warriors from various lands who assailed other men with no right and no reason other than their own passions, iniquity, malice, and hope of gain, and yet [67] were called the Great Company.[68] These miscreants, united in a large band and under arms, drew near to Avignon, desiring to subdue our lord the supreme pontiff, the cardinals, and the Holy Church of God. They came to Pont-Saint-Esprit, a city near Avignon, and took it by force of arms. There they passed some time wasting the adjacent countryside horribly. They planned in some fashion or other to subjugate ultimately the whole city of Avignon, the residence of Pope Innocent VI and the cardinals, and the other towns and fortresses of that region as well, Montpellier and Toulouse, Narbonne and Carcassonne. Finally, however, after receiving large sums of money from the pope and with his absolution, it is said, they left the country round Avignon and scattered in various directions through the world, doing harm wherever they went.[69]

The same year there was such a shortage of wine and fruit that a full cask of wine cost 25 or more florins at Paris and there were no cherries and little wheat to be had. An apple cost 3 or 4 denarii at Paris. There was a great plague that year in Flanders and Picardy and the next year at Paris.[70]

1361

IN A.D. 1361 THERE WAS A VERY GREAT[1] ABUNDANCE OF FRUIT AND WINE, BUT BEfore they could come to maturity a great dearth of wine, wheat and fruit resulting from the failure of the crops the year before made itself felt in France. The winter was long, the spring very dry, and the summer temperate. There were many deaths at Paris, especially among the poor who kept pouring into the city from the villages, straitened by hunger, penury, and want. Seventy or eighty dead bodies were commonly carried out [daily?] from the Hôtel-Dieu this spring and summer. There were many deaths in England as well.[2] The count of Saint-Pol, one of the hostages for King John and the peace, and several other hostages, both knights and burgesses, died there.[3]

The same year some Bretons and Gascons came to certain places in Poitou and Anjou and pillaged and plundered the whole region, for no reason at all. They took several fortresses and castles, seized the priory of Cunault on the Loire, and pillaged the whole district. Under the leadership of an Englishman called Robert Markaunt, they took the castle of Vendôme at night and with it the countess and her daughter and many lords and ladies who were there. Markaunt, who was not of noble birth and came from nothing, reached undue elevation by steps of this kind. He became a nobleman and a vigorous supporter of the king of France, although he was English and had always been on the English side.[4]

Soon after this, many Bretons went through the regions around Chartres and Orléans in the manner of freebooters[5] and plundered the whole region, with the result that the country population fled from the villages and took refuge in Paris. The freebooters came so close to Paris on the west that the inhabitants of the faubourgs were very much alarmed. None of the nobles prescribed any remedy. On the contrary, the princes and the councilors forbade [6] the burgesses to interfere in any way with these Bretons and Gascons and to busy themselves with their buying and selling as best they could. Thus the poor and the country dwellers were plundered, and there was none to help. Hardly anyone dared to go from Paris to Orléans and Chartres and other cities in those parts. These ills all had their beginning this year, but they continued throughout the next, becoming steadily worse all the time.

This [7] year in Lent a very large and brilliant star, hitherto unknown and rather like a comet, was seen several times before dawn in Touraine and Anjou.[8]

This year the winter was unnaturally wet and warm. As a result many trees in various parts of the world blossomed before the feast of our Lord's Nativity, but they bore no fruit either that year or the year following.

The same year the king of France issued some very good coins, silver gros of the value of 12 Parisian denarii. They were not so large as the former gros, which had been worth 16 denarii.[9] There were heavy taxes on sales and gabelles on salt, and the plague raged in several towns and localities.

1362 IN A.D. 1362, RECKONING THE YEAR FROM EASTER, WHICH FELL ON APRIL 17, THE TREES and vines gave every sign of great fruitfulness. But in Easter week there was a very heavy frost which ruined the vines in the Ile de France, in Touraine, in Anjou, and even in Lorraine, and killed nut trees and fruit trees. As a result of this frost and the wet, almost continuously rainy, winter, there was a great dearth of wine, nuts and fruit, except in a few localities.[1] There was not so much wheat as usual either, but everyone got through the year very well, thanks to the great abundance of wine, fruit and wheat in the preceding year. Oats were abundant as a result of copious rains.

In October of this year Pope Innocent VI died at Avignon and the lord cardinals proceeded to the election of a new pope.[2] After they had been shut up together some time and had found it impossible to agree on a member of the college, they chose Guillaume Grimouart, the abbot of Saint Victor of Marseilles in the Benedictine order. He was called Urban V and was consecrated at Avignon within the octave of All Saints.[3] There arose a great murmur from the clergy and the people against the cardinals because they had not cared to elect one of the many worthy and suitable members of their own college, but I firmly believe that the cause is not hidden from the Holy Spirit.[4]

At this time King John went to the consecration of the new pope at Avignon in order to betroth himself to Jeanne, widowed queen of Apulia and Sicily.[5] Just as John had had two wives, Bonne of Bohemia and Jeanne,[6] daughter of the Count of Boulogne and widow of Philip of Burgundy, son of the lord previously mentioned,[7] so Jeanne had had two husbands, King Andrew, brother of the king of Hungary, first, and after him, Count Louis.[8] King John never took Jeanne to wife, however.

Before this, in the same year, the young duke of Burgundy who had married the daughter of Louis, count of Flanders, died. His marriage had never been consummated on account of the extreme youth and immaturity of both husband and wife.[9] The duchy of Burgundy fell to King John by the law of inheritance because his mother, Queen Jeanne, had been the aunt of the late duke.[10] The dowager countess of Flanders, the mother of Louis, the present count of Flanders, inherited the counties of Artois and Arras.[11]

In the same year the plague was at its height in Poitou, Brittany,[12] and Anjou. As before, men died everywhere and indiscriminately of this disease characterized by swellings. The freebooters did not cease their depredations, for all this, and pillaged the countryside and the inhabitants of the Beauce, in the Ile de France near Paris, of Orléans[13] and of Chartres more ruthlessly than they had[14] the year before. The country folk were forced to flee to places of greater safety.[15]

This year the duke of Lancaster died. He was an Englishman, noble and valiant in arms, whose counsel the king of England had followed in the conduct of his wars against France.[16]

The same year the king and his councilors imposed very heavy imposts and tailles, sometimes called *maltôtes,* on all salable articles and on every sort of merchandise. A cask of Burgundy, for example, was taxed at 64 solidi of Paris, and for every cask of French wine 32 solidi of Paris were paid to the royal tax collectors. The merchants had to pay taxes on this scale for everything they sold.[17] Thus the people were heavily burdened and did all they could to get concessions. Many men, with their wives and children, changed [18] their residences to other regions.

The same year the count of Armagnac in Gascony was defeated and captured [19] by the count of Foix, and many of his men were killed.[20]

This year, on Maundy Thursday at night,[21] the English and other freebooters who were occupying the district came up by stealth to the walls of Orléans, in number about five hundred, though all of them were not visible. They proceeded with caution [22] and would have entered the town by scaling the walls and thus have taken [23] it and pillaged it, had it not been for a little boy on the walls who was awake while those whose duty it was to keep watch were sleeping. He saw the enemy and shouted out a warning. A miller saw them [24] too and roused others by his shouts. The freebooters were frightened away by the clamor and hastily retreated. They passed an establishment of Carmelite friars which stood outside the city walls in their flight, entered it, and seized and carried off [25] whatever they could find there, chalices,[26] vestments, and the like, after the manner of freebooters.

This year Robert Markaunt, the Englishman who had taken the castle of Vendôme, as I have told, came in the guise of a friend and well-wisher to the castle of Toutvoie [27] near Le Mans, which belongs to the bishop of Le Mans. He left a large following hiding in a wood near the castle and went up to it with only a few men, planning to take it by craft [28] and guile. He told the men of the castle who were on the wall that he had come out of friendship for them and that he was planning no injury to them. The keepers of the castle, however, knew his cunning and in addition saw the men-at-arms hiding in the wood. Accordingly they tampered with the drawbridge by removing the pegs which held the planks and beams together, and

thus prevented them from tilting up, and by putting worthless imi-
tations in the place of the pegs in such a way that the substitution was
not perceptible. Then they lowered the bridge and permitted Robert
and the sixteen men with him to step onto it. When they were in the
middle of the bridge, the substitute pegs gave way, the planks of
the bridge up-ended and precipitated them all into the water where
it was very deep. Thus Robert and the greater part of his companions[29] were drowned. Only those lightest in weight escaped. The
men hiding in the wood beheld the mischance and fled in grief and
confusion. The bishop of Le Mans,[30] in return for large sums of
money, delivered the bodies of those who had been drowned to the
wives and friends at Chartres.

1363 IN A.D. 1363, RECKONING THE YEAR FROM
EASTER,[1] THE PEOPLE THROUGHOUT THE ILE
de France and Normandy as far as Poitou and Brittany were afflicted
and distressed on the one hand by the large number of robbers and
thieves on the road and in the villages, and on the other by very
heavy imposts and taxes. Murders were common on the highways[2]
and in the woods. There was none to defend the people nor to meet
these dangers and perils. Rather did the burdens which bore so
heavily upon the people seem to please the lords and princes whose
duty it was to oppose[3] and remedy these evils with a strong hand.

The same year, for several days beginning with Holy Trinity Eve,[4]
a very small star was seen at Paris before noon, about the third hour,
in the part of the sky where the sun commonly is at noon. The astronomers of Paris said that it signified peril to women in childbirth.
This was clearly so in some cases, but in truth we believe that by
God's will many more astonishing events than this followed upon
the portent. For from July to the feast of Saint Luke[5] of the same
year 1363, the plague raged at Paris to an extent that was wonderful
and fearful. More men than women died, and more children and
young people than adults.[6] When death entered a house, it carried
off the children of the family first and their parents only in the second
place.[7] It was impossible to enumerate accurately the dead, both old
and young, rich and poor. A very striking fact was that a man who

was well and happy one day would be dead two or three days later. Nor did death spare religious or priests or curates at this time. On the contrary, it seized great numbers of them suddenly, by God's will, in Paris and on its confines. It is said, furthermore, that men died in as great numbers in many little villages as at Paris and in the same way. This was especially true of Argenteuil, where there were seventeen hundred hearths or manors before the plague and it is said only four or five hundred after it.[8] It would stun anyone to read or hear the exact truth about the number of deaths which occurred every day at this time in the Hôtel-Dieu at Paris. Who could count the black-clad women, many of them young,[9] whom he saw about the city at that time? In many cases they had been bereaved and deprived of the comfort of both husband and children. Jean de Meulan, a man at once noble, venerable and discreet, bishop of Paris, died as the plague was slackening on the feast of Saint Cecilia, Virgin and Martyr,[10] in the twelfth year of his episcopate and in the eightieth year of his life. Master Etienne de Paris, Doctor of Laws, dean of Paris, succeeded him.[11]

This same [12] year, about the feast of All Saints,[13] a few of the enemies and the robbers who were in the Beauce and the country round Orléans and Chartres disguised themselves as dealers in swine and cowherds, concealed their arms, and went to the castle of Murs near Corbeil.[14] They found the knight who was lord of the castle standing in front of the castle gate and besought him to give them back their swine which, so they said, his servants had taken from them the day before. This they said mendaciously, for it was false. The lord of the castle said that if this were the case they might come in to identify their swine and take them away with them. Lo, the moment the brigands set foot on the drawbridge, they put off their disguise, appearing strongly armed, and laid hold on the lord. At a blast from their trumpets, their companions who were hiding in a wood nearby came up at once. In this way they took the castle with its lord and lady and all their household. Very shortly afterward they began to overrun the neighboring country, plundering the people and provisioning the castle ever more amply with the food which they stole from them. Many men-at-arms came to drive out the enemy who had taken the castle by fraud, or rather who had pilfered it, and to recover it from them by force of arms. After making one assault, however, they did nothing further and merely withdrew to Corbeil and established themselves there. They too began to waste the country round them, exactly as the enemy were doing, and to carry off wine and food supplies from the little villages, paying nothing, to provision Corbeil. They conducted themselves in such a way that they were even more feared by the people of this village and of the villages round about than was the enemy. Wherefore, very soon after their arrival, the men and women of the neighboring villages abandoned their labors and their houses and, with their children and such property as had been left them, hastened to Paris to find safety from friend and foe alike.[15] Nonetheless, under color and pretext of defending the country and of expelling [16] the enemy, the heaviest and most burdensome tailles and imposts imaginable and extraordinary charges were levied on wines and other merchandise both in Paris and outside. Thus at this time the people, both in the city of Paris [17] and outside, were as grievously oppressed by their friends and protectors as by their enemies. Indeed, the story that is commonly told [18] of the dog and the wolf seemed to have come true. Once upon a time there was a very strong dog in whom his master had complete confidence. He thought that this dog of his would keep his sheep safe and would drive off any wolf that would try to devour them. This was the case on several occasions. At length, however, in the course of time, the dog contracted a great friendship with a wolf. He told the wolf that he was to attack and seize a sheep boldly and that he would run eagerly after the wolf as if to recover the sheep and bring it back to his master, but that so soon as both were hidden in a wood and well out of sight of the master and [19] his shepherd they would together devour the poor sheep whole. This they often did with success.[20] When the dog came back, he was praised by his master, who had been deceived by his pursuit of the wolf into thinking that he had done all that he could to recover the sheep. That accursed dog repeated the trick successfully until he and the wolf between them had iniquitously and fraudulently devoured all his master's sheep.[21] That is all.

Earlier in the same year there was a great war which had been going on for some time near Metz in Lorraine between the count of

Vaudemont, sire de Joinville,[22] on the one hand, and the duke of Lorraine and the duke of Bar[23] and many Germans on the other. The count of Vaudemont had in his company a brave knight called the Archpriest[24] and many brave Breton men-at-arms who did great harm to the whole country and especially to this neighborhood. The so-called Archpriest and his Bretons then went on to plunder Burgundy in the same way. They inflicted many injuries on that land and on all wayfarers there.[25] Men could travel only with difficulty and at the risk of being robbed and could defend themselves only at the risk of being killed. This was true also of the country around Orléans and Chartres and in Normandy across the Seine in Neustria.[26]

Freebooters held the tower of Rolleboise at this time[27] and overran the whole country as far as Poissy, and farther, at their pleasure. Some frequently crossed the Seine and overran the French Vexin as far as Pontoise, plundering as they went.[28] Had it not been for the men of Rouen who kept them out of the waters of the Seine, no ships could have plied safely back and forth between Paris and Rouen.[29]

This present year King John, before his return to France and during his summer's sojourn in the Roman Curia, together with the king of Cyprus, took the cross at the wish and with the assent of Pope Urban V as the pledge of a pilgrimage and journey overseas to fight against Saracens and unbelievers, in the company of many other nobles and, should it please God, to recover the Holy Land from their hands. They arranged to set out two years from this present year. When matters had been thus arranged, the king returned without delay to France.[30] The king of Cyprus accompanied him and then went on to Rouen and Caen where he was given a magnificent reception in September of that year by Charles, duke of Normandy, the eldest son of the king, and by nobles and burgesses. Very soon afterward he crossed over to England in order to stir up the English to take the cross as the pledge of an expedition overseas.[31]

About the feast of Saint Andrew[32] this year King John went to Amiens and there convoked nobles and prelates, abbots and burgesses, that he might ask of them advice and subsidies toward the remainder of his ransom.[33] No small part of this sum had already been received in England. What the king did afterward shall be told. The land and people of France meantime remained a prey to the oppression of robbers and to the dangers described above.

On the feast of Saint Thomas the Apostle [34] the count of Auxerre [35] besieged the robbers who were without right occupying the castle of Murs near Corbeil. When the robbers felt the force of the stones which were hurled in upon them by machines outside, they finally surrendered on condition that their lives be spared. They withdrew unharmed and were even [36] escorted by our men-at-arms beyond the Chartrain that they might, safe and uninjured, join their allies who were established in fortresses in Maine. The minute they had been taken leave of and dismissed by our men, they began to plunder and pillage everyone as lustily as they had before. Extraordinary that men like these, wretches, robbers and rascals that they were, who ought to have been killed as a warning to other robbers, should not only have been allowed to depart freely [37] but even have been escorted past the nearest frontiers. Perhaps they received such consideration because they held the lord of the castle prisoner and were given these terms lest they kill him.

About this time or a little before, Louis, duke of Anjou, one of the sons of the king of France, who had been in England for some time as a hostage for his father with other nobles and burgesses of France,[38] left England secretly,[39] without permission from the king of England and with no companions,[40] and speedily joined his wife in Guise castle.[41] He went on to Paris after our Lord's Nativity and in the presence of his brother, Charles, duke of Normandy, eldest son of King John and regent of the kingdom in his father's absence, and of the king of Cyprus then in Paris, and of the burgesses of Paris [42] assembled in the palace, he said that when his father, the king, and the people knew the reasons for his departure they would all hold him honorably excused. He said further that he desired to ride under arms over the countryside to extirpate all robbers and thieves, to expel all those wrongfully occupying castles and fortresses throughout the country, and to restore peace to the land by force of arms with God's aid. He begged the assistance and good will of his brother the duke of Normandy in this enterprise. The duke replied that he would take counsel on these matters as was meet.[43] What came of it will perhaps appear below.

About the time of our Lord's Nativity in this same year, King John had left Amiens and had gone to England, either because he had not yet paid his ransom in full or because he desired to keep his agreement and faith with the king of England now that his son, a hostage for him, had left England without permission. There were those who said that he went back to England merely for diversion and against the will and counsel of his nobles who repeatedly and in all humility sought to dissuade him from sailing. They were with reason concerned about him and feared lest the voyage injure his health.[44] He had entrusted the government of his kingdom to his eldest son, Charles, the illustrious duke of Normandy.[45] Thus King John crossed over to England a second time, notwithstanding the fact that he had taken the cross at the hands of Pope Urban V in Avignon and was pledged to go overseas [46] to subdue the enemies of the Crucified in company with the king of Cyprus and many nobles from his own kingdom. Alas! He was not to return from England alive.

The winter of this year 1363 was very severe and long. A hard frost accompanied by frequent snowfalls persisted almost to the end of March, when it broke at last. In midwinter [47] it had frozen the vines even to their roots, in several localities, and had destroyed many nut trees. The sheep and lambs of many districts perished as a result of the cold and the lack of fodder. Bread and other foodstuffs were stored to protect them from the cold in very deep vaults and cellars which had always before kept warm all winter. Yet I saw supplies thus protected brought up frozen even when they had been covered with straw down below, a most extraordinary fact. Vines and trees were frozen in root and branch as we have seen.[48] With God's favor I shall describe what sort of season for vines and fruit ensued [49] when I treat and write of the events of the next year.

I do not write here of events in Brittany [50] and elsewhere, however numerous, but I leave them to other writers who know the truth about them more fully than I. I shall apply myself to the recital of what befell the following year, though not of all, rudely, in rude words, since I am rude.

1364

TOWARD THE END OF THE YEAR 1364, RECK-ONING THE YEAR FROM EASTER, THE OC-tave of which fell that year on Sunday at the end of March, on the eve of the feast of the Annunciation,[1] when King John was in Eng-land, as I have said, Jean de Craon, archbishop of Reims,[2] procured a decree from Parlement that the very large, thick, high walls in front of his castle gate, that is, the Porte de Mars, which the men of Reims had built before in the time of the English wars and had re-cently strengthened, should be utterly destroyed. He hastened from Paris within the octave of Easter with commissioners deputed to the task by Parlement. The decree was executed in the presence of all the citizens, who remained silent and did not make their anger known, though they were greatly displeased. It was then arranged that the walls be erected elsewhere without derogation of the bishop's dignity or damage to his castle, which as I have said was called the Porte de Mars. Thus this point of difference, together with many others which had been creating discord between the citizens of Reims and their lord the archbishop, were amicably composed or yielded.[3]

About this time, Charles of Evreux, king of Navarre, of whose royal blood and marriage with a daughter of King John of France I have already spoken above,[4] had, while sojourning in his kingdom of Navarre, made many alliances with numerous kings of various nations, among others with the king of Aragon it is said,[5] and with many barons and lords, who held a large part of the land in Nor-mandy, especially in Neustria, and in the French part also held many places, for example, Evreux, Mantes, Meulan, Pacy-sur-Eure,[6] and Anet. He then openly renounced his allegiance to the lord of whom he held these lands in fee, namely Charles, duke of Normandy and dauphin of Vienne, regent of the kingdom during his father's ab-sence in England.[7] At once the regent sent to the king of Navarre's part of Normandy many powerful and noble men-at-arms, among whom were the count of Auxerre with his men and Bertrand du Guesclin,[8] a brave knight from French [9] Brittany, with many sol-diers from France and French Brittany. They went [10] first to Mantes, a handsome and pleasant castle situated on the Seine beyond Poissy, which had a high keep, powerful walls, and a bridge. They entered the town, not by force of arms but by a stratagem which went undetected by the inhabitants, took it, and pillaged it completely, slaughtering all those who offered resistance. They did not kill such as they found defenseless, but they robbed the burgesses of everything they had and cast them out of the city destitute and destined to be paupers and mendicants henceforth. Then they assailed the keep or tower and took it by force at the cost of many lives. In the keep, together with the Navarrese and the native inhabitants, they found men from Paris and Saint-Denis in the Ile de France and from other parts of the Ile de France valiantly defending themselves and the tower.[11] These were finally taken by force and brought to Paris, some twenty-eight men in all.[12] Some were beheaded on their arrival in Paris and then their bodies affixed to the gibbet, and others were handed over to the prévôt of Saint-Denis, who executed the same sentence on them.[13]

After this the regent's men took the very strong castle and town of Meulan-sur-Seine. They stormed[14] its tower, which was very big, and leveled most of its walls to the ground.[15] Thus in a short space of time they had reduced many of the lands and possessions of the king of Navarre to unsightly ruins.[16] Their hangers-on overran the region and plundered all travelers, without distinguishing friend from foe, to such a degree that no one could safely traverse the district on his way to Rouen from Paris or from Rouen to Paris. The nobles and their followers who conducted these sieges permitted such pillaging. Thus the castle and town of Mantes, which had up to now been rich and prosperous and had in days of old, according to the chronicles, been very warlike and valiant, had been exposed to this great peril because of the favor which its inhabitants, those of the immediate vicinity, in Meulan for example, and of all the adjacent countryside, alas! had shown the king of Navarre. At least the men who took the church of Mantes, a magnificent stone structure, did it the least possible harm.[17] All this destruction was wrought to the end that the king of Navarre, in case he should attack France and the neighborhood of Paris, might not find in these castles the aid and comfort which would enable him to do great harm,[18] and could not interfere with shipping going from Rouen to Paris and from Paris to Rouen as he did formerly, according to our account of 1358.[19]

The king of Navarre's reason for renouncing all allegiance to the duke and to the king, the duke's father,[20] was his claim to the duchy of Burgundy. He declared that he was a more immediate heir than John, king of France, who was at this time in peaceful possession of the duchy. The barons of Burgundy and all the duchy had long since done homage to John as to their rightful lord, as I have said above. Nevertheless the king of Navarre was striving with all his might, but without just cause, to controvert his claim.[21]

The men-at-arms of the party of the king of Navarre who were at Evreux heard of these exploits, and for fear lest the French troops attack Evreux in the same way and take by assault the castle or fortress, they immediately set about strengthening the defenses of the whole town.[22]

At this time an accusation was brought to Duke Albert, son of Lewis the late duke of Bavaria, who in time past had usurped the empire against the will of the church, and representative for his brother,[23] the count of Hainaut, in Hainaut, against Engelbert d'Enghien near Brabant. It was said that this very noble prince and valiant knight had plotted treason to the land and county of Hainaut. On this account Duke Albert seized the count at night in Kyurna near Valenciennes, whither he had come in the course of a journey, and took him to Quesnoy,[24] three leagues from Valenciennes. He had him beheaded in the castle there without delay and without the formality[25] of a trial. The men of Hainaut feared lest many misfortunes to their land originate with this deed, since the count was of high and noble birth and renowned in distant lands.[26]

That year, very soon after Easter, on the eighth or tenth day of April,[27] the illustrious prince and noble lord, John, king of France, of worthy[28] memory, died and departed this world in England. Edward, king of England, and all England with him lamented John bitterly. The king and the queen and their children and the nobles of the kingdom all donned mourning garments for him. The king had John's obsequies performed in Saint Paul's cathedral in London, and dignified, magnificent, and sumptuous they were.[29] For the occasion Edward provided horses caparisoned from head to foot with the arms and lilies[30] of France and riders fittingly and magnificently adorned[31] with the same emblems;[32] also, eighty great lights,[33] each twelve feet high, according to those who claim to have been there, and four thousand wax tapers, each containing six pounds of wax, for the bier or rather the ornate wooden canopy which had been erected over the king's body in the cathedral.[34] The English escorted [35] the king's lifeless body to the shores of the sea. There they said farewell to the household of the dead king whom they were sending back with the body and then returned with tears, it is said,[36] to London. They took with them the hostages from France who had been in England before John returned. The illustrious [37] corpse was taken first to the church of the nuns of Saint-Antoine outside Paris and then, on the Sunday within the octave of the feast of the Ascension which was the eve of the feast of Saint John before the Latin Gate,[38] to the cathedral of Notre Dame at Paris, with the greatest ceremony on the part of all the clergy, including the University of Paris, and of an innumerable multitude. There were present many prelates, barons, and nobles. The king of Cyprus accompanied the three sons of the dead king, Duke Charles, the eldest, and his two brothers. On the next day, after the performance of solemn obsequies, the devout celebration of masses and the recital of the office for the dead, with appropriate rites,[39] the body of the king was escorted by the cortege just described to the church of Saint Denis in the Ile de France and there, on the day after the feast of Saint John [40] before the Latin Gate, given Christian burial with great solemnity close to the high altar of the monks' church. John rests with his fathers in a well-built stone tomb. When the tomb was opened to prepare it, rings set with gems of great value and a golden crown of great price were found, but no bones whatever.

After the burial of King John of France in Saint-Denis', Charles, his eldest son, duke of Normandy and dauphin of Vienne, reigned. On the feast of the Holy Trinity [41] he, together with his wife, Jeanne of Bourbon, received in Reims the holy unction and the crown at the hands of Jean de Craon, archbishop of Reims.

While the dauphin was in Reims for his coronation, Charles of Evreux, king of Navarre, of whom there has been sufficient mention above, who had renounced his allegiance to the dauphin long before his coronation,[42] heard in Navarre how Bertrand du Guesclin on behalf of the king of France had taken his towns of Mantes and

Meulan and had placed them in the hands of the king of France while he was yet but regent. The king of Navarre was very sorry and very much astonished to hear this news. Desiring to do all he could to recover his towns speedily and to defend his land at Evreux and on the confines of Evreux, he sent thither a great army composed of Gascon mercenaries and of his own Navarrese with the Captal de Buch,[43] a nobleman very valiant in arms, in his place as their captain. He sent in addition an abundant supply of knights and men-at-arms with their captains. They descended upon various parts of Normandy,[44] especially upon Neustria, and took and held stoutly many castles and fortresses. At length the Captal de Buch and all his men reached the district[45] of Evreux and entered the city. The great multitude of Navarrese who were holding Evreux for their lord, the king of Navarre, in his absence and defending it stoutly against the French received the Captal with the greatest joy.[46] The king of France, on learning of his arrival in Normandy, sent the count of Auxerre and Bertrand du Guesclin against him and his troops. They took with them a great multitude of Bretons and men of other nations to fight[47] against the Gascons and Navarrese. After an interchange of many words between the two armies, the place and time of a pitched battle were agreed upon.[48] On the appointed day, namely the Thursday within the octave of Pentecost,[49] both armies, full of courage, met together at the appointed place, namely, a field near Croix-Saint-Leufroi.[50] The battle began and was hotly contested from the start.[51] The Gascons and Navarrese and the rest attacked[52] our Frenchmen and Bretons valiantly, and they in their turn defended themselves stoutly with lances, swords, and bows and arrows. Most of the action[53] took place on foot, not on horseback. The close array of the Gascons, Navarrese, and Normans in the king of Navarre's service offered an impenetrable wall, so to speak, to the first attacks of our Frenchmen and Bretons, with the result that they were vigorously repulsed and many of them killed or mortally wounded.[54] Of the French, the sire d'Annequin, a valiant Picard knight, who was in command of the French crossbowmen,[55] the viscount of Beaumont[56] in Anjou, the sire de Béthencourt in Caux,[57] the sire de Villequier who was captain of Caudebec, and many other nobles whose names I do not know fell dead on that field. Bertrand du Guesclin, who was one of the French captains, as I have said,[58] realizing that his troops could not easily [59] penetrate the close formation of the Gascon and Navarrese men-at-arms and thus could not easily vanquish them,[60] bethought himself of a stratagem, as became an experienced soldier.[61] With a few of his Bretons he withdrew from the battle a little way and, still armed, mounted a horse. Then he and his men returned all together suddenly and attacked the Gascons and the rest from the rear. They valiantly broke into [62] the whole phalanx of Gascons and Navarrese and the rest while the count of Auxerre and his men went on fighting none the less bravely [63] in front. In this way the Gascons and the others of their army were separated a little way from each other, and an opening was made in their ranks.[64] The fighting became very hard and fierce and many were killed and wounded on both sides, but more Gascons and Navarrese than French. Among the dead on the Gascon side in this battle were John Jowel, captain of Rolleboise [65] and of many other fortresses, who had been in the habit of boasting that he was the duke of Normandy, and the Bascon de Mareuil,[66] a very strong and active man, and James Plantain, an Englishman.[67] They were all valiant knights.[68] The sire de Sacquenville, a Norman upon whose counsel the king of Navarre had to a large extent relied in his opposition to the king of France and who had done great harm in Normandy, was taken prisoner.[69] He was afterwards led captive to Rouen and was publicly beheaded in the chief square of that city. His head affixed to a stake is there for all to see to this very day.[70]

When, then, the Gascons and the Navarrese and the rest [71] saw that many of their men had been killed and that the French and the Bretons as if unwearied continued to rage against them, they felt that there had already been quite sufficient [72] carnage in their midst and decided to entrust their lives at once to the benefits of flight rather than to the protection of arms. They were, however, so hindered by the sallies and onsets of our men by whom they were surrounded that they could not flee to any great distance. Indeed, the greater part of that company [73] of Gascons and others, captains and soldiers alike, either perished by the sword or surrendered to the French and Bretons on condition that their lives be spared. The Captal de Buch, their principal captain, a Gascon, and many other captains on the side of Navarre who had escaped death, surrendered to Bertrand du Guesclin and became prisoners and captives. Since the Captal de Buch was such an illustrious baron that he was the equivalent of several other captains, he was incontinently taken to Rouen for Charles, the new king of France, to dispose of according to his own good pleasure so soon as he should have returned from his sacred anointing and coronation at Reims.[74] This, then, is how the battle was won and how the French and the Bretons triumphed over the Gascons and the Navarrese. Great joy and exultation filled the hearts of men throughout France. All praised God Who succors His own when such is His pleasure. For in truth if our men had succumbed and the other side had triumphed, misfortunes, perils, and injuries would have increased in France as a result of the invasion of the Navarrese and their overweening pride and luxury.[75]

At this time the nobles and burgesses of Normandy fought against the Navarrese in the diocese of Coutances, on behalf of the king of France and by his command, and won many victories and private wars.[76] I shall make no mention here of these private wars and victories, but I do say and I know that neither there nor elsewhere, whether in Anjou, Touraine, Maine, Beauce, the Orléanais or in the confines of these regions as far as Paris, was there a single district free of robbers and thieves. Indeed, they were everywhere in such numbers in the numerous fortresses they held, or in the villages,[77] hamlets and towns, that no merchant or anyone else could travel the roads safely [78] without incurring losses and risks. Furthermore, the friends whose duty it was to protect our peasants and wayfarers were themselves, alas! all basely intent upon plundering and robbing travelers indiscriminately as if they were foes.[79] The like was true of Burgundy and of all [80] that region. Certain knights who kept light-armed foot soldiers [81] in their company did just the same sort of thing, although they pretended quite falsely to be devoted friends of the king and of the king's majesty. I shall not write their names here. Even more amazing is the fact that though they were known to all and frequently recognized,[82] yet no avenging hand was ever raised [83] against them in their descents upon Paris and other cities. I have heard that some of these freebooters who were for the time being in Paris with their lords entered one night some houses in the faubourg Saint-Germain-des-Prés while the inhabitants were asleep and looted them by stealth. Although the thieves were discovered and forcibly seized and imprisoned in the Châtelet, they were in the end held excused and innocent and set at liberty without suffering any penalty. In easy indulgence of this sort they had an incentive to still further wrongdoing.

The king of France, after his return from his coronation at Reims, heard reports of the victory won by Bertrand du Guesclin and by the count of Auxerre. He generously gave Bertrand, to whom credit for the victory was given by popular acclaim, the magnificent gift of the whole county of Longueville in Caux in the diocese of Rouen.[84] It had once belonged to Philip of Navarre and now belonged to his brother,[85] the king of Navarre. Bertrand accepted possession of the county and in return promised the king of France that he would expel by force of arms all enemies of the kingdom and robbers and thieves from this region. But in truth he did nothing of the sort. On the contrary, his Bretons on their way back from Rouen stole everything they could find in the villages or in the possession of travelers [86] on the highways: money, clothing, horses, sheep, oxen, cattle, or beasts of burden.[87]

At this time the Navarrese who were holding the city of Evreux for their lord provisioned the castle abundantly, fortified it,[88] and, that they might not sustain injuries from any other fortress, destroyed utterly the churches and dwellings of the Preaching Friars and of the Minorites there.[89] They were left only a few huts. Thus, alas! misfortune was added [90] to misfortune almost continually throughout the land.

Then King Charles of France, who bore the title of dauphin of Vienne left Reims and came to Paris, where he was received with the greatest ceremony.[91] (Humbert, the former rightful dauphin of Vienne, had with the consent of his barons bestowed Dauphiné upon Charles because of his kinship with Philip, grandfather to Charles, and because being childless he had become a Preaching Friar. However, he did not long remain a friar. He abandoned the habit and was made patriarch of Alexandria and archbishop of Reims *in commendam*. He had adopted Charles as his son. For these reasons Charles is called dauphin.) [92] Very soon after this, about the time of the feast of Saint Barnabas the Apostle, he went to Rouen, where he was received in like manner with all honor by all the Norman burgesses.[93] Then he returned to Paris. It was after this that the sire de Sacquenville, of whom I have already spoken, was beheaded.[94] At the same time Kieret, a native of Amiens and a canon of the cathedral there, was taken prisoner and beheaded on account of his activity in the interests of the king of Navarre against the king of France. He was not given over to the ecclesiastical court because the church demanded him indifferently, almost as if the matter [95] did not concern it. Indeed he was hateful [96] to the church as a man-at-arms and a malefactor, with more than one crime to his charge.[97] If the church had pressed its claim vigorously, the royal courts would indubitably have been willing to surrender him. The Lord left him, so it seems, in accordance with his demerits, to be punished in the end by laymen.[98]

After this, in the same year, 1364, a great war broke out [99] between the count of Flanders, the new sire d'Enghien, and their men, on the one hand, and the count or regent of Hainaut, namely Duke Albert,[100] son of that Lewis, duke of Bavaria, who in his time had unlawfully acted as emperor, on the other. The cause of this war was the death of the sire d'Enghien whom, as I have said, Duke Albert had had beheaded at Quesnoy without any legal or judicial forms. The Flemings and other friends of the dead lord entered Hainaut this year and did much damage in that region, devastating and laying waste [101] many towns and churches in a lamentable manner. As a result the whole land feared and mourned, and peasants and monks and nuns left their abodes in great numbers and fled dismayed to seek refuge for themselves, their goods,[102] and their children in strongholds and walled towns. The Flemings burned a great many towns in Hainaut, Soignes and Havré [103] among many others at this time. Duke Albert, regent of Hainaut in the place of his brother, Count William, who lay demented in Quesnoy, wished to levy imposts on the people after the French fashion, gabelles on wine and other merchandise, in order to provide funds for war and defense. But the town of Valenciennes would not agree to them in spite of all its lord could do, and opposed with great vigor the imposition of unprecedented taxes. The other towns of Hainaut followed the lead of the principal town among them and, like Valenciennes, refused to pay the tailles, to the great indignation of their lord. Yet they all offered to contribute at any time according to their means to the costs of war and defense, provided that churchmen, knights and nobles did likewise. Their unwillingness to assent to imposts, exactions, and gabelles in accordance with their lord's will filled Duke Albert with great indignation. The citizens of Valenciennes and the other towns of Hainaut were little [104] troubled thereat, for they said among themselves, "If we were to do as men in Paris and elsewhere in France do now, we should become slaves and ruined men. Also, most of those who are employed in the wool industry would at once leave Hainaut and go to strange [105] parts. And perhaps, as we fear, these exactions would never cease." Thus, the people desired to continue in their liberty without oppression by their lords.[106] What the outcome of that war was, is not at present known. Let us now turn to other matters.[107]

The same year, 1364, during the reign of Charles the dauphin in France, a lamentable war took place in Brittany. Yet we believe that by God's will this war was the end of war [108] in that land and the beginning of a good peace. As the common [109] proverb has it, "The end of war is peace." Charles of Blois, who was acting as duke of Brittany in his wife's right, concerning both of whom enough has been said above, and John of Montfort, who claimed the duchy through his father, both of whom have been mentioned above, held many parleys concerning peace at this time in Brittany.[110] I do not wish to speak of these parleys lest I stray from the truth in my account. This I should be unwilling to do. When neither side could reach a final settlement, they both agreed to fight a pitched battle.[111] On the feast of Saint Michael in the month of September,[112] a great multitude of nobles in arms assembled and drew up their lines in a large field near the castle of Auray in the diocese of Vannes in Brittany. Each side attacked fiercely and fighting began. In this battle many nobles from France as well as from Brittany fought on the side of Charles of Blois,[113] who was himself present, and large numbers of Englishmen as well as Bretons fought on the side of John of Montfort.[114] Both sides fought hard, but John of Montfort's side prevailed, so it pleased God in Whose hands all things lie. His army overcame the other and won the field.[115] In this battle, alas!

Charles of Blois fell. Thus died an illustrious nobleman, valiant and gentle, courteous and handsome. With him died likewise the brother of the count of Auxerre, a noble knight,[116] and Guillaume de Roche-fort in French Brittany, and many other knights and nobles as well as 777 men-at-arms.[117] All these lay dead upon the field of battle, and two thousand more stricken with mortal wounds were carried to hospices. On the losing side the count of Auxerre, the count of Joigny,[118] Bertrand du Guesclin, a valiant knight, and many others gave themselves up. They were all ransomed in the end for large sums of money.[119] I do not concern myself here with the fugitives since I am not fully informed about them.

The body of Charles of Blois, that noble warrior and most gracious knight, was borne with many tears and groans to Guingamp in that part of Brittany and was given honorable burial there in the church of the Minorites. It is impossible for me to narrate fully and accurately the grief, the anxieties, the unspeakable groans and tearful sighs which tortured his wife, Jeanne of Brittany, in whose right he had justly claimed possession of the duchy, when she heard of his violent death.[120] But what became of her? The moment she heard the dolorous tidings, she and her little son left the castle of Nantes with a small train, to avoid notice, and went to the city of Angers where her daughter, who had married the duke of Anjou, son of the late King John, often sojourned in the castle.[121]

John of Montfort, the victor in this conflict, rode triumphantly about Brittany, vigorously stormed various castles, which had re-belled against him at one time or another, and took several fortifi-cations, which he subjected to himself and from which he drove out the rebels. At length he came with a multitude of armed men to storm the city of Nantes, which was fortified very strongly and effectively with walls, ditches, and other defenses. His men had already entered and taken by a ruse the noble and strong tower of Pirmil, which was at the head of the bridge over the Loire on the side the wood was on. They had also destroyed the faubourg next the tower, and the church used by a priory of monks, and had given them over to devouring flames.[122] While John of Montfort was there and was disturbing that region and its fortresses, Charles, king of France, sent thither ambassadors of distinction, Jean de Craon, archbishop of Reims, and many other nobles, to negotiate a peace in conjunction with the barons of Brittany between John of Montfort and the widow of Charles of Blois, who still considered herself as duchess of Brittany, and to interpose their good offices between them.[123] By the will of God, Who had compassion on the land and people of Brittany afflicted for years by war and spoliation and other miseries and Who willed to grant them peace and quiet henceforth, and by the intervention of the arbitrators mentioned above, a good peace was established amid great rejoicing.[124] The opposing parties were to be united by the marriage of their children. Other provisions were that the whole duchy and county of Nantes should remain in the possession of John of Montfort and that he should be entitled duke of Brittany ever after; that the widow of Charles of Blois should keep the lands which had formed part of her patrimony, such as Penthièvre, and should receive from the duchy an annual rent of 14,000 librae in addition; furthermore that one of her sons should marry another child, the sister of John of Montfort, and should have the viscounty of Limoges. Thus, praise God, was peace established in that land. John, now duke of Brittany, was greeted with rejoicing by everyone and welcomed by cities and castles as he went about the duchy to receive the homage of his nobles and to expel all enemies and freebooters from his castles. In this way he obtained the duchy of Brittany and did what his father, John, count of Montfort, brother of John, the former duke of Brittany, could not do so long as he lived, even though Edward, king of England, had crossed over to Brittany to aid him with a strong hand, when John, his son, was [125] but a little boy. But of this aid and of those [126] events I have already said enough under the years 1341 and 1342. There are those who doubt whether this peace will be lasting and whether its terms will be adhered to. Such men say that the widow of Charles of Blois was wrongly advised and deluded and that therefore the treaty will be set aside or annulled and that as a consequence a worse war than before, so they fear, will break out. May Almighty God, the King of Peace, avert this danger! What comes of all this will perchance be seen or told in the future and then written down, if I live.

The same year a great dispute arose between the populace or less powerful men of the city of Tournai on the one hand and the burgesses or the greater and richer men on the other. The burgesses assented to the levy of gabelles and heavy exactions on merchandise by the king of France to meet the expenses of the wars, whereas the populace opposed it altogether. They gainsaid the burgesses vigorously and said loudly [127] that the rich agreed to the imposts and gabelles because they themselves had at other times been responsible for their collection and were now, and because they were farming them out and paying [128] less themselves than the rest of the population. The populace therefore considered itself oppressed by the acquiescence of the burgesses in the levy and consequently refused to make any payment at all.[129] A fatal war would soon have grown out of the dissension and discord in the city,[130] had not God and certain wise men found a remedy. All the populace ran to arms. Some hastened to the belfry and rang the bells incessantly for many days and nights to rouse the city; others ran like madmen through the public squares and roamed about, ready for mischief. No one worked at his craft but all under the protection of arms rioted in the market places and squares both day and night for many days. As a result of their fury many prominent burgesses fled to escape being murdered. Some hid in silence in their own houses; others with like fears prudently withdrew from the city for a time in order to be safe.[131] And so these taxes and gabelles were stopped completely for the time being because of the wild resistance of the townsmen. Both parties to the dispute wrote to the king of France and sent messengers to present their reasons and motives as forcibly as possible. After the king and the council had considered the matter, they remitted the taxes up to that time and quickly arranged to appease and pacify both parties by the agency of discreet men.[132] Oudard de Renty, a Picard knight who was valiant in arms and wise, was appointed governor of the city. He governed in the king's behalf discreetly and pacifically, overlooking much that had happened and making several concessions to the populace in the interests of peace.[133]

1365 IN A.D. 1365, BEGINNING THE YEAR, ACCORDING TO THE CUSTOM OF FRANCE, WITH Easter, which fell that year on the thirteenth day of April, the freebooters withdrew at Easter time from the tower of Rolleboise, in return for money received. This tower stood about two leagues from Mantes and Vernon near Rosni on a hill overlooking the Seine. A handful of men, six or ten, it is said, and an elderly [1] woman held it and defended it so stoutly that although it had been assaulted many times by the men of Rouen and by others of that region, it had never been taken. It was very high and was considered almost impregnable. By it had come many misfortunes, as I have said elsewhere,[2] for no one could travel by the roads or the Seine in its neighborhood without sustaining serious damages at the hands of the men who then held it. After they had been bought off and had gone away, as I have said, the tower was completely demolished and destroyed by the people of that region in accordance with the king's will, to the end that wicked men might not again establish themselves in it to work harm.[3] It is said that the wall surrounding [4] the tower was so thick that it was only with the greatest difficulty and after a long time that very strong men using iron hammers succeeded in demolishing it. It was more than nine feet thick and was built of very large stones held firmly together by mortar. This tower, which I have often seen, rose to an extraordinary height. Now it lies prostrate on the ground, humbled and brought low.

At the same time the French likewise completely demolished Meulan; both the town, which had formerly been rich and had been enclosed by ditches and very strong walls, and also all its fortifications including a fine square tower, strong and very high. Like Mantes, Meulan belonged to the king of Navarre.[5] The war between the two kings, Charles, king of France, and Charles of Evreux, king of Navarre, of whom I have said enough elsewhere,[6] was still going on at that time. This town and castle belonged to him as part of the county of Evreux, which was at once his birthplace and his domain. Meulan was by the Seine and was a fair and pleasant and exceedingly rich town. It had a fine priory on its island, belonging to the monastery of Bec, and it also had a bridge over the Seine which is still standing, firmly and solidly constructed of stone. It was and is a fertile spot, adorned with many vines and other good things. It was a necessary and extremely useful stopping place [7] for travelers by land and by water, both day and night; by God's grace, it will be so again.

In the same year the knight called the Archpriest, a partisan of the king of France, of whom I have spoken elsewhere, hearing that a peace was being negotiated between the king of France and the king of Navarre,[8] left France for Lorraine. As long as war lasted his men had plundered the land extensively under color of provisioning themselves for the conduct of war. Now Bretons and other robbers accompanied or followed him in great numbers. As they passed through the county of Champagne, they rapidly despoiled its merchants and other inhabitants of horses, money, goods, furnishings, and food wherever opportunity offered, in the unfortified country villages, along the roads, in the houses, or in the fields. Then when they had added unto themselves other companies of robbers like themselves,[9] they entered the duchy of Bar, which but a short time before had been called a county,[10] thence the duchy of Lorraine and finally betook themselves, unopposed, to the district round Verdun and beyond as far as Metz, a very rich city, everywhere plundering and devastating.[11]

At this time, Charles, king of Bohemia and Roman emperor, an illustrious knight and a faithful and religious man, obedient to the church, journeyed to the Roman Curia at Avignon to see Pope Urban V. Many nobles from Germany and elsewhere also assembled there, in answer to the summons of our lord the pope, it is said.[12] Charles, king of France, sent thither as his representatives his brother, the duke of Anjou, and many barons and prelates, among others Guillaume de Melun, archbishop of Sens, and Guillaume de Dormans, chancellor of Normandy.[13] The pope's aim was to obtain the succor from these princes for the Christians and the lands which were being grievously troubled by the Turks and other infidels. It was said at Paris while these words were being written that the emperor had offered the pope the tithes and half the rents of his kingdom for the maintenance of mercenary troops for three years for this cause.[14] It was also the intention of the pope and the emperor to dispatch thither many prominent nobles, valiant in arms, such as the king of Cyprus who long before had journeyed to the Roman Curia and

France in the interests of this cause. They also planned to summon all the robbers who had long been in France and were now devastating Lorraine and other companies like them as well and, if they would agree to go, to grant them the remission [15] and absolution of their sins, provided they were penitent, to give them generous pay, and immediately to assign them the task of aiding and defending the faithful in the name of Christ against the infidels and the enemies of the cross of Christ.[16] I shall perhaps describe later what became of it.

For several days after Pentecost [17] this year violent and dangerous storms accompanied by thunder and lightning raged in France and Burgundy both day and night. In some localities the rain beat down the wheat in the fields so that a scarcity of grain [18] resulted which grew steadily worse. Many men and many houses were injured or destroyed by lightning. A horseman riding from Paris to Saint-Denis was killed by a stroke of lightning. A church of some holy nuns outside [19] Paris was struck with such force that the nuns and some ladies who had come there on pilgrimage from Paris fell to the floor in terror and lay there as if dead. In the church of the Minorites in the city of Trèves, where the friars had assembled to pray God to avert the horror of the thunder and lightning, a friar who had that very day celebrated mass was mortally struck by lightning in the midst of his devotions and breathed his last. The friar who was pulling the bell rope felt lightning run down the belfry and up his arm through the wide sleeve of his habit, which fell back as he lifted his arm. The hair under his arms was burned but his flesh was completely uninjured. For this, as was meet, he praised the Lord. Surprisingly enough, this same flash of lightning burned and blackened the sandals of the friars who were praying there without in any way injuring or hurting their feet. That bolt also struck the repository or chest in which their relics lay, though it did no damage to the windows above it, and burned the cloths in which the relics were wrapped. The vessels and reliquaries remained whole and uninjured, aside from a certain amount of blackening. No opening or crack was visible by which the lightning could have gone into the chest or come out. The belfry of the cathedral of Trèves, which was unusually high, was thrown to the ground by a thunderbolt. Furthermore, at the same time in a certain village near Dijon in Burgundy the thunder was accompanied by an inundation of rain. So great was [20] the deluge that it was as if a cloud had burst and had sent a waterfall down from heaven. The village, which was built on a hill, and all that was in it, houses, men and women, and infants in the cradle, was swept away by the fearful force of the torrent and the rapacity of the falling rains to a valley far below, and completely demolished. Every animate being found a lamentable death in the whirlpool of waters. At Dijon most of the walls round the town, which had been almost completely rebuilt to meet the perils of war, collapsed under the assault of abundant torrents of rain. The vines too, on which clusters of grapes were already visible though not fully formed, suffered damage which brought sadness to all good topers and losses to their cultivators and owners. Very soon, however, fair and warm and dry weather returned, and after the feast of Saint John the Baptist [21] it was so fine that vines and other fruits of the earth recovered and grew more abundantly than before, by God's will, and the shortage moderated. Now let us turn to other events which, like the foregoing, relate the glory of God, the great joy of the kingdom of France, the gladness and salvation of the people, and the solace and quietness of the afflicted. [22]

As the feast of Saint John the Baptist, our Lord's forerunner [23] and glorious herald, at whose birth many faithful and devout persons rejoiced, as we learn from the Holy Gospel, approached in the year 1365, our Lord Jesus Christ willed to have compassion on the people of France. For the space of twenty-five years, as is clear from the course of the narrative in this little book to anyone who has perused it [24] from the beginning thus far, they had almost continuously sustained and endured all these [25] tribulations, afflictions, oppressions, perils, losses, many evils, homicides, and exactions; devastations of towns, churches, monasteries, and castles; depopulation, plagues, violences, rapes, and, to make an end, perturbations [26] innumerable as a result of the divisions and strife [27] caused by the wars long waged by the king of France, or rather two successive kings, Philip of Valois and his son John, on the one hand, and Edward, king of England on the other, and also the war between these same two French kings and a third one, namely Lord Charles, dauphin and king of France after them, on the one hand, and Lord Charles of Evreux, king of Navarre, on the other. I have described the course of these wars, albeit rudely, in this manuscript, if not in every detail at least in part. Wherefore the Lord God, as I have said, seeing the long duration of these afflictions, willed to convert[28] the sadness and sorrow of his people into joy and solace, for He it is Who will not desert forever those who trust in His mercy and in His help in due time and Who wills to establish peace among His people. Wherefore at this time by His inspiration, negotiations for peace between the king of France and the king of Navarre, Charles of Evreux, count of Evreux in his father's right and king of Navarres in his mother's, were entered upon.[29] The Captal de Buch, though at the time a prisoner of the king of France, served as an intermediary. He was first sent to the king of Navarre to arrange for peace and concord. Then he returned as the emissary of the king of Navarre and reported that king's peace terms and demands to the king of France and his council.[30] These conditions were so displeasing to the French that no peace was made,[31] though many pitied the afflicted people and took deep thought, grieving that a way of peace had not been found. At length God, Who of old had aroused the spirit and wisdom of young Daniel, inspired one of the lords of the council who seemed young in comparison with the others but who was no less prudent and of good counsel[32] than they. He was a prudent man named Louis, count of Etampes, noble, honorable, good and merciful,[33] manifesting bowels of compassion to the poor and afflicted. He was of the royal lineage of France and had been nurtured in the royal household with the king of France.[34] He foresaw the ills and perils which would result from this refusal of peace and, having compassion on the afflicted people, besought the king to reassemble his council. He said that if no one else were willing to propose reopening negotiations, he himself would do so publicly for the sake of the common good. The king assented and agreed to his petition. Accordingly, a few days before the feast of Saint John the Baptist, at the time of the fair of Lendit,[35] the count of Etampes, having first sent messengers to the religious of Paris to ask them to pray God for peace,[36] called the council together again in the king's name and to the king's presence. When it had assembled, the same Lord Who opened the lips of Zachariah His prophet on the birthday of Saint John in like manner opened the lips of this count. Speaking in the midst of wise men, he showed his prudence by making clear how many and what great benefits would accrue to the king and to the whole realm if peace were made and, on the other hand, the innumerable ills which would befall the people if peace were not made and how greatly all the people everywhere had suffered incessantly all this time from these wars. The Holy Spirit taught him so to speak that by his counsel and his prayers he inclined the king and his council wholly toward the establishment of good peace and quietness of mind. The praise be God's, from Whom all good things do proceed! The terms were a combination of those demands of the king of Navarre which seemed reasonable and of the decisions of the king and his council which seemed reasonable. They were, in part, that the king of Navarre should keep the lands which he held in Normandy, namely in Neustria, round Coutances and the county of Evreux, except Mantes and Meulan. He was also to have the whole barony of Montpellier with the very rich town and castle of that name, but he was bound to make no claims on Champagne nor, so it is believed, on Burgundy.[37] I have not made it my concern to write down here the sums of money involved. Heralds then proclaimed the peace in the public squares of Paris, in the palace of the king, and at the fair at Lendit on the fourth day before the feast of the birth of John the Baptist,[38] so that all [39] the people might thank God on this festal day and abide in joy and gladness. And indeed this was the case, for it would take long to write of the great joy that there was in the hearts of the people and of the thanks which they offered to God.

So then, when the wars in the kingdom of France, in Gaul and Brittany alike, had been composed by this peace, the thieves and robbers who in time of war had heaped ill upon ill and loss upon loss on the people were alarmed and began little by little to decrease and diminish in numbers. They either sought out other lands or warily refrained from raids and evil deeds. Those who had wrongfully occupied castles and fortresses, in many instances abandoned them for fear or for money given them by neighboring cities or their lords. But even though they withdrew from these strongholds, many of them could not abstain from robbery on the highroads and in the country, so used were they to plundering. But what availed them gains thus extorted? Truly, little or nothing. They all seemed to vanish from their hands like snow before the sun. Yea verily, coming into cities and expensive places, they were soon forced to sell their horses and to contract debts if they could find anyone to trust them, and in the end they became paupers and miserable wretches in the sight of all, thus providing the truth of the popular saying, "Gains ill got will be ill spent." [40] Thus their end was ruin and lamentation. But the end of the righteous is said to be precious in the sight of the Lord. Therefore blessed be the Lord God in all things. Amen.

At this time and during the wars [41] just ended, nearly all the nobles, except a few of the more reputable, deformed themselves monstrously by their dress, departing to their shame from the modesty of decent men of old time. They wore the tightest possible tunics, cut off above the hips and, what was even more monstrous, they affected shoes with very long points in front like horns, which sometimes stretched straight out and sometimes slanted up like the talon on the back of a griffon's foot which it uses in accordance with its nature as a claw. This point or beak is called a *poulaine* in French. It was a truly shameful fashion, in that it went quite contrary to the natural shape of the human foot and thus seemed an abuse of nature. King Charles of France caused heralds to proclaim publicly in Paris that no one, whosoever he might be, should dare to wear them more and that no shoemaker should presume, under threat of heavy penalties, to make or sell pointed shoes or hose.[42] Urban V had in like manner strictly forbidden them in the Roman Curia. Those who deplore such follies hope [43] that by the inspiration of God [44] within a short time scanty robes also and other indecencies of dress worn by men and women alike will be firmly prohibited by prelates and princes, both ecclesiastical and secular, and the whole kingdom will be changed for the better.

1366 IN A.D. 1366 [1] THE ENEMIES AND ROBBERS WHO WERE OCCUPYING FORTRESSES IN NORmandy and elsewhere left them and set out for Spain, where Peter, king of Spain, and his brother Henry were disputing the possession of the kingdom of Spain.[2] Henry said that though Peter had obtained the kingdom a long time before, he had done so contrary to God

and justice and that the kingdom belonged rather to him. He charged
Peter with being a changeling, not a true son of the dead king but
a child of Jewish parentage secretly substituted by the queen for
the daughter to whom she had just given birth. He said that knights
in the queen's confidence had sworn to this when they were at the
point of death; that they had stolen the boy secretly from the Jews
and had hidden the girl, because the king had sworn to kill the queen
if she did not bring forth a son at that time. In fear of the king, who
was kept in ignorance of the whole matter, Peter, the present king,
of Jewish birth, was secretly substituted by the queen for her newly
born daughter. So at least Henry strongly alleged.[3] He also charged
Peter with being a heretic and, worse, an adherent of the Jews and
of their law who set at naught and contemned the law of Christ our
Lord, and declared that according to the ancient laws of the kingdom
he should therefore be deposed and expelled from the kingdom and
that another king should be chosen and appointed in his place. This
was done, for the people of Spain, or so at least it was said, had
chosen Henry after deposing and rejecting Peter. Peter [4] was also a
man who thirsted for the blood of his own, a man of vile and disgrace-
ful life. This is clear from the fact that he had his wife of the royal
lineage of France, a modest, chaste, saintly, and honorable lady, killed
by strangling, for no just cause and for the sake of a concubine, a
Jewess, so it was said. The whole country lamented and deplored her
unjust death.[5] It is said furthermore that Peter ruled himself and
his household and governed his whole kingdom through Jews, who
are found in great numbers in Spain.[6] These and many other enormities are reported of Peter by a great many people. Wherefore
Henry his brother, with the support and assistance of many Spanish
barons, burgesses, and knights, invaded Spain and proffered himself
as the rightful king in the place of the deposed Peter. Hence there
was great discord in the land, and wars of no slight proportions broke
out between the common people and the nobles. News of this came
to many nobles and knights in France, Brittany, and Germany who,
ever desirous as covetous men are of a greater abundance of lucre and
booty, hastened to Spain. Among the number was Bertrand du
Guesclin, a very valiant Breton knight, who with his men had for
some time past been holding high revel in Normandy and France

after the manner of freebooters, spoiling and devastating the country and the peasants. He advanced with a great multitude of men-at-arms to the support of Henry and there with his Bretons performed many valiant feats of arms. Especially did he slaughter with overwhelming might countless Jews who had joined Peter in force of arms.[7] Those that were not slain escaped only to perish miserably elsewhere. There are many living in Paris and various other cities today who subtly despoil our Christian brothers through usury.[8] But woe to the despoiler![9] For as we believe, they shall finally be driven out and be despoiled themselves. This has been seen many times elsewhere.

Peter was not strong enough to withstand the courage and might of Henry and of his numerous Spanish adherents and of his strong supporters from Brittany and France and elsewhere, and was forced to leave the kingdom for the time being and to flee.[10] With a small following he made his way to Edward,[11] prince of Wales, eldest son of the king of England, duke of Aquitaine and count of Poitou, who was at that time in Bordeaux in Gascony, and, on the plea of their relationship, begged his assistance in the recovery of his kingdom of Spain.[12] The prince assembled the largest possible number of men-at-arms from England, Gascony, Poitou, and La Rochelle and in the winter of that year went to Spain. There, as a result of winter storms and rains and cold, and of an inadequate food supply as well, he lost a large proportion of his men and of his horses and wagons.[13] His standard-bearer, William Felton, seneschal of Poitou, a valiant and noble knight, of good counsel, prudent and devout, fell in battle there with the Spaniards.[14] At the same time Charles of Evreux, king of Navarre, was taken prisoner by the king of Aragon, it is said, but he was afterwards surrendered and given back.[15] In another battle, between Prince Edward and Henry, Henry retreated from battle, and Bertrand du Guesclin, who was fighting on his side, together with many of his Bretons and many famous nobles, was taken prisoner by the English, because, it is said, Henry and his men fought languidly and indifferently and soon abandoned the field and fled.[16] But what the outcome of this war was had not been reported here at the time these words were being written.[17]

1367 IN A.D. 1367, BEGINNING WITH EASTER,[1] POPE URBAN V FOUNDED A HANDSOME NEW MONastery of black monks of the order of Saint Benedict in honor of Saint Germain at Montpellier.[2] Then he returned to Avignon and immediately after Easter, that is the month of May, with all his cardinals and the whole Curia set out on a journey to Rome, that great city.[3] On the way he stopped at Viterbo with all his following.[4] While he was there with his cardinals, a quarrel broke out between one of the household of a cardinal and a citizen of Viterbo. The quarrel grew so violent that most of the citizens ran to arms and attacked certain cardinals' servants in their masters' houses and, once battle had been joined, killed many of them. The citizens reached such a point of madness and insanity that they would even have laid sacrilegious and violent hands upon the person of a cardinal, had not he in terror wisely sought safety in flight.[5] What is even more reprehensible, they proposed, it is said, to massacre the pope and his cardinals together, but God did not will that the church should endure so scandalous a wrong. The pope, seeing all this and desiring to repress and punish the excesses of these men as they deserved, called out a great army against them. Then, as many of the citizens and malefactors as had been taken and examined by his marshals [6] he ordered to be hanged from gibbets in front of their houses, and he ordered the fortifications and walls of Viterbo to be destroyed.[7] This done, the pope and the cardinals and the whole Curia departed and journeyed to the illustrious and famous city of Rome and there the papal see and the Curia are to this day.[8] All this happened in the year 1367.

The same year in the month of December, on the night of the feast of Saint Lucy the Virgin,[9] a violent gale of wind from the north off the sea blew all night long in Flanders, Picardy, and Brabant. Its like had never before been seen or heard of.[10] Many houses and churches were blown down by the violence and force of the blast. Even the strongest buildings which remained standing lost their thatched or tiled roofs and stood open to the sky. Many grown people and children were killed by falling houses and chimneys as they slept in their beds. Their lifeless bodies, alas! were afterwards found crushed among the ruins.[11] A great number of windmills were found lying on the ground. One extraordinary thing was that the very beautiful and strongly built belfry of the church of Saint Mary of regular canons in Boulogne [12] was blown down that night by the great force of the wind. In its fall it broke in the roof of the choir below and the stone vaulting under the roof. Many other great belfries were blown down as well, as I myself saw, and many houses collapsed that night [13] under the violence of the wind. The gale's fury piled the ocean in these regions into such great waves and billows that it exceeded its accustomed bounds. It rose so high that without warning it swept over and submerged houses and villages along the shore which had up to this time always been safe. They were destroyed and all their inhabitants perished.[14]

In Advent of the same year, on the night of the feast of Saint Nicholas,[15] the sergeants of the guard at Paris [16] who make the rounds of the city by night violently assaulted some students who were singing and making merry in honor of the saint and, quite without cause and contrary to the liberties and privileges of the University of Paris, haled several to the Châtelet, wounding atrociously the students who tried to defend themselves. Most horrible of all, they dealt one a mortal blow and then hurled him into the Seine which was near at hand. In the darkness of night no one saw this save the perpetrators of the crime. When the university learned of this execrable crime on the next day, it waited on King Charles and quite properly lodged a grave complaint against the sergeants. A heavy fine was exacted of them. This fine was, however, not commensurate with their guilt, since the body of the student thrown into the Seine could not be found and the sergeants claimed that he had secretly retired to his lodgings in order that it might appear that the sergeants had killed him. It was not remarkable that the body was not found near the scene of the crime, for the swift current of the river had carried it to a point far downstream. After the lapse of some time when the river was lower, the body with a broken lung showed above the surface of the water and was recovered on the confines of the city beyond the buildings of the Augustinian Friars of Paris, near the last houses. The corpse was taken from the water and was buried in the house of the Carmelite Friars at Paris with the greatest honors by the whole university, solemnly and publicly. And then a new complaint against the sergeants was lodged with the king by the university and its friends. Some of the sergeants fled; others were taken, but what justice was done on them I do not know.[17]

1368 IN A.D. 1368 THE MOON RAN THROUGH ONE, THAT IS, THE GOLDEN NUMBER OF THE moon ran through one.[1] On Easter Day, the ninth day of the month of April, a comet was visible. It had already been seen on several days of the preceding Holy Week and was visible for . . .[2] It appeared with the oncoming of night or early in the night in the northwest. The head of the comet, the star itself, was on the ocean side, and its tail extended toward the northeast. Its rays mounted skyward and looked like a very high belfry completely enveloped in flames. When I suddenly saw it for the first time, I thought that it was a high belfry on fire, emitting flames in the most extraordinary way. It sent up a red pyramid or spear point of light like a flame into the sky toward the place where I was at the time, namely Reims. Nearly everyone in Reims, and especially the men keeping watch and ward on the walls by night, saw this comet clearly and with amazement. And so it was throughout France.[3] Bede, as quoted by Friar Bartholomew in his compilation,[4] tells what the apparition of the comet signifies, and I have taken pains to note it here. He says that a comet is a star surrounded by flames which springs suddenly into being and which signifies some great change or a plague or wars or winds or heats or the like. I know that this Easter time the air was clear, for otherwise the comet would not have been visible, but the weather was very cold and the wind cold and biting and the air also cold and noxious. Although Bede says that comets always appear in the north, as this one did, yet in the year 1340 a comet appeared in the south and sent out its rays toward the northeast. This comet was the sign of great tribulations to come in France. Great pestilence and dreadful mortality and other unprecedented events which began in 1348, as everyone knows, followed after it. Then came horrible wars and unsupportable burdens and deaths innumerable as a result of these long and cruelly protracted wars between Edward, king of England,

and the king of France. This little book sets them forth in order and makes brief mention of all these matters from the like of which may the power of our Savior deliver us in the future.

I have thought fit to write down here in order the events and tribulations in various parts of the kingdom of France which occurred shortly before, at the same time with, and after the apparition of that comet on Easter Day, as I saw them or heard them accurately reported, as a record for future generations.

Notes

Notes

In these notes all material from H. Géraud, ed., *Chronique latine de Guillaume de Nangis de 1113 à 1300 avec les continuations de cette chronique de 1300 à 1368,* 2 vols. (Paris, 1843), is cited as "Géraud." This work contains the text of Jean de Venette's chronicle as well as that of the chronicle of Guillaume and his continuators. The Arundel manuscript of Jean de Venette (British Museum, Arundel MS 28) is cited as "A." The abbreviation MGH refers to *Monumenta Germaniae historica.*

INTRODUCTION

I. THE AUTHOR AND HIS WORK

1. *Mémoirs de l'Académie des inscriptions,* XIII (1735), 520 ff.
2. See p. 51.
3. Wessels, ed., *Acta capitulorum,* I, 37–63; *idem, Bibliotheca Carmelitana,* II, 131, No. clii: Zimmerman, ed., *Monumenta historica Carmelitana,* I, 208–9, 388. The chronicle of the order is in *Speculum Carmelitana* (Antwerp, 1680), I, 202–5. The British Museum has an earlier edition published in 1507 at Venice. In our chronicle of events in France special Carmelite touches will be found on pages 35, 46, 62, 99, 110, 140.
4. See p. 93.   5. Géraud, I, xxxi.
6. A. Molinier, *Les Sources de l'histoire de France,* IV, 21.
7. Calmette, *L'Elaboration de monde moderne,* p. 44.
8. See p. 66.   9. See pp. 60, 63, 66, 73, 75–78, 84, 94, 105, 108, 118.
10. See p. 111, 1363.   11. See p. 113.   12. See p. 219, n. 40.
13. See p. 214, n. 22.   14. See p. 68.   15. See p. 50.
16. See pp. 62, 109.
17. English writers call him John of Rupescissa. For his career and significance see p. 211, n. 2; p. 264, n. 67.
18. See pp. 61–62.
19. A. Molinier, *Les Sources de l'histoire de France,* IV, 21.
20. See p. 96.   21. See p. 97.   22. See p. 250, n. 112.
23. See p. 251, n. 116; p. 255, n. 148; p. 256, n. 4; p. 259, n. 25; p. 262, nn. 56, 58.   24. See p. 185, n. 29; p. 277, n. 9.
25. See p. 195, n. 17.   26. See p. 67.   27. See p. 69.
28. See p. 72.   29. See p. 231, n. 47.
30. See pp. 41, 47, 48, 53, 58, 60, 61, 63, 67–69, 71, 79, 84.
31. See p. 93.   32. See p. 90.   33. See p. 203, n. 6.
34. See p. 60.   35. See p. 201, n. 1.

36. This is where the author of the *Chronique des règnes de Jean II et de Charles V* (I, 37 ff.) puts these events.

37. This is what he seems to have done for the year 1351, where he devotes all his space to the controversy between the regular clergy and the mendicants which actually happened in 1350.

38. In 1346, pp. 40, 41, 43; 1348, p. 48; 1350, p. 54.

39. Six, if we include a repetition.   40. See pp. 57, 69, 70, 75, 80.

41. See p. 69.   42. See p. 83.   43. See p. 226, n. 21.

44. See p. 97.   45. See p. 98.   46. See p. 60.

47. See pp. 31–32.   48. See p. 173, n. 41.   49. See p. 182, n. 17.

50. P. 67, "and I shall speak of the matter again in the following pages"; p. 69, "as you will see in part hereafter"; p. 58, "as shall be told; p. 84, "Of this I shall speak under the year following."

51. Probably the paragraph on the currency (p. 98) is the conclusion of the first part. The following paragraphs for 1360 are contemporary with the events they describe, and the sections on the later years were written at varying periods afterwards.

52. See p. 35.   53. See p. 178, n. 70; p. 66; p. 277, n. 7.

54. See p. 195, n. 17.   55. See p. 130.   56. See p. 108.

57. See p. 114.   58. See p. 116.   59. See p. 116.

60. See pp. 109, 110.   61. See p. 108.   62. See p. 127.

63. See p. 295, nn. 84, 87.   64. See p. 300, n. 133.

65. See p. 286, n. 3.   66. See p. 302, nn. 14, 16.

67. See p. 128.   68. See p. 136.   69. See p. 128.

70. See p. 132.   71. See p. 139.   72. See p. 140.

73. See p. 140.   74. This is discussed on p. 311, n. 2.

75. See p. 142.

76. If we had only Géraud's text we would be embarrassed at this point by the sentence concerning Pope Urban's appointment of the bishop of Paris to be a cardinal, which happened Sept. 22, 1368. The sentence as it stands could have been written only after Urban's return to Avignon and death, contradicting Jean's statement that the Curia was still in Rome. See the discussion on p. 279, n. 11.

2. THE MANUSCRIPT

1. Brit. Mus., Arundel MS 28.

2. *Mémoires de la Société de l'histoire de Paris,* IV (1878), 225–26.

3. *Mélanges d'archéologie et d'histoire de l'Ecole française de Rome,* XIX (1899), 131–41.

4. Bib. Nat., fonds latin 4921 A.

5. There are more than sixty corrections, mostly in the margins, but sometimes between the lines. Some of them were made by the copyist and are in the same letters as the text, but most of them are in a different but contemporary hand. See pp. 26–27; p. 241, n. 44.

6. See p. 94; Géraud, II, 294; Arundel MS, fol. 14.

7. Géraud, II, 293: *suam hachiam ponderosam.*

8. See p. 141; Géraud, II, 376.   9. See p. 28, n. 8.

10. College of Arms, Arundel MS VII: this is the text published in the "Rolls Series," London, 1863; see I, x.

11. See p. 199, n. 6.   12. (Oxford, 1913). Appendix XIII, pp. 374–75.

13. Delisle, *Recherches sur la librairie de Charles V,* I, 4.

14. J. W. Thompson, *The Medieval Library* (Chicago, 1939), pp. 427–28.

THE CHRONICLE

1340

1. The Arundel manuscript differs from Géraud's text by adding *qui in regno francie* after *mirandorum,* and *evenerit* after the date. Hereafter the Arundel text will be referred to as A.

2. A adds *Parisius* after *apices.*   3. A reads *quidem* for *quasi.*

4. A adds *prognosticationes seu* before *prophetiae.*

5. For an interesting but not exhaustive study of the medieval interest in this sort of prognostication see Taylor, *The Political Prophecy in England.*

6. A adds *Est autem una talem.*

7. There are five main sections to the Mass: (1) The Preparation; (2) The Oblation; (3) The Consecration; (4) The Communion; (5) The Dismissal. The Secret is the final prayer of the Oblation, following the Prayer for Acceptance. It is an offertory prayer, asking God's grace in return for the offering, whispered by the celebrant while the choir chants. Young, *The Drama of the Medieval Church,* I, 19; Fortescue, *The Mass,* pp. 311–14.

8. A omits *Domino;* the translation follows Géraud.

9. A adds *vituperabatur* after *Petri.*

10. A omits *ignoratur* after *veraciter;* the translation follows Géraud.

11. See Lucas, "The Great European Famine of 1315, 1316, and 1317," *Speculum,* V (1930), 343–77. The first continuator of the chronicle of Guillaume de Nangis refers to this famine. Géraud, I, 421–22, 426.

12. A adds *tam* before *gravis.*   13. A adds *aquas* after *transibit.*

14. A reads *pellem* for *carnem.*

15. A omits *hominis;* the translation follows Géraud.

16. Jean de Murs flourished 1318–45. His works on astronomy, arithmetic, and music were very popular in the fourteenth and fifteenth centuries. Like many astronomers, he was interested in astrology and enjoyed considerable reputation as a prognosticator. See Symon de Phares, *Recueil des plus célèbres astrologues,* pp. 216 ff., 231 ff. There is an undated letter from him to Clement VI (died 1352) describing the conjunction of Saturn and Jupiter in the sign of Scorpion on Oct. 30, 1365, along with Mars, and informing him that this sign had preceded the advent of Mahomet. Its return, therefore, is believed to signify great changes in the Moslem world. If the Christians can strike then great results should be accomplished. Also on June 8, 1357, there will be a grand conjunction of Saturn and Mars in the sign of Cancer, which indicates some great disaster for France. Duhem, *Le Système du monde,* IV, 35–37, corrected in Thorndike, *History of Magic and Experimental Science,* III, 319–21. This passage, which Jean de Venette opens with the word *Filius,* appears in quite a number of copies with *Lilium* as the opening word. It is called "The Prophecy of the Lily, the Lion, and the Son of Man." The earliest example of it is ascribed by H. L. D. Ward to "about 1340." It would seem to describe an attack by France (the lily) against Brabant (the lion), repulsed by aid from England (the son of man) with help from the emperor (the eagle). Ward, *Catalogue of Romances in . . . the British Museum,* I, 302, 314, 316–19, 321. A manuscript copy of this prophecy, dated 1380 and ascribed to Sextus of Ireland, is said to be at Trinity College, Dublin. There are verbal differences from Jean de Venette's version, but it is interesting to note that this Dublin version agrees with two of the verbal peculiarities, which distinguish A from Géraud's text: "transiet *aquas*" and *"pellem* dilaceraverint." Todd, ed., *The Last Age of the Church,* Notes, pp. lxxxiii ff.

A discussion of this reference to Jean de Murs as a help in dating Jean de Venette's record will be found in Déprez, "Une Tentative de réforme du calendrier sous Clément VI," *Mélanges d'archéologie et d'histoire de l'Ecole française de Rome,* IX (1899), 131–43. He argues that the chronicle must have been begun after 1345, since this reference implies that Jean de Murs was long dead. This can very readily be accepted, since it is supported by many other indications in the chronicle. It is surprising that Jean de Venette, with all his interest in portents, seems ignorant of the famous conjunction of Saturn, Jupiter, and Mars in March, 1345, an unusual astrological event which led to several prognostications, one of which was by Jean de Murs. See Thorndike, *History of Magic and Experimental Science,* Vol. III, Chap. 20. These record that Jupiter and Mars will meet March 1, 1345, "after midnight, and the result for the world will be wars, slaughters, floods, corruptions of the air, epidemics, discords, and unexpected castastrophes from above. [Saturn and Mars] will be joined on the fourth day of the same month at daybreak, threatening or sowing discords, deceits and frauds, wars, violent winds, and disease. [Saturn and Jupiter will meet on March 20] and ordain changes of kingdoms, famine, wars, seditions, and marvelous innovations unheard of since distant times. The three . . . are in complete accord that there shall ensue destruction of sects, changes of kingdoms, appearance of prophets, sedition of peoples, new rites, and finally a horrible blowing of winds. All this, however, will not come to pass the same year but at different times."—*Ibid.,* III, 306. A contemporary chronicler, Gilles li Muisis, abbot of Saint Martin's at Tournai, under the year 1349 in his annals, after describing the Flagellants, wrote, "Moreover, while I was writing the above, there occurred to me and came back to my mind the prophecy of Master Jean de Murs, wherein among other things he spoke of the conjunction of stars and planets, that there would be destruction of sects, sedition of peoples, new rites, epidemics: and it seemed to me that in this year 1349 the greater part of these predictions had come to pass, so that we heard them and saw them in Tournai, in as much as the sects of Jews, wherever they were found among the Christians, were destroyed with divers tortures. Furthermore all the people were stirred up in a very great sedition by the appearance of the Penitents and their forms of penance." Later he wonders whether it might be said that these "were the new rites and the appearance of prophets according to the prognostications of Master Jean de Murs."—Gilles li Muisis, *Chronique,* pp. 238, 248. See also the *Petite Chronique françoise,* in *Mélanges . . . Soc. des bibliophiles français,* 1867, Part 2, p. 20. The author of *Les Grandes Chroniques de France* wrote, "The last day of February there was a conjunction of the three most important planets, namely, Mars, Jupiter, and Saturn; and according to the opinion of wise astronomers then resident in Paris this conjunction, as they said, was equivalent to three conjunctions, that is a great conjunction, a very great, and a medium, and such an one could not happen again for at least . . . [omitted] years. For this showed and signified great and wonderful things which only happen very infrequently, such as changes of laws, generations and kingdoms, and the appearance of prophets. And these things should happen especially near Jerusalem and in Syria."—IX, 252–53. Giovanni Villani, another contemporary chronicler, shared the contemporary interest in astrology and its relation to historical events.

17. This refers to the prophecy of Jean de la Roche-Taillade with which Jean de Venette introduces his section on 1356 (p. 61), showing that he began writing his chronicle after that date. See Introduction, p. 16.

18. Presumably this refers to the comet of 1337, which attracted considerable attention. The first continuator of the chronicle of Guillaume de Nangis had considerable astrological discussion in connection with his record of this comet, which appeared about St. John's day (June 24). Géraud, II, 156. *Les Grandes Chroniques* (IX, 159) has practically the same passage. For other references see Thomas Walsingham, *Historia Anglicana*, I, 222; Giovanni Villani, *Cronica*, Book XI, Chaps. 67 and 68; Heinricus Rebdorfensis, *Annales,* in Böhmer, ed., *Fontes,* IV, 520–21. The author of *Les Grandes Chroniques* (IX, 167), the first continuator (Géraud, II, 160), and Villani mention a second comet within the space of a year, on April 15, 1338. Villani (*Cronica,* Book XI, Chap. 68) comments on these phenomena: "But whatever they may be, every comet is the sign of some event in the world and generally a malignant one: and sometimes it is the sign of death of great lords or of revolution in kingdoms and among people more particularly in that planet which has given birth to the comet. And wheresoever the comet extends its mastery, it produces many evils, such as famine, pestilence, revolution, and other grave occurrences, as any man of good understanding may find out for himself by reading in this book."—Quotation in translation in Schevill, *History of Florence,* p. 233. Geoffroi de Meaux, a contemporary of Jean de Venette who was at the University of Paris in the 1340s, wrote a treatise on this comet of 1337. Thorndike notes a fourteenth-century manuscript at Paris containing predictions relative to the conjunction of planets in 1345, one of which is ascribed to Jean de Murs, preceded by a prognostication by Geoffroi de Meaux respecting the comet of 1337. *History of Magic and Experimental Science,* III, 283, 304. Another of Jean de Venette's Paris contemporaries, Nicolas Oresme, at almost the same time Jean was writing his chronicle, was writing his treatise *De divinationibus,* challenging the notion that comets necessarily bring evil. Thorndike, *op. cit.,* III, 401, 417–18. In Villani (*Cronica,* Book XI, Chap. 114), however, there is also mention of a comet appearing for a short time in March, 1340. This merely adds another detail to the confused chronology of Jean de Venette's early sections, where he seems to have mixed together events of 1337–38 and those of 1340.

19. The twelfth year of Philip VI, dating from his coronation, would be May 29, 1339, to May 28, 1340. On July 16, 1339, Edward set forth at length the arguments for his claim to the French crown in a letter addressed to the pope and cardinals. Walsingham, *Historia Anglicana,* I, 201–8. On Feb. 8, 1340, he issued letters patent from Ghent addressed to the clergy, nobles, and commons of France asserting those claims. Rymer, *Foedera,* Vol. II, Part 4, p. 64. The classic discussion of this succession question is Viollet's

"Comment les femmes ont été exclues en France de la succession à la couronne," *Mémoires de l'Académie des inscriptions et belles-lettres,* Vol. XXXIV, Part 2 (1895); also his *Histoire des institutions politiques et administratives de la France,* II, 55 ff. See also Potter, "The Development and Significance of the Salic Law of the French," *Eng. Hist. Rev.,* LII (1937), 235–53; "La Question dynastique," Chap. 6 in Déprez, *Les Préliminaires de la guerre de cent ans;* and Viard, "Philippe VI de Valois: la succession au trone," *Le Moyen Age,* XXXII (1921), 218–22, and the same author's "Philippe VI de Valois: début du règne (fevrier-juillet 1328)," *Bib. de l'Ecole des chartes,* XCV (1934), 259–83. The genealogical chart at pp. 312–13 illustrates the fact that Edward was in the second degree of relationship to Charles IV (1328), last king in the direct Capetian line, being his nephew, while Philip of Valois was in the third degree, being his first cousin. Edward's genealogical position was again stronger than Philip's because he was a grandson, through his mother, of Philip IV, while Philip was a grandson, through his father, of Philip III. This made Edward of nearer kin than Philip to two recent French kings unless female relationship was ruled out of consideration. It is sometimes remarked that Charles of Navarre had a claim to the succession like Edward's, i.e., through his mother, but derived from Louis X. But if a claim of this sort were valid, then Edward's took precedence, because his became valid in 1328 and Charles was born in 1332.

20. On June 6, 1329, Edward had done homage in person, in provisional form, to Philip at Amiens for the duchy of Guyenne and the county of Ponthieu. By letters patent of March 30, 1331, he recognized this as liege homage. See Déprez, *Les Préliminaires de la guerre de cent ans,* Chap. 3, "L'Hommage (1329–1331)"; also Lowe, "The Considerations Which Induced Edward III to Assume the Title King of France," in American Historical Association, *Annual Report,* I (1900), 535–83. There is a letter of defiance from Edward to Philip dated Oct. 19, 1337, referring to his closer degree of relationship to Charles IV. *Froissart,* ed. Luce, I, 404.

21. Robert of Artois was the pretender to the county of Artois, where, although his claims rested on unquestionable primogeniture in the male line, decision in the Court of Peers at Paris had twice (1308, 1316) been given against him in favor of a female heir, Robert's aunt Matilda, his father's younger sister. The first count of Artois, Robert I, was son of King Louis VIII. His son and successor, Robert II, had a son Philip, father of Robert of Artois the pretender, who died in 1298, four years before Count Robert II. Robert of Artois' claim rested on the right of representation, i.e., that his dead father's right to inherit passed to him, but the court alleged that

local custom in Artois did not permit this. Decision in favor of Matilda
meant that her two daughters would be second and third in line of succession to Artois, after her son (who actually died in 1315, fourteen years
before his mother). These two daughters, Jeanne and Blanche, in 1307
married the second and third sons of King Philip IV (later Philip V and
Charles IV), bringing the succession to Artois into the royal family,
through the female line. Had Philip V and Jeanne I had a son, Artois would
have become part of the royal domain. It went in fact to his daughter
Jeanne. Robert of Artois attached himself to the Valois fortunes in 1317
when he married Jeanne of Valois, half sister of Philip of Valois. But the
following year Eudes IV, duke of Burgundy, brother of Philip of Valois'
wife Jeanne, married Jeanne II of Artois, Matilda's granddaughter and heir
to Jeanne I. Robert of Artois gave active support to Philip of Valois' claim
to the throne in 1328. Robert reasserted his claim to Artois in 1329, but his
evidence was successfully challenged as perjured and forged. When, very
soon after, his aunt and her daughter died within three months of each
other (November, 1329–January, 1330) Robert was charged with poisoning
them. In the fall of 1331 he fled to Brabant and sentence of banishment and
confiscation was passed against him in the following April and May. For
some time he plotted against Philip and attempted to employ magic and
assassins against him. When this became known, Robert fled in the spring
of 1334 to England. See Richard, *Mahaut, comtesse d'Artois et de Bourgogne,*
pp. 20–27; *Froissart,* ed. Kervyn de Lettenhove, XX, 144–83; Moranvillé,
"Guillaume du Breuil et Robert d'Artois," *Bib. de l'Ecole des chartes,*
XLVIII (1887), 641–50; Lancelot, "Mémoires pour servir à l'histoire de
Robert d'Artois," *Mémoires de littérature tirez des registres de l'Académie
royale des inscriptions et belles-lettres,* X (1736), 571–663. For the chroniclers on this subject see Froissart, ed. Luce, I, 100 ff., 307–16; Jean le Bel,
Chronique, I, 95 ff.; first continuator of Guillaume de Nangis (Géraud, II,
124 ff.); *Les Grandes Chroniques,* IX, 123 ff. There are all the appearances
of a personal feud in the relations of Robert and Philip. As to Robert's influence on Edward, see the comment by Lucas, *The Low Countries,* p. 179.
This work is the most recent and most detailed study of a confused period.
Pocquet du Haut-Jussé has remarked upon questions of inheritance and
succession, pointing out that before the thirteenth century they were settled
by wager of battle or private war, and that in the thirteenth and fourteenth
centuries, by the extension of royal jurisdiction, they came to be settled in
court or by royal arbitration. Under the Valois a series of these, in which the
decisions seemed to favor the royal family, took on major political significance. "The quarrel over Artois threw the heir disinherited by the Court

of Peers into the arms of England; the quarrel over Brittany threw the heir disinherited by the Parlement into the arms of England; the quarrel over Burgundy would have thrown Charles of Navarre into the arms of England if he had not already been there."—"La Succession de Bourgogne en 1361," *Annales de Bourgogne,* X (1938), 55.

22. A reads *Johanne* for *Guillelmo.* This is clearly a copyist's error. In the margin is a note of correction, apparently written there by William Howard, calling attention to the use of *Guillelmo* on the preceding page.

23. Jean de Venette seems to fail to distinguish between William I, count of Hainaut (III of Holland and Zeeland), and his son William II. The former was the father of Queen Philippa, who married Edward III in 1328. His other daughter, Margaret, had married the Emperor Lewis the Bavarian in 1324. William I died June 7, 1337. It seems very probable that Jean de Venette has confused the events of 1337 and 1339–1340. Edward's alliance at the time of his invasion of France was with William II, his brother-in-law. The reference is to John III, duke of Brabant, Limburg, and Lorraine (1312–55). The "many Germans" presumably refers to William, count of Juliers, Queen Philippa's brother-in-law, Reginald, count of Guelders, Edward's brother-in-law, Lewis, elector of Brandenburg, Queen Philippa's nephew, the count palatine of the Rhine, the dukes of Austria, Styria, and Carinthia, with all of whom, at one time or another, Edward made alliances. The Anglo-Flemish alliance was published at Ghent in January, 1340. For detailed discussion of this diplomacy see Lucas, *The Low Countries,* Chaps. 7–9, and Déprez, *Les Préliminaires de la guerre de cent ans,* Chaps. 5, 7–8. See also Sturler, *Les Relations politiques et les échanges commerciaux entre le duché de Brabant et l'Angleterre au moyen âge,* Chap. 4. See also Templeman, "Edward III and the Beginnings of the Hundred Years War," in *Transactions of the Royal Historical Society,* 5th series, II (1952), 69–88. An excellent summary will be found in Perroy, *The Hundred Years War.*

24. Jacques van Artevelde was chosen captain of Ghent, Jan. 3, 1338. Count Louis I of Flanders fled by ruse from Ghent in December, 1339, rather than participate in the Anglo-Flemish alliance. Lucas, *The Low Countries,* pp. 264–360. For Van Artevelde see Lucas, "The Sources and Literature on Jacob van Artevelde," *Speculum,* VIII (1933), 125–49. Jean de Venette has so little to say about Van Artevelde that it is not quite clear exactly what Lucas had in mind when he said that the Saint-Denis chroniclers wrote in a "very biased manner, inspired by the official hatred of a man who was esteemed a rebel and whose motives the ruling class never took the least trouble to understand," and then adds that Jean de Venette's

"account differs considerably from that of his predecessors [the Saint-Denis chroniclers] especially in connection with Van Artevelde and the problems confronting the towns of Flanders." Can he be referring to the first continuator of Guillaume de Nangis instead of the last?

25. All manuscripts give John instead of Nicholas as his first name. Whatever may have been Behuchet's origin, he was not a burgess in 1340, having been ennobled in September, 1328, and Luce calls him a Norman. See "La Marine normande à la bataille de l'Ecluse," *Bulletin de la Société des antiquaires de Normandie,* XIII (1885), 7. This article is reprinted in Luce's *La France pendant la guerre de cent ans,* 2d series. He shared the command of the French fleet with Hugh Quiéret, admiral of France. See Dufourmantelle, *La Marine militaire au commencement de la guerre de cent ans.* The author of *Les Grandes Chroniques* (IX, 182) reflects a hostile attitude in his comment that Behuchet refused to enlist gentlemen for this enterprise because they demanded too high pay, but he retained poor fishermen and sailors because he could get them cheaply. Behuchet was treasurer in 1331, and a master of accounts as well as admiral in 1338. A memoir of 1339 by Behuchet on the conduct of the war at sea against the English will be found with other documents in the article by Jusselin, "Comment la France se préparait à la guerre de cent ans," *Bib. de l'Ecole des chartes,* LXXIII (1912), 209–236.

26. For the battle of Sluys (June 24, 1340) see La Roncière, "Quatrième Guerre navale entre la France et l'Angleterre," *Revue maritime,* February, 1898, and in his *Histoire de la marine française,* I, 349–457. See also Nicolas, *A History of the Royal Navy,* Vol. II, Chap. 1; and Clowes, *The Royal Navy,* I, 235–57. The latter has a translation of Edward III's letter describing the battle, written June 28, 1340, which this author calls "the earliest English naval dispatch." Behuchet was hanged by the English from the mast of a ship, probably as reprisal for his depredations along the English coast where, among other things, he had plundered and burned Portsmouth. First continuator of Guillaume de Nangis in Géraud, II, 169 (Nicolas, *op. cit.,* II, 57, note *h,* confused this writer with Jean de Venette).

27. It is a well recognized custom for the defeated party to emphasize the losses which were inflicted on the victors. The casualties at Sluys excited widespread comment. In England, however, "so many French and Normans were killed there that it was said of them in ridicule, if God had given the ability to talk to the fish of the sea, from then on they would have spoken French because they had eaten so many [French] corpses." *Chronica monasterii de Melsa,* III, 45. Lucas doubts if the English losses were par-

ticularly heavy. He has a section on the battle of Sluys in *The Low Countries,* pp. 395–403.

28. This is an error. Edward went to Ghent, not Antwerp. Probably Jean de Venette has confused Edward's journey to Flanders in January–February 1340, which he describes in the third paragraph after this, with the events following the battle of Sluys. Lucas, *The Low Countries,* pp. 364 ff., 404 ff. An itinerary for Edward in 1338–40 based on records of the privy seal will be found in the appendix (pp. 204–7) of Richard Lescot, *Chronique.*

29. A adds *et contra regnum* after *comitem.*

30. A adds *valde* after *clero.*

31. In the treaty of Melun, April, 1226, which marked the end of an unsuccessful effort of the count of Flanders to escape from vassalage to the French crown, the count surrendered to the king the bull of Honorius III of April 22, 1224, addressed to the archbishop of Reims and the bishop of Senlis, empowering them to excommunicate the count and countess of Flanders if they violate the treaty with the king of France, and recognized that these prelates had power to launch this sentence of excommunication, at the king's request, against the count and his subjects. The papal bull authorized the bishops to act on the king's demand. In 1305, after the battle of Courtrai, Philip IV imposed the treaty of Athis upon the defeated Flemings wherein the latter, in renewing their oaths of fidelity, were required themselves to request the pope to excommunicate them in case they failed to fulfill their obligations. Funck-Brentano, *Les Origines de la guerre de cent ans,* pp. 7–8, 500–501. This religious censure was to be supported, according to a later report, by a fine of 12,000 *écus.* Viollet, *Histoire des institutions politiques et administratives de la France,* II, 79, n. 1. The power to excommunicate had been invoked unsuccessfully in 1338 against Ghent to force the citizens to destroy their fortifications. *Les Grandes Chroniques,* IX, 166; Lucas, *The Low Countries,* pp. 273–78. Can it be that Jean de Venette's confused chronology arises from his failure to realize that there were two sentences of excommunication, one in 1338 and the other in 1340? His later discussion shows that he is referring to the ban pronounced on April 4, 1340, by the bishop of Senlis and the abbot of Saint-Denis at Tournai, described in *Istore et croniques de Flandres,* II, 155, as "an excommunication so great that there was not a priest who dared celebrate divine service." Lucas (*op. cit.,* pp. 372–73) does not think it was very well enforced. According to the *Annales Flandriae,* p. 14, clergy from abroad came into Flanders, some of them sent by Edward III, said mass, and enabled the people to communicate.

32. For this campaign in Thiérache, which was in October, 1339, see

Lucas, *The Low Countries,* pp. 333–39. Jean de Venette is in error as to the truce. There was none. His confused chronology appears again when we note that he discusses the operations against Cambrai of September, 1339, two paragraphs afterward.

33. A reads *applicavit* for *applicuit.*

34. A adds *similiter* after *cremando:* it is not translated.

35. A reads *provinciam* for *totam terram.*

36. A adds *similiter* after *Parisienses;* it is not translated.

37. This paragraph and the following illustrate still further how Jean de Venette has confused the events of 1338 and 1340. It was between Jan. 23 and 26, 1340, that Edward assumed the title of king of France at Ghent. Our author is confused when he says that Edward returned to England and came back to Flanders between the campaign of Thiérache and the assumption of the French arms. The approach of the two armies to each other at Buironfosse had been Oct. 23–24, 1339. Edward retired to Brussels and Ghent, and spent the period from Nov. 12, 1339 to Jan. 20, 1340, at Antwerp. For discussion of this topic see Lowe, "The Considerations Which Induced Edward III to Assume the Title King of France," in American Historical Association, *Annual Report,* I (1900), 535–83, as well as Déprez and Lucas.

38. A reads *venerat* for *advenerat.*

39. Jean de Venette has confused the birth of Lionel of Clarence at Antwerp on Nov. 29, 1338, with that of John of Gaunt at Ghent in March, 1340, after the assumption of the title and arms of France. Presumably Edward's sojourn at Antwerp, as noted above, helped to confuse him. The name Lionel referred to the arms of Edward's ally the duke of Brabant.

40. With respect to the reaction at the French court to Edward's assumption of the title and arms of France, Geoffrey the Baker in his chronicle records, "As for the before-mentioned title and arms, it is reported that the French usurper remarked to certain Englishmen, who had been sent to him, 'It does not displease us that our cousin has quartered the arms of England and France together, inasmuch as we freely permit poor young men of our kindred to bear our royal arms, but it does distress us that on his seal and in his letters he names himself first as king of England rather than of France, and that he places the quarter of his arms with the leopards in the first place above the quarter with the lilies, since this does greater honor to the small island of England than to the great kingdom of France.' To which Sir John Shoreditch, the king's envoy, made reply, that, in accordance with modern usage, his lord, the king of England, as was right and proper, gave to the title and arms inherited from his father pre-

cedence over those which he bore by right of his mother."—Geoffrey the Baker, *Chronicon,* pp. 66–67.

41. Like a good cleric, our author supports the papal position, which dated from October, 1323, when Pope John XXII issued a bull declaring that in a disputed imperial election the pope decided between the candidates. For Lewis of Bavaria to assume the title of king of the Romans without awaiting such decision and receiving apostolic sanction was declared a usurpation, and he was threatened with excommunication unless he submitted within three months. MGH, *Constitutiones,* Vol. V, Nos. 616, 881, 944.

42. The latest study is by Offler, "England and Germany at the beginning of the Hundred Years' War," *Eng. Hist. Rev.,* LIV (1939), 608–31. This author shows that appointment of Edward as imperial vicar was made, not on Sept. 5, 1338, at the *Reichstag* of Coblenz, but by letters issued from Frankfort on September 15. Jean de Venette's seeming restriction of the vicariate to Hainaut and Cambrai fits in with Offler's thesis that part of the emperor's purpose was to resist French encroachment on the Empire in this region.

43. For the political competition between the emperor, the counts of Hainaut, and kings of France relative to Cambrai, see the chapter, "Le Cambrésis pendant la première partie de la guerre de cent ans" in Dubrulle, *Cambrai à la fin du moyen âge,* pp. 275 ff.

44. Géraud (II, 184, n. 3) remarks that all his MSS read *eos sustinentibus.* He proposes to change *eos* to *eum* and to add *perpessi* after *sustinentibus.* A omits *eos.*

45. For the invasion and devastation of the Cambrésis see Lucas, *The Low Countries,* pp. 329–31. The city of Cambrai was besieged from Sept. 24 to Oct. 8, 1339. During this siege there is one of the earliest recorded uses of cannon in the defense of the city. Lacabane, "De la poudre à canon et de son introduction en France," *Bib. de l'Ecole des chartes,* VI (1844), 51.

46. This error and the confusion in chronology has already been noted above (p. 155, n. 32). Our author is probably confused with the siege of Tournai and the truce of Esplechin, which was in 1340 after the assumption of the arms of France, but which he describes under 1341. The subject of papal mediation in this period is discussed in Jenkins, *Papal Efforts for Peace under Benedict XII.*

47. A adds *quamplurimum* after *seipsos;* this does not appear in the translation.

48. A adds *postea* after *pluries.*

49. The author refers again to this subject under the year 1356 as a prelude to the defeat at Poitiers. Can it be that he inserts this here merely as a literary, moralizing device in preparation for later disasters? There is some ground for thinking that when Jean de Venette started writing he began with 1354, and wrote the earlier and introductory part either simultaneously or as an afterthought. This would explain the repetition. There is little in the pictorial records of the period to confirm his statement, but as a contemporary eye-witness with no apparent reason for falsification he should be entitled to credence. In Brooke and Laver, *English Costume,* there is reference to satire on long beards (p. 16), but the authors comment that it must have been a very temporary fashion, since the fourteenth-century pictures show very few beards. An injunction issued in 1342 by the archbishop of Canterbury complains that some of the clergy were not wearing clerical garb, but were walking about "with an outer habit very short and tight-fitting . . . with long beards, rings on their fingers, and girded belts studded with precious stones of wonderful size . . . their boots of red and green peaked and cut in many ways." Such costume was forbidden under penalty of suspension. Quoted at length from Lyndewode's "Provinciale" in E. L. Cutts, *Parish Priests and Their People* (London, 1914), pp. 165–66. The portrait of King John (Delachenal, *Histoire de Charles V,* Vol. I, frontispiece) shows him with a very short beard.

A miniature showing King John founding his Order of the Star in 1352 pictures the members of the order with short beards similar to the king's. Piton, *Le Costume civil en France,* p. 58. A miniature portrait of the Dauphin Charles shows him with a beard of the same cut. Delisle, *Recherches sur la librairie de Charles V,* album, Plate I. The figure in the foreground of Lorenzetti's "Crucifixion" in the lower church of St. Francis at Assisi (Rusconi, *Assisi,* p. 113), which is a portrait of Walter of Brienne, duke of Athens, constable of France, is also bearded, but this is certainly not a long beard. In 1357 the chapter general of the Carmelite order, meeting at Ferrara, made rules relative to dress, one of which forbade members of the order to grow long beards, and another prescribed that their tunics must come down as far as the middle of the tibia. Jean de Venette was present at this meeting. Wessels, ed., *Acta capitulorum,* I, 46, 56. In the *Brut,* under the year 1345, appears the following passage.

In this time Englishmen so much practised and cleaved to the madness and folly of the strangers, that from the time of the coming of the Hainauters (1326), 18 years past, they regulated and changed every year divers shapes and disguising of clothing, of long, large and wide clothes, departing from all old honest and good usage; and another time short clothes and straight-waisted, dagged and cut, and on every side slashed and boned, with sleeves and embroidered sur-coats, and hoods over long and large, and overmuch hanging, that if I shall speak truly, they were more like to tormenters and devils in their clothing and appearance and other array. And the women more dreadfully surpassed the men in array and curiouser; for they were so straight clothed that they let hang fox tails sewed beneath within their clothes for to conceal and hide their behind; the which disguising and pride peradventure afterward brought forth many mishaps and mischiefs in the realm of England.

—*The Brut, or, the Chronicles of England,* ed. by F. W. D. Brie (London, Early English Text Society, 1908), pp. 296–97. Déprez thinks that this sec-tion of the Brut is based upon a lost chronicle by William of Packington, which, he claims, was also used by John of Reading ("La Bataille de Najera," *Rev. hist.,* CXXXVI [1921], 45). There may be a reflection of this association of beards with cowardice in a passage in John Stow, *The Annals or General Chronicle of England* (London, 1615), p. 263, which reads: "After this taking of King John of France Englishmen (which before were bearded and the hair of their heads short rounded) then used long hair on their heads and their beards be shaven." Quicherat (*Histoire du costume en France,* Chap. X) discusses this excitement over styles, pointing out that there had been no changes in costume for a long time, and that the novelties were very marked changes. This author seems to draw much of his in-formation from Jean de Venette and the Saint-Denis chroniclers.

50. A reads *tempore* and adds *rex* where Géraud has *anno.*

51. Robert of Artois' wife was Jeanne of Valois, half sister of Philip VI. Some credit her with responsibility for Robert's activity against the king. There were four children, Jean, Charles, Jacques, and Robert. (The author of the *Chronique des quatre premiers Valois,* p. 2, seems to be in error in calling the third son Louis.) They were arrested and imprisoned in 1334, and not in 1340, as Jean de Venette seems to record, although they were still detained in that year, and the sons remained so until King John's time. See Jean le Bel, *Chronique,* I, 96, n. 4; *Les Grandes Chroniques,* IX, 142; Félibien and Lobineau, *Histoire de la ville de Paris,* I, 585; Moranvillé, "Charles d'Artois," *Bib. de l'Ecole des chartes,* LXVIII (1907), 433–80. The eldest son became count of Eu. See p. 272, n. 57.

1341

1. Jean de Venette is confused as to the numerals of the dukes of Brit-tany. Géraud, in editing his text, attempted to correct him by changing the passage *Johannes secundus filius ducis Arturi* to read *Johannes filius ducis Arturi secundi,* since it does refer to John III, son of Arthur II; but A not

only has the original reading of this phrase, but, unlike Géraud's manu-scripts, repeats a few lines later the expression *dictus Johannes secundus,* where Géraud has only *Johannes.* It is unusual for a medieval chronicler to use the numeral in a reference like this and in this form. The correct form would be John III. He died April 30, 1341 at Caen in Normandy. Jeanne of Savoy was his third wife. She survived him by three years.

2. The Carmelite convent at Ploërmel, one of the first of this order in France, had been founded by Duke John II in 1284, and the founder was buried there on Dec. 15, 1305. Duke Arthur's heart was buried in his father's tomb in 1312. In 1318 Duke John III erected a monumental tomb for his grandfather. His own tomb was not erected until 1365, by his nephew John IV. The statues from these two tombs are still to be seen in the church of Saint-Armel, where they have been since 1821, having survived the destruction of the original Carmelite church by the Huguenots in 1591, and of its successor by the Jacobins. See Bellevue, "Monographie de l'église Saint-Armel de Ploërmel," *Association bretonne: Mémoires,* 3d series, XXVIII (1910), 22–43.

3. This is another of Jean de Venette's errors. Mauclerc is the term ap-plied to Peter of Dreux, founder of the Breton house, who was duke in 1237. He was in fact grandfather of the real Duke John II. Since Jean de Venette, writing in 1360 or thereabouts, uses this term, it may be worth noting that the name Mauclerc applied to Duke Peter is now regarded as a fourteenth-century novelty which cannot be traced back of the arrêt de Conflans of Sept. 7, 1341, the decree awarding Brittany to Charles of Blois. Pocquet du Haut-Jussé, *Les Papes et les ducs de Bretagne,* I, 48–49. The author of the chronicle of Saint-Brieuc, which is regarded as an original source from 1363, applies the term to Duke Peter. Berthou, "Essai sur la Chronique de Saint-Brieuc," *Bulletin archéologique de l'Association bre-tonne: Mémoires,* XIX (1900–1901).

4. The genealogical table on the page following will illustrate the prob-lem of the Breton succession.

It can be noted that John of Montfort and Edward III, by their descent from Henry III of England, were second cousins. There is a similar relation-ship between Edward and King John of France, by common descent from King Philip III of France. John of Montfort was only a half brother of Duke John III. Charles of Blois was nephew to King Philip of Valois, being son of his half sister Marguerite of Valois, wife of Guy de Châtillon, count of Blois. The claim to Brittany by right of representation advanced by Charles in his wife's name was the same as that made unsuccessfully by Robert of Artois with respect to Artois. See p. 151, n. 21.

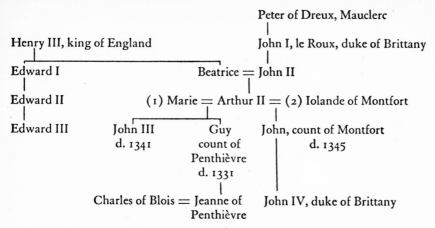

Peter of Dreux, Mauclerc

Henry III, king of England   John I, le Roux, duke of Brittany

Edward I   Beatrice = John II

Edward II   (1) Marie = Arthur II = (2) Iolande of Montfort

Edward III   John III   Guy   John, count of Montfort
                  d. 1341   count of   d. 1345
                             Penthièvre
                               d. 1331

            Charles of Blois = Jeanne of   John IV, duke of Brittany
                              Penthièvre

5. The claim to Brittany advanced by John of Montfort, the replies thereto, and the decision of the Parlement are set forth in detail in Morice, *Mémoires,* I, 1415–24. La Borderie discusses "La Question de droit" on this matter in his *Histoire de Bretagne,* III, 411–20, and concludes that John of Montfort had the better claim. See also for the succession question Plaine, *La Guerre de la succession de Bretagne.*

6. The French chroniclers are very confused and inaccurate in their accounts of the Breton war, and Jean de Venette is no better than the others. His narrative must be corrected at almost every point. John of Montfort was active in occupying Nantes and gaining support in Brittany in the summer of 1341 before the decision in favor of Charles was made, Sept. 7, 1341. His wife was not sent to England but remained in Brittany directing the Montfort forces until early in 1343. Readers of Froissart (ed. Luce, II, 141–47) will recall his romantic account of her heroism in directing the defense of Hennebont in June, 1342. The duke of Normandy's expedition started late in September, 1341, took Champtoceaux by the end of October, and received the surrender of Nantes, at the latest, by November 21. John of Montfort had not withdrawn into Lower Brittany but was taken prisoner at the surrender of Nantes. He remained a captive until Sept. 1, 1343, when he was released provisionally until March 27, 1345, on giving pledges not to go to Brittany. On Jan. 20, 1345, the pope asked King Philip to extend this a year, but the latter refused. In March John fled in disguise to England. On May 20, 1345, he did liege homage for the duchy to Edward as king of France. Rymer, *Foedera,* Vol. II, Part 4, p. 179. He returned to Brittany with the earl of Northampton in the following June. La Borderie, *Histoire de Bretagne,* III, 440, 493; Pocquet du Haut-Jussé,

Les Papes et les ducs de Bretagne, I, 295; Denifle, *La Désolation des églises,* II, 23, n. 9; II, 24.

7. A adds *procedens* before *propugnavit.*

8. A adds *civitatis* after *claves.*

9. A adds *de cetero* after *observare.*

10. A reads *profundiores* for *inferiores.*

11. The reader should remember that part of Brittany was French-speaking and part Celtic (Breton).

12. A reads *remanserunt* for *permanserunt.*

13. A adds *forsitan* after *inferius.*

14. This is another example of confused chronology as already noted above, p. 153, note 23. This refers under 1341 to the death of Count William I, the Good, on June 7, 1337.

15. A adds *fallaciter* after *imperatore.*

16. Jeanne of Valois, wife of William the Good, sister of Philip of Valois, mother of Queen Philippa, who was wife of Edward III of England. It is surprising that Jean de Venette ignores her part as a mediator of truces, particularly the truce of Esplechin; see below, n. 25.

17. A adds the king's name.

18. This is another example of our author's confused chronology. The Tournai campaign here described followed the battle of Sluys, which he discussed under 1340 (above, p. 33). The siege of Tournai lasted from August 1 until September 27, 1340. See Jean le Bel, *Chronique,* I, 183, n. 1, and Gilles li Muisis, *Chronique,* pp. 128–33.

19. For the details of this devastation see Déprez, *Les Préliminaires de la guerre de cent ans,* p. 332.

20. Saint-Amand-les-Eaux (dép. Nord). The town was destroyed Aug. 2, 1340. *Ibid.; Froissart,* ed. Luce, Vol. II, pp. xxiv ff., 54 ff.; Hossart, *Histoire ecclésiastique et profane de Hainaut,* II, 128.

21. A omits *obsidere civitatem;* the translation follows Géraud.

22. A reads *qui erat dux* for *ducem.*

23. This expedition of John, duke of Normandy, did not take place at this time but in the preceding spring. Déprez, *Les Préliminaires de la guerre de cent ans,* pp. 289–99 and notes. *Froissart,* ed. Luce, Vol. II, Chaps. 35–36, has a detailed account of this campaign, followed by a chapter on the battle of Sluys.

24. A omits *habere;* the translation follows Géraud.

25. Sept. 25, 1340, the truce of Esplechin, negotiated through the mediation of Jeanne of Valois, abbess of Fontenelles. The text of this agreement closes the work of the actual continuators of Guillaume de Nangis. There is

nothing to indicate that Jean de Venette had seen this. On the other hand, he did have some knowledge of the renunciation by Philip of Valois, as part of the general agreement, of his right to invoke excommunication and interdict against the Flemings. A document of this date renouncing such right is published by Kervyn de Lettenhove in his edition of Froissart, XVIII, 176. For Philip's efforts with the pope relative to lifting the sentence of excommunication, and their failure, see Lucas, *The Low Countries,* pp. 456–62. When in 1342 the papal envoys attempted to negotiate a general peace, the Flemings refused unless first the interdict was raised. Richard Lescot, *Chronique,* p. 58.

26. A adds *cum gaudio* after *organa.*

27. According to Vanderkindere, *Le Siècle des Artevelde,* p. 307, Pope Clement VI refused to recognize the validity of Philip's renunciation relative to the interdict. There is a passage somewhat similar to Jean de Venette's in the *Breve chronicon clerici anonymi,* in De Smet, ed., *Corpus chronicorum Flandriae,* III, 8, about the resumption by the Flemings of singing and organ music.

28. A reads *dicam relaxationem* for *ipsam restitutionem.*

29. The exact date for this relaxation remains somewhat obscure. In May, 1353, the interdict is referred to as still in force. Berlière, ed., *Suppliques d'Innocent VI,* p. 83. Hutton, in *James and Philip van Artevelde,* p. 212, connects the relaxation with the arrangements for the marriage of Marguerite of Flanders and Philip de Rouvre, duke of Burgundy. Royal authorization for this marriage is dated Aug. 5, 1354. Plancher, *Histoire générale et particulière de Bourgogne,* II, Preuves, p. 291. This helps to establish a date after which Jean de Venette was writing this section of his chronicle.

30. Jacques van Artevelde was killed in July 1345. Discussion as to the exact date, July 17 or July 24, will be found in Pirenne, *Histoire de Belgique,* II, 130, n. 1. Kervyn de Lettenhove in his edition of Froissart, IV, 464, argues for July 24, and Pirenne accepts this date (*op. cit.,* II, 119, n. 1), as do also Viard and Déprez (Jean le Bel, *Chronique,* II, 38, n. 1). It would appear that the Flemish rebellion against the count ended with the submission of Ghent to Louis de Mâle in January, 1349. Gilles li Muisis, *Chronique,* p. 214.

1342

1. A adds *niger* after *monachus.*

2. Pope Benedict XII (Jacques Fournier) died April 25, 1342. The most recent discussion of his life and works is by P. Fournier in *Histoire littéraire de la France,* XXXVII, 174–209. In the *Revue historique,* LXXXIII (1903), 58–76, Déprez has an article, "La Guerre de cent ans à la mort de Benoît

XII; l'intervention des cardinaux avant le conclave et du pape Clément VI avant son couronnement (25 avril—19 mai 1342)." Pierre Roger was born at the village of Roziers-Saint-Georges, about twenty-five miles from Limoges. He became a monk at the Benedictine abbey of Saint-Robert-la-Chaise-Dieu. A papal bull of May 23, 1323 directs the chancellor at the University of Paris to make him a master in theology. In *Les Grandes Chroniques* (IX, 224) he is called "a man of great learning and a doctor in theology superior to all his contemporaries." Jean de Venette ignores the fact that he was prior of Saint-Bausile, abbot of Fécamp (1326), bishop of Arras (1328), and archbishop of Sens (1329), before becoming archbishop of Rouen in 1330. Philip VI employed him frequently as an ambassador after 1328 and made him a royal councilor in 1334. He participated in the revival of the title Duke of Normandy and the coronation of the heir apparent John as duke in 1332–33. In 1338 he resigned his archbishopric to become cardinal priest of the church of Saints Nereus and Achilleus. He was the French king's candidate in 1342 for the papal throne. At that time he was the youngest cardinal. *Les Grandes Chroniques,* IX, 225; see also P. Fournier, in *Histoire littéraire de la France,* XXXVII, 209–38; and Fallue, *Histoire . . . de Rouen,* II, 210–23.

3. Negotiations between John of Montfort and Edward began in the summer of 1341. By Sept. 24, 1341, Edward had recognized John as duke of Brittany, had received his homage, had allied with him, and had conferred upon him, as heir to his predecessor John III, the county of Richmond. Preparations for an expedition to Brittany were started. Rymer, *Foedera,* Vol. II, Part 4, p. 112. The truce between Edward and Philip, made Sept. 25, 1340 (see above, p. 162, n. 25) and twice extended, would expire June 24, 1342. According to Jean le Bel (*Chronique,* II, 2–4), an appeal came to Edward in August, 1342, from the countess of Montfort reporting that Charles of Blois had conquered most of Brittany and asked for English assistance to prevent his conquering the rest of the duchy. Charles took Vannes, May 31, 1342. Denifle, *La Désolation des églises,* II, 21, n. 2, correcting Dom Morice. For Edward's expedition to Brittany, see Jean le Bel, *Chronique,* II, 8–21.

4. A adds *britanniae* after *magnam.*

5. A adds the king's name; omitted in the translation.

6. A reads *interfuerunt* for *fuerunt.*

7. A adds *regorum* after *utriusque.*

8. A adds *vel tres* after *duos.*

9. A reads *concordatum* for *ordinatum.*

10. For the course of the Breton war and the English activities in Brittany

during 1341 and 1342 see La Borderie, *Histoire de Bretagne,* III, 441–71. This is the period of Countess Jeanne's heroic defense of Hennebont described in Froissart (ed. Luce, II, 143 ff.). Jean de Venette ignores all these matters (see p. 161, n. 6). Edward III landed in Brittany Oct. 27, 1342 (Denifle, *La Désolation des églises,* II, 22, n. 3). He besieged but did not take Vannes. Kervyn de Lettenhove (*Froissart,* XVIII, 200) publishes a letter dated Dec. 5, 1342 from Edward, besieging Vannes, to the prince of Wales, reporting the submission of Ploërmel, Malestroit, and other places. The king remained before Vannes until Jan. 23, 1343. Richard Lescot, *Chronique,* p. 208. One of the significant differences between A and the texts used by Géraud is that the latter err in reading *Nannetensem* (Nantes) while A reads *Ventensem* (Vannes), which is historically correct for Edward's main operations. But *Les Grandes Chroniques* (IX, 229) records that part of the English army besieged Vannes and another part besieged Nantes, where they burned the suburbs and remained before the city until the French forces led by King Philip approached. The two cardinals were Pierre Desprès de Montpezat, cardinal of Praeneste and archbishop of Aix, and Annibal Caietani, cardinal of Tusculum and archbishop of Naples. Pocquet du Haut-Jussé, *Les Papes et les ducs de Bretagne,* I, 272. The truce of Malestroit was concluded Jan. 19, 1343. It merely arranged for an armistice until Sept. 29, 1346. Vannes was to be put in the hands of the papal legates to be held in the pope's name during the truce, then to be disposed of as they saw fit. They had already agreed to restore the city to the French king. *Ibid.,* I, 274. The question at issue in Brittany remained undecided. For the attempt to negotiate following this truce see Déprez, "La Conférence d'Avignon (1344)," in *Essays in Medieval History Presented to Thomas Frederick Tout,* ed. by A. G. Little and F. M. Powicke (Manchester, 1925), pp. 300–320.

11. Dagworth seems to have impressed his contemporaries. He was brother-in-law to his predecessor in Brittany, the earl of Northampton. Reporting on the return from Brittany of Northampton and the other English magnates, Adam Murimuth writes, "On their return home Lord Thomas Dagworth, a most valiant knight, who had been commissioned to rule Brittany after the departure of the magnates, conducted himself against the French and Bretons in such successful and praiseworthy fashion that his name became worthy of honor to all future time."—Thompson, ed., *Adae Murimuth continuatio chronicarum,* p. 244. Sir Thomas Gray speaks of him as "a man of too high courage to flee," and comments on the battle of Mauron as "one of the most wonderful affairs that happened in the war of Brittany, always excepting the affair of Lankaderet, where Thomas

de Dagworth, an English knight, admirably defeated the barons of Brittany."—*Scalacronica*, pp. 117, 137. He is referring to a battle of June 17, 1345 *in landa Cadoreti.* See *Chronicon Britannicum,* in Morice, *Histoire ecclésiastique et civile de Bretagne,* "Preuves," I, 8; Denifle *La Désolation des églises,* II, 24; Richard Lescot, *Chronique,* p. 78, n. 4. The earl of Northampton was Edward's lieutenant-general in Brittany in 1342 and afterwards. Rymer, *Foedera,* Vol. II, Part 4, pp. 131, 175–76. Dagworth's commission as royal lieutenant is of Jan. 10, 1347. *Ibid.,* Vol. III, Part 1, p. 2.

12. In *Les Grandes Chroniques* (IX, 258) the chronicler wrote, "At this time Lord John of Brittany, count of Montfort, died in complete dispair, as many say; and it is also said that on his death bed he saw evil spirits. And an astounding thing happened inasmuch as there gathered over the house at the hour of his death such a huge flock of ravens that it was hard to believe that there could be so many in the entire kingdom." The count died at Hennebont on Sept. 26, 1345. His wife and son John, afterwards duke, had been in England since early in 1343, having accompanied King Edward on his return after the truce of Malestroit. Young John, before his father's death, had been betrothed to Edward's daughter Mary, born in 1344. Ramsay, *Genesis of Lancaster,* II, 314. There is a document of Nov. 15, 1345, relative to his wardship. Rymer, *Foedera,* Vol. II, Part 4, p. 189.

1343–1345

1. A adds *comitis Montisfortis* after *filius.*

2. A adds *finaliter atque* after *captus.*

3. This is another serious chronological error since in fact the battle of La Roche-Derrien was fought on June 20, 1347. Dagworth's letter reporting the victory and the capture of Charles of Blois is in Robert of Avesbury, *De gestis mirabilibus,* pp. 388–90. There is a long account also in *Les Grandes Chroniques,* IX, 297–306; see also Richard Lescot, *Chronique,* p. 79, n. 2; Jean le Bel, *Chronique,* II, 145–49; Denifle, *La Désolation des églises,* II, 18–24, 49–52. None of the events of the Breton war mentioned in this section come within the years 1343–1345.

4. A adds *ad uxorem propriam* after *britannicas.* The treaty-making arrangement for Charles' ransom and return is dated Aug. 10, 1356. Rymer, *Foedera,* Vol. III, Part 1, pp. 126–28.

5. The ransom of Charles was set at 700,000 florins, each worth 40 d. sterling, to be paid in seven equal installments, with his two sons John and Guy as hostages. Déprez estimated the modern (1926) equivalent, in terms of gold weight, at about nine million francs. Déprez, "La Querelle de Bretagne," *Mémoires de la Soc. d'hist. et d'archéologie de Bretagne,* Vol.

VII (1926), Part 1, pp. 49–52. But see also Bock, "Some New Documents Illustrating the Early Years of the Hundred Years War," *Bulletin of the John Rylands Library,* XV (1931), 60–99. Bock takes issue with Déprez on the size of the ransom, and has some very interesting details relative to relations between Edward and Charles. There is a royal letter of Sept. 4, 1348, granting Dagworth 25,000 écus for his capture of Charles of Blois. Jean le Bel, *Chronique,* Vol. II, Appendix, p. 352, No. xxviii.

6. Where Géraud has Nantes, A has Vannes, which is historically correct.

7. A adds *Blani.*

8. A vivid contemporary description of conditions in Brittany (1352) will be found in "The petitions made to our lord the King and his council by Walter Bentley, captain of Brittany, and the responses thereto," published in *Froissart,* ed. Kervyn de Lettenhove, XVII, 339–43.

9. This fight is located at Auray by other chroniclers. It took place early in August, 1350. Dagworth's death is ascribed to treachery inasmuch as, during a period of truce, he was ambushed by Raoul de Cahors, who had hitherto been a Montfort partisan. Robert of Avesbury, *De gestis mirabilibus,* p. 411; *Les Grandes Chroniques,* IX, 326; the text cited in Luce's *Froissart* (IV, 400) is the same as that of the *Les Grandes Chroniques.* Luce, *Histoire de Bertrand du Guesclin,* p. 99, n. 1, dates this fight Aug. 1.

10. This combat of the thirties took place March 27, 1351. *Froissart,* ed. Luce, Vol. IV, pp. xlv, 110–15, 338–40; La Borderie, *Histoire de Bretagne,* Vol. III, Chap. 11, sections 2–4. This chapter in La Borderie also appeared in the *Revue de Bretagne, de Vendee et d'Anjou,* XXII (1899), 164–92.

11. The battle of Mauron occurred Aug. 14, 1352. A letter describing it is in Robert of Avesbury, *De gestis mirabilibus,* p. 416. This lists the seneschal of Anjou among the dead but omits mention of Guy de Nesle. The latter's death is mentioned in the *Chronique normande du XIVe siècle,* pp. 105–6. This battle is discussed by Tout in "Some Neglected Fights between Crécy and Poitiers," *Eng. Hist. Rev.,* XX (1904), 726–30, and by Bentley in *A Brief Note upon the Battles of Saintes and Mauron.* Guy de Nesle was captain-general of the king of France for Brittany, Anjou, Maine, and southwestern Normandy, and lieutenant of Charles of Blois. Déprez, "La Querelle de Bretagne," *Mémoires de la Soc. d'hist. et d'archéologie de Bretagne,* Vol. VII (1926), Part 1, p. 52. He was succeeded by Arnoul d'Audrehem. E. Molinier, *Etude sur la vie d'Arnoul d'Audrehem,* p. 39; *Chronique . . . de Jean II,* I, 35–36; Jean le Bel, *Chronique,* II, 206; *Froissart,* ed. Luce, Vol. IV, pp. xlix–l, 126–28, 348–49. It was at this battle that King John's new Order of the Star was ruined by the heavy losses in its membership due to the oath required of its knights never to flee the battlefield.

12. A adds *armatorum* after *multitudine*.

13. The relations of the Frisians with Count William are discussed by Lucas, *The Low Countries,* pp. 505–9. See also the story of these events in the Bourgeois of Valenciennes, *Récits,* pp. 193–205. This battle of Staveren, at which Count William was killed, is usually dated Sept. 26 or 27, 1345, but Froissart puts it on or about Oct. 18 (ed. Luce, Vol. III, pp. xxvii, 105, 322), and Viard, *Les Journaux du trésor,* p. 49, notes that expenses for the man sent to Count William's funeral are dated November, which he thinks supports the October date. See also *Les Grandes Chroniques,* IX, 256–58. This death ended the male line of the house of Avesnes. The inheritance of Holland and Hainaut passed to William's sister Margaret, wife of Emperor Lewis the Bavarian.

14. A adds *deinceps in Francia* after *postea*.

15. A adds *annos et* before *tempore*.

1346

1. A reads *inmiscendo jam permixerat;* Géraud omits the first word.

2. Robert of Artois died in Brittany Nov. 20, 1342, from wounds received at the siege of Vannes. Déprez, "La Mort de Robert d'Artois," *Rev. hist.,* XCIV (1907), 63–66. On the evidence of contemporary documents this corrects the accounts found in Jean le Bel and Froissart.

3. Edward set sail July 2 for the Isle of Wight, where he remained until July 11. Rymer, *Foedera,* Vol. II, Part 4, p. 202; *Froissart,* ed. Luce, Vol. III, p. xxxiv. He landed in Normandy July 12, 1346. An itinerary of this expedition, from this date until the army arrived before Calais Sept. 4, has been compiled from the contemporary English sources by E. M. Thompson and published as an appendix (pp. 252–57) to his edition of Geoffrey the Baker, *Chronicon.*

4. A adds *accedere et* before *capere.*

5. A adds the king's name; omitted in the translation.

6. Raoul III de Brienne, count of Eu and of Guînes. He had been at the siege of Aiguillon with John, duke of Normandy, and had been sent to report to King Philip, who sent him to defend Caen. *Froissart,* ed. Luce, III, 128, 132. According to Jean le Bel (*Chronique,* II, 198), he was "so courteous and so amiable in every way that he was beloved and admired by great lords, knights, ladies and *damoiselles* and by everyone, as well in England as in France." A reads *conestabularius* for *connestabilis.*

7. Jean II, viscount of Melun, was heir, through his mother, to the sires of Tancarville, who were hereditary grand chamberlains of Normandy. This explains the title used by Jean de Venette. In 1352 King John made

him count of Tancarville. Delville, *Histoire du château et des sires de Tancarville*. Géraud (II, 196, n. 2) remarks that his MSS read *gamellingum de Ancarvilla*. A reads *carmellingum de Tancarvilla*.

8. King Philip took the oriflamme at Saint-Denis on July 22, 1346. Gilles li Muisis, *Chronique*, p. 152. He was at Rouen Aug. 2. *Chronique des quatre premiers Valois*, p. 15.

9. Henri Prentout, "La Prise de Caen par Edouard III," *Mémoires de l'Acad. nat. des sciences, arts et belles-lettres de Caen*, 1904. This author discusses the problem of the existence of gates at Caen in 1346, and the general testimony that the city was unfortified, and concludes that fortifications were either unfinished or were not high enough (pp. 243–45). He regards Jean de Venette's story as the French account written nearest to the event and finds it in agreement with the English sources (p. 240). Viard cites royal letters from King Philip of December 1346 authorizing the citizens of Caen to fortify their town, because the lack of fortifications laid it open to the enemy. "La Campagne de juillet-août 1346 et la bataille de Crécy," *Le Moyen Age*, XXXVI (1926), 19.

10. Geoffrey of Harcourt, a younger son of John III of Harcourt, was lord of Saint-Sauveur-le-Vicomte. He was involved in the opposition of part of the Norman nobility to the power of the Valois kings. He was also involved in a feud with the Bertrand family, who played a leading part under Robert Bertrand, lord of Bricquebec, marshal of France, and William Bertrand, bishop of Bayeux, in the local resistance to Edward's army at Caen. Geoffrey had been in exile from Normandy since 1343. He went from Brabant to England early in 1345. The previous July he had been condemned by the French king's courts to banishment and confiscation of goods in connection with Philip's arrest and execution of certain Norman lords, who were charged with treasonable conspiracy to make Geoffrey duke of Normandy. Geoffrey is credited with persuading Edward to land in Normandy instead of proceeding to Guienne to relieve Aiguillon, and this move is alleged to have taken the French by surprise. See Dupont, *Histoire du Cotentin et de ses îles*, Vol. II, Book IV, and Book V, Chaps. 1–4; Delisle, *Histoire du château et des sires de Saint-Sauveur-le-Vicomte*, Chap. 3; *Froissart*, ed. Kervyn de Lettenhove, XVIII, 273; XXI, 514.

11. A reads *villam caperent* for *eam depraedarentur*.

12. A repeats the names of the constable and chamberlain; omitted in the translation.

13. A reads *nunc edificatum castelletum sive castrum primi ad modum valde* for *nunc aedificatum castrum valde pulchrum*.

14. Prentout ("La Prise de Caen par Edouard III," *Mémoires de l'Acad.*

nat. des sciences, arts et belles-lettres de Caen, 1904, p. 245), noting this comment, conjectures that the castle at the Pont Saint-Pierre was built between 1346 and 1367. The latter date seems unnecessarily late. We have assumed that this part of the chronicle was finished by the summer of 1360. Even if that assumption be doubted there can be no question that all the earlier part was completed when Jean de Venette was writing of the events of 1365 (p. 133). The section preceding this relating to the Breton war (pp. 38–39) must have been written before the renewal of that war in 1363, and the section following this is clearly written before the death of the young duke of Burgundy in 1361 (p. 109).

15. A adds *Franciae* after *conestabularius.*

16. According to Jean le Bel (*Chronique,* II, 82) the count and the chamberlain were being pushed very hard in their defense of the gate. English archers were killing the French "Sans deffense et sans pitie." Recognizing among the English, presumably by his shield, Sir Thomas Holland, with whom they had campaigned in Prussia and Granada, they called out to him and surrendered themselves. According to another account, contemporary and detailed but anonymous, the count surrendered himself to Sir Thomas Holland, but the chamberlain became the prisoner of Sir Thomas Dommer. This is published as an appendix to Moisant's *Le Prince Noir en Aquitaine, 1355–70,* p. 166.

17. A adds *cum suis* after *Anglici;* omitted in the translation.

18. The contemporary English account of the capture of Caen on July 26, 1346, appears in a letter written to the queen in London by Michael of Northburgh, one of King Edward's clerks.

And on the Monday the king marched and quartered in the country towns, and on Tuesday also. And on the Wednesday betimes he came before the city of Caen at the hour of nones, and had news that great plenty of men of arms were within the city. And the king made array his battles, fair and great, and sent certain men to the city to spy it out. And they found the castle fair and strong; and within was the bishop of Bayeux, knights and men of arms, who held it. And on that side the water is the city very fair and large; and at one end of the city is an abbey, as noble as can be, where William the Conqueror lieth; and it is closed in with walls and embattled towers, great and strong. In the which abbey was no man found. And at the other end of the city is another noble abbey for women. And no man was found abiding in the said abbeys nor in the town on that side of the water save only in the castle. And the men of the city were drawn into the city on the other side of the water, where was the constable of France, and the chamberlain of Tancarville, who is a very great lord, and much people, to the number of five or six hundred, and the commons of the city. And the men of our host without accord and without array assailed the bridge, which was much strengthened with a stockade and portcullis, and they had hard fighting; and the French defended the said bridge bravely and bore up against them right well, before it could be taken. And then were taken the said constable and chamberlain, and to the number of one hundred knights, and six or seven score squires, and knights and squires slain and other people of the city very many, in the streets and houses and gardens; one cannot know what number of men of substance, for that they were presently stripped, so that they could not be known. And no gentleman was slain on our side, save one squire who was wounded and two days after died. And there were found in the city wines and victuals and other goods and chattels without number. And the city is greater than any town of England, save London.

—Robert of Avesbury, *De gestis mirabilibus,* p. 361. Another letter from the king to the citizens of London describing the English successes, dated Aug. 3, 1346, is in Delpit, *Collection générale des documents français qui se trouvent en Angleterre,* p. 71.

19. For the successful resistance of Caen castle, see *Chronique normande du XIVe siècle,* p. 77, n. 1; *Chronographia,* II, 225–26, and Richard Lescot, *Chronique,* p. 72, n. 1.

20. A reads *Rothomagum cum suis dirixit* for *Rothomagum dirigens.*

21. A reads *Trouchart* for *Crouchart.* Presumably this refers to Troarn, mentioned in various contemporary English records as "Troard," "Treward," or "Troward." Edward's headquarters were there July 31, 1346. Geoffrey the Baker, *Chronicon,* pp. 80, 252–53.

22. A adds *Anglici* after *partes.*

23. None of the English records mentions Bec, but it could have served as headquarters on Aug. 5. Geoffrey the Baker, *Chronicon,* pp. 252–53.

24. A reads *primo* for *principio.*

25. On Aug. 7 the English reached Elbeuf on the Seine about twenty miles south of Rouen. This was their nearest approach to the city. Geoffrey the Baker, *Chronicon,* pp. 252–53. According to the *Chronique normande de Pierre Cochon,* pp. 67–68,

Geoffrey [of Harcourt] with ten men rode over toward Rouen to know the state of the town and to encounter any of those there. And he went beyond the forest [of Moulineaux] and passed by a building called La Salle as Puchellez [a home for lepers in the parish of Petit-Quevilly] and he found no one there but a crazy woman who was at the edge of the wood toward Rouen begging alms from passers-by on the road. And Geoffrey stopped and demanded of her what was the news and where was the king. And she told him that King Philip and all his men were in the castle and town and that they had broken two of the arches of Rouen bridge, because they had learned of King Edward's approach and how he had pillaged Caen, and that there was great to-do at Rouen. At this

Geoffrey left the woman and returned to the English king and said, "Go no farther, for King Philip and all his power is in the town; you can hear the alarm bells ringing and the town is all aroused. They are well informed [of your approach] and if you enter the town you will never escape alive because they are holding no one for ransom but are putting all to the sword."

From *Les Grandes Chroniques* (IX, 279) we learn that Harcourt always rode on ahead of the English, ravaging the country. The Bourgeois of Valenciennes, *Récits,* p. 220, has a story of how Sir Richard de la Marche and Sir Thomas Holland rode into Rouen as far as the broken bridge crying "St. George for Edward!" and attacking those whom they encountered. When the citizens began to gather they spurred their horses back to King Edward, who blamed them for their action. The bridge crossing from Rouen to the south bank of the Seine was made of stone except for the part nearest the city, which was of wood so that it could be destroyed in time of emergency. Chéruel, *Histoire de Rouen sous la domination anglaise,* p. 4. A picture of a bridge of this sort, the Pont d'Auxonne, is in Petit, *Histoire des ducs de Bourgogne,* Vol. IX, facing p. 161.

26. This priory of Notre-Dame-du-Pré, sometimes called "Bonne Nouvelle," was to the south of the Seine in the neighborhood of Rouen. No other chronicler mentions this place in connection with these events. A adds *in parte Rothomagensis qui est.* This is a correction written in a small hand over *aliquibus domunculis.*

27. According to Thompson's itinerary (cited above, n. 21) the English passed Pont-de-l'Arche on Aug. 8. A reads *in littore Secane* for *in littore maris.*

28. The English reached the vicinity of Vernon on Aug. 9.

29. A reads *notabiliter devastando* for *miserabiliter devastando;* the translation ignores the adverb altogether.

30. The English passed Meulan on Aug. 11.

31. The English reached Poissy on Aug. 13 and halted there two days while raiding up to the walls of Paris, as Jean de Venette relates.

32. A adds *fluminis* before *Sequanae;* omitted in the translation.

33. According to *Les Grandes Chroniques* (IX, 274, 276) King Philip at Pont-de-l'Arche challenged the English to battle. Edward replied that he would fight the French before Paris. Whereupon Philip returned to Paris and took up headquarters Aug. 13 on the south bank at Saint-Germain-des-Prés. A reads *remanente* for *manente.*

34. *Les Grandes Chroniques* (IX, 274–76) has an account even more detailed than Jean de Venette's. It tells how "in our house at Rueil, a gift to our church from Charles the Bald, king and emperor, they set fires many

times, but always because of the merits of our lord Saint Denis, as we firmly believe, there was no damage."

35. A adds *Anglici* before *cremaverunt;* omitted in the translation.

36. This castle was in the forest of Marly near Saint-Germain-en-Laye. Its destruction by the English seems to have excited the attention of contemporaries to a considerable degree. The author of the *Chronica monasterii de Melsa* (III, 57) wrote, "They burned in particular the manor of Montjoye, which was the favorite among the manors belonging to the French king, in order better to provoke Philip to fight." The *Anonimalle Chronicle* also mentions it (p. 21). Probably the reason for this is to be found in *Les Grandes Chroniques,* where the author wrote, "And in order that I may write the truth for those who come after, the places where the king of England and his son were, these were regarded as the principle residences and the favorite abodes of the king of France, which was a great dishonor to the kingdom of France, and a proof of treason inasmuch as none of the French nobles drove out the English king [from the French king's own dwellings] where he consumed and wasted the king's wines and his other possessions."

37. A reads *istos* after *autem* instead of *hos.*

38. A adds *eos* before *videre poterant.*

39. This is one of the personal references which Jean de Venette occasionally inserts. Is there any possible relationship between this and the passage in *Les Grandes Chroniques* (IX, 275) reporting that while Edward was at Poissy and his son at Saint-Germain-en-Laye, "raiders went about setting fire to all the towns roundabout even as far as Saint-Cloud near Paris, so that all the Parisians could see clearly from Paris itself the fire and smoke; wherefore they were very much alarmed and with good reason"?

40. A adds *quiquidem ignes et appropinquatio tanta de Parisius omnibus hoc stuporem et admirationem non modicam nec mirum tunc temporis videntibus gravabant non credentes qui unquam talia videre debuissent.*

41. This vague allusion seems to offer some help in dating the composition of this section. Would it have been written before March, 1360, when the English army again appeared before Paris, considering the events which preceded that appearance? We can do no more than surmise, but it seems that to associate this particular event with future events, disastrous as they were, before repetition suggested this particular association would be less likely than not. See p. 99.

42. A adds *apud Poyssiacum* after *Anglicorum.*

43. A adds *astutus* after *miles.*

44. A adds *taciter* before *expectabat*.

45. A omits *beatae Mariae virginis*.

46. A reads *cum suis transire usque partes Carnotenses* for *cum suis versus partes Tornacences*. This reading is not only more probable but it also conforms to the statement earlier in this paragraph.

47. A adds *versus* before *Belvacum*.

48. A reads *remanente* for *exspectante*. *Les Grandes Chroniques* (IX, 276–78) gives a longer account of King Philip's movements in these circumstances, and one to which Jean de Venette's story may possibly have some relation. This tells how Philip came with his army to Saint-Denis on the vigil of the Assumption (Aug. 14) and celebrated the feast the next day. A man, who had been captured by the English and ransomed, was brought before the king and reported that the English were repairing the bridge at Poissy, but the king's advisers mocked him as a liar. So Philip and his army went to Antony beyond Bourg-la-Reine on the south side of the river, and there set up headquarters Aug. 16. On the following day, learning the facts, he returned to Paris. (Viard, "La Campagne de juillet-août 1346 et la bataille de Crécy," *Le Moyen Age,* XXXVI [1926], 51). In Jean le Bel (*Chronique,* II, 86–87) there is a commentary to the effect that the surprising things in this campaign were that the English, without any boats, could repair Poissy bridge so quickly; that King Philip, who was so near in Paris in such great strength, did not defend the crossing; and that he did not cross the Seine and attack Edward, knowing that the latter could not escape over the Seine because all the bridges were broken. The French king's counselors were said to have advised against battle for fear of treason. The alarm of the Parisians, in expectation of an English attack, and their astonishment at Philip's failure to fight is described in the Bourgeois of Valenciennes, *Récits,* pp. 224–25.

49. Géraud, in a footnote (II, 199), remarks that all his texts read *comitem Ambianensem,* but that D'Achery, the earlier editor, judiciously corrected this to read *communiam Ambianensem,* which reading he follows. Since A also reads *comitatem Ambianensem* this earlier correction has been ignored in this translation. This adds another error of detail to Jean de Venette's story, because Edward would not come to the county of Amiens until he had passed Beauvais. The castle of Poix, mentioned five sentences later, is in the county. It is also true that men from the commune of Amiens did oppose Edward's passage of the Seine. But this serves better to explain Jean de Venette's carelessness and confusion than to justify an emendation of his text.

50. A omits *viri*.

51. A reads *omnes illos* for *omnes alios.*

52. This phrase would help in determining the date of composition for this section of the chronicle if we knew more precisely than we do when the walls of Beauvais were extended to include this monastery, since Jean de Venette implies that such was the situation when he was writing. That it may have been about 1360, but not earlier, seems possible from such scanty information as is at hand. See Doyen, *Histoire de la ville de Beauvais,* I, 44; Delettre, *Histoire du diocèse de Beauvais,* II, 427–29, 444–45, 457–58; Labaude, *Histoire de Beauvais,* p. 248. The phrase *et sumptuose aedificatum,* which Géraud (II, 200, n. 1) takes from his two late texts, does not appear in the Arundel text, but it is included in the translation.

53. Jean de Venette correctly labels Godemar du Fay a Burgundian. He was seigneur de Boutheon. See Viard, "Lettres d'état," *Annuaire-Bulletin de la Soc. de l'hist. de France,* XXXIV–XXXV (1897–98), No. 247, n. 1. Jean le Bel, followed by Froissart, credits him with putting up a good fight. The other chroniclers agree with Jean de Venette. The Chandos Herald also describes a vigorous defense of Blanchetaque (*Life of the Black Prince,* pp. 7, 137, 183). A reads *divertens* for *revertens.*

54. A adds *Anglici* before *Sommam.*

55. On Aug. 17, while Edward was marching north from the Seine toward Beauvais, Philip left Antony and returned to Paris. For his movements before and at this time see Viard, "Itinéraire de Philippe VI de Valois," *Bib. de l'Ecole des chartes,* LXXIV (1913), 74–128, 525–619.

56. For the intimate relations of John of Luxemburg, king of Bohemia, with the Valois, see Puymaigre," Jean l'Aveugle en France," *Rev. des quest. hist.,* LII (1892), 391–452.

57. Charles became Emperor Charles IV in 1347. The marriage of Duke John and Bonne of Luxemburg took place July 28, 1332. The passage *dominus Johannes dux Normanniae primogenitus regis Philippi nunc regnantis* is a troublesome one. The translation assumes that Jean de Venette's Latin is as rude as he admits it to be, and that the last two words really refer to John and not to Philip. An alternative assumption is that he meant *tunc* for *nunc.* The translation would then read "the eldest son of King Philip who was then reigning." Considering the context, however, it would seem peculiarly superfluous, at this point, to remind the reader that King Philip was reigning at that time. It seems even more superfluous to accept a literal translation and the assumption from it that this passage indicates composition before Philip's death in August, 1350. Jean de Venette has mentioned King Philip so many times before without feeling any necessity for telling his reader that he was "now reigning" that it is ex-

tremely difficult to see why such a phrase would be called for at this point. As an aside, however, explaining the change in John's position, it becomes comprehensible. There is no other evidence for early composition of this section, while there is considerable for a later date.

58. Jean de Venette commits an error of one day at this point. Saint Louis' day is Aug. 25, and King Philip remained that day at Abbeville out of respect for the royal saint. Battle was joined the next day about vespers. *Les Grandes Chroniques,* IX, 281–82. Vespers is shortly after the ninth hour.

59. A adds *qui balistarii* before *venerant,* and reads *pro Gallicis* for *pro Francis.*

60. A adds *ad pugnandum* after *aciebus.*

61. A reads *cognantes cordes* for *cogentes cordas.*

62. A adds *super praedictum* after *impedimentum;* Géraud omits *super.* The translation ignores this phrase.

63. The subject of rain at Crécy and its effect on the crossbow cords is discussed at length by Viard in "La Campagne de juillet-août 1346 et la bataille de Crécy," *Le Moyen Age,* XXXVI (1926), 73–74, n. 2. This passage of Jean de Venette is one of the earliest recordings of the story. The passage in the continuator of the chronicle of Richard Lescot (p. 74), as indeed most of his story for this period, seems to be based on Jean de Venette. In *Les Grandes Chroniques* (IX, 282) the flight of the Genoese is ascribed to the fire of three English cannon. This author also remarks upon suspicion of treason, and reports that it was commonly said that the rain had so *softened* (*si moilliées*) the crossbow cords that they were useless. This is just the opposite of Jean de Venette's statement that the cords were shrunk by the rain, but it is more in accord with the facts as described by Payne-Gallwey in his book, *The Crossbow.* He discusses this matter at some length (pp. 5–6).

Although much doubt has been thrown on the statement that the crossbows of the Genoese failed to act on this occasion, owing to their strings being slackened by wet weather, it is possible that the incident occurred, without, however, in any measure influencing the result of the battle. The strings might easily have been rendered less effective than usual by the heavy rain that fell just before the battle, and by the bright sun which is known to have succeeded the rain. This combination of water and heat would certainly relax in some degree the strings of the crossbows used at the time of Crécy, if they were uncovered, and would make the strings too loose to be of good service till they could be removed from the bows in order to be shortened by twisting, and then replaced; all of which would entail, of course, time and care. It should be remembered that the bows of the Genoese crossbowmen at Crécy were doubtless composite ones, made of horn, sinew, and glue, bows of steel being of later introduction. The composite bow was straight, hence its bowstring was fixed to it in a necessarily rather slack condition; for this reason the threads composing its string, being more or less detached, were liable to absorb moisture. On the other hand, the threads that composed the tighly strained string of a steel crossbow, lay closely packed together, and as in this case the string was always thickly smeared, both inside and outside, with beeswax to preserve it, it was impervious to water. To test the matter, I have sunk a steel crossbow in a tank of water for a day and a night and have found no appreciable alteration in the tightness of its string. I have also placed in water a crossbow with a comparatively loose string—such as those which I believe were used by the Genoese at Crécy—and found that after half an hour's submersion, the application of a lever to bend the bow caused the string subsequently to stretch down the stock an inch further than its proper position, its tautness and consequent effectiveness thus being lost.

There are reasonable grounds for believing that the military crossbow was of wood and not steel, and that it "was bent either by hands alone, or, as was more probable, by a thong and pulley, a claw fixed to the girdle, or by means of a goat's-foot lever," but not by a windlass. The probable maximum range of a crossbow at Crécy was 200 yards. The long bow has a greater effective range (from 220 to 400 yards) and can be fired more rapidly than the crossbow, which explains sufficiently the discomfiture of the Genoese. One of the best contemporary French chroniclers of this region, Gilles li Muisis, says the crossbowmen were without the protection of their shields, which were well to the rear in the wagon train (*Chronique,* pp. 161–62). There is no good reason for accepting Jean de Venette's explanation for French defeat as of any weight. As an example of popular tradition it is interesting. An alibi for defeat which could be ascribed to nature, to the foreigner, and to the man of low degree, would have a wide appeal.

64. A adds *et plus* before *gladio.*   65. A reads *ibidem* for *ibi.*

66. A reads *erat eiectus* for *expulsus fuerat.*

67. A adds *ut credo* after *dux.*

68. This casualty list for the French at Crécy contains two errors when compared with the lists given in other chronicles. The first of these relates to the count of Bar, who was not killed at Crécy. Possibly Jean de Venette confused in his memory Henry IV, count of Bar, who died in 1344, with Henry IV, count of Vaudemont, who was killed at Crécy. The latter was son-in-law to King John of Bohemia. The other error relates to the second duke, whose name could not be recalled. None of the other lists include another duke. Could it be that Jean de Venette is merely exhibiting further confusion about his first error? The count of Bar in 1355, after Crécy and before the time when Jean de Venette was writing, resumed the title of duke. The most extensive lists are found in the contemporary English

chroniclers, Geoffrey the Baker, Robert of Avesbury, and Adam Murimuth. The Chandos Herald reports one king, one duke, seven counts, and sixty bannerets as the French killed. The persons referred to by Jean de Venette are Charles II (the Magnanimous), count of Alençon, second son of Charles of Valois and brother of King Philip; Louis I de Châtillon, count of Blois, son of King Philip's sister Marguerite of Valois and older brother of Charles of Blois, claimant to Brittany; Louis I, count of Flanders and Nevers, son-in-law to King Philip V; John IV, count of Harcourt, older brother of Geoffrey of Harcourt and father of John, count of Aumâle, who was wounded at Crécy and whom we will encounter again as the chief victim of King John's coup of April 5, 1356 (see p. 59); Louis II, count of Sançerre; Raoul, duke of Lorraine, brother-in-law to Louis and Charles of Blois. Harcourt had been raised from a barony to a county in March, 1339, as recorded in the couplet:

> Harcourt fut Comte neuf
> Treize cens trente neuf.

See La Roque, *Histoire de la maison de Harcourt,* I, 357; III, 247–49. See also Moranvillé, "Philippe VI à la bataille de Crécy," *Bib. de l'Ecole des chartes,* L (1889), 295–97.

69. A reads *revertens postea venit Parisius* for *reversus est et post Parisius.*

70. Jean de Venette is again mistaken when he calls Philip the duke of Burgundy. He was in fact, by marriage, count of Auvergne and Boulogne, and heir to Duke Eudes IV of Burgundy, who was reigning duke until his death in 1350. This Count Philip was father of Philip de Rouvre, the last Capetian duke of Burgundy. He did not die of natural infirmity but as the result of a fall while riding (Jean le Bel, *Chronique,* II, 116). But the author of the *Chronique normande du XIVe siècle* (p. 72), after recording the count's death, adds, "and in this army died many other noble men, more from sickness than from other causes." Petit puts this fatal accident on Aug. 10, 1346 (*Histoire des ducs de Bourgogne,* VIII, 10–11). Preparations for the funeral are dated Aug. 11 (Bertrandy, *Etude sur les chroniques de Froissart,* p. 343).

71. Jean de Venette makes very few references to events in southern France. He seems, in this case, to be quite ignorant of the events preceding the siege of Aiguillon, the very successful campaign of the earl of Derby, which caused Duke John's expedition. See Denifle's section, "The Campaign of the Earl of Derby in Guienne," in *La Désolation des églises,* II, 24–33. Our author even ignores the destruction of the Carmelite convent in the suburbs of Aiguillon, a fact which might have come to his attention and have been considered significant. Marie-Joseph, "Les Convents des grands-

carmes," *Etudes carmélitaines,* IX (1924), 64. But he does not fall into the error of Jean le Bel (*Chronique,* II, 116), who reports that Duke John did not raise the siege until he received news of Crécy, and even then hesitated for consideration of honor. Jean de Venette is unique in his statement about the garb of a hospitaler, an interesting detail not likely to have been invented if untrue. Was such a pilgrim dress a disguise? Would it make it easier for the duke to travel northward in a hurry with only a small retinue? Would it help to save his honor? Can it have any possible connection with Adam Murimuth's statement (*Adami Murimuthensis Chronica sui temporis,* ed. Thomas Hog, [London, 1846], p. 169) that John had sworn on the sacraments not to withdraw until he captured the town? There has been some debate on the dates for the siege of Aiguillon by Bertrandy (*Etude sur les chroniques de Froissart*), Moranvillé (*Chronographia,* II, 220, n. 2; 235, n. 2), Luce (*Froissart,* Vol. III, pp. xxxii, 1–2), and Viard (*Les Journaux du trésor,* p. 90, n. 1). The last two present arguments for March 25–Aug. 24, 1346. The last existing document issued at the siege is dated Aug. 19, 1346 (Bertrandy, *op. cit.,* p. 345), and the earl of Derby reports the siege raised on the next day (Robert of Avesbury, *De gestis mirabilibus,* p. 373). On Aug. 26 the duke started north from Moissac (Bertrandy, *op. cit.,* p. 353; Devic and Vaissete, *Histoire générale de Languedoc,* IX, 586–94). According to the Bourgeois of Valenciennes (*Récits,* p. 237), Duke John learned of Crécy at "le Sousterine" on the borders of the Limousin. On arriving at Paris, he learned that the king was at Pont-Sainte-Maxence and went out to meet him on the road. King Philip had remained at Amiens until Sept. 8 (Viard, "Le Siège de Calais," *Le Moyen Age,* XXXIX [1929], 143, n. 65).

72. Under 1343 in *Les Grandes Chroniques* (IX, 235) we find: "In this same year the king levied a tax on salt which was called gabelle, which is to say that no one could sell salt anywhere in the kingdom unless he had bought it from the king, and royal salt garners were established. This excited the indignation and ill will of both great and small, and of everyone, against the king." To the popular complaints in 1341 King Philip had retorted that the idea of the gabelle on salt had come to him from God as if by angelic messenger, as a means whereby all, both great and small, might equally share the burdens of war costs. M. Ménard, *Histoire de la ville de Nismes* (Paris, 1750–58), II, Preuves, p. 121. The gabelle had been established by an ordonnance of March 16, 1341, and reorganized by one of March 20, 1343. In 1340 a sales tax of 4 d. per livre, i.e., one and two thirds percent, was established. This was called the *maletote.* In February, 1346, the king declared that both the sales tax and the gabelle were only temporary and would be abolished as soon as other revenue became available. See

in general Viard, "Les Ressources extraordinaires de la royauté sous Philippe VI de Valois," *Rev. des quest. hist.,* XLIV (1888), 167–218.

73. See A. Vuitry, *Etudes sur le régime financier de la France avant la révolution de 1789. Nouvelle série: Philippe le Bel et ses trois fils 1285–1328, les trois premiers Valois 1328–1380* (Paris, 1877–83), II, 232 ff.; A. Despaux, *Les Dévaluations monétaires dans l'histoire* (Paris, 1936), Part III, Chap. 6. There was a popular song to the effect that:

> L'an mil ccc xliii
> Fist Philippe de Valloys
> xv deniers venir a trois.
> —Pierre Cochon, *Chronique normande,* p. 66.

74. A reads *possidentis* for *quantitatis.*

75. A adds *et postea* after *similiter.*

76. As early as 1332 Pope John XXII gave Philip permission to levy tithes for a crusade. J. Viard, "Les Projets de croisade de Philippe VI de Valois," *Bib. de l'Ecole des chartes,* XCVII (1936), 305–16. On March 27, 1338, Pope Benedict XII granted a tenth for two years. Viard, *Les Journaux du trésor,* p. 68, n. 5. On June 20, 1344, Pope Clement VI gave the king permission to keep the tenths collected for the crusade. Viard, "Les Ressources extraordinaires de la royauté sous Philippe VI de Valois," *Rev. des quest. hist.,* XLIV (1888), 213. On these matters see also *Mémoires de la Soc. de l'hist. de Paris,* XI (1884), 175–76.

1347

1. As for the Crécy campaign so also for the siege of Calais the most complete, scholarly account is by Viard, "Le Siège de Calais," *Le Moyen Age,* XXXIX (1929), 129–90.

2. Early in April, 1347, a fleet of thirty ships, with supplies for the besieged, successfully forced the English blockade, but these were the last to do so. The English then increased their efforts, both by fortifications with artillery on shore and by squadrons at sea, and these effectively cut off the city. Geoffrey the Baker, *Chronicon,* p. 90; Jean le Bel, *Chronique,* II, 152; *Froissart,* ed. Luce, IV, 45, 273. Jean de Venette's blame for the corrupt French officials is important as an indication of current rumor and public opinion rather than as a record of fact. A final effort to re-victual Calais was made June 25, 1347, and failed (Viard, "Le Siège de Calais," *Le Moyen Age,* XXXIX [1929], 174–75).

3. A reads *copia* for *multitudine.*

4. An army for the relief of Calais began to gather in March, 1347, at the

time when the last blockade-running convoy was sent by sea. King Philip intended it to start for the siege early in May, but, as usual, it was delayed. By May 21 he was at Arras, where fighting men continued to assemble until June 19. From June 23 until July 17 he was at Hesdin, some seventy miles from Calais.

5. A reads *obiebant* for *moriebantur*.

6. June 26, 1347, the captain of Calais sent the following letter to King Philip. It was captured by the English, but was afterward sent on to the French king.

Right dear and dread lord, I recommend me unto you with all my might, as one who much desireth to know that you are in good estate, whom may our Lord ever keep in happiness by His grace. And, if it please you to know the estate of our town of Calais, be certified that, when these present letters were written, we were all well and of good cheer and right willing to serve you and to do whatever might be your honor and profit. But, right dear and dread lord, know that, although the people be all well and of good cheer, yet the town is in sore need of corn, wine, and meat. For know that there is nothing therein which hath not been eaten, both dogs and cats and horses so that victuals we can no more find in the town, except we eat men's flesh. For formerly you wrote that I should hold the town so long as there should be food. And now we are at that point that we have not wherewithal to live. So we have resolved amongst us that, if we have not succour quickly, we shall sally forth from the town into the open field, to fight for life or death. For it were better to die with honor in the field than to eat one another. Wherefore, right dear and dread lord, apply what remedy shall seem you fitting; for, if remedy and counsel be not briefly found, never more will you have letters from me, and the town will be lost and we that are therein. Our Lord grant you a good life and long and give you the will, if we die for you, to requite it to our heirs.

—Knighton, *Chronicon,* pp. 49–50. See also Robert of Avesbury, *De gestis mirabilibus,* pp. 386–88.

7. A reads *eum videntes* for *illum videntes*.

8. A reads *ostensos* for *accensos*.

9. On July 27 the French army arrived before Calais. Geoffrey the Baker (*Chronicon,* pp. 90–91), who was in the English camp, describes in detail how the besieged signaled to King Philip by setting up his standard on the chief tower of the city, with the banners of the French dukes and counts on the other towers. Then at nightfall they kindled a great fire on the highest tower toward the French army, and, for about an hour, made a great clamor with shouting, trumpets, and drums. The next night they repeated this, but with a smaller fire and not so much noise. And on the third night they

showed a fire so small that it was scarcely visible to the French, and made a sorrowful outcry for about an hour, indicating in this way that they were at the end of their resistance. That same night they took down all the banners except their own.

10. A reads *protractaret* for *tractaret*.

11. Géraud (II, 206, n. 2) found some difficulties in this passage which in his texts reads *Et tunc interim Anglici fossata magna fecerunt inter villam Calesiensem et exercitum regis Franciae et ita manu valida et veloci per prata et per paludes quod impossibile etc.* A differs from this by adding *talia* before *fossata* and *et ita* after it, reading *exercitu* for *exercitum,* and putting *valida* before *manu.*

12. A adds *neccessaria* after *et alia.*

13. A reads *nullo modo poterat* for *posset.*

14. The story of these parleys and the English activities to improve their defenses appears in very similar form in Gilles li Muisis (*Chronique,* p. 181), and the *Chronographia* (II, 244). The idea that King Philip was badly advised and tricked is an idea of Jean de Venette's. It probably represents current opinion rather than fact. Its currency may be inferred from a passage in Knighton (*Chronicon,* II, 51), which looks like an English retort, to the effect that King Edward offered to fill up all the ditches and to clear away all the obstacles so that the French could have free approach to do battle on either Thursday or Friday Aug. 2 or 3, but during the night (Wednesday-Thursday) the French retreated. The fact seems to be that the French broke camp at dawn on Aug. 2, which would be an early hour at that time of year in this latitude.

15. A reads *quam non poterat* for *nec.*

16. Géraud (II, 207, n. 1) prints from all his MSS *inimicos evadere* but indicates that the verb should be *invadere.* A has this latter reading.

17. It seems very probable that Jean de Venette had the story of the Calais siege from one of these Carmelite refugees. One of the brothers at Paris in 1348 was Jean Belini from Calais, who sustained losses in the siege, which makes it probable that he was present or had Calais connections. He was sufficiently skilled in astronomy to be able to predict an eclipse. This alone would have made a bond of interest with Jean de Venette. Zimmerman, ed., *Monumenta historica Carmelitana,* pp. 389–90. For the French efforts to help these expelled citizens see E. Molinier, "Documents relatifs aux Calaisiens expulsés par Edouard III," *Cabinet historique,* XXIV (1878), 254–80; also in Viard and Déprez's edition of Jean le Bel, *Chronique,* II, 169, n. 1. One of these refugees was Jean du Fresne, an ancestor of the great scholar Charles du Fresne du Cange. For Edward's arrangements for

English settlers at Calais see a document of Aug. 12, 1347, in Rymer, *Foedera,* Vol. III, Part 1, p. 130. In general consult Daumet, *Calais sous la domination anglaise,* and Sandeman, *Calais under English Rule.*

18. According to the French, Guînes was betrayed to the English by Hugh de Beauconroy in January, 1352. It is surmised that this might have been in consequence of King John's summary execution of the count of Guînes (see p. 54). See *Froissart,* ed. Luce, Vol. IV, p. xlviii, nn. 1 and 2; see also the discussion by the editor of the *Chronique normande du XIVe siècle,* p. 292, n. 2. According to the Englishman Geoffrey the Baker (*Chronicon,* pp. 116–19), who has a detailed account of the surprise and capture of Guînes, it was a very different affair. An English archer named John Doncaster had been held prisoner at Guînes. During his captivity he gained sufficient information about the castle to effect a *coup de main* on his own account. He then sold the place to the English king. See also Gilles li Muisis, *Chronique,* pp. 301–2. Possibly Hugh de Beauconroy was a scapegoat rather than a traitor.

19. This coronation should have taken place at Aix-la-Chapelle, but that town was held for Lewis the Bavarian, so, by a papal dispensation, Charles was crowned at Bonn, Nov. 26, 1346. He had been elected July 11 preceding. Werunsky, *Geschichte Kaiser Karls IV,* II, 72–78. Géraud (p. 208, n. 1) corrects the earlier editors on the phrase *in villa quae Boenna dicitur.* A reads *in villa quae Bonna.* Why Jean de Venette puts this in the wrong year is obscure, but his chronology here, as elsewhere, is badly confused. The phrase opening the next paragraph indicates a casual attitude towards chronological exactitude which is sufficient explanation.

20. This refers to the battle of Neville's Cross, Oct. 17, 1346, which was no nearer to London than Durham. King David remained captive for eleven years. A adds *sed tunc bello inito inter ipsum et Anglico qui in Anglia ad terram custodiendam remanserant.*

21. For previous reference to the usurpation and excommunication of Lewis the Bavarian, see p. 41, n. 157. He died Oct. 11, 1347, from an apoplectic stroke while bear hunting. Heinricus Rebdorfensis, *Annales,* in Böhmer, ed., *Fontes,* IV, 531; Henricus de Hervordia, *Chronicon,* pp. 270–72. The association in Paris of Lewis the Bavarian with heresy is indicated in the *Petite Chronique françoise,* in *Mélanges . . . Soc. des bibliophiles français,* 1867, Part 2, p. 21, which is contemporary with Jean de Venette. "In these same times there was brought from the Roman court to Paris by a papal chamberlain the copy of certain letters from a great heretic who was said to live on Mount Zion, and whom the Parisians regard as Antichrist, sent to Lewis of Bavaria. Wherein, among other things, it was stated that he

could perform such miracles that it was astonishing, and how he had appointed Lewis his vicar in the East and his chamberlain. Many in France copied these letters, which begin with the following words, *Messias, Dei filius, paraclitus spiritus, dilecto filio Ludovico de Bavaria, regi Romanorum, semper augusto, nostram gratiam obtinere,* etc." This looks like a bit of papal propaganda against the Bavarian emperor. Emperor Charles IV was crowned at Aix-la-Chapelle July 25, 1349; at Milan Jan. 6, 1355; and at Rome April 5, 1355. This would suffice to explain the expression about the customary activities of emperors. See Werunsky, *Geschichte Kaiser Karls IV*, II, 195–97; Westermann, "Emperor Charles IV and Pope Innocent VI," *University of Colorado Studies,* I (1941), 301–6. But Charles also revived the coronation at Arles, June 4, 1365. Prou, *Etude sur les relations politiques du pape Urbain V avec les rois de France,* pp. 51, 86. There had not been a coronation at Arles for two centuries. Fournier, *Le Royaume d'Arles et de Vienne,* pp. 472–73. It is obvious that Jean de Venette was writing this section after 1355, but it seems doubtful that it was after 1365.

22. A reads *ubi aderat diligentissime reservatus* for *ubi erat diligentissme observatus.*

23. A reads *in campis* for *in equis.*

24. A adds *sive iuxta* after *Parisius.*

25. A adds *comitem* after *iuvenem.*   26. A adds *alii* after *Artevella.*

27. A detailed, scholarly, and thoroughly documented account of this episode will be found in Lucas, *The Low Countries,* pp. 559–65. The meeting of Count Louis and King Edward was early in March, 1347, at Bergen. Royal letters patent dated March 13 issued at Bergen and relating to the marriage settlement are discussed by Wilkinson, "A Letter to Louis de Mâle, Count of Flanders," *Bulletin of the John Rylands Library,* IX (1925), 177–87. See also Rymer, *Foedera,* Vol. III, Part 1, pp. 111–12. For ten years King Edward had been aiming at a marriage alliance of this sort (*ibid.,* Vol. II, Part 2, pp. 967, 978, 1063, 1097, 1106), with either his first or his second daughter. The present negotiation involved the former, Isabella, who was nearly fifteen. Count Louis was a year older. The objection based upon the death of his father was remarked upon both by Count Louis and King Edward, according to Jean le Bel (*Chronique,* II, 137–38). March 28, 1347, is given as the date of the count's flight by Gilles li Muisis (*Chronique,* pp. 169–70) and accepted by Viard, although it is earlier than the dates suggested by other authorities, viz., Luce in his edition of *Froissart,* Vol. IV, p. xiv, n. 2; Molinier in *Chronique normande du XIVe siècle,* p. 85; p. 276, n. 7; p. 277, n. 3; *Les Grandes Chroniques,* IX, 292. In *Chronographia* (p. 239, n. 1) there is a letter dated April 28, 1347, of King Philip on this

affair. The king was not in Paris but at Moncel-lez-Pont-Sainte-Maxence. Viard, "Le Siège de Calais," *Le Moyen Age*, XXXIX (1929), 161, n. 152. Reference to Jacques van Artevelde is an error, since he had been dead for nearly two years, but it is accurate to associate him with the policy represented by the proposed marriage (Lucas, *The Low Countries*, p. 359). The jilted princess eighteen years later (July 27, 1356) married Enguerrand VII of Coucy. He had been a hostage in England in 1360–65. The affair is said to have been a love match. John of Reading, *Chronica*, p. 170; Savage, "Enguerrand de Coucy," *Speculum*, XIV (1939), 423–42. Efforts to find out more about this popular song have proved fruitless.

28. The implication that Count Louis's marriage followed King Edward's return to England and his own return to Flanders is erroneous. His marriage with Marguerite of Brabant took place near Brussels July 1, 1347, while the siege of Calais was still in progress. Gilles li Muisis, *Chronique*, p. 180. They had been betrothed a year previous. Viard, "Le Siège de Calais," *Le Moyen Age*, XXXIX (1929), 155, n. 121. See also Laurent, "Les Conventions de Saint-Quentin," *Bulletin de la Commission royale d'histoire*, XCI (1927), 89–180; *Froissart*, ed. Luce, IV, xxxv–xxxvi. The count did not return peacefully to Flanders before September, 1348. *Les Grandes Chroniques*, IX, 317–18.

29. This reference to the marriage of Marguerite of Flanders to Philip de Rouvre, duke of Burgundy, helps to date the writing of this section as probably between 1357 and 1361. It is true that the first project for this marriage was Aug. 6, 1354. This had required a papal dispensation, and such dispensation is probably to be associated with the unsuccessful efforts of Pope Innocent VI to negotiate a general peace. The project and the dispensation were renewed Jan. 5, 1357, and on March 21, 1357, there was a gathering at Paris to seal the contract, followed by the marriage ceremony at Arras on May 14. The young duke died Nov. 21, 1361. E. Petit, *Histoire des ducs de Bourgogne*, IX, 38, 78–81, 250; Mollat, "Innocent VI et les tentatives de paix entre la France et l'Angleterre," *Revue d'histoire ecclésiastique*, X (1909), 729–43.

1348

1. A omits *longe* after *multum;* the translation follows Géraud.

2. A adds *aeris* after *exhalationibus*.

3. A reads *relinquatur* for *derelinquo*.

4. We have already noted (p. 148, n. 16) Jean de Venette's surprising ignorance of the triple conjunction of the planets, which some of his contemporaries regarded as the portent for the plague. Yet Jean de Venette does

have this astrological observation of his own, of which no one else makes mention. In *Bib. de l'Ecole des chartes,* II (1841), 201–43, E. Littré published "Opuscula relatif à la peste de 1348 composé par un contemporain," which is a long Latin poem entitled *De judicio solis in conviviis Saturni,* written in 1350 by Simon de Covino of Liége. This is based on the astronomical works of Jean de Murs, Firmin de Beauval, and Leo Judaeos of Montpellier. It describes the plague and ascribes it to the triple conjunction of Jupiter, Saturn, and Mars in 1345. The pope's physician, Guy de Chauliac, makes a similar ascription. In consequence both of these authors get notices in Symon de Phares's *Recueil des plus célèbres astrologues,* pp. 219–20. Jean de Venette, with all his interest in the prophecies of Jean de la Roche-Taillade, also ignores the latter's remarks on the plague in his commentary on the prophecies of Cyril, priest and hermit. See Baluze, *Vitae paparum,* II, 394.

5. A reads *obiebant* for *moriebantur.*

6. A short but useful account of the plague, with many translations from contemporary sources, is Coulton's *The Black Death.* See also Coville, "Ecrits contemporains sur la peste de 1348 à 1350," in *Hist. litt. de la France,* XXXVII, 325–90; and Stein, "Comment on luttait autrefois contre les épidémies," *Annuaire-Bulletin de la Soc. de l'hist. de France,* 1918, pp. 125–50. A very useful summary of the contemporary medical approach to the plague will be found in Campbell, *The Black Death and Men of Learning.* This book also has an extensive bibliography. For references as to the effects of the plague in France see Denifle, *La Désolation des églises,* II, 57–63, and his section on "La Dépopulation en France pendant la seconde moitié du XIVe siècle," *Ibid.,* II, 592 ff. Careful study, based upon statistical data as a corrective for the excited and impressionistic statements of the chroniclers, is more possible for England than for France. See Creighton, *A History of Epidemics in Britain,* Vol. I, Chap. 3, and Levett and Ballard, *The Black Death,* especially Chap. 2, "The Immediate Effects of the Black Death, 1348–50." For one abbey it is recorded that forty out of fifty monks and lay brethren died in 1349. *Chronica monasterii de Melsa,* III, 37. Later studies of the statistics of mortality will be found in G. G. Coulton, *Medieval Panorama* (Cambridge, 1938), Chap. 38, and in Russell, *British Medieval Population,* pp. 214–34. For France there is one local record discussed by Gras, "Le Registre paroissial de Givry," *Bib. de l'Ecole des chartes,* C (1939), 295–308. This shows, for the period Aug. 1–Nov. 19, 1348, 615 deaths. The total parish population is unknown, but this figure indicates more deaths in four months than in the preceding twenty years. A contemporary account of

the plague at Tournai is in Gilles li Muisis, *Chronique,* pp. 195–98, 253–58, 267–68. See also A. C. Klebs, "A Catalan Plague-Tract of April 24, 1348, by Jacme d'Agramont," in *VIme Congrès international d'histoire de la médecine* (Anvers, 1929), pp. 229–32.

7. A adds *utrum pluribus* after *assellis vel.*

8. It is suggested that Jean de Venette would not have written thus had he been writing after the recurrence of the epidemic in 1362 and 1363. See pp. 109, 111.

9. The discovery of the fact of contagion is regarded as one of the results of this plague. Winslow, in *The Conquest of Epidemic Disease,* entitles his chapter on this plague "The Great Teacher." The best contemporary account of the symptoms of this disease is in Guy de Chauliac, *La Grande Chirugie.* He describes the plague as taking on two forms, one characterized by fever and the spitting of blood, with death on the third day, the other by fever and the appearance of abscesses and carbuncles, chiefly in the armpit or groin, with death in five days. But, if God so willed, those afflicted with the second form sometimes recovered. And this disease was very contagious, particularly in its blood-spitting form. (*Ibid.,* pp. 170, 172.) A letter from Avignon reports that the pope directed the dissection of some plague victims, in order to learn the cause of the disease, and that it was observed that all who spat blood and died quickly had badly infected lungs. *Breve chronicon clerici anonymi,* in De Smet, ed., *Corpus chronicorum Flandriae,* III, 14–18. An opportunity for a scientific study of this disease, making possible an understanding of the accuracy of Guy de Chauliac's observations and providing an explanation for the two forms of the disease, offered itself in 1910–11, when there was a great epidemic of this plague in Manchuria. This originated with a small fur-bearing marmot, which is itself subject to the disease in epidemic form. When such epidemics occur among these animals the disease spreads to trappers, who catch and skin diseased animals. There is only one bacillus, but if it is taken into the human system through the respiratory passages the disease takes on the first of Guy de Chauliac's forms (pneumonic plague), becomes extremely contagious from the victim's coughing and spitting, and is 100 percent fatal. If the bacillus is taken into the blood stream, by means, for instance, of body lice or other vermin as carriers from a diseased to a healthy person, it takes on the second form (bubonic plague). The resistance of the lymphatic system lessens the virulence of the bacillus sufficiently so that some victims do recover. Hendrick, "Fighting the 'Black Death' in Manchuria," *World's Work,* XXVII (1913–14), 210–22.

10. *Les Grandes Chroniques,* IX, 315–16, seems to refer to a mission of two monks from the abbey of Saint-Denis sent out on a sacramental mission to towns suffering from the plague.

11. A adds *devotissime* after *curribus.*

12. Géraud (II, 212, n. 1) remarks that all his MSS read *quingenti* (500), but he thinks this an excessive figure and suggests *quinquaginta* (50) instead. A agrees with the other MSS and the translation follows that text. The English records seem to indicate that half the beneficed clergy died of the plague. F. A. Gasquet, *The Black Death,* 2d ed. (London, 1908), pp. 86, 118 ff., 156, 171, 178, 181, 236. Recent studies question this. See above, n. 6. The church and the cemetery of the Innocents was located near Les Halles in that part of Paris north of the Seine. According to Raoul de Presles's "Description de la ville de Paris sous Charles V" (1371), this church was located far outside the ancient bounds of the city "because they located cemeteries and slaughter houses far outside the city to avoid the bad smells and the corruption."—In Le Roux de Lincy and Tisserand, *Paris et ses historiens,* p. 110. By March, 1349, this cemetery was closed, and arrangements were made for burying plague victims outside the walls. Félibien and Lobineau, *Histoire de la ville de Paris,* III, 70.

13. A adds *infirmos* after *timentes.*

14. See letters of King John, November, 1350, with respect to the Filles Dieu of Paris reduced in numbers by the plague. Félibien and Lobineau, *Histoire de la ville de Paris,* pp. 116–17. See also Le Roux de Lincy and Tisserand, *Paris et ses historiens,* p. 188, n. 2; and Viard, "La Messe pour la peste," *Bib. de l'Ecole des chartes,* LXI (1900), 334–38. Account of a consultation on the plague by the medical faculty at the University of Paris will be found in Michon, *Documents inédits sur la grande peste,* and in Rebouis, *Etude . . . sur la peste.*

15. Between May and August, 1348, seven cardinals, one quarter of the college, died. Campbell, *The Black Death and Men of Learning,* p. 135.

16. The pope's action would appear to have been local and special. We learn from the *Chronica monasterii de Melsa* (III, 40, 69) that at the request of the archbishop of York "the pope sent to England general absolution to last for three months from its publication for all those who during those three months should die of the plague" (April–June, 1349). See also John of Reading, *Chronica,* p. 108; Knighton, *Chronicon,* II, 61.

17. A reads *obiebant* for *moriebantur.*

18. A reads *heredes propinquos et liberos* for *proprios haeredes.*

19. A adds *aliquid* after *dicebant.*

20. A adds *et valide* after *subitae.*

21. A adds *firma sed* before *fatua*.

22. In the Manchurian epidemic the Russians accused the Japanese of poisoning the wells. Steveni, "The Ravages of the Black Death," *Fortnightly Review*, CI (1914), 159. Jean de Venette's statements seem to echo the letter of the castellan of Chillon on Lake Geneva to the city of Strasbourg recounting the persecution of the Jews at Chillon in September and October, 1348. This included a copy of confessions made under torture by certain Jews and also refers to certain Christians punished for similar guilt. Hecker, *Epidemics of the Middle Ages*, pp. 74–78. An extensive account of the German pogroms will be found in Heinricus Truchsess von Diessenhoven, *Chronicon*, in Böhmer, ed., *Fontes*, IV, 68–71. There is a passage in Jean le Bel (*Chronique*, I, 225–26), which also contains the charge that the Jews poisoned the wells

in order to poison all Christendom and to have the lordship over all the world, wherefore both great and small were so enraged against them that they were all burned and put to death by lords and judges of the places along the route of the Flagellants [see p. 52]. And they all went to their death dancing and singing joyously as though they were going to a wedding, and they would not be converted, nor would fathers nor mothers permit their children to be baptised . . . saying that they had found in the books of the prophets that as soon as the sect of the Flagellants had overrun the world, that all Jewry would be destroyed by fire, and that the souls of those who remained firm in their faith would go to paradise. Wherefore as soon as they saw the fire, men and women leaped into it, always singing and carrying their little infants with them for fear that they might become Christians.

It is possible that the events at Cologne are the background for all this. The first continuator of Guillaume de Nangis (ed. Géraud, II, 31–35) tells how the Jews in southern France in 1322 were charged with hiring lepers to poison the wells. Persecution and a royal ordonnance expelling the Jews from France followed. Werunsky, *Geschichte Kaiser Karls IV* (III, 239–324), devotes a long chapter to the persecution of the Jews, the Flagellants, and the plague in Germany.

23. This skepticism of Jean de Venette's was not peculiar to him. Gilles li Muisis (*Chronique*, I, 222 ff.) shows similar reserve. Pope Clement VI attempted to protect the innocent, both Jews and Christians, issuing bulls forbidding the plunder and slaughter of Jews (July 4 and Sept. 26, 1348). A bull of Urban V (June 7, 1365) repeats the orders of Clement. *Bullarium magnum Romanorum*, IV, 523; Baluze, *Vitae paparum* I, 251–52; II, 394–95. In Germany, following the Chillon letter accusing the Jews, there is a letter from the authorities at Cologne to those at Strasbourg expressing conviction

that the Jews were not guilty, as rumor made them, but that the plague was a visitation from God. Nohl, *The Black Death,* pp. 196–97. It may be noted that none of these outbreaks against the Jews are ascribed to places in France. Isidore Loeb concludes that, after their expulsion in 1322, there were no Jews in France until 1359, when the regent Charles permitted them to return. "Les Expulsions des Juifs," in *Jubelschrift . . . H. Graetz,* I, 38–56; Luce, "Les Juifs sous Charles V," *Rev. hist.,* VII (1878), 362–70.

24. This idea of corrupt humors was widely current and quite in accord with medical thinking. See Campbell, *The Black Death and Men of Learning,* Chap. 3. To combat such corruption, which was particularly dangerous because of the plague, King Philip, at the petition of the citizens of Troyes, prohibited the raising of pigs within the city. Isambert, *Recueil général des anciennes lois françaises,* Vol. IV, p. 545, No. 151.

25. Jean de Venette's contemporary, Guillaume de Machaut, wrote a description of the situation produced by the plague. "For lack of men you saw many a fair and fine heritage lying unploughed. No one could have his fields tilled, his wheat sowed, his vines trimmed without paying triple wages, so many were dead; and it happened that in the fields the dumb animals lay all bewildered, and went among the wheat and vines wherever they would; they had neither lord nor shepherd nor man to go with them. No one claimed them, nor demanded his own. Many heritages were left without lords. The living dared not stay at all at the manors where death had been, whether in winter or in summer; and if anyone did so he put himself in peril of death."—Translation in Winslow, *The Conquest of Epidemic Disease,* p. 97.

26. This quaint statement seems hard to understand since on its face it appears so obvious as to be banal. But the parish register from Givry offers some appropriate and interesting statistics. The period of great mortality was August–November, 1348. The register shows no marriages between the octave of Epiphany and the end of the year 1348. But in 1349 there were eighty-six marriages, of which forty-two were before the end of February. Gras, "Le Registre paroissial de Givry," *Bib. de l'Ecole des chartes* (1939), 307. See below, n. 33.

27. The monk of Malmesbury reports the contrary. *Eulogium historiarum,* III, 213–14.

28. A adds *liberos* after *geminos.*

29. A adds *tanta diminutio* before *numerus* and omits *iste* after it.

30. The earliest mention of this shortage of teeth appears in a tract called *The Last Age of the Church,* which is dated 1356. In this occurs the passage (p. xxxii): "That this tribulacioun is nyghe and whanne it schal

come bi hem that tretith this matir is whanne men schulle wante teeth and comynly alle children boren siththen the first pestylence ben such that wanten eighte grete teeth." It may be remarked that in normal circumstances children born after 1349 would not have their molar teeth by 1356. This tract has been mentioned previously (p. 148, n. 16) in connection with the so-called "Prophecy of the Lily," which Jean de Venette used for his introduction. May we infer that this observation on dentition is to be associated with the prophetic groups among the friars? Our author quite clearly regards this phenomenon as an omen of some sort. A variant appears in John of Reading, *Chronica* (p. 110), where it is stated that all those born after the plague lacked two molar teeth. This author is also much concerned with portents. He is contemporary with Jean de Venette. Did he write this passage when the post-plague children had cut their six-year molars but not their twelve-year ones, or is he referring to their wisdom teeth? Géraud (II, 215, n. 1) calls attention to a passage in Rigord's *Gesta Philippi Augusti* in which that author closes his account of the events of 1187 with the sentence "And observe that, from this same year of the Lord in which the Lord's cross overseas was captured by this same Saladin, infants born at that time had only twenty-two teeth or even twenty, whereas before they ordinarily had thirty or thirty-two."—In Delaborde, ed., *Œuvres de Rigord, et de Guillaume le Breton*, I, 82–83.

31. A adds *sed in peius* after *commutatus*.

32. A adds *amplius* before *conturbantes*.

33. This seems to have been a fairly common complaint; John of Reading voices it in this connection (*Chronica*, pp. 109–10). See also Campbell, *The Black Death and Men of Learning*, pp. 142 ff. For a detailed discussion of the demoralization of society caused by the plague, the illegal appropriation of property belonging to plague victims, and the frequent remarriages of widows see Jessopp, "The Black Death in East Anglia," *The Nineteenth Century*, XVI (1884), 915–34; XVII (1885), 599–622. Court records show how the pestilence provided the opportunity for robbery. W. Rees, "The Black Death in Wales," *Transactions of the Royal Historical Society*, 4th series, III (1920), 127. In 1350 the archbishop of Canterbury issued a mandate, *Effrenata generis humani cupiditas*. Miss Putnam summarizes the opening paragraph of this document as follows: "The unbridled covetousness of the human race would grow to such height as to banish charity out of the world, if it were not repressed by justice. Many complaints and long experience reveal that priests who have survived the plague, not realizing that they have been saved merely in order to serve God and his people, and not in the least ashamed of setting a pernicious example to lay work-

men, completely neglected the cure of souls, preferring to celebrate annals
and insisting on exorbitant salaries; unless their irrational appetites can be
checked many churches will remain empty."—Bertha H. Putnam, "Maximum Wage-Law for Priests after the Black Death, 1348–1381," *Amer.
Hist. Rev.*, XXI (1915–16), 20–21.

34. A adds *valde* before *mirabile*.

35. A omits *de mercimoniis;* the translation follows Géraud.

36. For similar complaint about agricultural workers in England see
Robert of Avesbury, *De gestis mirabilibus,* pp. 406–7; Knighton, *Chronicon,*
II, 58–65; Geoffrey the Baker, *Chronicon,* pp. 98–100.

37. An attempt to estimate the influence of the plague on elementary education will be found in Campbell, *The Black Death and Men of Learning,*
pp. 174–78.

38. A reads *beatus Yvo;* see Géraud, II, 216, n. 1.

39. There is a slight chronological error here. The bull of canonization
for Saint Yves was issued May 19, 1347, and King Philip was informed of
this about a month later (June 21, 1347). This completed a process begun
nearly thirty-five years earlier. The saint's tomb was in one of the churches
in Tréguier. The original plan had been to exhume the remains Oct. 27,
1347, and translate them to a provisional tomb in the cathedral. But the
English were demolishing some of the Tréguier churches to prevent their
use as strongholds, so the bishop and chapter appealed to the pope for delay. On Sept. 1, 1348, the pope gave permission for a secret exhumation, the
body to be kept in a safe place until a solemn translation could be undertaken safely. On May 12, 1349, permission for the latter was granted. See
La Borderie, Daniel, Perquis, and Tempier, *Monuments originaux de l'histoire de Saint Yves,* pp. 2–3, 483–87; Denifle, *La Désolation des églises,* II,
50; Pocquet du Haute-Jussé, *Les Papes et les ducs de Bretagne,* I, 290–92;
Baluze, *Vitae paparum,* II, 393–94. Pope Clement's sermon on the canonization of Saint Yves is referred to in Mollat, "L'Œuvre oratoire de Clément
VI," *Archives d'histoire doctrinale et littéraire du moyen âge,* III (1928),
246, No. 16; 256, No. 64. For one instance of miracle in this connection see
Les Grandes Chroniques, IX, 264.

40. This church on the rue Saint-Jacques was at the western end of the
rue des Noyers. The Carmelite monastery, where Jean de Venette lived,
was at the eastern end of this street about two hundred yards away. On
Aug. 19, 1348, the bishop of Paris gave permission for erecting this building. It was demolished in 1796, but there is a picture of it in F. Hoffbauer,
Paris à travers les âges (Paris, 1875–82), II, 11. The site has since been
obliterated by the boulevard Saint-Germain. Jaillot, *Recherches . . . sur la*

ville de Paris, VII, 107; Hoffbauer, *op. cit.,* II, 7, 11. Probably the reference to this chapel being founded in 1354 by King John refers to its completion and dedication. See "Fragments inédits de la chronique de Jean de Noyal" ed. Molinier, *Annuaire-Bulletin de la Soc. de l'hist. de France,* XX (1883), 255; J. Lebeuf, *Histoire . . . de Paris,* II, 67–68, 117–20. Géraud remarks (II, 216, n. 2) on the phrase *et ecclesia nomine ejus Parisius,* stating that *Parisius* is found only in the Citeaux manuscript. It is also in A. Géraud also observes (II, 216, n. 3) that all the manuscripts read *in ecclesia Trigonensi,* which was corrected by D'Achery to read *Tregorensi.* A is the same as the other MSS on this point.

1349

1. A reads *conbinate* for *conglobati,* and *flagellantes* for *affligentes.* See Coville, "Documents sur les Flagellants," *Hist. litt. de la France,* XXXVII, 390–411. One of the best eyewitness accounts is that of Gilles li Muisis (*Chronique,* pp. 227–41). See also *Gesta abbatum Trudonensium,* in MGH, *Scriptores,* X, 431–32; Heinricus Rebdorfensis, *Annales,* in Böhmer, ed., *Fontes,* IV, 561. There is an extensive account of the Flagellants with a long astrological discussion respecting them, illustrated by a diagram, in Henricus de Hervordia, *Chronicon,* pp. 280–84.

2. According to the chapter heading in the printed edition of his short chronicle of the Carmelite order (see Introduction, p. 4), Jean de Venette himself was a master of theology.

3. The University of Paris condemned the Flagellants, March 1, 1349. Du Boulay, *Histoire de l'Université de Paris,* IV, 314. Pope Clement's letter of condemnation will be found copied into the *Breve chronicon clerici anonymi,* in De Smet, ed., *Corpus chronicorum Flandriae,* III, 23–26; Baluze, *Vitae paparum,* I, 256. A reads *sub anathemate* for *sub auctoritate.*

4. At this point Géraud (II, 218) corrected his text to read *minus bene et minus sane quod ad fidem catholicam spectabat;* but A reads *quod minus bene et minus sane ad fidem catholicam sapiebant.* A series of documents illustrating the ideas of the Flagellants, viz., a letter alleged to have been brought by an angel to the Flagellants of Malines, the rules of the sect, a sermon, their rites and ceremonies, and a prayer, are published by Kervyn de Lettenhove in his edition of Froissart, Vol. XVIII, pp. 305–17, No. 73.

5. The description given by Gilles li Muisis (see above, n. 1) does not give quite the same impression of calm submission as does Jean de Venette.

In this same year, in the first week of Lent [Feb. 14–21, 1350, N.S.], public proclamation was made in the city square, by the rulers of the city [of Tournai], that everyone should cease practicing this public penance voluntarily assumed, on pain of perpetual banishment. There was a proclamation from the king also that they should cease under pain of losing body and goods, because the king in his letter called them a sect.

Also, the lord bishop of Tournai, the dean and chapter, and the rulers of the city agreed that in the second week of Lent, namely on the night of Saint Peter's Throne [Feb. 22, 1350, N.S.], in the church of Notre Dame de Tournai, the word of God should be expounded. And the priest of Saint Piatus preached a sermon; and an immense crowd gathered; and the papal bull ordering the Penitents to disband [Oct. 20, 1349] was to have been published, but this was not done, for fear there would be great outcry from the people. But in this sermon the priest announced the plenary indulgence agreed upon by the pope and the cardinals for all those who visit Rome and its churches and the tombs of the blessed apostles Peter and Paul.

6. *Les Grandes Chroniques* (IX, 320) records that Jeanne died on Monday, Oct. 4, 1349, but this is in error, since Oct. 4 was a Sunday in 1349. Delachenal puts her death on Oct. 6 (*Histoire de Charles V*, I, 80). She was thirty-seven. Her exclusion from the throne on the death of her father, King Louis X (1314), was the first step in that assertion of the so-called Salic law in France which led to the wars described by our chronicler. Her claim to succeed King Louis was the basis for the future claim of her son, Charles of Navarre. King Louis, her father, had inherited the crown of Navarre from his mother, the wife of King Philip IV. Jeanne's claim to succeed in Navarre had been challenged by her uncles, Philip V and Charles IV, who excluded her from the throne of France, but Philip of Valois could make no such claim as these did, since he was descended not from Philip IV but from Philip III.

7. A reads *dominum Philippum* for *nomine Philippum*.

8. Philip of Evreux was the son of Louis, count of Evreux, youngest brother of King Philip IV and of Charles of Valois. Jeanne was his first cousin once removed. He had died at Xeres, Sept. 16, 1343, from a disease contracted at the siege of Algeciras, where he was serving with King Alphonso XI of Castile. *Les Grandes Chroniques*, IX, 237, 240; *Annuaire-Bulletin de la Soc. de l'hist. de France*, XXXIV (1897), p. 246, No. 199 and n. 1. Jean de Venette's uncertainty as to whether he had been fighting in Prussia or in Granada suggests Chaucer's description of the knight who had fought in both places. Those were the customary regions where knights seeking adventure could fight infidels.

9. A adds *alii duo fuerant* after *primogenitus;* the translation does not show this.

10. The family of Navarre was larger than this by three daughters. In addition to Blanche, mentioned here, were Jeanne, a nun at Longchamp,

Marie, queen to Peter IV of Aragon, Agnes, wife of Gaston III, count of Foix, and Jeanne the younger, married to the viscount of Rohan.

11. Charles was eighteen. He was crowned king at Pampeluna, June 27, 1350. Meyer, *Charles II*, p. 25. Would Jean de Venette have written, "Of him I shall speak hereafter" except after the events of 1357–58? There is an interesting article by Honoré-Duvergé, "L'Origine du surnom de Charles le Mauvais," in *Mélanges d'histoire du moyen âge dédiés à la mémoire de Louis Halphen*, pp. 345–50.

12. A omits *domina;* the translation follows Géraud.

13. Sept. 11, 1349 (Viard, *Les Journaux du trésor,* p. 68, n. 1). This is Bonne of Luxemburg, daughter of King John of Bohemia and sister of the emperor Charles IV. She was married to Duke John July 28, 1332. Villani (*Istorie fiorentine,* in Muratori, *Scriptores,* XIV, 36), ascribes her death to the plague.

14. A adds *de Burgundia* after *francorum*.

15. Dec. 12, 1349. *Les Grandes chroniques,* IX, 320. She was the sister of Duke Eudes IV of Burgundy and the great-aunt of Duke Philip de Rouvre. The author of the *Chronique des quatre premiers Valois* (p. 18) calls her "the bad, lame queen." She too was probably a plague victim.

16. A reads *dominus* for *dux*.

17. Jean de Venette is badly confused at this point. Géraud (II, 220, n. 1) thinks that so much confusion must be due to careless copying, and he suggests considerable editing of the text. But the reading in A is almost identical with the published text, which fact makes it hard to accept the suggestion. The three daughters whom Jean de Venette ascribes to Philip of Valois and Queen Jeanne are really the daughters of John and Bonne of Luxemburg. Jeanne of France, at the age of seven, was married in February, 1352, to Charles of Navarre; Isabella was betrothed in May and married in September, 1360, to Gian Galeazzo (not Bernabo) Visconti, who was then only nine years old and who did not become duke until after Jean de Venette had concluded his chronicle. The marriage of Marie to Robert of Bar did not actually take place until June, 1364, but from 1356 King John considered Robert his son-in-law and spoke of him so in public. Baudot, *Les Princesses Yolande,* pp. 22–23; Prou, *Etude sur les relations politiques du pape Urbain V avec les rois de France,* p. 39; Cordey, *Les Comtes de Savoie,* pp. 155–57; Meyer, *Charles II,* p. 30; Delachenal, *Histoire de Charles V,* I, 61. This passage must have been written after May, 1360, at the earliest.

18. Jan. 11, 1350, a month after his first wife's death. Jean le Bel (*Chronique,* II, 183–85) calls her a beautiful young maid, whom Duke John had desired to marry. By his father's advice the latter, on Feb. 9, 1350, married

Jeanne, countess of Boulogne (the widow of that Philip of Burgundy who had been killed at Aiguillon) and mother of Duke Philip de Rouvre. "These two marriages," says Jean le Bel, "were clearly contrary to the laws of Holy Church, but Pope Clement consented to them because he was unwilling to oppose them."

1350

1. A reads *incarnatione* for *in circumcisione*.

2. A adds *hominum* after *malitia*.

3. The initiative for the fifty-year Jubilee came from the Romans in 1343, presumably for reasons which will be obvious to modern readers. Baluze, *Vitae paparum*, I, 245. Pope Clement issued the bull *Unigenitus Dei filius* on Jan. 27, 1349. According to this, all Christians who during the following year came to Rome and stayed two weeks, visiting the churches of Saint Peter, Saint Paul without the Walls, and Saint John Lateran, with true contrition, would acquire the most complete pardon for their sins. The original Jubilee in 1300 had not included the church of Saint John Lateran, but Pope Clement added this because it contained an image of Christ which had miraculously appeared to Pope Sylvester when he dedicated the church, and it also contained the baptismal fount where the emperor Constantine had been baptized and cleansed of his leprosy. Rodocanachi, "Le Premier Jubilé de 1350," in *Etudes et fantaisies historiques*, pp. 153–64. Heinricus Rebdorfensis reports (*Annales*, in Böhmer, ed., *Fontes*, IV, 562) that during the Jubilee he was in Saint Peter's when Saint Veronica's napkin was shown, and that the crowd was so great that many were suffocated. Gilles li Muisis (*Chronique*, p. 266), after recording the pope's proclamation of a general indulgence, reports, "but the king of France, I know not by whose advice, had his baillis proclaim that none of his subjects should leave the kingdom on any sort of journey nor absent themselves therefrom under certain penalties. . . . Wherefore all pilgrimages were stopped all over the kingdom. The king pretended that the reason was that he did not wish people to leave his kingdom so that he might better resist his enemies. This restriction lasted for a little while, but in Lent and after Easter many people undertook pilgrimages to Rome, Santiago, and elsewhere." King Edward also prohibited his subjects from going to Rome for the Jubilee because of the wars in France. Knighton, *Chronicon*, II, 65. In the summer of 1349 he sent Richard Fitz-Ralph, archbishop of Armagh, to Avignon to request that "the inhabitants of Great Britain and Ireland [enjoy the benefits of the Jubilee indulgence] without making the pilgrimage to Rome, because the trip was hard and costly from these distant islands, and par-

ticularly dangerous now because of pirates, war with the French, and the plague." In August Fitz-Ralph set this proposal before the pope. Hammerich, *Beginning of the Strife between Richard Fitzralph and the Mendicants*, p. 14; Gwynn, "The Black Death in Ireland," *Studies*, XXIV (1935), 25-42. In "Extraits du compte de la vicomté de Montivilliers, 1350" (Appendix X to Richard Lescot, *Chronique*, p. 233) there is reference to royal letters from King Philip to the bailli of Caux directing him to proclaim by the public crier "that no one was to leave the kingdom to go to the holy pardon or elsewhere unless each one be provided with arms and horses according to his estate." This was at the end of June.

4. The night of Aug. 22-23, 1350, at the abbey of Coulombs near Nogenle-Roi. Jean le Bel, *Chronique*, II, 185, n. 3. A discussion of Philip VI and his son John will be found in the first chapter of Dodu, *Les Valois*.

5. Jean de Venette again makes an error of a day (see above, p. 176, n. 58). Sunday and the coronation were Sept. 26, 1350. Jean le Bel, *Chronique*, II, 186; *Chronique . . . de Jean II*, I, 25.

6. A reads *doctorum in legibus* for *legum*.

7. None of the documents setting forth the legal basis for the Valois succession is known. Could the ones referred to here be those drawn up for pleading the issue in 1340 before Pope Benedict XII? Secousse (*Memoires*, p. 8, n. 2) suggests that this may refer to a treatise by Richard Lescot, which has not survived, but was known in the fifteenth century. See Potter, "The Development and Significance of the Salic Law of the French," *Eng. Hist. Rev.*, LII (1937), 235-53. For a summary of modern scholarship on this topic see Perroy, "Franco-English Relations, 1350-1400," *History*, XXI (1936-37), 148 ff.

8. A adds *inquit* after *sic enim*.

9. Philip had received the county of Valois in appanage on April 13, 1344.

10. Having reported the death of King Philip on Sunday, Aug. 22, 1350, the author of *Les Grandes Chroniques* (IX, 326-27) adds, "and he was carried to Notre-Dame in Paris on the following Thursday. And on the following Saturday the body was buried at Saint-Denis, on the left side of the great altar, and his entrails were buried at the Jacobins in Paris and his heart at Bourgfontaine in Valois."

11. He was back in Paris by Oct. 17, 1350. *Chronique . . . de Jean II*, I, 27; *Chronographia*, p. 249, n. 4.

12. This was Raoul III de Brienne, count of Eu and Guînes, constable of France. He had been captured by the English in 1346 at Caen and was in France seeking money for his ransom. He is reputed to have been very popular (see above, p. 168, n. 6). On Nov. 16, 1350, he was arrested and two

days later was beheaded without any form of trial. Jean de Venette shows none of the surpise reflected in the other chroniclers, nor the attempts to explain this act of violence. Surmise included treason, jealousy, and the sudden discovery of an amour between the constable and the late Bonne of Luxemburg, King John's former wife. This was the first of a series of summary executions during King John's reign. See Jean le Bel, *Chronique*, II, 198–200; *Chronique . . . de Jean II*, I, 28–30; Gilles li Muisis, *Chronique*, pp. 279–82; *Froissart*, ed. Luce, Vol. IV, p. xlviii, n. 1; *Chronique normande du XIVe siècle*, p. 97; p. 287, nn. 1–2; *Chronographia*, p. 250, n. 3. The affair is discussed at length by Delachenal, *Histoire de Charles V*, I, 67–69.

1351

1. A adds *Avinonnense* after *curia Romana*.

2. This passage suggests that Jean de Venette had seen the memorial from the English clergy headed *Propositio . . . ex parte praelatorum et omnium curatorum totius Ecclesiae coram papa in pleno consistorio . . . adversus ordines mendicantes,* published in Hammerich, *Beginning of the Strife between Richard Fitzralph and the Mendicants,* pp. 53 ff. It would seem as if Jean de Venette was a year off on this topic, since the controversy took place in 1350.

3. The controversy between the friars and the priests was of long standing. In February, 1300, Boniface VIII attempted, by the bull *Super cathedram,* to define the limits of the privileges enjoyed by the mendicant orders respecting confession, preaching, and burial. Under this bull, whenever any of the faithful chose to be buried in the mendicant churches, rather than in the parish church, the friars were required to pay to the parish priest one fourth of the burial fees. Boase, *Boniface VIII,* Chap. 7. Trouble arose from the failure of the friars to conform to this requirement. See also Jean L. Copeland, "The Relations between the Secular Clergy and the Mendicant Friars in England during the Century after the Issue of the Bull *Super cathedram* (1300)," Summaries of Theses No. clxii, *Bulletin of the Institute of Historical Research,* XVI (1938–39), 34–35; and Hammerich, *op. cit.,* Section 1, "The Pope and the Friars until 1350." The matter may have come to an issue at this time in consequence of the following case. The parish priest of Saint-Pierre, in the diocese of Langres, brought suit in the bishop's court against the friars for their failure to make the payments required under the bull *Super cathedram.* The court found for the priest. The friars appealed the case to the pope. This was under Benedict XII, who died before giving a decision. Clement VI referred the issue to one of his chaplains, who confirmed the finding of the bishop's court against the

friars. Notification of this was given the friars at Langres on Oct. 9, 1350. Mortier, *Histoire des maîtres généraux de l'ordre des frères prêcheurs*, III, 282. Gwynn writes, "At some date which cannot now be determined, most probably in the year 1349, the spokesmen of the four mendicant orders appeared before the Pope and begged him, in a formal *Proposicio* to issue a fresh bull. This bull, so they hoped, would interpret in their favour some doubtful clauses in the famous *Super cathedram* of Boniface VIII, and mitigate other points which were clear enough, but which the friars had found troublesome in their apostolate." He cites the heading of this *Proposicio* from a Bodleian manuscript.—*The English Austin Friars*, pp. 82–83. The case against the friars to which Jean de Venette refers was presented in papal consistory July 5, 1350, by Richard Fitz-Ralph, archbishop of Armagh, preaching from the text, "Let every man abide in the same calling wherein he was called" (I Cor. 7:20), and urging the abolition of the privileges enjoyed by the mendicants. This *Proposicio* (see n. 2 preceding) has been edited and published in full by Hammerich (*op. cit.*,). Inasmuch as Jean de Venette comments later in his text on Fitz-Ralph it seems strange that he fails to mention him by name or title at this point. Some time in the preceding year (VIII Clement VI, viz., May 9, 1349–May 8, 1350) the pope had appointed Fitz-Ralph one of a committee of three doctors to investigate certain matters relating to property and possession which had been troubling the mendicants, but we do not know what resulted. It would appear to be related to the controversy over poverty, about which Fitz-Ralph wrote *De pauperie salvatoris*. R. L. Poole, ed., *Iohannis Wycliffe De dominio divino*, pp. xxxv, xxxvii, 273. Pierre Raymond, prior general of Jean de Venette's order, the Carmelites (1342–57), is described as one very diligent in the business of the order, who sought many privileges from the Apostolic See. Zimmerman, ed., *Monumenta historica Carmelitana*, I (1907), 234.

4. Exodus 14:14.

5. A adds *curiositatibus magni sumptuosi* after *aliis*.

6. A reads *vos estis magis tenaces [magis avari et magis] cupidi;* the words in brackets are not in Géraud. At this point A has in the margin a gloss written in a fifteenth-century hand reading *Nota quomodo papa arguebat defensione statum mendicantium* ("See how the pope argues in defense of the mendicant position.") A later commentator has added a hand pointing to this gloss with the remark *ecce nihil notandum preter simplicitas asini* ("Behold nothing worthy of note except to a silly ass").

7. A reads *morienturi* for *mendicantium*.

8. A adds *honestis* before *edificiis*.

9. For the conditions exciting complaint to which the pope's words seem to be a retort, see Gwynn, *The English Austin Friars,* Part III, Chap. 1, "The English Provinces after the Black Death." This includes the translation of a passage from John of Reading, which elaborates a theme similar to that which Jean de Venette puts at the end of his discussion of the plague (see p. 50).

10. A reads *corruptibilia* for *temporalia.*

11. A reads *ostendit* for *dixit.*

12. Pope Clement was regarded as one of the most eloquent men of his time. Some of his discourses were written down in résumé by a *reportator* named Bernardin, an Augustinian friar. This passage in Jean de Venette has been ignored by the scholars who have studied the pope's sermons and speeches. *Hist. litt. de la France,* XXXVII, 223–24; Mollat, "L'Œuvre oratoire de Clément VI," *Archives d'hist. doct. et litt. du moyen âge,* III (1928); Baluze, *Vitae paparum,* II, 422, n. 1.

1352

1. A reads *doctor* for *magister.*

2. A reads *ad gubernandum appostolici* for *ad papatum;* the translation follows Géraud.

3. For Pierre Roger's career before his election as pope see Baluze, *Vitae paparum,* I, 241–42; for his doctorate see Mollat's note, *ibid.,* II, 342, with references, and Denifle and Chatelain, *Chartularium,* Vol. II, No. 784. A reads *illo in abbatia* for *unde in abbatia.*

4. A adds *et consecratus* after *papam.*

5. Baluze, *Vitae paparum,* II, 434–42.

1353

1. The most extensive account of this local warfare is in the *Chronique normande du XIVe siècle,* pp. 97–108, 287–98. A glimpse of the general situation appears in letters patent of Philip VI, Nov. 13, 1346, in favor of Pierre Morin "to whom, because he is serving us of his good will and harming our enemies, we, of our special grace, direct, and by these letters order, that any towns, castles, fortresses, inheritances, or goods belonging to us or to any of our subjects, now occupied by our enemies, which the said Pierre and his followers can conquer, recover, and deliver from the hands of our enemies and bring into our obedience, by whatever means he may, the said Pierre and his followers shall have all the fruits, profits, and emoluments of the said towns, castles, and fortresses for the period of a whole year from the day when they are brought into our obedience."—*Archives*

du Poitou, XIII (1883), 329–30. Conditions in the diocese of Coutances were such that the bishop refused to remain there. His cathedral was fortified as a place of refuge for the people. The records for Bayeux are very scant. Lecanu, *Histoire des évêques de Coutances,* pp. 215–17; Farcy, *Abbayes de l'évêché de Bayeux,* I, 103. Domfront, according to Luce, was occupied by the duke of Lancaster early in 1356. Luce, *Histoire de Bertrand du Guesclin,* pp. 494, 606–7.

1354

1. A adds *unde tunc eram* after *Remis.* Although he makes particular note of his own experience of this earthquake, Jean de Venette at this point makes an error of two years, because it actually occurred in 1356. It must have been sufficiently unusual for him to be at Reims so that he might have been expected to remember the year. He is correct as to the day, which was also the day of the first sitting of the Estates General, but since he was not in Paris he would not make any association in his memory with this event. The anonymous author of the *Petite Chronique françoise* in *Mélanges . . . Soc. des bibliophiles français,* 1867, Part 2, pp. 29–30, writes, "In this year a little after [the battle of Poitiers], namely on the following October 18, there was a great and terrifying earthquake a short while after curfew. And the next day there was a great to-do in Paris on the part of all those who had felt the earthquake, as well those of the city as those beyond the large bridge and across the little bridge." Another French chronicler wrote, "In the year 1356 there was such a great earthquake at Basle that the greater part of one of the streets back of Notre-Dame fell into the Rhine. It happened in like manner in Burgundy, where the biggest tower of Montront castle shook and fell down. This was on Saint Luke's day about dinner time. . . . Then everything quieted down, but about bedtime there was another shock worse than before, so that the poor people rushed aghast from their houses. The Vayte tower at Besançon was cracked in several places."— Quoted in Petit, *Histoire des ducs de Bourgogne,* IX, 69–70, from a manuscript in the Bib. nat. The German chroniclers take considerable note of this event. *Chronicon Moguntinum,* in *Die Chroniken der deutschen Städte,* XVIII, 159; Königshofen, *Chronik,* in *ibid.,* IX, 862–63; Closener, *Chronik,* in *ibid.,* VIII, 136, 292; *Chronikalien der Rathsbücher,* in *Basler Chroniken,* IV, 17; Heinricus Rebdorfensis, *Annales,* in Böhmer, ed., *Fontes,* IV, 543; Heinricus Truchsess von Diessenhoven, *Chronicon,* in *ibid.,* IV, 104–5; Conrad Justinger, *Die Berner-Chronik,* p. 122; *Chronicon Elwacense,* in MGH, *Scriptores,* X, 41.

2. Inasmuch as this murder was done Jan. 8, 1354, N.S., we might expect

Jean de Venette to put it in 1353, according to the practice of reckoning the year from Easter to Easter. With respect to the account later of the king's arrest of Charles of Navarre on April 5, 1356, N.S., he does date that event in 1355 "during Lent," i.e., at the end of the year. See p. 59. The author of the *Chronique . . . de Jean II* (I, 37) puts the constable's murder in 1353.

3. Charles of Spain was one of the De la Cerda line, whose pretensions to the throne of Castile at one time had been supported by France. He was a great-great-grandson of Louis IX and a third cousin to King John. The genealogy showing four generations between Louis IX and Charles of Spain was demonstrated by Delaborde, "Un Arrière Petit-Fils de Saint Louis, Alfonse d'Espagne," in *Mélanges Julien Havet,* pp. 411–27. Charles was son-in-law to John's cousin, Charles of Blois. The office of constable was conferred upon him immediately after the execution of Raoul de Brienne, and in some quarters Charles was credited with responsibility for that execution. His intimacy with King John, according to Villani (*Istorie fiorentine,* in Muratori, *Scriptores,* XIV, 219–20), was such as to excite scandalous imputations. Mollat has a long note on him in his edition of Baluze, *Vitae paparum* (II, 445–46).

4. A adds *cum lacrimis* after *pietatem.*

5. The most detailed account of this episode is in the *Chronique des quatre premiers Valois,* pp. 25–28. According to this story, the exchange of bitter words was between Charles of Spain and Philip of Navarre, younger brother to King Charles. The latter was not actually present at the murder but remained at a village nearby while the others killed the constable. The date was Jan. 8, 1354, N.S. King Charles immediately assumed responsibility for the crime in letters of Jan. 10 to the English king, the duke of Lancaster, and elsewhere. *Froissart,* ed. Kervyn de Lettenhove, XVIII, 350–61; Secousse, *Mémoires,* p. 33; *Bulletin de la Soc. de l'hist. de France* Vol. I, Part 2 (1834), pp. 25–27. There is a deposition made by one of the murderers which declares the motive to have been that the constable had taken an inheritance due to Charles of Navarre, as well as speaking ill of him and estranging the king from him (Secousse, *op. cit.,* pp. 49–59). This refers presumably to the county of Angoulême, which both Jean le Bel (*Chronique,* II, 201) and the Bourgeois of Valenciennes (*Récits,* p. 271) name as the matter at issue. King John had taken this county from the queen of Navarre in exchange for other lands, which he never delivered to her. He then conferred it upon Charles of Spain (Pocquet du Haut-Jussé, "La Succession de Bourgogne en 1361," *Annales de Bourgogne,* X [1938], p. 58). The persons mentioned here are John V, count of Harcourt, son and successor to the count killed at Crécy, Jean Malet, sire de Graville, Sir Wil-

liam de Mainmares, nicknamed "Maubue," and Colin (not Nicholas) Doublel, who seems to have been personal squire to Charles of Navarre. *Froissart,* ed. Luce, Vol. IV, p. li, n. 1; *Chronique . . . de Jean II,* I, 38–39.

6. The author of the *Chronique du Mont-Saint-Michel* (I, 2), in record-ing how the king of Navarre, by evil counsel, caused the constable to be murdered at Laigle, added, "and there began 'les rumours, doulours et mes-chiefs' which have since been in the French kingdom." We can easily be-lieve that Jean de Venette would have agreed with this.

7. Feb. 12, 1352, marriage of Jeanne of France and Charles of Navarre. Delachenal, *Histoire de Charles V,* I, 81.

8. Géraud's text reads *Guido de Valonia,* but Géraud (II, 228, n. 2) re-marks that it should read *de Bolonia.* A has this correct reading. Guy of Boulogne was a younger son of Robert VII, count of Auvergne and Boulogne, by his second wife. This made him half brother to the father of King John's queen, Jeanne of Boulogne. He had been archbishop of Lyons but resigned this see in 1342 on becoming cardinal priest of Saint Cecilia. In 1350 he became cardinal bishop of Porto. He was a prominent and active figure in Valois and papal circles. For papal efforts to negotiate peace, see Mollat, "Innocent VI et les tentatives de paix entre la France et l'Angleterre, *Revue d'histoire ecclésiastique,* X (1909), 729–43. For further interesting details of these negotiations, see Bock, "Some New Documents Illustrating the Early Years of the Hundred Years War," *Bulletin of the John Rylands Library,* XV (1931), 60–99. For a brief summary of the cardinal's activity see Perroy, "Franco-English Relations, 1350–1400," *History,* XXI (1936–37), 149–50.

9. Géraud (II, 228, n. 3) calls attention to the error in using the term *matertera* (maternal aunt) with reference to Jeanne of Evreux instead of *amita* (paternal aunt). All the MSS agree in this reading. It is merely an-other example of Jean de Venette's confusion about royal personages. It is suggested that the only actual fact of which Jean de Venette was aware was the public, ceremonial reconciliation of March 4, 1354, in which the cardinal and the two queens figured. *Chronique . . . de Jean II,* I, 42–45. Behind this was considerable tortuous diplomatic negotiation, most of which has become known only to modern research historians. King John's willingness to pardon Charles appears to have been due to the latter's negotiations for an alliance with the English, which John wished to avoid. Delachenal, "Premières Négociations de Charles le Mauvais avec les Anglais (1354–1355)," *Bib. de l'Ecole des chartes,* LXI (1900), 1–30.

10. The actual terms of settlement between the two kings were embodied in a treaty drawn up at Mantes, Feb. 22, 1354. Secousse, *Recueil,* pp. 33–36.

These are summarized by the author of the *Chronique . . . de Jean II*
(I, 41–42), but there is nothing there about masses and chapels. In fact,
Jean de Venette ignores the actual terms completely. For the royal letters
of pardon, which name all those present at the constable's murder, see Secousse, *op. cit.,* pp. 38–45, and *Froissart,* ed. Luce, Vol. IV, p. li, n. 1. It is
suggested that Jean de Venette's statement is an error arising from certain
facts connected with a "brotherhood of pardon" formed for pilgrimage to
Rome at the time of the Jubilee (1350). Charles of Navarre did not found
it, but he joined and contributed to its endowment. A document of July,
1353, shows him establishing an altar in a "chapel of pardon" in the cathedral at Evreux, with an endowment for daily mass. As a churchman who
traveled about, Jean de Venette might well have seen this and have assumed
that it was connected with the pardon granted on March 4, 1354. Fossey,
Monographe de la cathédrale d'Evreux, p. 60; Le Batelier d'Aviron, *Le
Mémorial historique des évêques, ville et comté d'Evreux,* pp. 104–5; Bonin,
*Analectes historiques, recueil des documents inédits sur l'histoire de la
ville d'Evreux,* No. xvi. pp. 33–36. In the church of Notre-Dame at Mantes
there is a "chapel of Navarre," which some, presumably because of this
statement of Jean de Venette, have thought might have been constructed in
expiation for the murder of Charles of Spain. But it has none of the characteristics of an expiatory monument, and it is thought to be of a date earlier
than 1354. Durand and Grave, *Chronique de Mantes,* pp. 221–22, 258–59.
Can there be any connection in Jean de Venette's mind with the dedication
of the church of Notre-Dame-de-Mont-Carmel in Paris Sunday, March 16,
1354, by the cardinal of Boulogne, in the presence of the three queens whom
he mentions in his text? Charles of Navarre's aunt, Queen Jeanne, was a
special patron of the Carmelite friars. Félibien and Lobineau, *Histoire de la
ville de Paris,* III, 222–23. A adds *una cum omnibus illis qui ad praefatum
homicidium ducti fuerant* after *receptus.*

11. A adds *ut dicetur postea ea nec duravit* after *diu.*

1355

1. This short campaign was all that came of great preparations. King
Edward had intended originally to land during the summer in Normandy,
where he expected to cooperate with an army led by Charles of Navarre,
who had been negotiating during the year for an English alliance. King
John, however, offered Charles such attractive terms that on Sept. 10, 1355,
he signed a treaty at Valognes, and two weeks later there was another
public ceremonial of pardon and reconciliation. Delachenal, "Premières
négociations de Charles le Mauvais avec les Anglais (1354–1355)," *Bib. de
l'Ecole des chartes,* LVI (1900), 1–30. Edward then prepared to take his

army across to Calais, where he landed Oct. 26. For the English accounts of this campaign see Robert of Avesbury, *De gestis mirabilibus,* pp. 427–31; Geoffrey the Baker, *Chronicon,* pp. 125–26; Knighton, *Chronicon,* II, 83–88; Walsingham, *Historia Anglicana,* I, 280. John arrived at Amiens Oct. 28 and remained there until Nov. 7. There occurred one of those futile and insincere attempts to set a day for battle such as our author refers to. There was even a suggestion of personal combat. By Nov. 11 Edward was back in Calais, and within two weeks he was again in England. Months before, the French king had sent an envoy to Scotland

with huge store of pounds of gold, which was to be bestowed freely, on behalf of the [French] king, upon [Robert Stewart, the] guardian [of Scotland] and the lords of the kingdom: Provided, however, that the Scots should not maintain peace or any good understanding with the English, but should, on the contrary, bravely war them down. This, at all events, was settled and finally promised by the leading men of the kingdom, in sundry interviews and councils held in sundry places, before the aforesaid gold, which had been left behind in Flanders, came into Scotland; and the Scots, who often for a penny lose a shilling, were led away by lust for gold, to promise to fight England to the last. But afterwards, when it came to deeds, they achieved little worthy of remembrance. So the chiefs of the kingdom shared among themselves the aforesaid gold they had got from the French; and the others, of meaner sort, they sent empty away.

—John of Fordun, *Chronicle of the Scottish Nation,* in *The Historians of Scotland,* IV, 360–61. In fact the Scots did make a surprise attack on Berwick, capturing the town (Nov. 6) and besieging the castle. It was news of this which brought King Edward back to England. King John was still at Amiens on Nov. 22, 1355 (Delachenal, *Histoire de Charles V,* I, 128, n. 3), but on Nov. 30 he was in Paris for the opening session of the Estates General (*Chronique . . . de Jean II,* I, 55). For this brief campaign near Calais with references to all the sources see Denifle, *La Désolation des églises,* II, 95–98, for King John's itinerary, as far as it can be determined, see Petit, "Séjours de Jean II (1350–1356)," Comité des travaux historiques et scientifiques, *Bulletin historique et philologique,* 1896, pp. 587–612.

2. A adds *varii et diversi* after *nobiles.*

3. A adds *forsitan* before *evenerunt;* it is not translated. This is characteristic of Jean de Venette's caution on a controversial topic.

4. A reads *dum* for *cum.*   5. A adds *in mensem* after *adhuc.*

6. A reads *anterius* for *interius.*

7. After the phrase *manus apponens ad regem Navarrae* A adds *cepit eum faciens ipsum celeriter ibidem carcerari mancipari. Et statim sine mora fecit capi comitem de Haricura ac dominum de Gerdivilla et militem voca-*

tum Malbue atque Nicholaum Doubleti scutifer regis Navarrae. The copy-ist from whom Géraud's MSS were derived omitted this passage, presum-ably misled by the two appearances of the word *Navarrae.* This passage shows the form *Gerdivilla* instead of *Girardi-Villa* about which Géraud makes comment (II, 230, n. 2).

8. The date was April 5, 1356. A complete and scholarly discussion of this episode, the historical sources for our information, and the various theories respecting the motivation will be found in Delachenal, *Histoire de Charles V,* I, 140–57. Concerning the "something sinister reported to King John" the Bourgeois of Valenciennes writes (*Récits,* p. 284), "I do not know if it be true that the men of Navarre were planning to poison the king, or to deliver him and his sons to the English, but such is the report." Delachenal considers the possibility that John of Artois, count of Eu, may have in-formed the king of some sort of plot against his person (*op. cit.,* I, 143–44), and that this caused the king to act on a sudden impulse. May 14, 1356, Edward III wrote to the pope repudiating the charge of King John that his action against Charles was due to the fact that the latter and the Norman lords had traitorously agreed to deliver Normandy to the English. "Fear-ing that this [French] assertion may make a false impression upon Your Holiness, and wishing to clear the king of Navarre, who is my enemy but is also my kinsman, of the charge of treason falsely imputed to him, I de-clare, on my royal word, and I protest before God, that the king of Navarre and his friends have never made an alliance with me, that they have never promised to help me, and that I have always regarded them as powerful enemies."— Rymer, *Foedera,* Vol. III, Part 1, p. 123. We can now recognize that this is somewhat disingenuous. The most detailed account of the affair at Rouen, one which probably embodies the local tradition, and which connects the coup with the struggle of the Norman lords, including Geof-frey of Harcourt, for their local liberties against the Valois kings, is in Pierre Cochon, *Chronique normande,* pp. 75–87. This author calls King John "the worst and most cruel king there ever was, the son of that queen from Bur-gundy who had no love for any Norman" and accuses the royal advisers of counseling John to behead four or five important Normans in order to cow the rest. According to this version Colin Doublel was beheaded because he struck the king with his dagger when the latter arrested Charles of Navarre. He alone of the four was permitted to confess before execution.

9. Charles of Navarre, in the custody of Arnoul d'Audrehem, marshal of France, was taken to Château-Gaillard, to the Louvre, to the Châtelet, to Crèvecœur (near Cambrai), and finally to Arleux-en-Palluel (near Douai). Molinier, "Etude sur la vie d'Arnoul d'Audrehem, maréchal de France

130.–1370," *Mémoires de l'Académie des inscriptions et belles-lettres,* 2d series, Vol. VI, Part 1 (1883), 61; *Chronique . . . de Jean II,* I, 65, n. 3. Probably the item in the records at Péronne (Nov. 3, 1356) relating to the cost of guarding Charles at the castle of Péronne refers to a stopping place on his move northward. Dournel, *Histoire générale de Péronne,* p. 99.

10. In the latter part of 1355 there had been a scheme, the purpose of which is obscure, for the dauphin Charles, duke of Normandy, Charles of Navarre, and certain others, including those arrested the following April, to take refuge secretly with Emperor Charles IV. That the Valois court was a center of intrigue, in which Charles of Navarre played an active part, is obvious. Delachenal, *Histoire de Charles V,* I, 116–20.

11. A reads *sine remedio* for *sine medio.*

12. Jean le Bel (*Chronique,* II, 225) writes that "King John arrested a gentle young knight, who was with the king of Navarre, named Frisquet de Frisquan, and he sent the king of Navarre to be imprisoned at Château-Gaillard, and the knight, Messire Frisquet, at the Châtelet in Paris. And all the people marveled greatly and could not understand why King John had done this. Some said that they would cut off Messire Frisquet's skin in strips, drag him through the streets, and then hang him at Montfaucon, and that they would behead the king of Navarre at night just as they had the count of Guînes. Others said that they would put him into a narrow lead box wherein he could not live long, and so cause him to die a slow, painful death." It is not insignificant that much of our information is based upon three depositions of Jean de Fricamps, nicknamed Friquet, published by Secousse, (*Recueil,* pp. 49–60). Froissart (ed. Luce, IV, 182) also reports the practice of frequently telling Charles that he was about to be beheaded, or put into a sack and thrown into the river, and of his patience in the face of this treatment. Jean de Venette is accurate as to the length of Charles's imprisonment, which was slightly over a year and seven months (April 5, 1356–Nov. 8, 1357). Probably both these chroniclers are doing no more than echoing Charles's speeches after his release (see below, p. 69). A adds *non sine magno periculo interitus atque* after *amplius.*

13. *Froissart,* ed. Luce, Vol. IV, p. lxv, nn. 2–4; Delachenal, *Histoire de Charles V,* I, 163, nn. 2–5; I, 164, n. 1. Probably Mantes was taken into royal hands at this time. Durand and Grave, *Chronique de Mantes,* p. 217. A adds *et occisi* after *fuerant.*

14. This was probably late in April, 1356, after Easter (April 24), and this initial stage of the Franco-Navarrese war belongs in the next section of the chronicle. The town was taken, but the castle held out. *Chronique des quatre premiers Valois,* pp. 37–38.

15. A reads *Et videntes* for *quod videntes.*

16. According to the *Chronique normande du XIVe siècle* (pp. 110–11), "King John laid siege to Evreux and easily gained the town [i.e. the faubourgs], but the city and the castle held out. Then at the command of King John the count of Eu brought the king of Navarre thither, and he brought about the surrender of the castle. And I do not know who set fire in the city before it surrendered, but the whole city and the church of Notre-Dame were burned. And after this the king of Navarre was taken to Crèvecœur." The canons of the cathedral, at a later date, reported that most of their charters and title deeds were burned on this occasion. Statenrath, "Etat des fortifications et des enceintes de la ville d'Evreux, à diverses époques de son histoire," *Travaux de la Société d'agriculture de l'Eure,* 1st series, VI (1835), 341–72. There exists a pardon for a man charged with responsibility for burning Evreux. *Ibid.,* 4e série, Vol. VII (1886–88), p. 227; also, in part, Secousse, *Recueil,* p. 60. According to the *Chronique des quatre premiers Valois* (p. 38), "The Navarrese in the castle set fire to those houses of the city which were before the castle, and the fire spread to the church of Notre Dame. And then the French entered the city and pillaged it." *Froissart,* ed. Luce, IV, 192–93. Molinier, in his life of Arnoul d'Audrehem (p. 66), thinks Evreux was taken before June 9, 1356. Luce (*Froissart,* Vol. IV, p. lxviii, n. 1) puts it before June 20. But in *Chronographia* (p. 256, n. 3) there is record of one of Charles of Navarre's partisans, who was held a prisoner in the household of the archbishop of Rouen from April 10 until June 28, when he was taken to Evreux to be surrendered to the Navarrese in the castle, according to an agreement made with them. Géraud (II, 233, n. 1) comments on the disagreement in reading among his MSS at this point. He follows the reading of MS 435. A has the same reading.

17. The garrison of Evreux did not withdraw to Pont-Audemer, as Jean de Venette says, but to Breteuil. *Froissart,* ed. Luce, IV, 193. But Pont-Audemer had been besieged by French forces at the same time as Evreux. It was relieved June 29 by the Anglo-Navarrese forces under the duke of Lancaster (see below, n. 20). Reinvested, it held out until Dec. 4, 1356. *Chronique . . . de Jean II,* I, 90–91.

18. A reads *se adhesit* [*sic*] for *sibi invicem adhaeserunt.*

19. It would appear that Philip of Navarre attempted for about six weeks to negotiate the release of his brother, for whose life he was said to be apprehensive (Jean le Bel, *Chronique,* II, 226). May 28, 1356, from Cherbourg, he sent King John a letter of defiance, renouncing all bonds of allegiance to him. Delachenal (*Histoire de Charles V,* I, 165–68) discusses this episode and gives a modernized version of this letter. Navarrese negotiations with

the English began at the end of April, but the treaty, whereby Edward was recognized as king of France and duke of Normandy, was not signed until Sept. 4. What Philip demanded of Edward was the deliverance of Charles of Navarre, the recovery of his inheritance, and assurance that in the struggle against the French Philip should have any important prisoner of King John's following to be used in bargaining for his brother's release. *Ibid.*, pp. 168–70; *Froissart,* ed. Kervyn de Lettenhove, XVIII, 378–81, 397–401. In the following passage the words in brackets appear in A but are lacking in Géraud. *Nam dictus Philippus de Navarra frater regis Navarrae capti [sicut dictus] et detenti [se cum rege Anglice confederunt qui advitus per anglicos contra regen Francie rebellando per se et per suos amicos aliqua castra in Normannia tenuit] et multa gravamina illi patriae intulit.*

20. The activities of the English and Navarrese during June–July, 1356, are vividly described in an official report from the duke of Lancaster.

These are the daily marches of the expedition [made] by my lord the duke of Lancaster in Normandy, who had in his company my lord John of Montfort, who claims to be duke of Brittany and who has been brought up from childhood by the king of England, and a force of five hundred men-at-arms and eight hundred archers. And Lord Philip, brother of the king of Navarre, and Lord Geoffrey of Harcourt came to him with a hundred men-at-arms of the country, and Robert Knolles brought three hundred men-at-arms and five hundred archers from the garrisons of Brittany, so that my lord duke had nine hundred men-at-arms and fourteen hundred archers in all. And on the Wednesday next before the feast of Saint John the Baptist [June 22] he moved from the abbey of Mountbourge in the isle of the Cotentin to Carentan, outside the isle, five French leagues, each league being longer than two English leagues, and remained there the eve of that feast [June 23], and on Friday the feast day [June 24] he moved on passing before the strong town of Saint-Lô as far as Torigny, a distance of eight French leagues, and spent Saturday there [June 25]. On Sunday [June 26] he moved on to Evrecy, seven French leagues. On Monday [June 27] he moved on, passing Caen, to the town of Argences, seven French leagues. On Tuesday [June 28] he moved on, passing the bridge of Corbon, which is a great fortress and one of the best defended crossings in the whole kingdom, set in a marsh, seven French leagues, to the city of Lisieux. On Wednesday [June 29] he moved on six French leagues to the town and castle of Pont-Audemer, which belong to the king of Navarre, and which castle was besieged by a very large number of men-at-arms and arbalesters; but when they heard that my lord the duke had passed the bridge of Corbon, they fled by night in such great haste that they left behind all their engines and artillery, arbalests, pavys, and other different harness. He stayed there Thursday and Friday [June 30–31] to fill in the mines which they had made very well and very strong, which were so near the castle that they lacked only four feet of reaching the walls. He victualed the castle for a year and appointed my lord John de Luc, a Brabançon knight, castellan with fifty men-at-arms and fifty archers of his men. On Saturday [July 1] he moved on from there five French leagues to the abbey of Bec-Hellouin. On Sunday [July 2] he moved on from there as far as the town of Conches, eight French leagues, where he attacked the castle and gained the outwork of the castle by assault and set it on fire. On Monday [July 3] he went on to Breteuil, which belongs to the king of Navarre, and where there was a very strong castle besieged by the king's enemies. But before the duke's arrival they withdrew from there, and my lord victualed that castle adequately and went on the same day two leagues to one side to a great walled town called Verneuil, which belongs to the countess of Alençon. This town my lord took by assault, capturing many prisoners and taking much booty. At once, on the very same Monday, he made an attack on a very strong tower of this town of Verneuil, and the attack lasted all that day, and Tuesday [July 4] and Wednesday [July 5] until the hour of prime, at which time the tower surrendered with all the goods therein on condition that the men who were there should be spared and should not be made prisoners. In this attack many English were wounded with quarrels and stones. My lord destroyed this tower. There was much booty there. The town of Verneuil is only eighteen leagues from Paris. It is called the key to Normandy. On Thursday [July 6] my lord stayed there to rest his men. On Friday [July 7], turning back towards the isle of the Cotentin, my lord duke moved to a town called Laigle, where Lord Charles of Spain was put to death. . . . King John of France, his eldest son the dauphin of Vienne, his brother the duke of Orleans and many magnates of the country with eight thousand men-at-arms, arbalesters, and forty thousand other commoners, were on one side of that town a short league away; and there came to my lord the duke from the king two heralds, who said that the king knew well that inasmuch as my lord had ridden so far into his kingdom and had remained so near him at Verneuil, he was come to do battle, which he could have willingly if he wished. To this my lord answered that he had come into these parts to accomplish certain things, and that these being accomplished satisfactorily, thank God, he would return to the place where he had things to do. If King John wished to interfere with his march, he was ready for him. After that there was no further news of the king. On Saturday [July 8] he moved from Laigle to the town of Argentan. On Sunday [July 9] he moved on to the town of Torigny. On Monday [July 10] he moved on to the abbey of Saint-Fremond, where he crossed a very dangerous river because the French had broken the bridge. Hereabouts sixty men-at-arms and other soldiers lay in ambush to do whatever harm they could to our men, but fifteen of our men-at-arms from England encountered them and killed them all, which was regarded as a miracle. On Tuesday [July 11] my lord moved on to Carentan. On Wednesday [July 12] he came back to Mountebourg in the isle of the Cotentin. The same day that my lord first entered the isle, Robert Knolles with one hundred forty men-at-arms rode on in advance of my lord to find billets for him and his men, when suddenly he ran into one hundred forty men-at-arms, arbalesters, footsoldiers, and French, who had come forth from a neighboring castle to rob and burn a town in our obedience. And Robert with the one hundred forty men-at-arms killed them all except three, whom they held for ransom. And each one of the towns where my lord lodged was a fine town, large and rich; and every day his men took various strongholds with plenty of prisoners and booty, and they brought back with them two thousand of the enemy's horses; so that in this raid my lord had great good fortune and great honor, for no one ever saw so few men make such a raid in such country without loss of men: God be praised. Written at Mountbourg July 16, 1356.

—Robert of Avesbury, *De gestis mirabilibus,* pp. 462–65.

21. There is a letter as early as July 13, 1356, issued by Louis of Navarre at Pampeluna. Brutails, *Documents des archives de la chambre des comptes de Navarre,* No. 48. There is another of March 25, 1359, *Ibid.,* No. 54. Géraud's text reads *alter autem frater eorum Ludovicus illius junior ivit ad Navarram.* Géraud remarks (II, 233, n. 2) that *illius* is an embarrasment but that all his MSS have it. A reads *frater eorum junior videlicet Ludovicus.*

22. A reads *mirabilia* after *mala et.*

1356

1. A adds *et iam fuerat diu* after *erat.*

2. This refers to Jean de la Roche-Taillade, who may be regarded as the leading French representative of that prophetic millennarianism current from the days of the Spiritual Franciscans and their enthusiasm for Joachim of Flore's Everlasting Gospel. Modern discussion of this and of Jean will be found in Kampers, "Ueber die Prophezeiungen des Johannes de Rupescissa," in *Historisches Jahrbuch,* XV (1894), 796–802; the same author's *Die deutsche Kaiseridee in Prophetie und Sage;* Menéndez y Pelayo, *Historia de los heterodoxos españoles,* Vol. III, Bk. III, Chap. 4; Zimmerman, ed., *Monumenta historica Carmelitana,* I, 296 ff. A short life of Jean appears in Oudin's *Commentarius de scriptoribus ecclesiae antiquis,* III, 1011–15, but it is not very satisfactory. The most recent study is "John of Rupescissa: Chemist and Prophet," in Thorndike's *A History of Magic and Experimental Science,* Vol. III, Chap. XXII; but this is chiefly concerned with his alchemy. At the Ecole des chartes, Jeanne Odier has written a thesis on "Jean de Roquetaillade," in which she has utilized a Vatican manuscript (Rossiano, 753) of Jean's *Liber ostensor,* which gives a long recital of his tribulations. According to this, he was born at Marcolès, near Aurillac. For five years he studied philosophy at Toulouse, and he then became a Franciscan friar in 1332. In 1340 he was at Aurillac. Arrested Dec. 2, 1344, he was imprisoned during the next month in the convent at Figeac. The

provincial of Aquitaine directed that he be treated as a rebel. For nearly five years, with occasional short intervals of liberty, he was taken from prison to prison. During this time he broke his leg, was sick from the plague, and was interrogated by Jean de Molineyrie, the inquisitor at Toulouse. In 1349 the friar who was ordered to take him from Rieux to Custres took him instead to Avignon, where they arrived Aug 17. On Oct. 2 he appeared before a public consistory. Instead of being returned to the jurisdiction of his order, he was put in the papal prison called Soudan. Twice he was brought before the cardinals for questioning, about Christmas, 1350, and again on Aug. 10, 1351. Nothing is known of his career after 1356. Thorndike suggests that his imprisonment was not due to his prophesying, because his prophecies became so widely current during his imprisonment. His earliest extant prophecy is dated Nov. 11, 1349, from prison in Avignon (Thorndike, *op. cit.*, III, 349, n. 10). It is addresesed to Cardinal William Curti (see Devic and Vaissete, *Histoire générale de Languedoc,* IX, 479), who seems, with Cardinal Tallyrand de Périgord, to have taken a special interest in Jean. It recounts how a revelation came to him in July, 1345, while he was imprisoned at Figeac. This announced the near approach of Antichrist, the coming cruel death of King Andrew of Naples, the plague, the desolation of France, the choice of a saintly pope from outside the college of cardinals, followed by the recovery of Jerusalem by a French king, Charles. (Summarized by Kervyn de Lettenhove in his edition of Froissart, VI, 494–95.) At the same time (1346–50) Jean was writing a commentary on the divine oracles of Cyril, a Carmelite, who in 1287 wrote Joachimite prophecies which some regarded as revelation superior to the Bible, a notion condemned as heretical by the Inquisition in 1316. Froissart, who visited Avignon as a young man in 1360, records another of Jean's prophecies under his discussion of the events of 1390, and seems to suggest that he was held in prison because of his diatribes against the pomp and power of the higher clergy. (Léon Mirot ed., Vol. XII, p. lviii, n. 2; pp. 228–32.) Notice of Mme. Bignami-Odier's *Etudes sur Jean de Roquetaillade* (Paris, 1952) came too late to be included in the editing of this chronicle.

3. A omits *loqueretur*. The copyist also omitted the six words before; the corrector wrote them in the margin. The translation follows Géraud.

4. A reads *apparet* for *patet*.

5. The *Liber ostensor* (see above, p. 211, n. 2) was finished in the Avignon prison, Sept. 1, 1356. It is addressed to Cardinal Elie Talleyrand de Périgord. The *Vade mecum in tribulatione* was also written at the end of 1356. It is the best known of Jean's writings. There are twenty extant manuscripts of it. It is published in Brown, *Fasciculus,* II, 496–508. In this edition there is an

introduction made up of this letter quoted by Jean de Venette, combined with another letter addressed to an unnamed prelate, which blames the rulers of the church for the burdensome taxes levied by the church, especially tenths for waging war.

6. Stephen Aldebrandi became archbishop of Toulouse in 1351. He had previously been archbishop of Arles (1349), bishop of Saint-Pons, and papal chamberlain. Is there any possible connection between his interest in Jean and the fact that in 1351 he complained to King John of the severity with which the regular clergy imprisoned those of their orders who had committed grievous faults? Devic and Vaissete, *Histoire générale de Languedoc*, IX, 614, 625.

7. A adds *dicti Minoris in cedula ibidem haec formae* after *responsio*. Apparently this particular document had some currency, for it seems to have been used by Jean le Bel (*Chronique*, II, 273–75), from whom Froissart derives his account (ed. Luce, V, 228–30), and also by Heinricus Rebdorfensis (*Annales*, in Böhmer, ed., *Fontes*, IV, 563; 565–66). The latter, in his chronology, makes a change of two years, putting the prophecy in 1358, but changing the prediction about the cardinals' flight from Avignon from six years to four, so the predicted date for the flight remained the same. He is also familiar with the prophecy of 1349 (see above, p. 212, n. 2). The author of the *Chronicon Moguntinum* (in *Die Chroniken der deutschen Städte*, XVIII, 163) notes under 1359, "In these times a certain Minorite friar was imprisoned by Pope Innocent VI, for prophesying many different future happenings in the world, of which the greater part have come true." See also Baluze, *Vitae paparum*, I, 318; II, 456–57.

8. Where Géraud's text reads *et per civitates crudeliter occidentur*, A reads *per communitatos*. This gives a closer approximation to an apparent prophecy of the Jacquerie, which would make it particularly interesting to Jean de Venette. As published in Brown (*Fasciculus*, II, 494), this reads *per communitates occidentur*.

9. A adds *terrarum* after *populi*.

10. At this point the same hand which wrote the gloss about the pope's defense of the mendicants (see above, p. 199, n. 6), wrote in the margin of A, *Benedictus deus quod super hoc mentitus est* ("Thank God this proved false").

11. Since this explicit prediction for 1362 did not come to pass, may we infer from his silence that Jean de Venette was writing this section before that year?

12. A reads *qui faciet* for *qui facit*.

13. A reads *ad Christum* for *ad ipsum*.   14. A adds *pax* after *fere*.

15. Where Géraud reads *Dei vicarius futurus totius saeculi Dei reformator*, A reads *Christi vicarius futurus totius destructi seculi reformator*.

16. Jean de Venette's version of this text at this point has a peculiarly Carmelite variation. Where he writes *salvabuntur qui fugerint de medio malorum ad Montem Carmeli*, the version of this document published in Brown's *Fasciculus* (II, 494) reads *salvabuntur omnes qui ad montes fugerint*. Presumably Jean de la Roche-Taillade had in mind Matthew 24:16, *tunc qui in Judaea sunt, fugiant ad montes*.

17. A reads *hereditatis* for *hereditas*.

18. But Jean de Venette avoids stating, with respect to any specific event, whether or not he regards it as actually in fulfillment of this prophecy.

19. See above, p. 34. Jean de Venette is not alone in his outbursts against extravagant fashions. His English contemporary John of Reading, has two such in his chronicle, one under 1344, the other under 1365 (*Chronica*, pp. 88, 167). The monk of Malmesbury, who wrote the *Eulogium historiarum*, has a long discussion of the matter under the year 1362 (II, 230–231). In the following year there was another English sumptuary law relating to "the outrageous and excessive apparel of divers people against their estate and degree to the great destruction and impoverishment of all the land."—*Statutes of the Realm*, 37 Edward III, c. 8, 14. There had been earlier legislation in 1336. *Ibid.*, 10 Edward III, c. 3.

20. A reads *a minimo usque ad maximum* for *a magno usque ad parvum*.

21. A adds *parvas* after *margaritas*.

22. In 1367 in France, at the request of the consuls of Montpellier and the bishop of Maguelonne, Charles V issued royal letters (Oct. 17), regulating dress, in which articles I and XII put restrictions on the display of pearls. Devic and Vaissete, *Histoire générale de Languedoc*, Vol. X, No. 532. There is a poem, contemporary with Jean de Venette, ascribed to one of the clergy of Notre-Dame in Paris, called "Complainte sur la bataille de Poitiers" (ed. Beaurepaire, *Bib. de l'Ecole des chartes*, XII [1851], 257 ff.), which also complains of nobles' styles in a way similar to Jean de Venette.

> Bonbanz et vaine gloire, vesture deshoneste,
> Les ceintures dorees, la plume sur la teste,
> La grant barbe de bouc, qui est une orde beste,
> Les vous font estordiz comme fouldre et tempest.
>
> —p. 261, ll. 25–28

23. The Latin phrase is *pilae cum palma*, which seems to approximate the French phrase *jeu de paume*. This is the period when the game was developing from a form of handball to something more like modern tennis,

with a court and some sort of racquet. See Noel and Clark, *A History of Tennis*, I, 2–4; Jusserand, *Les Sports et jeux d'exercice*, Chap. 6.

24. A adds *missi* before *portabant*.

25. Géraud (II, 238, n. 2) remarks that his text, in order to be clear, should read *quam ab Anglicis*, but that *ab* is lacking in all his MSS. A has *ab*.

26. The author of the "Complainte sur la bataille de Poitiers" (see above, n. 22) has a passage to the effect that the regent would be well advised to include "Jaque Bonhome" in his following. It would seem as if this must have been written before the Jacquerie, i.e., before May, 1358. According to the *Chronique des quatre premiers Valois* (p. 64), the English at Honfleur in 1357, when the French abandoned their effort to take the town, jeered at the French, calling them by this name. The Bourgeois of Valenciennes (*Récits*, p. 295) remarks upon "a sort of foolish people, sturdy, brutal, clumsy and stupid, who were called 'Jaque Bonhomme,'" but this is relative to the Jacquerie. Later or more distant writers ascribe this name to the leader of the peasants when the latter revolted. Jean le Bel, *Chronique*, II, 260; *The Anonimalle Chronicle*, p. 41; Gray, *Scalacronica*, p. 145.

27. A reads *multi qui [eos] hoc tempore [tali nomine] deriserunt a quamplurimus [de ipsis] postmodum [letaliter] delusi sunt.* The words in brackets are omitted in Géraud.

28. A adds *crudeliter* before *occisi*.

29. For Edward of Woodstock, prince of Wales, see Peter Shaw, "The Black Prince," *History*, XXIV (1939–40), 1–15. The prince and his army sailed for Gascony in September, 1355. (Robert of Avesbury, *De gestis mirabilibus*, p. 424.) This was a phase of the great campaign planned in the summer of that year, when cooperation with Charles of Navarre in Normandy for the main English army under King Edward was anticipated (see above, p. 204, n. 1, and p. 58). For discussion of the numbers in this expedition, see Ramsay, "The Strength of English Armies in the Middle Ages," *Eng. Hist. Rev.*, XXIX (1914), 221–27; Prince, "The Strength of English Armies in the Reign of Edward III," *ibid.*, XLVI (1931), 352–71; Burne, "The Battle of Poitiers," *ibid.*, LIII (1938), 21–52. The scholarly estimates vary from three to six thousand men.

30. From Oct. 5 until Dec. 2, 1355, the prince carried on a devastating, plundering raid in southern France, without meeting any effective opposition. Ramsay, *Genesis of Lancaster*, I, 394–99. The prince's expedition in 1356 should be associated with the war between King John and the Navarrese-Norman-English combination following upon the arrest of Charles of Navarre in April (see above, p. 60). The prince began making preparations early in July, and his march northward from Gascony into

France started Aug. 4. By Sept. 7 this English army, plundering as it went, reached the Loire at Tours but was unable to find means of crossing the river. The return march towards Aquitaine began Sept. 11. The battle of Poitiers was fought Sept. 19. Ramsay, *op. cit.,* I, 402–8.

31. The Anglo-Navarrese expedition of the duke of Lancaster had relieved and provisioned Breteuil (July 3) and had taken Verneuil by storm (July 3–5), but no effort to hold this last place seems to have been made (see above, p. 210, n. 20). Only this chronicler mentions the French recovery of Verneuil. The siege of Breteuil, however, was a first-class military effort. Begun shortly after July 8, it lasted until the third week in August (between Aug. 12–19). Froissart describes it at some length (ed. Luce, Vol. IV, pp. 193–98; p. lxx, n. 2). The besieged were then granted easy terms, because King John wished to be free to march against the prince of Wales. By Aug. 28 John was at Chartres (*ibid.,* Vol. V, p. ii, n. 1). The siege of Pont-Audemer, which also began in July, 1356, continued until Dec. 5, when the Navarrese garrison was persuaded to evacuate by a payment of 6,000 florins. (*Chronique . . . de Jean II,* I, 90–91; *Chronique normande du XIVe siècle,* p. 118.) The large army was assembled for the siege of Breteuil. Delachenal, *Histoire de Charles V,* I, 181–87. But from Sept. 1 John concentrated his forces at Chartres, and they increased daily as he advanced southward. *Ibid.,* I, 202.

32. For King John's intinerary see *Froissart,* ed. Luce, Vol. V, pp. iv–v, nn. 1–4 and 1–3.

33. A long list of the nobles in this army is in *Chroniques des quatre premiers Valois,* pp. 40–41; see also *Froissart,* ed. Luce, Vol. IV, p. lxx, n. 2. Of the persons mentioned by Jean de Venette, Pierre, duke of Bourbon, was second cousin and brother-in-law to King Philip VI. He was also father-in-law to Charles, duke of Normandy, to John VI, count of Harcourt, and to King Peter of Castile. The duke of Athens was Walter VI of Brienne, who took his title from the duchy held by his father until it was conquered in 1311 by the Catalan Company. After an unsuccessful attempt to recover his inheritance in 1331–32, Duke Walter attached himself to the Angevin court at Naples. For a year, 1342–43, he was tyrant of Florence, and Villani gives an unflattering picture of him. His maternal grandfather, Gaucher de Châtillon, had been constable of France (1302–27). Raoul de Brienne, count of Guînes, the constable beheaded in 1350 (see above, p. 54), was his brother-in-law and also a distant cousin. He himself was made constable May 6, 1356. Miller, *The Latins in the Levant,* pp. 260–65; Schevill, *History of Florence,* pp. 218–22; *Chronique . . . de Jean II,* I, 30, n. 1. Two marshals are mentioned prominently in most of the chronicles, Arnoul d'Au-

drehem, appointed in late June, 1351, and Jean de Clermont, sire de Chan-
tilly, appointed in August, 1352, who was killed in the battle. Robert de
Waurin, sire de Saint-Venant, a marshal since 1344, was also present, attached to the person of Charles, duke of Normandy. According to some
accounts Jean le Maingre, called Bouçicaut, figured in the battle, but it
seems doubtful that he was a marshal at this time, and there is some
ground for thinking that, having been taken prisoner at Romorantin early
in September, he was not released until the following summer. *Chronique
normande du XIVe siècle*, p. 112; *Archives historiques du Poitou*, XVII
(1886), 279, n. 1; Sir Bartholomew Burghersh's letter printed in the appendix to H. O. Coxe's edition of the Chandos Herald (London, 1842),
"Roxburghe Club Publications," Vol. 58.

34. A reads *Meluno* for *Melduno*. William of Melun was brother to Jean
II, viscount of Melun and count of Tancarville, who figured at the defense
of Caen (see above, p. 40). He became archbishop in January, 1345. In the
events following Poitiers he appears as an active figure among the dauphin's
counselors. Reginald Chauveau was bishop of Châlons-sur-Marne from
February, 1352. According to the *Chronique des quatre premiers Valois*
(p. 50), a third prelate, Pierre de la Forêt, archbishop of Rouen, was also
present.

35. The Latin phrase is *de peditibus et aliis brigantibus erat numerus
valde magnus*. This is interesting as an example of the word "brigand"
with the meaning of a lightly armored footsoldier, wearing a brigandine or
light cuirass (see C. Enlart, *Manuel d'archéologie française* [Paris, 1902–
1916], Vol. III, Fig. 459). Other examples of this usage are common (Jean
le Bel, *Chronique*, II, 227; Robert of Avesbury, *De gestis mirabilibus*, p.
465; documents quoted in Denifle, *La Désolation des églises*, II, 197, n. 5,
and Perrens, *Etienne Marcel*, p. j., No. 20). But from the conditions so often
described by our author there arose those associations which eventually
gave this word its modern meaning. How soon this happened it is not easy
to say. The continuation of the chronicle of Richard Lescot (p. 138) mentions *balistarios quingentos cum mille servientibus levis armature armatis
qui* tunc *brigantes vocabantur*. Clearly this author, writing about 1390, regarded this usage as obsolete. See below, p. 237, n. 28; p. 295, n. 81.

36. Instructions from Pope Innocent VI to the two cardinals, Talleyrand
de Périgord and Nicolas Capocci, for negotiating peace between the French
and English are dated April 8, 1356. Moisant, *Le Prince Noir en Aquitaine*,
pp. 233–53. The first encounter of the prince and Cardinal Talleyrand occurred Sept. 12, but Jean de Venette is obviously referring to the negotiations during the two days immediately prior to the battle. Our author's

reference to the French confidence in victory accords with Froissart's detailed account of these negotiations (ed. Luce, V, 24–27), in which the
cardinal assured King John that the English army could not possibly escape,
and with the less reliable story of the Chandos Herald (*Life of the Black
Prince*, pp. 22–27, 141–42, 193) about the insistence upon fighting of some
of King John's advisers, including Marshal Audrehem and Bishop
Chauveau. The current English view of these negotiations finds an echo in
Sir Thomas Gray, who writes of this ecclesiastical mediation, "Now this
was not done with the intention that appeared, but the cardinal acted entirely for [the French] advantage, so as to test the purpose of the said prince,
and to prolong the affair to the detriment of the said prince, [who would]
run short of provisions and other munitions, while their forces should be
increased [by reenforcements] continually arriving."—*Scalacronica*, p. 123.
Similarly, the account in the monk of Malmesbury's *Eulogium historiarum*
(III, 223), which has some of the appearances of an eyewitness report, says,
"But the prince, seeing that the enemy was daily becoming stronger, preferred rather to engage than thus to prolong the matter to his own loss. For
he often perceived now 200, now 300, now 500 Frenchmen hurrying by
companies to the French column, a sight which worried him considerably."
—Translation by Burne, "The Battle of Poitiers," *Eng. Hist. Rev.*, LIII
(1938), 25.

37. A reads *pedes cum suis pugnare voluit* for *pedester cum suis bellare
disposuit*.

38. The practice of dismounting the men-at-arms and having them fight
the English on foot was a tactical innovation with the French. Usually it
has been assumed that the defeat at Crécy forced this experiment upon the
French, but we now know that the earliest example was the battle between
Charles of Blois and Sir Thomas Dagworth at Saint-Pol-de-Léon, June 9,
1346, more than two months before Crécy. Galbraith, "Extracts from the
Historia aurea and a French 'Brut' (1317–47)," *Eng. Hist. Rev.*, XLIII
(1928), 213, corrected by "The Strength of English Armies in the Reign of
Edward III," *ibid.*, XLVI (1931), 364–65. For the French development of
this maneuver in the decade preceding the battle of Poitiers, see Tout,
"Some Neglected Fights between Crécy and Poitiers," *ibid.*, XX (1905),
726–30. For the most complete study of the battle of Poitiers see Delachenal,
Histoire de Charles V, Vol. I, Chap. 6, pp. 189–244. This has been challenged in some of its details, and a new study of the evidence presented by
Burne, "The Battle of Poitiers," *Eng. Hist. Rev.*, LIII (1938), 21–52; but
Col. Burne's interpretation in its turn has been challenged and Delachenal's
defended by Galbraith, "The Battle of Poitiers," *ibid.*, LIV (1939), 473–75.

See also Tourneur-Aumont, "Conclusions de l'histoire militaire de la bataille de Poitiers (17, 18, 19 septembre 1356)," *Bulletin de la Société des antiquaires de l'Ouest,* 3d series, XI (1936–38), 433–64.

39. A adds *super omnia* after *gloriose.*

40. Jean de Venette, here and elsewhere, seems to be echoing a contemporary *libellus* by Brother Francis Beaumont, *Tragicum argumentum de miserabili statu regni Francie editum a fratre Francisco de Monte Bellima, ordinis Sancti Benedicti.* This is a highly rhetorical indictment to the effect that if the French chivalry had shown stability on the field of battle equal to the king's courage, the king's majesty would not be a subject for tragedy, nor the military display of the nobility a subject for satire, nor would we be mourning the ruin of the state, nor enduring the mockery of nearly all peoples. The cowardice of the French chivalry has made it the sport of the nations. How they laugh at the fierce French, who, softened by a long peace, permit their king, fighting for peace and liberty, to be captured in the heart of the kingdom! How they jeer at them for letting a small band of enemies march across part of the kingdom, carrying off their prince into captivity in a foreign land! The people throw all the blame on the nobles, saying they ran away like rabbits. But people and nobles are equally to blame. The nobles have neglected to learn discipline and the military art because they are devoted to pleasure and luxury. But the people too are to blame because "their God is their belly," and they permit their women to rule them. They are torn with discord. The clergy too are given over to vices and voluptuousness.—Published as "Un Pamphlet politique au XIVe siècle" by the Comité des travaux historiques et scientifiques in *Bulletin historique et philologique,* 1886, pp. 112–16.

41. A adds *constabularius* after *Atheniensi.* A list of 169 French nobles killed in this battle is printed by Belleval, *La Grande Guerre,* pp. 173–77. It is based on the record of those buried after the battle in the Minorite and Dominican churches at Poitiers. The prince of Wales, writing from Bordeaux a month afterwards to the bishop of Worcester, reported 2,445 French men-at-arms dead, including a bishop, two dukes, and sixteen bannerets, *Archaeologia,* I (1779), 213–15.

42. The dramatic story of young Philip standing at his father's side and warning him of blows from left and right is found in Villani (*Istorie fiorentine,* in Muratori, *Scriptores,* XIV, 417), but in no French and English accounts of the battle. The captor of King John was Denis de Saint-Omer, seigneur de Marbecque, but there were others who disputed his claims, or claimed to have shared in the capture. Delachenal, *Histoire de Charles V,* I, 242–43.

43. A reads *hominibus* for *omnibus*.

44. A adds *confusibiliter* after *valentes*.

45. Froissart (ed. Luce, V, 53) tells how "the pursuit of the fugitives continued up to the gates of Poitiers. At that point there was a great slaughter and overthrow of men-at-arms and horses, because the men of Poitiers closed their gates and let no one enter because of the danger. Consequently on the causeway and before the gate men were wounded, cut down, and killed with such butchery that it is frightful even to think of it. And often the French surrendered to any Englishman they could find, so that many English, both archers and others, had four, five, or six prisoners."

46. Belleval (*La Grande Guerre,* pp. 177–80) lists the names of seventy captives. In his letter to the bishop of Worcester the prince of Wales mentions 1,975 captives, including an archbishop, thirteen counts, five viscounts, and twenty-one barons. A royal letter of July 6, 1358 (Rymer, *Foedera,* Vol. III, Part 2, p. 169) shows that Robert Clinton was one of four who captured the archbishop. King Edward paid Robert a thousand pounds for his share of the captive.

47. A carter killed the fugitive bishop. *Chronique des quatre premiers Valois,* p. 57.

48. The itinerary is in the monk of Malmesbury, *Eulogium historiarum,* III, 225–26. They reached Bordeaux Oct. 2, 1356. Froissart (ed. Luce, V, 80–81) tells how reluctant the Gascons were to have King John, "whom they had helped to capture," taken to England, and how the prince had to pay a hundred thousand francs for their agreement.

49. Froissart's account (ed. Luce, V, 63–64) of the prince's courteous treatment of his royal captive has become one of the commonplaces in the story of chivalry.

50. A truce for two years was signed at Bordeaux, March 23, 1357. Delachenal, in his edition of the *Chronique . . . de Jean II* (I, 107, n. 1) asserts that "in reality the negotiators tried to conclude the peace and outlined a complete treaty, but this was something which could be completed only in England." The chronicle itself states that "a treaty of peace was made at Bordeaux between the king of France, who was then a prisoner, and the prince of Wales. But the nature thereof was kept secret because it was reserved for the consent of the king of England." See also Bock, "Some New Documents Illustrating the Early Years of the Hundred Years War (1353–1356)," *Bulletin of the John Rylands Library,* XV (1931), 60–99.

51. A adds *transporto* after *anglicos.*

52. In secret orders of Dec. 17, 1356, King Edward ordered the prince to come to London with his captive. Bock, in *Bulletin of the John Rylands*

Library, XV (1931), 77, 79, 99. The prince and King John embarked from Bordeaux April 11, 1357. They landed at Plymouth May 4, and made their entry into London May 24. *Froissart,* ed. Luce, Vol. V, p. xx, n. 3; p. xxi, n. 1.

53. A reads *Pictavensi* for *Pictaviae.*

54. A reads *dolentibus populis* for *dolentibus dominis* and adds *ab omnibus* after *honorifice.*

55. Sept. 19, 1356. *Chronique . . . de Jean II,* I, 74. For comment on the criticism of the French princes for fleeing from the battle see *ibid.,* n. 2.

56. A adds *Francorum* after *patria.*

57. A reads *ut videtur* for *ut providetur.*

58. The Estates General met Nov. 30, 1355, for a few days. Since then it had reassembled twice, March 1 and May 8, 1356, and had set Nov. 30, 1356, as the date for another session. Delachenal, *Histoire de Charles V,* I, 249. Particularly important is Delachenal, "Journal des Etats Généraux réunis à Paris au mois d'octobre 1356," *Nouvelle Revue historique de droit française et étranger,* XXIV (1900), 415–65. Duke Charles, on returning after Poitiers to Paris, Sept. 29, summoned the deputies to meet Oct. 15. The first session took place Oct. 17, 1356.

59. This is an error. Charles acted as royal lieutenant (Delachenal, *Histoire de Charles V,* I, 245, n. 1, and 246, n. 1), but did not assume the title of regent until March 14, 1358. Presumably Jean de Venette was writing this section after this latter date.

60. Géraud (II, 243, n. 1) remarks that his MSS lack a verb at this point, and he adds *voluerunt* to his text in order to make sense. A has the verb *decreverunt.*

61. Géraud (II, 243, n. 2) remarks that all his MSS read *tria millia pugnatorum,* which is historically incorrect. A reads *xxx milia armaturum,* which is correct.

62. A reads *communitatem* for *civitatum.*

63. Jean de Venette is not very well informed as to this session of the Estates General. By his own account (see p. 57), he was at Reims on Oct. 17, and he may not have been in Paris at all during the meeting. At no time in 1356 did Charles consent to the commission from the Estates General to conduct the business of government. This commisison was to have consisted of four prelates, twelve knights, and twelve commoners. The offer of an aid to support thirty thousand men was made on condition that Charles accept this commission, dismiss seven of the king's chief counselors, and hold them to answer charges before the commission. The release of Charles of Navarre was also demanded. Duke Charles prorogued the session Nov.

3 and left the city. It seems probable that Jean de Venette has made no effort to distinguish between the session of October-November, 1356, and the session of February–March, 1357, to which he makes very brief allusion a couple of paragraphs later. He seems quite oblivious to the true nature of the current personal and political struggle for the control of the government. For these phases of the subject, see Douët-d'Arcq, "Acte d'accusation contre Robert le Coq, évêque de Laon," *Bib. de l'Ecole des chartes,* II (1840–41), 350–87; N. Valois, "Le Gouvernment représentatif en France au XIVe siècle; étude sur le conseil du roi pendant la captivité de Jean le Bon," *Rev. des quest. hist.,* XXXVII (1885), 63–115 (reprinted with additions and corrections in Valois, *Le Conseil du roi,* Chap. 1); and Valois, "Notes sur la révolution parisienne de 1356–58: la revanche des frères Braque," *Mémoires de la Soc. de l'hist. de Paris,* X (1883), 100–126; Funk, "Robert le Coq and Etienne Marcel," *Speculum,* XIX (1944), 470–87. Jean de Venette never mentions the bishop of Laon.

64. Jean de Venette is equally oblivious to the political nature of this journey to Metz. Since May, plans had been made for an imperial diet to which Duke Charles should go, carrying as a gift for the emperor two thorns from the Holy Crown. Charles of Bohemia was uncle to the duke of Normandy, being brother to Bonne of Luxemburg, the duke's mother, who died in 1349. He was also husband to King John's aunt, Blanche of Valois, who died in 1348. The emperor reached Metz Nov. 17, 1356. The duke left Paris Dec. 5 and arrived at Metz Dec. 22. He did homage for Dauphiné and renewed the treaty of 1347, thus assuring the benevolent neutrality of the emperor in the war with King Edward. On Dec. 28 he left Metz and reached Paris Jan. 14, 1357. Mendl and Quicke, "Les Relations politiques entre l'empereur et le roi de France de 1355 à 1356," *Revue belge de philologie et d'histoire,* Vol. VIII, Part 1 (1929), pp. 469–512; Fournier, *Le Royaume d'Arles et de Vienne,* pp. 443–69; Leroux, *Recherches critiques,* pp. 263–65; Delachenal, *Histoire de Charles V,* I, 268–81.

65. Queen Jeanne had been regent in Burgundy for her infant son until 1353, when her second husband, King John, took over that position. Now he was a prisoner. The young duke was a child of ten. The queen again became an active figure in Burgundian affairs as early as the meeting of the Estates of Burgundy at Dijon in December, 1356. Her son was Philip de Rouvre (see p. 48), born in August or September, 1346, and duke of Burgundy since the death of his grandfather, Eudes IV, April 3, 1349. Jean de Venette repeats his former error in calling Philip of Burgundy, dead at Aiguillon, duke (see p. 44). Queen Jeanne was in Paris in March for the betrothal ceremonies of Duke Philip and Marguerite of Flanders (March

21, 1357). She left at the end of the month to go to Arras for the wedding, which took place May 14, 1357. In June and July she was at Meaux, but in August she returned to Burgundy and remained there. Petit, *Histoire des ducs de Bourgogne,* IX, 75, 78, 80–84.

66. A reads *permanserunt* for *remanserunt.*

67. Géraud (II, 244, n. 2) inserted *secedentes* in his text, although it did not appear in any of his MSS. This has been ignored in the translation. Where Géraud reads *volebant facere* A has *volebant solvere.*

68. The Estates General reassembled Feb. 5, 1357, and remained in session for nearly a month. The final session of March 3 is probably the one of which Jean de Venette was thinking when he wrote his account of the meeting before the duke went to Metz. It was the ordonnance of March 3, 1357, which sanctioned the scheme described in the earlier paragraph. The *Chronique . . . de Jean II* (I, 111), reads, "And about July 22 [1357] following, the power and influence of those chosen by the three estates, both members of the Great Council, officials for collecting the subsidy, and those chosen to make reforms, began to decline because the revenue was not as great as they had promised. . . . And the nobles left them and would no longer pay, and the clergy also. And many of the good towns, realizing the evils done by the chief governors, some ten or twelve men, also withdrew and would no longer pay." For a useful summary, see Coville, "Les Etats-Généraux de 1332 et 1357" *Le Moyen Age,* VI (1893), 57–63. The statement made here by Jean de Venette seems more like one in the *Chronique . . . de Jean II,* I, 147, referring to 1358, which reads, "On Sunday . . . February 11 [1358] there reassembled at Paris many [deputies] of the good towns and the clergy, but not a noble appeared." See also Viollet, "Les Etats de Paris en février 1358," *Mémoires de l'Académie des inscriptions et belles-lettres,* Vol. XXXIV, Part 2 (1895), pp. 261–92. It is possible that the sessions of February, 1357, and February, 1358, were confused in Jean de Venette's mind when he came to write.

69. A adds *latrones* after *deperire.*

70. A reads *ab aliis* for *et aliis.*

71. A omits *contemptu;* the translation follows Géraud.

72. A reads *praedones* for *peditis.*

73. This paragraph seems to echo the sentiments found in the speeches of Robert le Coq, bishop of Laon, before the Estates in 1356 and 1357 (see Douët-d'Arcq, "Acte d'accusation contre Robert Le Coq," *Bib. de l'Ecole des chartes,* II [1841], 350–87), as well as those in the *Tragicum argumentum* of Brother Francis Beaumont (see above, p. 219, n. 40), and the "Complainte sur la bataille de Poitiers," ed. Beaurepaire, *Bib. de l'Ecole des*

chartes, XII (1851), 257 ff. (see above, p. 214, n. 22). For Jan. 14, 1357, there is a letter from Marcel and the Parisians to the authorities at Arras enclosing a plea for help from the people at Dreux, dated Jan. 12, and reporting that the enemies of the kingdom were out in force, had just taken and pillaged Laigle, and were about to advance on Dreux under the leadership of Philip of Navarre. *Mémoires de la Soc. de l'hist. de Paris* XXIV (1897), 59–60.

74. A reads *carperent* for *caperent.*

75. A adds *et maneria* after *hospicia.*

76. According to the *Chronique . . . de Jean II* (I, 108–9) it was the proclamation, April 5, 1357, of royal letters from King John announcing the truce of Bordeaux and forbidding either the collection of the subsidy recently voted or the reassembling of the Estates General, which caused the Parisians "to set guards over the city with extreme care, by day and by night, so that on the side towards the Large Bridge only three gates were open during the day, and at night they were all closed." For comment and references on this work of fortification, see Delachenal, *Histoire de Charles V,* I, 313–14. At this point Jean de Venette is one of the most important primary sources.

1357

1. A reads *populares* for *plures.*

2. Géraud (II, 247, n. 1) inserts *et crudeliter* at this point, a phrase taken from his two late MSS. A has no such phrase, and the translation ignores it.

3. The places mentioned are all near Paris. No doubt Jean de Venette is drawing on his own vivid memories. The *Chronique . . . de Jean II* (I, 127–30) tells how the English and Navarrese from Normandy, in late December, 1357, and January, 1358, raided and pillaged close to Paris.

4. Géraud (II, 247, n. 2), following his earlier MS, reads *ad praedicta stupenda* after *nemine,* but he remarks that his two late MSS read *ad praedicta incommoda.* A reads *ad praedicta dispendia.*

5. The note of complaint against the duke and the nobles in this and the preceding paragraph sounds in many ways similar to that which appears in Marcel's letter of April 18, 1358. *Froissart,* ed. Kervyn de Lettenhove, VI, 462–64. Froissart's account of the murder of the marshals puts these complaints into a speech of Marcel to the duke just preceding the murder. Luce ed., V, 96.

6. In a pardon of August, 1358, Marcel and his accomplices are alleged to have asserted that whatever they did was for a good object (*à bonne fin*), for the recovery of the king and for the public weal. It was also stated that

the prévôt misled the people by giving out that the duke wished to destroy them and to have them pillaged by the men-at-arms, that he had abandoned Paris and other cities, and the open country, to the men-at-arms, and that he had no intention of doing anything to free the king from captivity. Secousse, *Recueil*, pp. 83–85. On Jan. 11, 1358, Duke Charles, speaking at Les Halles, contradicted these charges. The next day, speaking to a crowd gathered at Saint-Jacques-de-l'Hôpital, Charles Toussac said "that the said prévôt was a worthy man (*preudomme*) and that whatever he had done had been for the well-being and safety of the people."—*Chronique* . . . *de Jean II*, I, 135–38.

7. A reads *ipse* for *iste* before *praepositus*.

8. A adds *publice* before *confessus*.

9. It is suggested that Jean de Venette is referring here to the speech which Marcel made from the window of the Hôtel de Ville immediately after the murder of the marshals, justifying the murder. *Chronique* . . . *de Jean II*, I, 150.

10. These caps were adopted early in January, 1358. *Ibid.*, p. 130. The colors are those of the city of Paris. They were "a badge of agreement to live and die with the prévôt in opposition to everyone else." Secousse, *Recueil*, p. 84.

11. A reads *ei* for *sibi* before *Domini*.

12. A reads *faciatis* for *breviter facite;* the translation follows Géraud.

13. A adds *qui quidem omnes* before *aspicientes*.

14. A adds *similiter nullos duos* before *ensibus*.

15. Robert of Clermont was marshal of Normandy, not marshal of France. He was a brother to that marshal who was killed at Poitiers. See further *Froissart,* ed. Luce, Vol. V, p. xxvii, n. 2. Why does Jean de Venette ignore the fact that the marshal had been excommunicated by the bishop of Paris for violating the right of asylum at the cloister of Saint-Merry only a month before (Jan. 24, 1358)? *Chronique* . . . *de Jean II*, I, 142–43, 153; Jourdain, "L'Université de Paris au temps d'Etienne Marcel," *Rev. des quest. hist.,* XXIV (1878), 556.

16. Jean de Conflans, seigneur de Dampierre, marshal of Champagne.

17. A reads *attraxerunt* for *extraxerunt*.

18. This episode and the sources are discussed at length by Delachenal, *Histoire de Charles V,* I, 354–65. Jean de Venette is an important source, but here, as elsewhere, he seems oblivious to everything except the most obvious facts.

19. Reginald d'Acy was one of the king's advocates in the Parlement of Paris. His career and death are discussed in Delachenal, *Histoire des avocats,* pp. 332–35. Unlike Jean de Venette, the author of the *Chronique*

... *de Jean II* (I, 148–49) puts this murder before that of the marshals, and makes it appear the result of d'Acy's accidental encounter with the crowd headed for the palace.

20. A adds *festo* after *in*.

21. This date is Feb. 22, 1358. This is the first place where Jean de Venette uses the phrase, "according to the reckoning of France." This refers to the practice of reckoning the beginning of the year from Easter, as distinguished from the Roman practice of beginning at Christmas, which in fact meant the first of January. The distinction is illustrated clearly by the heading of a sermon of Clement VI: *Sermo quem fecit dominus Petrus Rothomagensis archiepiscopus in cappela d.n. pape dominica in Quadragesima anno Domini 1332 secundum computationem Ecclesie Romane, 1331 secundum computationem Ecclesie Gallicane, viii die martie.* Mollat, "L'Œuvre oratoire de Clément VI," *Archives d'hist. doct. et litt. du moyen âge,* Vol. III (1928), p. 247, No. 23. See also Poole, "The Beginning of the Year in the Middle Ages," in his *Studies in Chronology and History,* pp. 10, 23. Jean de Venette in his *Chronicon ordinis B. V. Mariae de Monte Carmeli* used the Roman reckoning. In *Speculum Carmelitanum,* I, 204. Why he wrote his account of the year 1357 backward is quite obscure. As it is, he includes in his accounts nothing of the events of 1357 that happened earlier than November, except some occurrences before Easter, 1357, which he includes in 1356.

22. The night of Nov. 8–9, 1357.

23. A adds *carcaribus* after *tempus*.

24. Jean de Picquigny was governor of Artois. He had played a prominent part in the sessions of the Estates General in October, 1356, and February–March, 1357, and had been one of those chosen by the Estates to the Great Council. He came of a family prominent in the region about Amiens. It should be remembered that one of the persistent demands made in the Estates General after Poitiers was for the release of Charles of Navarre. Of this Jean de Venette says nothing. The *Chronique . . . de Jean II* (I, 116–17) tells how some twenty-nine men, mostly citizens from Amiens, effected the rescue of Charles by ladders. Immediately on his release the king of Navarre wrote to the authorities at Arras, "My dear and particular friends, as you and all the people of the kingdom of France well know, we have been held captive and villainously detained for a long time in an obscure prison without reasonable cause. You also know the great exertions and legal appeals made on our behalf by our lords and friends, without avail. But now, by God's aid, and with the help of good friends, we are free. . . . Be assured, as we hope for God's grace, that we bear no

ill will to the good people of France, but we wish merely to be good friends with them, if they will have it so."—Guesnon, "Documents inédits sur l'invasion anglaise et les états au temps de Philippe VI et de Jean le Bon," *Bulletin historique et philologique* (1897), No. 20. Shortly afterward he wrote the count of Savoy, "Please be assured that, thanks to our Lord and to certain of my good friends, I departed from the place where I was, without saying farewell to my host, on November 9, in good health."—Delachenal, "Deux Prétendues Lettres du régent . . . au comte de Savoie, Amédée VI," *Bib. de l'Ecole des chartes,* LXXII (1911), 277.

25. He stayed with Canon Guy Quiéret, "who greatly loved him." —*Froissart,* ed. Luce, V, 97 (see p. 125; p. 297, n. 97). In his speech at Amiens Charles set forth his claims to Champagne and Brie, and asserted that his claim to the French crown was better than King Edward's because his grandfather, Louis of Evreux, was son of King Philip III. *Chronographia,* II, 267–68. For the development of Charles's claims according to the course of events see p. 79.

26. Nov. 29, 1357, "near nightfall." *Chronique . . . de Jean II,* I, 118.

27. The monastery was outside the city walls.

28. A adds *et timores* after *anxietatis.*

29. The impression of awaiting an opportunity is misleading, inasmuch as this occurred the morning following his arrival.

The next day, Saint Andrew's day, about Prime [8–9 A.M.], the king, who had let it be known throughout Paris that he wanted to address the citizens, was on a platform on the walls of the monastery of Saint-Germain, overlooking the Pré-aux-Clercs. This platform had been made so that the king of France could see the wagers of battle which sometimes took place in the lists which were in the Pré, adjoining the monastery walls. In these lists there was a great crowd, gathered through orders from the king of Navarre and the prévôt of the merchants to the local ward captains of Paris. So in the presence of more than ten thousand persons he said many things, showing how he had been arrested without cause and held in prison for nineteen months. . . . He spoke for such a long time that dinner was over in Paris when he finished. And his whole speech was to justify his actions and to denounce his arrest. It was like the speech he made at Amiens.

—*Chronique . . . de Jean II,* I, 119–20. It is suggested that this speech is the source of Jean de Venette's account, under 1355, of Charles of Navarre's sufferings for more than a year and a half (see above, p. 60). The text is Psalms 10:8.

30. A adds *regnum* after *nunc.*

31. The two queens had been active before in mediating between the

Valois and Navarrese kings (see above, p. 58). They are credited with having persuaded Duke Charles to send a safe-conduct for Charles of Navarre to Amiens. *Ibid.*, p. 117. It was at Queen Jeanne's hotel on Dec. 2, 1357, that the two were brought face to face for an interview. The chief "magnates" seem to have been Robert le Coq, bishop of Laon, and Etienne Marcel. *Ibid.*, pp. 120–24.

32. A adds *liberos* after *similiter*.

33. The terms of agreement appear in a letter patent issued by the duke of Normandy, Dec. 12, 1357. Secousse, *Recueil,* pp. 65–67. This reads, "also, according to the request and prayer of our said brother [Charles of Navarre], the bodies of those who were beheaded shall be taken down by our men, without ceremonial, from the place where they are, and shall be given to our said brother to do with as he wishes." The introduction to this document recounts the events of April 5, 1355, and summarizes the experiences of Charles of Navarre afterwards. It is suggested that this may have been one of Jean de Venette's sources.

34. One of his bids for popularity seems to have been to use his influence with the duke to secure the release of all prisoners, no matter what crimes they were charged with, from the Châtelet and elsewhere in Paris. Letters of Dec. 9 and Dec. 15, 1357, in Secousse, *Recueil,* pp. 64, 68–70. He is said to have done the same on his own authority in Amiens. *Chronique . . . de Jean II,* I, 117.

35. He left Paris Dec. 13, 1357, and arrived at Rouen Jan. 8, 1358. *Ibid.,* pp. 127, 130.

36. A adds *accensis* after *cereis.*

37. There are two errors in Jean de Venette's story of the Rouen funeral. He has the wrong date. Innocents' Day is Dec. 28, but this ceremony was on Jan. 10, 1358. The remains of the count of Harcourt were not on the gibbet, having disappeared long before. There were only three corpses in 1358, as Jean de Venette indicates, because there had been four victims. An empty coffin, with the Harcourt arms, was included in the Rouen funeral. A detailed account of the ceremonies is in *Chronique . . . de Jean II,* I, 131–33. The sixteenth-century printed edition of *Les Cronicques de Normendie* (*1223–1453*) has a paragraph added to the story of this affair which reads, "He gave them honorable sepulture in the chapel of the Innocents, which is at present the chapel of Saint-Romanus, in the church of Notre-Dame at Rouen, where one can still see to this day their helms, except that of the count of Harcourt, whose corpse was no longer on the gibbet with the others."—*Les Cronicques de Normendie,* ed. Hellot, p. 189, n. 28. Deville, in 1833, writing on *Tombeaux de la cathédrale de Rouen,* reports that no

sign of these tombs remained. The great chapel of Saint-Romanus is in the southeast corner of the south transept. Loth, *La Cathédrale de Rouen,* pp. 68, 71–72, 74–78. The actual interment took place on Jan. 11, at which time Charles preached from the text, Psalms 24:21. His speech is said to have been the same in substance as the one at Paris, with a commentary on the martyrdom of his four dead friends in addition.

38. A adds *tenuerant et* before *tenebant.*

39. This passage is very similar to, but less explicit than, that in the *Chronique . . . de Jean II,* I, 130, which says, "Those who guarded the castles of Breteuil, Evreux, Pont-Audemer, and Pacy[-sur-Eure] were unwilling to surrender them to the king of Navarre without an order from the king of France. And on this account the king of Navarre said that the agreement to surrender his castles, made by my lord the duke, was not being carried out. And he announced his intention of asserting his so-called rights." Early in February he sent Jean de Picquigny to Paris to complain of the failure to restore to him his fortresses, and the University of Paris supported this demand. *Ibid.,* I, 144–47.

40. A adds *circa Parisius* after *Francie.*

41. See above, p. 224, n. 3.

42. Jean de Venette has already discussed an earlier phase of this controversy under 1351 (see above, p. 55). Father Aubrey Gwynn, S.J., has recently published a series of learned articles on Richard Fitz-Ralph, archbishop of Armagh, in *Studies,* XXII (1933), 389–405, 591–607; XXIII (1934), 395–411; XXIV (1935), 25–42, 558–72; XXV (1936), 81–96; XXVI (1937), 50–67; also "The Sermon-Diary of Richard FitzRalph, Archbishop of Armagh," in *Proceedings of the Royal Irish Academy,* XLIV (1937), Section C, No. 1, pp. 2–66. In his volume *The English Austin Friars* he has two relevant chapters, "The English Province after the Black Death" and "Archbishop FitzRalph and the Friars" (pp. 75–89). Father Gwynn regards Fitz-Ralph as "an outstanding figure in the intellectual history of the fourteenth century," "one of the leading theologians of Europe." It would appear that new life had been put into the controversy when the clergy of the province of Canterbury made formal complaint to their archbishop, May 16, 1356, against the unrestrained begging of the friars and their abuse of their position as confessors by giving absolution on such easy terms that they encouraged sin. Already Archbishop Fitz-Ralph had had trouble in his own diocese because the friars absolved even those whom the archbishop himself had excommunicated. His public attack on the mendicants began with a sermon at Saint Paul's Cross, London, on June 26, 1356, which was followed at intervals by six other sermons developing his indictment, the

last on March 25, 1357. The friars, after trying vainly to get King Edward to forbid Fitz-Ralph's preaching against their privileges, appealed to the pope. *Studies*, XXVI (1937), 50–60. Fitz-Ralph had been a prominent figure at the papal court during the decade 1334–44, before he became archbishop. He was there again in 1349–51. The culmination of his attack on the friars is a sermon preached at Avignon, Nov. 8, 1357, from the text, "Judge not according to appearances, but judge righteous judgment" (John 7:24). This is usually known as *Defensorium curatorum.* "Texts of this famous philippic . . . seem to have been freely circulated throughout England and France almost immediately, and [copies] . . . usually dating from the late fourteenth or the early fifteenth century [are] to be found in more than fifty manuscripts through the libraries of Europe."—Gwynn, in *Proc. Royal Irish Acad.,* XLIV (1937), Section C, No. 1, p. 45.

43. Fitz-Ralph presented his arguments in certain tracts which Jean de Venette might have seen. These are *Informacio brevis pro clero et populo* and *Ordinacio prelatorum et curatorum regni ffrancie.* His great work is *De pauperie Salvatoris,* the eighth and final book of which is *De mendicitate fratrum et eorum privilegiis.* This was written between 1350 and 1356 as part of a study of the exact nature of Christ's poverty. Poole edited the first four books of *De pauperie* as an appendix to Wycliffe's *De dominio divino* (London, 1890). The rest of *De pauperie Salvatoris* and the complete *De mendicitate* are unedited. A copy of the latter is in MS. Ancien latin 3222 in the Bibliothèque nationale. Hammerich, *op. cit.,* p. 15. On Fitz-Ralph at Avignon see further Gwynn, in *Rev. of Eng. Studies,* XIX (1943), 22–23.

44. A adds *aliis* before *exemptionibus.*

45. In his London sermons Fitz-Ralph "asserted that voluntary poverty was neither of Christ's example nor of present obligation, and that mendicancy had no warrant in Scripture or primitive tradition."—Poole, in *Iohannis Wycliffe De dominio divino,* p. xxxvi. A convenient summary of the archbishop's views is in Lechler, *John Wiclif and his English Precursors,* I, 77–84. Two quotations will help to illustrate the indictment. "They [the friars] have churches finer than our cathedrals, their cellars are full of good wine, they have ornaments more splendid than those of any prelate in the world, save only our Lord Pope. They have more books and finer books than any prelate or doctor; their belfries are most costly; they have double cloisters in which armed knights could do battle with lances erect; they wear finer raiment than any prelates in the world."—Gwynn, *The English Austin Friars,* p. 87. (This author suggests that young Geoffrey Chaucer could have heard Fitz-Ralph.) "Let it only be remembered that the mendicant orders, since the time when they obtained the privilege of hearing

confessions, have built everywhere the most beautiful monasteries and truly princely palaces, which, before that time, they were in no condition to do. It is never heard that they impose alms upon those who confess to them, for the repairs of a parish church or a bridge, or for the upholding of a country road; they prefer to impose them entirely for their own benefit and that of their order."—Lechler, *op. cit.,* I, 81. A reads *et exemptionibus priventur et non amplius immunantur. Et contra autem religiosi praefati se deffendentes multos articulos,* etc. Géraud puts *non amplius* after *se,* and omits *et immunantur* and *deffendentes.*

46. The first retort of the friars to Fitz-Ralph was on March 7, 1357, when a meeting in London drew up a list of twenty-one errors in his public sermons and served it upon him. Gwynn, *The English Austin Friars,* pp. 85–86. Roger Conway, English provincial of the Franciscans, pressed the mendicant case at Avignon. His reply to Fitz-Ralph, *Contra proposiciones Armachani* or *Defensio religionis mendicancium* is published in Goldast, *Monarchia sancti Romani imperii,* II, 1410 ff. In 1357 the charges of heresy had no significance, but it is interesting to note that in some respects Fitz-Ralph was a forerunner of Wyclif, and the Lollards called him Saint Richard. Workman, *John Wyclif,* I, 130.

47. This obscure statement seems to indicate that Jean de Venette did not know the outcome when he was writing this section but that he intended to record it in its place. If this is a correct interpretation, it helps in surmising the date of composition for this section. Before the issue had been joined at Avignon the pope had issued orders (Aug. 25, 1357) charging certain monastic officials in England to see that the mendicants observed the bull *Super cathedram.* Mortier, *Histoire des maîtres généraux de l'ordre des frères prêcheurs,* III, 356. Some indication of the situation could be seen in Innocent VI's order of Oct. 1, 1356, to the prelates of England warning them not to hinder the mendicants in hearing confessions, preaching, burying and receiving alms, inasmuch as many false charges had been made against them, and the issue was still before the court. Theiner, *Vetera monumenta,* p. 313, No. 634. July 14, 1359, another bull of Innocent VI confirmed the bull *Vas electionis* (1321) of John XXII. In this roundabout way the attack on the mendicants was repulsed, because Pope John had condemned the views of an earlier teacher, with whom Fitz-Ralph agreed, and had asserted the efficacy of papal power in conferring privileges upon the friars. Gwynn, *The English Austin Friars,* pp. 81, 89. Fitz-Ralph died at Avignon, Nov. 16, 1360. Workman, *John Wyclif,* I, 130. It is hard to believe that Jean de Venette would have neglected to note this fact had he known it when writing this section. The friars are alleged to have rejoiced at his death. Final decision for the friars is said to have been

given five months after Fitz-Ralph's death, *ca.* April–May 1361. Baluze, *Vitae paparum,* I, 324; II, 465–66; Walsingham, *Historia Anglicana,* I, 285. John of Reading ascribes mendicant success to bribery (*Chronica,* pp. 130–31).

1358

1. A reads *succrescerunt* for *succreverunt.*

2. By March 1, 1358, Charles had assumed the title of regent. *Chronique . . . de Jean II,* I, 161, n. 2. Delachenal, *Histoire de Charles V,* I, 370–75, discusses the political significance of this move.

3. A reads *specialiter* for *principaliter* and then adds *principaliter* after *illos qui.*

4. Jean de Venette is somewhat confused here. The regent left Paris March 25, 1358, and went to Senlis, whither he and Charles of Navarre had summoned the nobles of Picardy and the Beauvaisis. Since these had not attended the meeting of the Estates General in February, they had not voted their share of the aid. Charles of Navarre sent his excuses, and very few nobles appeared. Before April 1 the regent moved on to Compiègne; on April 9 he entered Provins to meet the Estates of Champagne. *Chronique . . . de Jean II,* I, 163–65. He left Provins April 11 and proceeded by way of Preuilly and Montereau to Meaux, which he left April 18 to return to Compiègne, where he remained for a while. *Ibid.,* pp. 168–71. In an interview, May 2, near Clermont in Beauvaisis, between Charles of Navarre and the regent, the latter is reported to have said "that he loved the good town of Paris and he was well aware that there were good people there, but certain men had been guilty of very serious offenses, such as killing his followers in his very presence . . . and many other villainies. Consequently, until these things were made right he had no intention of coming to Paris." —*Ibid.,* p. 174.

5. A reads *attemptuerunt* for *praesumpserant.*

6. A adds *une* before *animo,* and *ei* before *uno corde.*

7. Among his items for late March, 1358, the author of the *Chronique . . . de Jean II* (I, 163) writes, "A knight called le Bègue de Villaines, who was a close friend to the late lord Robert of Clermont, who had been killed at Paris, declared himself an enemy to the men of Paris." According to the *Chronique normande du XIVe siècle* (p. 124), he led a company of knights who surprised Corbeil, because it was the chief town for supplying provisions to Paris. At the meeting of the Estates of Champagne the count of Braisne demanded to know if the regent knew of any villainy to be ascribed to the marshal of Champagne (Jean de Conflans), who had been killed at

Paris, explaining that he left it to the Normans to concern themselves with the case of Robert of Clermont. The regent replied that the marshals had always served him loyally. "And then the count of Braisne said to the regent, 'My lord, we men of Champagne, who are here, thank you for what you have said, and we trust you to execute justice upon those who have killed our friend without cause.' "—*Chronique . . . de Jean II,* I, 167. With respect to the situation in April, 1358, this same chronicler writes, "And at this time and previously, ever since the regent left the city, scarcely a gentleman came to Paris, wherefore the citizens were much concerned. And many believed that the gentlemen intended harm to them."—*Ibid.,* I, 170.

8. The *coup de main,* about April 15, 1358, by which the count of Joigny, acting for the regent, seized the Marché at Meaux, would have this result with respect to supplies coming down the Marne river. *Ibid.,* p. 169.

9. A reads *assumpserant* for *acceperant.*

10. A reads *pro bono communitatis* for *pro bono civitatis.*

11. The only source other than Jean de Venette for this academic deputation is a university record of May 2, 1358, to the effect that the university agreed that the rector, two masters, and the chief beadle from each nation should wait upon the regent in the interests of peace and concord. Du Boulay, *Histoire de l'Université de Paris,* IV, 344 (also quoted in *Rev. des quest. hist.,* XXIV [1878], 559). This was the time when the king of Navarre was meeting the regent between Mello and Clermont and urging the cause of the Parisians. *Chronique . . . de Jean II,* I, 173–74. Did the university delegation accompany him?

12. Géraud (II, 255, n. 3) remarks that the phrase *et non credentes quod* provides the sentence with a superfluous negative. It would appear that Jean de Venette was responsible for this, since A agrees with the other MSS.

13. This happened April 18, 1358. It particularly involved the seizure by Marcel and his partisans of royal artillery about to be sent to Meaux and Montereau, where it would help control the shipping of provisions down the river to Paris. *Chronique . . . de Jean II,* I, 170; Perrens, *Etienne Marcel,* p. 382; Secousse, *Recueil,* p. 100. The whole matter is discussed in Delachenal, *Histoire de Charles V,* I, 385–88. The same day Marcel wrote the following letter to the regent, the tone and content of which is very similar to Jean de Venette's story (*Froissart,* ed. Kervyn de Lettenhove, VI, 462–64).

Your Supreme Highness will remember how you agreed with us that if any reports unfavorable to us were brought to you that you would not believe them but would make them known to us. Likewise if anything concerning you was reported to us we would inform you. Consequently, Your Highness, we assure you truly that your people of Paris complain greatly of you and your government for three reasons. Firstly, those who are enemies to you, to us, and to the kingdom [of France] prey upon us and pillage us from all sides in the region towards Chartres, and you, who give direction in matters of this sort, do nothing about it. Likewise all the soldiers, who for some time past have been coming by your orders from Dauphiné, Burgundy, and elsewhere, for the defense of the realm, are neither a credit nor a profit to you nor to your people, because they eat up the whole countryside, pillaging and robbing the people, despite the fact that they have been well paid. And all this is well known to you because many complaints have been made to you, both by me and by other persons, on which account you should have ordered these soldiers to return to their homes. On the contrary, however, your people observe that you retain these in your following and that you have put some of them in garrison at the fortresses of Meaux and Montereau, which control the rivers Seine, Marne, and Yonne, by which your good town of Paris has to be supplied with provisions, as you well realize since you have very often been told. The third cause of complaint by the people is that you make no effort to garrison the fortresses facing your enemies, but you have been very quick to take possession of those past which provisions must come to us, and, what is worse, you have garrisoned them with men who wish us no good, as clearly appears to you and to us from letters intercepted at the gates of Paris, which were shown to you at a meeting of your Great Council. And yet you removed from your town of Paris artillery wherewith to strengthen the fortresses of Meaux and Montereau, which are garrisoned by men who wish us no good, as is reported and as clearly appears from the words which they have spoken to you, which you know well are to this effect: "Sire, whoever is lord of this castle, he can well boast that these villains at Paris are in his power and that he can easily clip their claws." May it please Your Supreme Highness to know that the men of Paris do not regard themselves as villains, but as good and loyal citizens, such as you have found them to be and will find them again; and furthermore, they assert that everyone who commits villainies is a villain. All these things are occasion for the great discontent of all your people, and not without cause, because in the first place it is your duty to provide defense and protection, while they owe you honor and obedience. If you are negligent of your duty then they are not held to theirs. Likewise, it seems right and just to your people that it would be better to use soldiers' pay for men who would fight against the enemies of the realm, rather than for those who take the king's money and rob and pillage the king's people. Likewise, it seems as if you and the fighting men, who are in your company, would be more creditably employed between Paris and Chartres, where the enemy is, than in the places where you are, which are in quiet country free from war. Also, it is a fact that the fortresses recently seized by you were in the hands of excellent men, unsuspected of any evil, that they were nowhere near the enemy lines, and that they cost you nothing to guard. Furthermore, it is the truth that whenever there are two places which need to be guarded and garrisoned, it is better and quicker to guard and garrison the one which is the most easily defended and contributes most to your honor and interests, rather than the one which is farthest away and least serviceable. But you, on the advice of your new council, wish to remove from Paris artillery with which to arm the fortresses referred to above, an action which your people are unwilling to permit, because it would help the destruction and loss of the kingdom, of yourself, and of all your people. So we very humbly petition Your Supreme Highness that you deign to enter your good city of Paris and afford it your defense and protection according to your duty, and that you dismiss from your presence all those men who are evilly disposed towards your said people, whom you can easily identify by the counsel which they give you, and at the same time, that you return the fortresses of Meaux and Montereau into the keeping of those your faithful and loyal subjects who had them before, so that your people of Paris, having no more cause for alarm about any shortage of supplies, shall cease to murmur against you. We also beseech you not to be angry because we have retained the artillery which had already been taken to the Louvre by Jean de Lyons, inasmuch as our intentions were good, and by so doing we prevented worse evils and dangers, because the people were so aroused by the order that great evils would have ensued if we had not quieted them by agreeing to keep it.

May it please Your Supreme Highness to know that the people of Paris still remember the many promises you made them by word of mouth at Saint-Jacques-de-l'Hôpital, at the market, and in your chamber, in addition to the promises to the effect that if you could leave the city with thirty or forty companions, you would not permit things to go on the way they were going; and, thank God, since then there has been a slight improvement.

May it please Your Supreme Highness to give orders respecting each and all of the matters here set forth, in such manner as will be to the glory of God, the honor of the king your father and yourself, and the well-being of the people, and that with all reasonable speed, and may you have us in your favor.

The Holy Spirit have you in His holy keeping and give you a long and happy life. Written at Paris, April 18, [1358].

14. A reads *armis* for *acrius*.

15. Félibien (*Histoire de la ville de Paris, V,* 818) says that in 1358 the prévôt of the merchants and the aldermen were ordered "to have ditches constructed about the walls of Paris and to build towers and bastilles for the defense thereof, and in recompense for the expense necessary for these works, the said prévôt and aldermen were to enjoy all profits and emoluments which might accrue from the rights of fishing in these ditches."

16. A reads *bastilas* for *balistas*.

17. A reads *puta porta Inferni;* Géraud omits *porta*.

18. Guillebert de Metz in his description of Paris, written in 1422, de-

votes Chap. 28 to the city gates on the southern bank of the Seine. He names them in order from east to west as follows:

The Victor gate, outside of which, near the town, is Saint Victor's abbey; and at that point there is a very large fir tree. The gate of Saint-Marcel, outside of which are the parish churches of Saint-Marcel, Saint-Médard, and Saint-Hippolyte; there also are the college of canons of Saint-Marcel and the Cordeliers nunnery. There is also a very large faubourg, almost like a separate town, where workers of various occupations live, especially butchers, dyers, makers of tomb-stones, knife-makers and others. The gate of Saint-Jacques, where there is a faubourg, and here is the hospital of Saint-Jacques-du-Haut-Pas and the church of Notre-Dame-des-Champs. The Porte d'Enfer, which is now called the gate of Saint-Michel, outside of which are the Carthusians. And there is the building called the press house of the Hôtel-Dieu, which extends from this gate as far as the Carthusians. The gate of Saint-Germain: there is a suburb here where many butchers dwell; there is Saint Vincent's abbey, now called the abbey of Saint-Germain-des-Prés, whose abbot exercises all three forms of justice, high, mesne and low. The Orléans gate (beyond which is the Nesle postern), outside of which is the place called Pré-aux-Clercs.

—Le Roux de Lincy and Tisserand, *Paris et ses historiens,* pp. 221–24.

19. A reads *capellas volcatas* for *capelas votatas.*

20. Géraud (II, 257, n. 4) thinks that *per domos civitatis* must be an error for *per muros,* but A agrees with the other MSS and the translation ignores Géraud's suggested correction.

21. A adds *suas* after *solum domus.*

22. A reads *sed etiam tam domos quam extra menia quam intras qui muris ab infra,* etc. for *sed etiam domos intra moenia et illas quae muris ab infra,* etc.

23. Jean de Venette is the only source for these activities. He is, of course, an eyewitness.

24. A ads *calcis et corti lateris aptatorum* after *cementorum.*

25. In the thirteenth century "the lord of Hautefeuille, head of the Ganelon family, gave to the Jacobins his castle, which adjoined their convent."—Félibien and Lobineau, *Histoire de la ville de Paris,* I, 261. As early as 1252 there was a street named Hautefeuille running next to the Jacobins, from the rue Saint-André-des-Arts to the rue des Cordeliers. Jaillot, *Recherches . . . sur la ville de Paris,* VII, 87. The notion, said to have prevailed in the sixteenth century, that the street derived its name from the fact that it was lined with tall trees seems unlikely when the connection with this region of the family name is so clearly established. Le Roux de Lincy and Tisserand, *Paris et ses historiens,* p. 175, n. 6. In Saint Louis' time (*ca.* 1270) that part of the Dominican convent abutting upon

the city wall and its moat was the castle of the seigneur de Hautefeuille. Du Breul, *Le Théâtre des antiquitez de Paris,* pp. 500–501. According to Jaillot, Earl Amaury, a grandnephew of Ganelon, one of the characters in "Huon of Bordeaux," had a castle of Hautefeuille, but the published version of this chanson does not confirm this. There is a character, Amauri de la Tour de Rivière, in "Huon of Bordeaux," who plays the role of a traitor, which would be expected from one of the Ganelon family. A castle named Hautefeuille is mentioned in "Gaydon" and "Gaufrey," but it is not located in Paris. The name is also the rallying cry of the Ganelon family in "Gaydon," "Fierabras," and "Renaut de Montauban." Langlois, *Table des noms propres de toute nature compris dans les chansons de geste imprimées, passim.* I am obliged to my colleague Professor Charles Grimm for assistance on this point.

26. On March 15, 1358, he was captain of Bonneval and Alluyes in the region south of Chartres. But the document showing this fact and this passage in Jean de Venette are the last notices we have of him. He was a younger son of Guy VIII, seigneur de Laval. There are scattered items relative to his activities in the lower Loire region for 1350 and following years. Broussillon, *La Maison de Laval, 1020–1605,* II, 112, 249, 254–59; Ch. de Sourdeval, "Les Sires de Retz et le château de Machecoul," *Mémoires de la Société archéologique de Touraine,* II (1843–44), 27–70; *Annuaire-Bulletin de la Soc. de l'hist. de France* (1898), p. 243, No. 595; *Archives historiques du Poitou,* XVII (1886), 29, n. 3; XX (1889), 272. Why this particular captain should be noticed by Jean de Venette is quite obscure. No other writer mentions him.

27. According to the *Chronique . . . de Jean II* (I, 142) on Tuesday, Jan. 16, 1358, "the enemies round about Paris and Chartres took Etampes and pillaged it, capturing large numbers of prisoners, whom they shut up in many fortresses which they held in the Chartrain and in Beauce." Presumably this is the first capture. Etampes is an important place on the Paris-Orléans road.

28. Jean le Bel (*Chronique,* II, 249–50) describes this state of affairs vividly.

At this time there went about a company of men-at-arms and foot soldiers [brigands] gathered together from every country, and they conquered and robbed whatever they found, and they ravaged the country between the Seine and the Loire so that no one could go between Paris and Vendôme, or between Paris and Orléans, or between Paris and Montargis, so that none of the country folk remained there, but all fled to Paris or Orléans. And this company had for captain one called Ruffin, and they made him a knight, and he became as rich as anyone could, so that he did not know how rich he was. Often they raided near Paris, at other times towards Orléans up to the gates, and they set fire to the suburbs. And there remained no town nor village in this region, no matter how large or populous, which was not raided and robbed, namely Saint-Arnoult, Gallardon, Bonneval, Cloyes [sur-le-Loire], Etampes, Châtres, Montlhéry, Pithivers-en-Gâtinois, Larchaut, Milly, Château-Landon, Montargis, and many other large towns, astonishing to tell, and they raided about the country in troops of twenty, thirty, or forty, and destroyed whatever they found.

Froissart copied this text. Ed. Luce, Vol. V, pp. xxiv–xxv, 94–95; see also *Chronique . . . de Jean II,* I, 159, 171, 175.

29. May 14, 1358 (*Ordonnances,* III, 221), is the date on the decisions of this session of the Estates General at Compiègne and presumably marks the end of the session. Géraud (II, 259, n. 1) includes here a passage of thirty-five words, which he took from the Citeaux MS, except for the verb *subigerent,* which he inserted in order to make sense. A has this passage and also has in addition the verb *debilitarent,* which makes Géraud's editing unnecessary. It is also clear that Géraud or the Citeaux copyist repeated needlessly the words *seu fortalitium quod ibi est,* which occur only once in A.

30. A adds *et patrie* before *capiendo.*

31. As before, there is a certain vagueness to Jean de Venette's chronology. The first invitation from Marcel to Charles of Navarre asking him to come to Paris was decided upon the evening of the day on which the marshals were murdered, Feb. 22, 1358. The king arrived four days later with a large body of men-at-arms, and remained until March 13. During this time he negotiated an agreement with the duke of Normandy. Possibly the "fresh discord" mentioned here refers to the interview between the two Charles's on May 2–3 in the Beauvaisis. The next day Charles of Navarre with large forces came again to Paris, where he was feted for ten or twelve days. Some wished to make him captain then. His suppression of the Jacquerie followed at the end of May and early in June. On June 14, 1358, he again returned to Paris, and at a great public assembly the next day was acclaimed captain. It is at this time that he insinuated his own claim to the French throne by explaining that his mother would have been king if she had been a man, because she was the only child of the king of France. *Chronique . . . de Jean II,* I, 153, 155–56, 161, 163–64, 173–74, 184–86.

32. Jean de Venette was a sympathetic chronicler who was himself in the city and who wrote only a few years after the event. He offers a reflection of the attitude prevailing in Paris which is in interesting contrast with the official, royal version of the *Chronique . . . de Jean II,* which records that "the men of Paris always maintained an attitude of haughty arrogance to-

wards the regent, their lord"; and again, "No man dared come out of Paris on that side [towards the regent's forces], nor to go in either; but frequently they came out to fight, but they always lost more than they gained and left many dead behind." The regent was moving his forces nearer to Paris; June 26 at Chelles, June 29 at Vincennes, Charenton bridge, and Conflans, ravaging the country and burning the towns (*ibid.*, I, 189–90). On July 11 there was a skirmish at the outworks of the Porte-Saint-Antoine. *Ibid.*, I, 193–94.

33. There is considerable confusion here. The bridge referred to was a bridge of boats thrown across the Seine from the quarries of Charenton to Ivry, completed July 12. Corbeil is much higher up the Seine and had no connection with the bridge. The attack on the bridge was made July 14. According to the official royal account, it was made by a force composed chiefly of English in the pay of Charles of Navarre and was a failure. *Ibid.*, I, 196–98. It seems very possible that Jean de Venette has confused this July expedition against the bridge with the expedition on or about Holy Thursday (March 29, 1358) against Corbeil, which is mentioned in the *Chronique normande du XIVe siècle* (p. 124). See above, p. 232, n. 7.

34. The official account has the duke with the forces in the neighborhood, which is much more probable.

35. A reads *eggressus* for *aggressus*.

36. Jean de Venette's statements sound more like the interview and negotiations of July 8 near the abbey of Saint-Antoine than anything else. Two days later, when Charles of Navarre explained these negotiations in Paris, the citizens complained that he had made his peace with the regent without consideration for them, and they told him "that they did not care because they could get on very well without him."—*Chronique . . . de Jean II*, I, 190–93. After the fighting at the bridge there were further negotiations until July 19, which brought about the withdrawal of the regent's army, July 21, and relieved the blockade of Paris on the east. But Charles of Navarre did not take part in these personally and Jean de Venette ignores them. *Ibid.*, I, 198–200.

37. A omits *de Parisius* after *exierunt;* the translation follows Géraud.

38. A adds *per totam patriam* before *ad omnem partem*.

39. Again Jean de Venette's chronology seems confused or incomplete. On July 10 Charles of Navarre was in Paris explaining his negotiations with the regent. The next day he brought into the city a body of English men-at-arms, who were in his pay. On July 12 he himself returned to his headquarters at Saint-Denis. But he was back in Paris on the twenty-first, when there was a popular outbreak against his English men-at-arms because of

the strong feeling against the English companies, who were ravaging the country west of Paris. On this occasion "about thirty-four English were killed, and forty-seven of the leaders were arrested at the hôtel de Nesle, where they were dining with the king of Navarre, and four hundred more in various other houses in the city, and they were thrown into prison at the Louvre." The next day, July 22, in order to satisfy the people, the king and Marcel agreed upon a military effort to drive off the plundering English. It was a column of Parisians, engaged in this enterprise, that was ambushed and annihilated in the Bois de Boulogne by the English. The Parisians blamed Charles for this failure. There was also a popular demand that the English prisoners in the Louvre be put to death. But on July 27 Marcel, at the request of the king of Navarre, released these prisoners and marched them with an escort of two hundred archers through the city to the Porte-Saint-Honoré, and permitted them to go to Saint-Denis, where Charles had been since July 22. *Chronique . . . de Jean II,* I, 194, 201–4.

40. A reads *circa* for *iuxta.*

41. A reads *crassabatur* for *grassabatur.*

42. Most of these details are peculiar to Jean de Venette's story and cannot be confirmed from other sources. With respect to the city of Orléans there is some information. Knighton (*Chronicon,* II, 102) reports an English force, presumably led by Robert Knolles, before Orléans after the feast of the Purification (Feb. 2, 1358), which burned the suburbs, and killed and plundered at will, the citizens not daring to come out against them. To confirm this there is a letter of Feb. 5, 1358, whereby Jean de Montmorency, bishop of Orléans, curtailed the customary ceremonial for his solemn entry into the episcopal church because of the great danger in going outside the city. Published in Saussaye, *Annales ecclesiae Aurelianensis,* pp. 567–72. In this year also the Carmelite monastery at Orléans was destroyed, "either by the English or by the inhabitants" of the city as a measure of defense. Dubois, *Histoire du siège d'Orléans,* p. 201, citing a *supplicat* of 1405 in the *Cartulaire de l'hôpital du pont.*

43. This is the peasant uprising known as the Jacquerie. The affair at Saint-Leu-d'Essérent, which was the first step in the revolt, took place May 28, 1358. The chief scholarly studies are Luce, *Histoire de la Jacquerie,* and Flammermont, "La Jacquerie en Beauvaisis," *Rev. hist.,* IX (1879), 123–43; an excellent summary in Delachenal, *Histoire de Charles V,* I, 394–410. Saint-Leu is near Creil.

44. Jean de Venette is the only source for this item about Cale's home town. Froissart says he was from Clermont, but Luce regards Jean de Venette as a better authority. *Froissart,* Vol. V, pp. xxix, 100. The name

Cale is a form of Charles, and so appears in the *Chronique des quatre premiers Valois,* p. 71. According to this source, Cale was forced to accept the leadership of the peasants. Géraud's text gives the name Karle in a passage reading, *rusticum magis astutum ordinarunt scilicet Guillelmum dictum Karle.* By italicizing it, Géraud seems to imply that he has made an editorial insertion of the name. A supports this reading in an interesting way. The copyist omitted the last four words in the passage quoted above, but the corrector has them in the margin. The latter himself first wrote *Kalre,* which he then crossed out and wrote *Karle.*

45. A omits *contenti erant* after *non solum sic.*

46. Géraud (II, 264, n. 1) remarks that his MSS read *Cironovilla* where they should read *Ermenovilla.* A reads *Ermonovilla.*

47. Ermenonville is near Senlis. The castle belonged to Robert de Lorris, chamberlain to King John and one of his most unpopular councilors. In this particular enterprise a force of three hundred men went out from Paris and cooperated with the peasants in capturing the castle. Probably this explains why this is the only particular episode of the Jacquerie that came to Jean de Venette's attention. Why he neglects to mention the Parisian cooperation is obscure. According to the *Chronique normande du XIVe siècle* (p. 130), those within the castle were saved from anything worse than pillage by Robert de Lorris's renunciation of "gentillesse," and his swearing that he loved the citizens of Paris better than the nobles. The capture of Ermenonville was probably June 7, 1358. Luce, *Histoire de la Jacquerie,* p. 151, n. 1. A reads *recenditos* for *qui se ibi tuebantur.*

48. A reads *cecidisset* for *in manibus eorum incidisset;* the translation follows Géraud.

49. A repeats *et eorum maneria cum uxoribus et liberis* between *nobiles* and *se aliquo.* This seems so clearly to be a copyist's error due to the double use of *nobiles* that the translation follows Géraud.

50. A reads *subito* for *cito.*

51. The atrocities attendant upon the Jacquerie impressed contemporaries and are dwelt upon at considerable length. See Jean le Bel, *Chronique,* II, 256–60; *The Anonimalle Chronicle,* p. 42; Gray, *Scalacronica,* p. 131. The echo of class antagonisms appears clearly in the latter: "The villagers and laborers of the commonality of France gathered in crowds after their King John was taken at Poitiers, despising the gentle folks and doing violence to those whom they could reach, throwing down their houses and declaring that gentle folk were no use except to oppress the commonality and poor people by their extortions." A reads *uxores* for *feminas.*

52. A reads *nec debebant* for *nec decebat.*

53. A reads *non adunatos* for *adunatos*.

54. The most detailed account of the Jacquerie is in the *Chronique des quatre premiers Valois* (pp. 71–77). According to this, the Picard nobles appealed to Charles of Navarre at his castle of Longueville saying, "Sire, you are the leading gentleman in the world. Do not permit the destruction of 'gentillesse.' If this crowd of Jacques carry on for any length of time and the townsmen come to their aid, gentlemen and all that they stand for will be completely destroyed." King Charles led an army into the Beauvaisis and encountered the peasants under Cale at Mello near Clermont on June 8, 1358. The latter had taken up such a strong position that the king hesitated to attack. Cale knew enough about war to wish to avoid battle, but his followers wanted to fight. The two forces faced each other throughout June 9. Then King Charles asked for a truce and a parley. The peasant captains neglected to demand hostages; whereupon, during the parley, they were treacherously seized. The leaderless peasants were then suddenly attacked and cut to pieces. Faithlessness in dealing with social inferiors has seldom seemed dishonorable. The episode of Wat Tyler thirty years later in England is another example of the same. After the battle Cale was taken to Clermont and beheaded. Why Jean de Venette mentions the count of Saint-Pol (Guy V de Châtillon) is obscure. The list, in the *Chronique des quatre premiers Valois,* of forty noblemen who were present at this battle does not include the count.

55. A adds *Et sic totam eorum fatua secta et male custodia qualia fuma evanuit et cessavit* after *peremit.*

56. Jean de Venette came from this region. Obviously he had seen the places which he mentions, and no doubt he is repeating the current report, which has the ring of truth. A adds *Ressonum* after *Compendium.*

57. The fortress of Meaux was that part of the city called the Marché. It was on an island formed by the river Marne and an old canal, and fortified with walls and towers. A single bridge over the Marne connected the fortress with the town of Meaux. Secousse (*Mémoires*, 244–47) has a detailed description which is quoted at length in Luce, *Histoire de la Jacquerie*, pp. 129–32. It will be recalled that the regent's men seized this place about the middle of April 1358 (see above, p. 233, n. 8). The citizens were much annoyed at this coup. The duchess took up her residence at Meaux apparently at this time. *Chronique . . . de Jean II,* I, 169–71, 187. The duke-regent left Meaux April 19. He may have returned after May 14, but early in June he departed again for Montereau, where he was June 7, and shortly afterwards for Sens, where he arrived June 9. He returned to Meaux June 23. *Froissart,* ed. Luce, Vol. V, p. xxix, n. 6.

58. The importance of Meaux in connection with the blockade of Paris has already been mentioned. At the same time that the Parisians sent a force of three hundred men to help in the attack on Ermenonville, they also sent another force of five hundred south of the Seine. On June 9 both these companies went to Meaux, where they were welcomed by the mayor and citizens. The official royal chronicler asserts that the mayor had sworn to be loyal to the regent. *Chronique . . . de Jean II,* I, 181–82. Jean le Bel (*Chronique,* II, 260–62) gives the story of these events from the aristocratic point of view, telling how maliciously the Parisians sent their forces to Meaux, how the wicked citizens opened their gates, how the Parisians rushed in like madmen to attack the nobles.

59. Froissart (ed. Luce, V, 103–4) tells how Gaston Phoebus, count of Foix, and Jean de Grailly, Captal de Buch, were returning from Prussia at this time. They arrived at Châlons at the time of the Jacquerie (i.e., after May 28) and came on to Meaux to protect the ladies there from harm. With the duke of Orléans they made a vigorous sortie, which, in the narrow fighting space at the bridge and in the streets, was entirely successful. They killed the Parisians "like pigs," says Jean le Bel (*Chronique,* II, 260–62), drove them out into the fields, and then returning set the town on fire, on the theory that the citizens were enemies because they had admitted the Parisians. See also *Chronique . . . de Jean II,* I, 181–84. Meaux burned for more than two weeks. "The mayor, Jean Soulas, was forced to leap from a window into the street onto their swords."—*Chronographia,* p. 274, n. 4.

60. A adds *priora* after *capitales.*

61. Jean le Bel says (*Chronographia,* II, 262), "This magnificent adventure . . . was the more admirable for them and for all good Christians because it was a turning point, inasmuch as those fellows had never before been repulsed, but were getting more and more arrogant in their deviltry, and were increasing daily in strength against the nobles, so that they would have overrun the world if God, because of His special pity for France, had not prevented it and provided a remedy." Froissart remarks that the Captal de Buch was English, but since there was a truce he could help the French nobles.

62. This attack on Senlis was on Wednesday June 13, 1358. Luce, *Histoire de la Jacquerie,* p. 145, n. 1, and see below, p. 273, n. 62. Jean de Venette is the only source for this episode. The short account in *Chronique des quatre premiers Valois* (pp. 76–77) looks like a summary of Jean de Venette. A plan of Senlis in the fourteenth century and a restored view of the city can be found in Le Roux de Lincy and Tisserand, *Paris et ses historiens,* p. 74.

63. A adds *ad recipiendos eos* before *se optime.*

64. A adds *statim* after *totum*.   65. A reads *balneati* for *ordinati*.

66. See above, p. 72.

67. A reads *cogitaverunt secrete ut* for *cogitaverunt ut secrete*.

68. A reads *miserunt* for *iverunt*.

69. A reads *ordinaverunt iterum ut secrete per ipsos vocaretur et insimul taliter fieret quod eorum regimen et defensionem contra dominum ducem*. Géraud differs from this by reading *secrete ut iterum* and omitting *insimul*. Géraud (II, 269, n. 1) thinks *quod* should be dropped.

70. A adds *ut dicitur* after *nam*.

71. A adds *sine venia* after *signata*.

72. It should be noted that Jean de Venette prefaces this outline of the Marcel program with the phrase, "So it was charged against them afterwards." According to A, which this translation follows, he also wrote *ut dicitur* in the sentence charging Charles of Navarre with aiming for a long time at the throne. Géraud's text lacks this phrase. This wording and the items in the indictment make it seem probable that Jean de Venette is merely summarizing the content or echoing the speech made by the regent Charles at the Hôtel de Ville on Aug. 4, 1358. *Chronique . . . de Jean II*, I, 212. This official point of view is set forth in the letter of Charles to the count of Savoy dated Aug. 31, 1358. If this be the real explanation of Jean de Venette's text, it hardly justifies the emphasis which Delachenal (*Histoire de Charles V*, I, 445, n. 2) places upon it as evidence against Marcel. At best it indicates that Jean de Venette accepted the official explanation, though apparently with reservations. That explanation may well have had some foundation, but we should hesitate to accept Jean de Venette as an independent authority in its favor. There are other places in his chronicle which show his disposition to accept the direction of the legitimate authorities, even when, at the same time, he creates the impression that he is somewhat doubtful. A person in his position would not ordinarily come in contact with anything but official explanations and the general notions current among the people.

73. A reads *et* for *sed*.

74. There seems to be a superficial parallelism between Jean de Venette's account of the events of July 31–Aug. 1, 1358, and that in the *Chronique . . . de Jean II* (I, 205–10).

Tuesday the last day of July, the aforesaid prévôt and many others with him went before dinner to the bastille Saint-Denis. And the prévôt commanded those who kept the keys of this bastille to deliver them to Josseran de Mâcon, treasurer for the king of Navarre. But those who kept the keys said they would give them to no one. At this the prévôt was much incensed and there was such a row at this bastille between the prévôt and those who kept the keys that a citizen named Jean Maillart, who was in charge of that quarter of the city next to this bastille, getting word of the argument, betook himself to the prévôt and told him that the keys ought not to be given over to Josseran. And there were many high words passed between the prévôt and Josseran on one side and Jean Maillart on the other. So Maillart got on a horse, and took a royal banner, and began to cry out, "Montjoye for the king of France and the duke," in such wise that everyone who saw him followed after him shouting the same slogan. And the prévôt and his companions did the same and they made for the bastille Saint-Antoine. Jean Maillart went toward Les Halles. And a knight named Pepin des Essars, knowing nothing of what Jean Maillart had done, likewise shortly afterwards took another royal banner, and raised a cry like that of Jean Maillart. Meanwhile the prévôt went to the bastille Saint-Antoine, and he took with him two boxes wherein, so they say, were letters sent him by the king of Navarre. And those at the bastille demanded to be shown these letters. And there was such a row at this bastille that some of those there rushed at Philip Giffart, who accompanied the prévôt. He defended himself boldly, being well armed, with a basinet on his head; nevertheless he was killed. And afterward the prévôt was killed and another of his companions named Simon la Paonnier. They were promptly stripped and stretched out all naked on the pavement. This done, the people rushed to hunt for others to treat them in like manner. Someone said that Jean de l'Isle the younger was at Hocans' house at the sign of the Bear near the Baudoyer gate. So a great crowd went in there, found this Jean de l'Isle and Gilles Marcel, secretary of the Paris merchants, and put them to death. These were promptly stripped like the others and dragged all naked into the street before the house and left there. Then the people departed and rushed off to hunt for others. And this day at the bastille Saint-Martin Jean Porret the younger was killed. And these five corpses were dragged as far as the court of Sainte-Katherine-du-Val-des-Escoliers, where they were stretched out all naked for everyone to see, just as they themselves had treated the marshals of Champagne and Clermont, wherefore many said it was God's judgment upon them since they had suffered the same fate as they had visited upon the marshals.

Géraud (II, 270, n. 1) comments on his texts which put this episode on Aug. 1 instead of July 31, but in A the corrector wrote *in vigil* in the margin to be inserted before *festo*.

75. A adds *mensis* after *die*.   76. A reads *in consiliis* for *in castris*.

77. A adds *tandem* before *ad portam*.

78. This was at that part of the city fortification where, some ten years later, the Bastille of French Revolutionary fame was built.

79. This statement about proclamations is peculiar to Jean de Venette. Delachenal (*Histoire de Charles V*, I, 455, n. 5) offers the very plausible theory that the issue really applied to the slogans, whether the cry should

be "Montjoye for the king and the duke" or merely "Montjoye for the king." It is also of interest that the Arundel text differs from Géraud's in a way better to indicate the suspicions involved in the dispute. Where Géraud reads *et de hoc mirabantur alii cives,* A has *et mirabantur alii cuius rege.* The translation follows the latter.

80. A adds *et suos* before *proditi.*

81. A reads *dicentibus et [ad invicem sic] altercantibus.* Géraud omits the words in brackets.

82. Géraud reads *cum magno impetu gladium vel hastam,* but A reads *hachiam.* Froissart (ed. Luce, V, 116) says Marcel was killed with an ax.

83. A adds *isti percussori* after *alii.*

84. Géraud reads *quinquaginta quatuor,* but A has *vel quatuor,* which conforms more nearly to the other account. Apparently a careless copyist mistook the last letter of *vel* for a numeral.

85. This church was several hundred yards from the Porte-Saint-Antoine, at the juncture of the grande rue Saint-Antoine and the rue Sainte-Katherine.

86. When one of the prisoners, Thomas de Ladit, was released from the Châtelet on Sept. 12 he was in such condition that he could not walk and had to be carried on a door. *Chronique . . . de Jean II,* I, 215–16.

87. A reads *tertium* for *certum.*

88. In the *Chronique . . . de Jean II* (I, 210–12) we learn that on Aug. 1, 1358, Charles Toussac, alderman (one of Marcel's chief lieutenants) and Josseran de Mâcon were arrested and imprisoned at the Châtelet. The next day, before the regent's arrival, they were beheaded. On Aug. 3 Pierre Gilles and Thomas de Ladit, chancellor to Charles of Navarre, were arrested. The next day the former and Sir Gilles Caillart, chatelain of the Louvre, were beheaded, Sir Gilles first having his tongue cut out because of the many evil things he had said against the king and the regent. In the next week on one day were beheaded Jean Prévost and Pierre le Blont, and on another two advocates, Pierre de Puiseux and Jean Godart. See Luce, "Un des meneurs de la commune de Paris en 1358; Pierre Gilles," in *La France pendant la guerre de cent ans,* I, 25–30.

89. The regent came to Paris Aug. 2, 1358.

90. It would appear that the regent immediately appointed a commission of ten to do justice upon those guilty of treason and rebellion in Paris. Delachenal, *Histoire de Charles V,* I, 462, n. 2. But on Aug. 10 he issued a general amnesty for the good people of Paris, "who, ignorant of the high treason and the wicked activities which the prévôt and his accomplices were secretly carrying on against the king's person and the royal majesty, had

```
         #  01-04-2016 10:42AM
Item(s) checked out to Brar, Jujar.

TITLE: The chronicle of Jean de Venette;
BARCODE: 31888009253668
DUE DATE: 02-05-16
```

agreed to accept the king of Navarre as governor, defender, and captain, and had made alliance with him." The man who "had attempted to balk the ransoming of the king, who wished to kill the king and the dauphin or to imprison them for life and make the king of Navarre king of France" were excepted from this amnesty. *Ordonnances*, IV, 346–48; Secousse, *Recueil*, pp. 81–83. On Oct. 25 some twenty citizens were arrested, but on Oct. 29 the people staged a demonstration, complaining that this was an act of vengeance. This forced the regent to appoint a special commission of inquiry, which released these citizens late in November. *Chronique . . . de Jean II*, I, 222–24.

91. The new prévôt would seem to have been Gencien Tristan, but evidently he did not hold office after 1358. Jean Culdoe then became prévôt of the merchants. *Ibid.*, I, 222, n. 1.

92. In Amiens there was a strong bourgeois group similar to the one at Paris, and similarly disposed to be anti-noble and pro-Navarre. It will be recalled that Charles of Navarre, immediately on his release from prison, went to Amiens and made there his first bid for popular support (see above, p. 69). In issuing an amnesty for Amiens in September, 1358, the regent outlined the hostile policy pursued by the city. Its representatives had been involved in the activities of the Third Estate in the Estates General of 1356. With the other townsmen they had urged the release of the king of Navarre. When the regent, in 1358, attempted to avoid calling the Estates General by appealing to local assemblies, the men of Amiens refused to answer his summons, nor would they permit him to come to Amiens unless he dispensed with his armed escort, of which the citizens were suspicious and fearful. "Also [the men of Amiens] had adopted caps, part blue and part red, as a sign of their union and alliance with the city of Paris. . . . And they had agreed to have the king of Navarre for their captain, because the city of Paris wrote them that this had been agreed to, among other things, between [the regent] and the king."—Thierry, *Recueil des monuments inédits de l'histoire du Tiers Etat*, I, 583–89, No. 235. There was political division at Amiens as at Paris. In the late spring of 1358 the mayor "many times assembled the citizens in arms, and those who came asked why they were called to arms; and one time when they were armed and assembled in the market place, a man named [Stephen] Gelee demanded to know why they were armed and urged that the good men should range themselves on one side and the Navarrese on the other: the regent Charles was then at Montdidier. Then Jacques [de Saint-Fuscien, captain of the town] told the men of Amiens that [the regent] wished to come to the city to pillage it, and he prevented the townsmen going to the regent or permit-

ting him to come to the city."—*Ibid.*, I, 604, No. 604. See also Maugis, *Documents inédits concernant la ville et le siège du bailliage d'Amiens*, I, 86–87, 107–10. Presumably it was at this time that the mayor warned "that if they permitted the regent to enter Amiens he would cut off the heads of the leading men."—Secousse, *Recueil*, p. 132.

93. A reads *majorem dictae villae* for Géraud's *majorem partem dictae villae*.

94. The mayor was Firmin Cocquerel. The neighboring monastery was Notre-Dame-du-Gard, about ten miles from Amiens near Picquigny. We know only that the abbot was named Nicholas. He had been elected in 1357. *Gallia Christiana* (X, 1330) makes no mention of him. Thierry, *op. cit.*, I, 590; Delgove, "L'Abbaye du Gard," *Mémoires de la Société des antiquaires de Picardie*, XXII (1868), 117–316; Beaunier, *Recueil historique, chronologique et topographique des archevechez, evêchez, abbayes et prieurez de France*, II, 640; Desnoyers, *Topographie ecclésiastique de la France*, Part 2, p. 541; *Froissart*, ed. Luce, Vol. V, p. xl, n. 3. Jean de Venette neglects the two most important actors in this episode, Jean de Picquigny, who headed the Navarrese, and Jacques de Saint-Fuscien, captain of Amiens. The former planned the affair. It seems very doubtful that Charles of Navarre himself was present. Only Jean de Venette says that he was. The wives of two partisans of Navarre (Jean de Picquigny and the viscount of Poix) were staying at Amiens. It is said that this effort to surprise Amiens was caused by an order from the regent to imprison these ladies and hold them as hostages. *Chronique normande du XIVe siècle*, pp. 137–38, 316; Secousse, *Recueil*, p. 150.

95. A adds *de Ternoys* after *Sancti Pauli*.

96. Géraud's text has a reading from one of the late MSS, *fuisset illa die capta penitus*, but Géraud (II, 275, n. 2) indicates that his early MS reads *fuisset illo tunc capta*. A reads *fuisset illo tunc penitus et capta*.

97. A reads *properantem* for *concurrentem*.

98. A reads *suburbibus itaque* for *suburbibus civitatis*.

99. A adds *voracibus* after *flammis*.

100. During August, 1358, the partisans of Navarre were occupying and seizing strongholds west and north of Paris. Among these was La Hérelle, "three leagues from Amiens," where Jean de Picquigny commanded (*Froissart*, ed. Luce, V, 120). According to arrangements between him and the mayor and the captain of Amiens, Navarrese soldiers were brought secretly into the faubourgs and hidden in the houses, particularly the refuge of the abbey of Gard. On Sunday night, Sept. 16, 1358, Jean de Picquigny with five hundred men appeared before the city. Some pro-

Navarre citizens had left open one of the gates, which Picquigny's men seized. The hidden soldiers appeared suddenly in the streets shouting "Navarre! Navarre!" The citizens rang their bells and rushed to arms crying "Treason!" The Navarrese easily mastered the faubourgs but hesitated to attack the bourg. After vainly waiting for the mayor's orders the citizens took up the defense of the fortified gate leading into the bourg, and held off the Navarrese until the arrival from Corbie of Robert de Fiennes, constable of France, and his nephew, Guy de Châtillon, count of Saint-Pol, recently appointed royal lieutenant in Picardy, Vermandois, and the Beauvaisis. These occupied the bourg and Picquigny withdrew. The Navarrese burned the faubourgs, including about three thousand houses, the churches of Saint-Michael, Saint-Jacques, the convents of the Jacobins, Cordeliers, and Augustinians, and the abbey of Saint-Jean-les-Amiens. The constable, the next day, arrested seventeen suspects, including the captain and the abbot, and had them beheaded. The mayor was arrested, questioned, and deposed, along with the aldermen. The constable's letter of Nov. 30, 1358, does not mention his execution, but at some later date he must have been executed, because in 1371 his son received permission to take down his remains and bury them. He may have been among those beheaded Jan. 1, 1359 (*Chronique . . . de Jean II*, I, 225). The new mayor was Jean du Gard. Thierry, *Recueil des monuments inédits de l'histoire du Tiers Etat*, I, 590–99, Nos. 236, 238, 240; Janvier, *Les Clabault, famille municipale amienoise*, p. 11; Maugis, *Documents inédits concernant la ville et le siège du bailliage d'Amiens*, I, 59–128; Calonne, *Histoire d'Amiens*, I, 282.

101. Charles of Navarre had been at Saint-Denis during the latter part of July, "awaiting his brother, that good knight, Philip of Navarre, count of Longueville and Beaumont, who was collecting the English and Navarrese garrisons of Brittany and Normandy in the Cotentin."—*Chronique des quatre premiers Valois*, pp. 81–83. By Aug. 9, 1358, he was at Mantes (*Froissart*, ed. Luce, Vol. V, p. xxxvii, n. 1).

102. On Aug. 3 Charles of Navarre sent his defiance to the regent. *Chronique . . . de Jean II*, I, 211.

103. For the Anglo-Navarrese agreement of Aug. 1, 1358, see Rymer, *Foedera*, Vol. III, Part 1, p. 70. Rymer's error in dating this document (1351 instead of 1358) was first corrected by Secousse (*Mémoires*, p. 318, n. 1). Luce, "Négociations des Anglais avec le roi de Navarre pendant la révolution parisienne de 1358," *Mémoires de la Soc. de l'hist. de Paris*, I (1875), reprinted in his *La France pendant la guerre de cent ans*, I, 33–46, interpreted this as an arrangement for the partition of France between King Edward and King Charles. But Déprez, "Une Conference anglo-navarrese

en 1358," *Rev. hist.,* XCIX (1908), 34–39, reviews the previous discussion, provides a complete and corrected text, outlines the diplomatic background, and shows that Luce's interpretation is much too lurid and epoch-making. There was an essential contradiction in any Anglo-Navarrese alliance. The matter is summarized in Delachenal, *Histoire de Charles V,* II, 2–7. The latest contribution to this topic is Perroy, "France, England, and Navarre from 1359 to 1364," *Bulletin of the Institute of Historical Research,* XIII (1935–36), 151–54.

104. For events in Normandy, see *Chronique des quatre premiers Valois,* p. 86 ff., and *Chronique normande du XIVe siècle,* pp. 139–42.

105. Only Jean de Venette mentions Vernon. Charles was at Mantes Aug. 9, 1358. *Froissart,* ed. Luce, Vol. V, p. xxxvii, n. 1, and Delachenal, *Histoire de Charles V,* II, 11, n. 3. For Meulan see *ibid.,* n. 2. Why does the Navarrese recovery of Evreux go unnoticed? It took place before September, 1358. *Froissart,* ed. Luce, Vol. V, pp. 87–93; p. xxiii, n. 2.

106. A reads *domina* for *regina;* the translation follows Géraud.

107. Melun was occupied Aug. 4, 1358, by a mixture of surprise and deceit in which Queen Blanche's officials certainly played a part. Some of the details are to be found in the letters of pardon issued to persons involved in the episode. Secousse, *Receuil,* pp. 88–89, 102; *Froissart,* ed. Luce, Vol. V, pp. 119–20; p. xxxvi, n. 3; Delachenal, *Histoire de Charles V,* II, 8–10. Why Jean de Venette dates this by stating that the queen was staying there before Christmas is obscure.

108. A omits *vel ascendere;* the translation follows Géraud.

109. A adds *nec* after *quia.*

110. Jean le Bel (*Chronique,* II, 272) records that no merchants could leave Paris because of the Navarrese at Melun and Mantes, and that nothing could come to Paris. In consequence prices were so high that a cask of herrings cost 30 or 40 écus. According to him most of the Parisians favored Charles of Navarre, and in consequence the regent dared not leave the city for fear it would be turned over to the Navarrese.

111. This unsuccessful attack on Melun lasted from June 18 until July 31, 1359. *Froissart,* ed. Luce, Vol. V, p. xlviii, n. 2.

112. This refers to the peace of Pontoise of Aug. 21, 1359. For the difficulties and delays relative to Melun see Delachenal, *Histoire de Charles V,* II, 130–31.

113. Jean le Bel (*Chronique,* II, 268–69) expresses himself in similar vein. "Thus the noble kingdom of France, the noblest of the noble, which should have been a refuge of peace and security, was unjustly confounded and oppressed." For although the French "guarded each good town as best they

could, they left the countryside to be pillaged and ravaged, [because] always they were fearful of treason, and always they had great suspicion of each other. Wherefore the knights and gentlemen of the kingdom dared not undertake to do anything, because if they had any misadventure, at once they were suspected of treason." A adds *pro illo tunc* after *apposito*.

114. A reads *notabile* for *nobile*.

115. Jean de Venette is slightly confused here. The English took the castle presumably some time in August. The regent ordered its recovery, and the bishop, certain Picard nobles, and the communal militia from Tournai and elsewhere laid siege. Jean de Picquigny, captain of La Hérelle, and Robert de Picquigny, captain of Creil, gathered together an Anglo-Navarrese relieving force. Battle was joined Aug. 23, 1358. The besiegers were defeated because "the men of the towns took to flight while the gentlemen were taken prisoner, to the number of six score or thereabouts. And the bishop of Noyon was captured and carried off to Creil."—*Chronique . . . de Jean II,* I, 213–14. Froissart says that a hundred knights and squires were captured, and fifteen hundred men were killed, of whom seven hundred were men from Tournai (ed. Luce, V, 124–25). Sir Thomas Gray reports one bishop, four barons, and fifty knights captured (*Scalacronica,* p. 134). The bishop was Gilles de Lorris, son of Robert de Lorris, seigneur d'Erme-nonville. *Froissart,* ed. Luce, Vol. V, p. xxxviii, n. 3; p. xxxix, n. 2. He became prisoner of King Edward, presumably by purchase and because of his importance, and was held for a ransom of 9,000 écus, 50 marks of silver, and a good courser worth 100 gold moutons. Rymer, *Foedera,* Vol. III, Part 2, p. 217.

116. There is a small controversy as to the date of the English occupation of Creil. Luce (*Froissart,* Vol. V, p. xxxvii, n. 5) puts it before the middle of July, 1358. He bases this on an act of pardon given to a man, who describes how he escaped on Oct. 13, 1358, after thirteen weeks of captivity at Creil. This document is published in Boursier, *Histoire de la ville et châtellenie de Creil,* pp. 93–94. While this document seems to be quite explicit, both Meyer (*Charles II,* p. 128) and Delachenal (*Histoire de Charles V,* II, 6, 12) insist that it must have been in early August. Sir Thomas Gray, after telling of the Navarrese forces around Paris when Marcel was killed and when King Charles issued his defiance (Aug. 3), remarks, "In marching thence they took the town of Creil by assault."—*Scalacronica,* p. 133. This supports the theory of an early August date. If we may assume, even with hesitation, a certain amount of accuracy as to detail in Jean de Venette's account, his assertion as to Creil, Remy, and La Hérelle, that the English "now hold" (*jam tenebant*) these places, helps to date the writing of this

section as before October–November, 1359, when the Anglo-Navarrese occupation of Creil ended (see p. 95). It is also after Aug. 21, 1359, because he refers to the peace of Pontoise.

117. Luce has compiled a "Tableau des lieux forts occupés en France par les compagnies anglo-navarraises de 1356 à 1364" as an appendix to his *Histoire de Bertrand du Guesclin,* 2d ed. (Paris, 1882), pp. 459–509. For the occupation of Remy near Compiègne Jean de Venette is the only source. *Ibid.,* p. 493.

118. Ibid., pp. 491–92. Occupied by the Navarrese sometime in 1358; evacuated under the treaty of Pontoise.

119. *Ibid.,* pp. 499–500. About July, 1359, it was surrendered to the regent's men.

120. Robert Knolles took this place in October, 1358. *Chronique . . . de Jean II,* I, 218–19.

121. Luce, *op. cit.,* p. 480, gives Jean de Venette as the only source.

122. A adds *ecclesia et* after *monasteria.*

123. See p. 95.

124. Géraud (II, 279) prints *nequeo* in brackets but without comment. The word is lacking in A but is included in the translation since the context clearly demands it.

125. A reads *resistentibus* for *obsistentibus.* Knighton, *Chronicon,* II, 102. This was part of the raid by Knolles in October, 1358, referred to above.

126. A adds *super menia* after *excubias.*

127. A reads *festina* for *serotina.*

128. A reads *tractactis* for *pulsatis.*

129. This was on Jan. 8, 1359. *Chronique . . . de Jean II,* I, 225.

130. A reads *homines* for *nobiles.*

131. A reads *ad* for *apud.*

132. The English occupied La Ferté, Nov. 6, 1358. Delachenal, *Histoire de Charles V,* II, 14, n. 1. It was at this point that they stopped traffic on the Marne. *Chronique . . . de Jean II,* I, 218.

133. A puts *de se* after *fortalitia* instead of after *munierunt.*

134. A adds *forsitan* after *invaderunt.*

135. A reads *Et in hiis locis de nocte cum uxoribus et liberis tuicior accubabant et de die supra turres,* etc. for *Et de nocte supra turres,* etc.

136. A reads *ad ecclesias [sic forterias] citissime currentes [in illo refugio].* The words in brackets are lacking in Géraud.

137. A reads *logiis et tuguriis tam in naviculis quam in insulis ad sui salvationem cum familia et pecudibus [manufaciis].* With the exception of the last word in brackets this agrees with the reading in Géraud's early MS

(II, 280, n. 3) which he does not put in his text. A contemporary letter deals with this same subject.

In A.D. 1358 the English came to Chantecocq and took the castle on the eve of All Saints [Oct. 31]. At the same time they burned almost all of the town and afterwards reduced the whole countryside to their control, ordering the towns, both great and small, to ransom all their possessions, viz., bodies, goods, and movables, or else they would burn the houses. This they did in many places. Confounded and completely terrorized in this fashion, very many of the people submitted to the English, paying them money by way of ransom and agreeing to provide them with cash, flour, oats, and many other necessary supplies, if they would stop for a while the aforementioned persecution, because they had already killed many men in different places. Some they shut up in very dark dungeons, threatening them daily with death, and continually punishing them with whippings, wounds, hunger, and want beyond belief. But others had nothing with which to pay ransom or they were unwilling to submit to the power of the English. To escape from their hands these made themselves huts in the woods and there ate their bread with fear, sorrow, and great anguish. But the English learned of this and they resolutely sought out these hiding places, searching numerous woods and putting many men to death there. Some they killed, others they captured, still others escaped. Among the latter I, Hugh de Montgeron, prior of Brailet in the parish of Domats, in the deanery of Courtenay, the diocese of Sens, contrived a hiding place in the Bois de les Queues beyond the swamp of the lord of Villebon and there remained with many of my neighbors seeing and hearing every day about the vicious and wicked deeds of our enemies, namely, houses burned and many dead left lying in brutal fashion through the villages and hamlets. Seeing and hearing such things, I decided on the Sunday [Oct. 20] after Saint Luke's day to go to the city and remain there. But it happened that very night that these wicked English found their way to my hut so quietly that, in spite of the watchfulness of our sentinels, they almost captured me while I was asleep. But by God's grace and through the help of the Blessed Virgin Mary I was awakened by the noise they made and escaped naked, taking nothing with me because of my haste except a habit with a hood. Crossing into the middle of the swamp I stayed there shivering and shaking with the cold, which was very great at the time, while my hut was completely despoiled. Afterwards I went to Sens to the house of John Paysan, a priest and one of my relations, who received me kindly, showing me such charity from the goods that God had bestowed upon him that it is impossible for me adequately to describe it. And still [the English] never stopped coming to our aforementioned house, sending me letters threatening destruction and intimating that they would set it on fire unless I came to them under safe conduct which they would send me. On this account I went and obtained from them a respite from the feast of Saint Peter's throne [Feb. 22, 1359] until the feast of Saint John the Baptist [June 24, 1359]. But little good this did because the man who was captain at that time was taken prisoner by the French, and so all my trouble went for nothing. So I lived in the midst of troubles from the feast of All Saints until the feast of the Baptist. But again they took me prisoner, but, not recognizing me, they left their booty behind because there was so little of it, for which God be praised. During this time they stripped the house of all movable goods, they drank up four *queues* of wine, they carried off a *modius* of oats according to the measure in use at Courtenay, they took all my clothes, and at Easter [April 21, 1359] and again on the Sunday [June 30, 1359] after the feast of Saint Peter and Saint Paul they ate up the pigeons. And so by God's grace, I have escaped in the name of the Lord out of their hands up until now. But unless I wish to lose thirty arpents of the best grain, it is necessary to make again a settlement with these fellows lest worse happen and the last state of affairs be worse than the first.

I am writing this out behind our barn on Wednesday, the festival of Saint Martin, 1359, because I do not dare write elsewhere. Do you who live in cities and castles ever see trouble equal to my trouble? Farewell.

HUGH

—Published in *Bib. de l'Ecole des chartes,* XVIII (1857), 357–60. The feast of the Translation of Saint Martin, July 4, was on Wednesday in 1358; in 1359 it was on Thursday.

138. A adds *ceperunt* after *intraverunt.*

139. A reads *relinquerunt* for *abierunt.* Since Dec. 8, 1358, Robert Knolles had been established at Regennes castle near Auxerre. An English attack on Auxerre on Jan. 10, 1359, had been repulsed. But on March 10 the city was taken by surprise. The booty gained on this occasion is remarked upon by other chroniclers. The English destroyed the defenses of the city and withdrew April 30. *Chronique . . . de Jean II,* I, 226–29; Delachenal, *Histoire de Charles V,* II, 34–36. Sir Thomas Gray (*Scalacronica,* p. 140) tells how the English "threw to the ground a great deal of the city wall, and went off to their fortresses in the neighborhood, which seemed more convenient to them than the city, because they could not well live together, as each one claimed to be master." According to him the citizens promised to pay a large ransom, but succeeded in evading payment. If this last is true, it becomes easier to understand why Robert Knolles in 1366, for the good of his soul, forgave the citizens their debt to him. Abbé Lebeuf, *Mémoires concernant l'histoire civile et ecclésiastique d'Auxerre,* IV, 194, No. 311.

140. Jean le Bel, *Chronique,* II, 277; *Froissart,* ed. Luce, V, 135, 184, 352; Gray, *Scalacronica,* p. 142. Like Jean de Venette, these other chroniclers merely mention this. A reads *Espernatum* for *Spernacum.*

141. A adds *Velly.* Occupied by the English and Navarrese in September, 1358. *Froissart,* ed. Luce, Vol. V, p. xxxix, n. 5; Gray, *Scalacronica,* p. 143.

142. No other chronicler has anything to this effect about Soissons, but Froissart (ed. Luce, V, 152–57) has a story about Châlons which sounds enough like this so that it is possible that the two chroniclers are referring to the same event. Géraud lacks the last three sentences of this paragraph. A reads *sic quam patriam* [*circa Remensum usque Catalanum et Suessionem*] *equitabant nemine resistente. Everunt post haec Suessionis et civitatem intraverunt fortiter praeliantes et eam tunc cepissent. Sed ibi fuit unus miles nomine incognitus qui cum suis se viriliter opposuit et ipsos eiecit. Modo* [*similiter*], etc. The words in brackets appear in Géraud, except that it reads *circa Remis*.

143. A reads *triumphum* for *victoriam*.

144. A reads *ii°et lx* for *ducenti et quadraginta*.

145. Henry of Poitiers was bishop of Troyes, and Henry V, sire de Joinville, was count of Vaudemont. This affair took place on Jan. 12, 1359. *Chronique . . . de Jean II,* I, 225. Sir Thomas Gray (*Scalacronica*, p. 139) writes, "In the same season the English before Troyes were defeated through their own bad management by Count Wadmond, who sallied from the city before which the English were in ambush, having sent their scouts to the barriers of the said city, placing them unskillfully, so that the enemy, unperceived by them, sent some light horse into the middle of the ambush, which was in a village, where [the English] were dispersed in the houses, so that they could not rally, but it was each one for himself. Some were taken; [but] the knight John of Dalton and others withdrew in good order."

146. According to the *Chronique . . . de Jean II* (I, 180) the houses and castles of the seigneur de Montmorency had been destroyed during the Jacquerie.

147. A reads *captivos deducentes* for *ducentes*.

148. The captain of Creil for about a year, 1358–59, was John Fotheringay. "He provided safe conducts for all men who wished to go from Paris to Noyon, or from Paris to Compiègne, or from Compiègne to Soissons or Laon and the neighboring frontiers, and the issuing of safe-conducts during the time he was at Creil was worth a hundred thousand francs." *Froissart,* ed. Luce, V, 121. A reads *brevatore* for *litteratorie*.

149. A adds *eorum* before *nobilia*.

1359

1. Easter was April 21, 1359.

2. See Garnier, "Notice sur Robert de Fiennes, connétable de France (1320–1384)," *Bib. de l'Ecole des chartes,* XIII (1852), 23–52. He was also

called Moreau de Fiennes. He became constable in succession to the duke of Athens, killed at Poitiers.

3. Froissart's story of a siege of Saint-Valéry from August, 1358, until Easter, 1359 (ed. Luce, V, 131–33, 141–44), is not now accepted. Luce (*Histoire de Bertrand du Guesclin*, p. 506) puts the English occupation of Saint-Valéry a little before October, 1358 (*Chronique normande du XIVe siècle,* p. 121). His study of the documents relative to the constable and the count of Saint-Pol demonstrates that the siege was between March 15 and April 29, 1359 (*Froissart,* Vol. V, p. xliv, n. 1). Jean de Venette fails to indicate that the expedition of Philip of Navarre into Vermandois, which he describes a couple of paragraphs farther on, was made as an attempt to raise the siege of Saint-Valéry.

4. Froissart (ed. Luce, V, 176) says the men of Noyon paid 12,000 moutons and that the English withdrew to Creil, Clermont, La Hérelle, Vailly, Pierrepont, Roucy, and Sissonne. Luce has nothing to offer in support of this passage in Froissart except this section of Jean de Venette (*ibid.,* Vol. V, p. lii, n. 2). A adds *et specialiter turrem qui fortis erat et sollempnis* after *dictum castrum.*

5. A reads *securiora* for *secura.*

6. A adds *liquide* before *manifestant.*

7. A reads *Frafagues* for *Frasagnes.*

8. A adds *de patria velociter* after *comitiva.*

9. A adds *videbant non posse illos evadere si eis insultus citissime conferietur* after *cupiebat.* This clarifies the meaning of the words which follow, upon which Géraud (II, 284, n. 1) has a comment.

10. A omits *et aliis* after *patria.*   11. A reads *inhibuit* for *prohibuit.*

12. A omits *ad suum libitum* before *spoliis,* and *ultionem* after *corporibus.*

13. Froissart (ed. Luce, V, 144–52) is the chief source for this successful maneuver. Delachenal (*Histoire de Charles V,* II, 43–45) interprets this as the account of a very skillful retreat in the face of superior numbers. It may be noted that the aristocratic Froissart places the ultimate blame for failure on the citizens of Saint-Quentin, in contrast with Jean de Venette's echoes of the popular discontent with the constable. Sir Thomas Gray (*Scalacronica,* pp. 142–43) tells how, near Saint-Quentin, the six hundred English under Philip of Navarre, faced forty-five hundred French, "scarcely further off than the range of an arblast . . . and lay before them all day without fighting. In the evening the said English billeted themselves in a village near at hand, and marched off at noon on the next day, in the direction of Soissons, burning the country without any interference from the said French."

14. For an extensive study of the attack on Melun see Delachenal, *Histoire de Charles V*, II, 108–19. For later historians the participation of Bertrand du Guesclin in this attack is a matter of interest, but to Jean de Venette, writing in 1359–60, this meant nothing.

15. A omits *et notabiles* after *nobiles*.

16. A adds *partis* after *utriusque*.

17. Géraud edited the text to read *recusabant,* although indicating (II, 285, n. 3) that all his MSS read *recusantes*. A agrees with the other MSS.

18. A adds *diu* after *consulibus*.

19. Jean de Venette is somewhat confused as to details of the points at issue. The original basis of agreement was "that the regent should return to the king of Navarre all the lands and fortresses which he held of him, and in addition lands bringing in 12,000 livres annually and 6,000 écus of King John, and for twelve years to pay him 50,000 livres a year." This does not signify Champagne, to which Charles of Navarre had laid claim publicly. As to towns and castles in Normandy, the negotiations broke down after both parties had agreed to the terms as set forth, because Charles of Navarre demanded that the lands bringing in 12,000 livres a year should be the Norman vicomtés of Falaise, Bayeux, Auge, and Vire. *Chronique . . . de Jean II,* I, 238, 242.

20. "And many said that God had inspired the king to speak as he did." —*Chronique . . . de Jean II,* I, 243.

21. A adds *vel per similia* before *prout*.

22. A reads *assistentibus* for *existentibus*.

23. A adds *immensum* after *laetantibus*.

24. The account of this episode in the official chronicle (*ibid.*) is more detailed, but is in general agreement with Jean de Venette's account. In some respects the latter seems to echo the letter of Aug. 21, 1359, sent by the regent to the city of Montpellier (and presumably to other cities) as a sort of official communiqué. Delachenal, *Histoire de Charles V,* II, 437, No. xxxiv. Philip of Navarre refused to abandon the English alliance and retired into the Cotentin. *Froissart,* ed. Luce, V, 163.

25. The story of this episode is the special feature of Jean de Venette's chronicle. It is suggested that it was the news of this affair which gave Jean the impulse to write his history. The affair attracted enough attention to be recorded in another version, omitting Grandferré, which was widely copied, although Géraud does not seem to have known of any other account (II, 288, n. 1). This other account is inferior to that of Jean de Venette. The continuator of the chronicle of Richard Lescot mentions Grandferré, but it seems quite clear that he is merely summarizing Jean de Venette. For the

correct name of Guillaume l'Aloue, see S. Luce, "Notice sur Guillaume l'Aloue," *Annuaire-Bulletin de la Soc. de l'hist. de France,* 1875, pp. 149–56, reprinted in his *La France pendant la guerre de cent ans;* see also *Froissart,* ed. Luce, Vol. V, p. xxxvii, n. 5. Luce becomes lyrical in his enthusiasm for this peasant who should occupy a place of honor in French annals and whose name should appear in every history of France, even the most elementary. Michelet eloquently couples his name with that of Jeanne d'Arc. Neither of these authors, presumably, ever saw Sir Thomas Gray's *Scala-cronica.* The following translation of the more common French account of this affair is from the chronicle of Jean de Noyal ("Fragment de la chronique inédite de Jean de Noyal, abbé de Saint-Vincent-de-Laon, relatif à Guillaume l'Aloue," *Annuaire-Bulletin de la Soc. de l'hist. de France,* 1875, pp. 155–56, p. j. No. 2 of Luce's "Notice sur Guillaume l'Aloue").

In the year 1359 Philip of Navarre and Robert Knolles took the city of Auxerre [March 10, 1359], which certain citizens betrayed to them for money. And after this atrocity there gathered together in arms about three hundred peasants of the Beauvaisis, and their leader was named Guillaume l'Aloue; and they waged war against the English who were then in many fortresses in that region, repeatedly committing great depredation. And the peasants had their retreat at Longueil-Sainte-Marie. It was a house surrounded with walls but without other means of defense, except that the gate was defensible. Then more than seventeen hundred English from many fortresses gathered together and went in broad daylight to attack this house. And some six hundred of them got over the walls because the peasants could not defend them. And the peasants took refuge in a tall building, where they had lodged their wives and children to be out of the way because of their outcry. And the English rushed about seizing provisions and horses and whatever they could find. Others brought fire and threatened to set the building ablaze if the peasants did not surrender, to be killed without ransom. Then the peasants took counsel together and decided that it was better to die defending themselves. So they all came down together making great outcry and shouting many slogans, and rushed on the English and defeated them. More than eight score of the latter were killed, of whom twenty-four were knights. But of the peasants only two were killed, of whom Guillaume l'Aloue, their captain, was one. And because of his death they were unwilling to hold anyone for ransom, except one named Sancho Lopez, in return for whom were exchanged a hundred captives from Compiègne whom the English held in many fortresses. And after this event these peasants dug ditches around that building, and named Colart Sade captain. And they received into their stronghouse all those of the countryside who wished to protect themselves in bodies and goods, except men of noble lineage, but no noble could take refuge in their place. And they sustained many strong attacks on the part of their enemies and held their place throughout the whole course of the war.

This same account in Latin is in the *Chronographia,* II, 287–88. It will also be found in the *Chronique normande du XIVe siècle,* pp. 146–48, and in the *Chronique des Pays-bas* (in De Smet, ed., *Corpus chronicorum Flandriae,* III, 198), and in the *Chronique de Berne,* quoted by Kervyn de Lettenhove in his edition of Froissart (VI, 487–88). The last paragraph shows that this account was written longer after the event than was Jean de Venette's. These two French accounts should be compared with the contemporary English version of this affair which is told by Sir Thomas Gray in *Scalacronica* (pp. 140–41).

John of Fotheringay, with other English captains [coming] out of the town of Creil, attacked a fortress and an abbey which the French had fortified between the said Creil and Compiègne, carried the palisade and the fosses with the base court,[when] those within treated for their lives with those without. The captain of the garrison came out and surrendered to the pennon of one of the English commanders, whereat one and another of the English took offense, wrangling for a share in his ransom, so that in the strife he was murdered among them. He to whom [the captain] had surrendered went off straightway in a rage, telling them that it served them right. Those within the fortress, seeing that they were bound to die, with one consent descended a vaulted stair with such din— shouting and clattering of shields and staves, with other noises, yelling the different war cries of the chief men of the country—that the English who had remained fell into such a sudden panic, believing that they had been betrayed, partly because of the departure of the said captain who had gone off in a rage in the manner [described], partly by the bold front and spirit of the enemy, that they fell back in disorder, each man falling over the others in the deep water of the ditches, where five or six English knights and several others were drowned. Others who could get on horseback fled, and thus the people of the fortress were saved, being for the most part only *Brigauntz* and common folk of the band of Jacques Bonhomme.

This English report of the behavior of the local French captain may be compared with Jean de Venette's story of the French leaders at Châtres. See pp. 100–101.

26. In Géraud the name is spelled *Longolium,* but in A, at this point, it appears as *Longovolium.* Later the shorter form is used.

27. Géraud reads *Ysarae adjacente,* but there is an editorial comment (II, 288, n. 2) stating that *interjacente* should be substituted. A reads *Ysarae mediante* which requires no substitution.

28. A adds *forsitan* before *locum.*

29. A adds *de unicis fortiter* before *defensarent.*

30. A reads *saltantes* for *salientes.*

31. Géraud reads *sic viam se inter et fossatum,* but indicates (II, 291, n. 1)

that his oldest MS reads *sic viam et inter fossatum,* and his two late MSS read *sic viam inter fossatum.* A reads *sic viam et inter ad fossatum.*

32. A reads *Grandus Ferratus* for *Magnus Ferratus,* but later the latter form is used.

33. A reads *lx* for *quadraginta.*

34. A adds *in primo aggressu* after *praelio.*

35. A adds *audierant* before *ponderosis.*

36. A adds *et valorem* after *fortitudinem.*

37. A reads *huic vice* for *illa die;* the translation follows Géraud.

38. A adds *cum uxore* after *propriam.*

39. A reads *in grabato* for *in lecto.*

40. A adds *seu guysarmiam* before *ponderosam.*

41. A adds *plures* before *percusserat.*

42. A reads *potenter immittit* for *mittit.*

43. A adds *confusabiliter* after *fugam.*

44. A reads *convalescente* for *invalescente.*

45. A reads *putate* for *factae.*

46. A reads *acuriate* for *activatae.*   47. A reads *aves* for *oves.*

48. This descriptive passage is peculiar to the Arundel text (fol. 14), and gives strong support to the greater authenticity of that text, because this is the sort of passage which a copyist might well omit, but which he would never insert. The Latin text follows:

Gallus non cantavit pro horis profunde noctis nunciandis. Sed nec gallina provocavit pullos suos. Non erat opus milvo insidiari pulliculis in Marcio huius anni, nec puelli per latibula ova quere gallinarum. Non faciebat in illis partibus agniculus balatum post matrem sed nec vitulus mugitabat. Querere poterat alibi lupus predam suam et de herbis virentibus replere et non de arietibus capaces fauces suos. Tunc saltabant per desertos agros libere cuniculi et lepores canes venaticos non timentes cum nemo esset ausus eos ducere per solaciosos decursus nemorum vel agrorum. Alaude tute levabantur per aera exaltando garribundos cantus suos nisi vel falconis sibilosos impetus nescientes. Non procedebant per itinera viatores. Ad forum autem caseos meliores et lactionia non ferebant. Per parochias et villagia pro confessionibus et predicationibus in xl, prohdolor!, non exiebant pauperes mendicantes sed pocius predones et latrones qui quidquid invenire poterant publice rapiebant.

This passage seems to have a sort of literary kinship with the description of conditions produced by the Black Death written by Jean de Venette's contemporary Guillaume de Machaut and quoted above (p. 190, n. 25). This term "eyas" (Latin *nisus*) signifies "a young hawk taken from the nest for the purpose of training, or one whose training is incomplete" (*Oxford*

English Dictionary). For a study of the desolated countryside see Boutruche, "La Dévastation des campagnes pendant la guerre de cent ans et
la reconstruction agricole de la France," in *Mélanges 1945,* Vol. III, *Etudes
historiques,* pp. 127–63.

49. Géraud's text reads *flammis voracibus consumpta* in accordance with
the two late MSS, but Géraud (II, 294, n. 1) remarks that his early MS
reads *flammis voracibus crebris.* A has this latter reading.

50. Géraud's text reads *ante solentibus,* but Géraud (II, 294, n. 2) remarks
that there should be a verb here. A reads *videre solentibus.*

51. A omits *eorum;* the translation follows Géraud.

52. A reads *inimici* for *Anglici.*

53. A reads *versus Laudunensis* for *Laudunensis dioecesis.*

54. According to Jean le Bel (*Chronique,* II, 278 ff., 283–84) and Froissart (ed. Luce, V, 136–37) the English company at Vailly-sur-Aisne (see
p. 85) ravaged the region about Soissons, Laon, and Reims. On Christmas,
1358, Robert Scot, one of the English captains, very savagely took Roucy
castle by surprise, capturing Count Robert II, with his wife and daughter,
and holding them for a ransom of 12,000 florins. After paying this the
count went to Laon. In the following spring he joined with the count of
Porcien and the citizens of Laon to attack the English company at Sissonne.
Here Count Robert was captured a second time, and his captors turned him
over to Robert Scot, who imprisoned him in his own castle of Roucy, where
he still remained in May, 1359, at the time Jean le Bel was writing. About
mid-August, 1359, a force gathered from Reims, Champagne, and Rethel,
led by the archbishop of Reims and the count of Porcien, besieged Roucy for
about three weeks, and regained it by an agreement releasing the count and
permitting the safe departure of the English garrison. "But the greater
part of them were killed by the common people, contrary to the agreement
made by the lords," and the English captain, Frank Hannequin, was taken
to Reims to be executed, contrary to the promise of the lords, but in the
end they got him released. "It was a pity and an evil thing that all those who
were found in that castle did not die a cruel death, or that God did not make
them all mad, because Saracens could not have been more inhuman to
Christians than they had been to the countryside. For time and again,
which is wonderful to relate, when they had laid a siege so that no one
could possibly escape, instead of ransoming the great crowd of prisoners,
they made them, men and women, mount the walls all naked and then
with two or three blows of their swords made them leap down." An example of what one of these companies could do appears in the story of the
garrison at Beauvoir (in the Bourbonnais) "where the English had dug a

hole named 'Hell' . . . so that when they have taken any prisoners who will not or cannot pay ransoms, they say 'To Hell with them' (*menez les en enfer*), and they throw them into this hole full of fire, so that everyone is so terrified that when anyone is captured he pays whatever they desire for fear of being thrown into 'Hell.' " When the French ultimately took this place all the survivors of the English garrison except the captain were thrown into their own "Hell."—*La Chronique du bon duc Loys de Bourbon,* pp. 16, 19–20.

55. A reads *de Credolio seu Creillio.*

56. According to the *Chronique . . . de Jean II* (I, 247–48) Charles of Navarre, after the peace of Pontoise, in September 1359, could not carry out his promise to surrender Creil, because he owed the captain 6,000 royals. The city of Paris loaned him this sum, but the captain refused unless he were paid more. Sir Thomas Gray (*Scalacronica*, p. 147) writes, "An English knight, John of Fotheringay, held this town of Creil in keeping for the king of Navarre, on sworn condition to deliver it on notice from the said king. He often received summons [to deliver it], but refused to do so failing a large sum of money which he declared the said king owed him, which money he received from the French in discharge of the said debt and handed over the said town to them." Delachenal (*Histoire de Charles V,* II, 131) comments that he does not know by what arrangement the English agreed to evacuate Creil late in October, 1359 (see below, n. 58), but it would seem a reasonable assumption, combining the statements of Jean de Venette and Sir Thomas Gray, that the men of Senlis and Compiègne added enough to the sum provided by Paris to meet Fotheringay's demands. A diplomatic document of Nov. 15, 1361, shows that Fotheringay was paid 24,000 royals plus 2,000 royals paid for ransoming Sancho Lopez and John Scot. Chaplais, "Some Documents Regarding the Fulfilment and Interpretation of the Treaty of Bretigny (1361–1369)," in *Camden Miscellany,* XIX (1952), 44.

57. *Chronique . . . de Jean II* (I, 250) says that on Nov. 12, 1359, the tower at Ponte-Sainte-Maxence was captured by certain English prisoners held therein. This seems more explicit than Jean de Venette, and, in general, this chronicle is more accurate as to chronology than Jean de Venette. A question of the date for the evacuation of Creil is involved here. If this statement about Pont-Sainte-Maxence is true, presumably the garrison of Creil did not take Pont-Sainte-Maxence, but withdrew to it after it had been taken. See following note.

58. The same chronicle (p. 250) says that on Monday, Nov. 18, 1359, "before daybreak the castle of Clermont in Beauvaisis was taken by escalade

and the town also by a Gascon called the Captal de Buch [Jean de Grailly], a partisan of the English king, who had come to the king of Navarre, his cousin and very dear friend, at Mantes, under a safe-conduct from the regent, issued by the regent at the urgent request of the king of Navarre. And he took the castle and town of Clermont during the safe conduct." This last explains Jean de Venette's "dishonestly." According to Sir Thomas Gray (*Scalacronica,* p. 147) the Captal de Buch "came to Creil, which was then held by the English, from which town he took the castle of Clermont." He then recounts the English sale of Creil as quoted above, n. 56. He also states that Fotheringay "strengthened" Pont-Sainte-Maxence and remained there, not that he took it. If the sequence indicated here is valid, the English evacuation of Creil should be put late in November instead of October. This has some bearing on the question of dating the writing of this section (see p. 11).

59. For record of this destruction, see Denifle, *La Désolation des églises,* Vol. I, Nos. 105–7, 109, 110, 140, 954.

60. Sir Thomas Gray (*Scalacronica,* pp. 130–31) has an interesting passage on this.

In the same season, truce having been struck as aforesaid (April 5, 1357–June 24, 1359), numbers of Englishmen who lived by war invaded Normandy, plundered castles, seized manors, and carried on such warlike operations in the country by help of those of the English commonalty who flocked to them daily against the king's prohibition. It was astonishing how they went in bands, each on his own account, without an appointed chieftain, and wrought much oppression in the country. They levied tribute from nearly all Normandy and the borders of the neighboring lands, securing for themselves good fortresses in Poitou, Anjou, and Maine, and into fair France itself within six leagues of Paris. They were scattered in so many places over different parts of the country that nobody could recount the combats and deeds of arms which befell them during this time; but they so acted that all Christian people were filled with astonishment. And yet they were but a gathering of commons, young fellows who hitherto had been but small account, who became exceedingly rich and skillful in this [kind of] war, wherefore the youth of many parts of England went to join them.

See also *Froissart,* ed. Luce, V, 125–26.

61. Edward crossed from Sandwich to Calais on Oct. 28, 1359. Delachenal, *Histoire de Charles V,* II, 148 n. 4. He was accompanied by four of his sons. The poet Chaucer was in the retinue of Lionel of Clarence. Sir Thomas Gray participated in this expedition. Ramsay, *Genesis of Lancaster,* I, 434–35.

62. Henry Plantagenet was King Edward's second cousin and chief

counselor. Created earl of Derby in 1337, he became the first duke of Lancaster in 1351. His daughter Blanche married the king's third son, John of Gaunt, and the latter, as her husband, eventually succeeded to the Lancaster title. Hitherto Jean de Venette has ignored Lancaster, although the latter had been playing a very active part in the war, particularly in Guienne during 1345–47 (see p. 178, n. 71) and in the Norman-Breton campaigns of 1356–57. On this expedition of 1359 he crossed in advance of the king, landing at Calais Oct. 1, 1359. See *Froissart,* ed. Luce, V, 191–93.

63. This army numbered about twelve thousand men, "a vast expeditionary force, only surpassed by the Crécy-Calais armies."—Prince, "The Strength of English Armies in the Reign of Edward III," *Eng. Hist. Rev.,* XLVI (1931), 367–68.

64. A reads *iterum est ingressus* for *iterum est reversus.*

65. This refers to Lancaster's activity during October. The attack on Bray must have been Oct. 30. The impression made by its brave defense is reflected in letters from the regent in January rewarding the townsmen. *Froissart,* ed. Luce, Vol. V, p. 193; p. lvii, n. 2; Gray, *Scalacronica,* pp. 145–46.

66. Sir Thomas Gray gives a detailed account of the march to Reims (*Scalacronica,* pp. 146–50). See also *Froissart,* ed. Luce, V, 199–211. The English king set out from Calais Nov. 4, 1359. He arrived before Reims Dec. 4. Delachenal, *Histoire de Charles V,* II, 150–54.

67. This peculiar expression is probably to be associated with the prophecies of Jean de la Roche-Taillade, wherein he tells of a struggle between the league of Antichrist, viz., the emperor supported by the duke of Aquitaine, the king of England, several Spanish kings, and certain German princes related to Lewis the Bavarian, with "the new Maccabees," viz., the pope, the king of France, and Charles of Bohemia. An opponent of the "new Maccabees" would be a new Antiochus. Kampers, *Die deutsche Kaiseridee in Prophetie und Sage,* p. 117.

68. H. Moranvillé, "Le Siège de Reims, 1359–1360," *Bib. de l'Ecole des chartes,* LVI (1895), 90–98.

69. A reads *circa civitatem* for *ante civitatem.*

70. Even in Scotland reports of Edward's devastation excited comment. "Respecting no spot or province, he reduced to an endless waste even the noblest monasteries, and other stately places of sundry religious orders, as well as abbeys of nuns, after having destroyed all their substance upon earth. No one in the French kingdom durst lift his head against him, or fight against him in any way; but with unhindered foot went he into boroughs and fortresses, towns and cities, perpetrating countless massacres."

—John of Fordun, *Chronicle,* in *The Historians of Scotland,* IV, 368. Sir Thomas Gray (*Scalacronica,* pp. 161–62) shows the point of view of one of Edward's followers when he writes of the "grievous labors" of this campaign "which . . . lasted nine months, in which [the English] had traversed as much of France as they were able, courting combat to maintain the right of their lord, finding nowhere encouragement in this task, but subsisting all the time upon the country, sometimes in plenty, at other times according to what they could find in a country wasted and raided before their coming."

71. *Chronique . . . de Jean II,* I, 253–54; *Chronique des quatre premiers Valois,* pp. 105–6. For Edward's itinerary, see Richard Lescot, *Chronique,* Appendix, pp. 208–9.

72. This refers to the treaty of Guillon, March 10, 1360, published in Rymer, *Foedera,* Vol. III, Part 1, pp. 195–97.

73. This dates the writing of this section with considerable exactitude.

74. A reads *aliquod facere* for *hoc facere.*

75. The account in the *Scalacronica* is:

At the same time William de Aldborough, captain of Honfleur in Normandy, was taken by the French in a sortie and his people were defeated. An English knight, Thomas Fog, [captain of Auvillers], who was in a fortress of his in the neighborhood, hearing of this affair, threw himself into the said Honfleur, found it displenished of provender, and rode forth with other English garrisons in the neighborhood, foraging in the country for supplies to the said town. They came suddenly upon 250 French men-at-arms and 200 archers and arblasters, who were ambushed on the English line of march, Monsire Louis d'Harcourt and Baudric de la Huse being in command of the French. The English, numbering forty men-at-arms and a hundred archers, had the protection of a hedge. Both sides dismounted and engaged smartly. The French were defeated, their two leaders being captured, and with them several knights and esquires, and several were killed in the melee. Louis d'Harcourt soon afterwards was released by the same English who took him, and they became Frenchmen with him.

—Gray, *Scalacronica,* pp. 151–52. See also *Chronique normande du XIVe siècle,* p. 150, which places this fight at Le Favril, about twenty miles from Pont-Audemer. There is quite a long account of this affair in *Chronique des quatres premiers Valois,* pp. 107–110, 113. The capture of the leading military and naval officials in Normandy seriously crippled the plans for the descent on England described in the next paragraph. Guillaume Martel de Saint-Vigor was captain of Château-Gaillard. Louis of Harcourt, younger brother to Count John V who was beheaded in 1355, had been appointed by the regent lieutenant general for Normandy in March, 1359.

Le Baudrain de la Heuse, marshal of Normandy, had been appointed admiral of France, June 3, 1359. Hellot, *Essai historique sur les Martel de Basqueville;* Secousse, *Recueil,* p. 134.

76. This refers to the period prior to Easter, April 5, 1360.

77. Géraud reads *nolente Domino* and the translation follows this reading, but A reads *volente Domino,* which would make the translation "by God's will or perchance by reason of their own demerits."

78. A reads *maris intraverunt;* Géraud omits *maris.*

79. The actual attack on Winchelsea was on Sunday, March 15, 1360. See La Roncière, *Histoire de la marine française,* I, 513–16; Delachenal, *Histoire de Charles V,* II, 176–84. The English accounts emphasize the atrocities committed by the French and the losses inflicted upon them by the English. Gray, *Scalacronica,* pp. 152–53; John of Reading, *Chronica,* pp. 134–35; Knighton, *Chronicon,* II, 109–10. Delachenal refers to "this enterprise [as] badly conceived, poorly prepared, and of mediocre leadership. It had been organized at first with high hopes. But it degenerated into an exploit of ordinary piracy, without appreciable results, which immediately provoked unfortunate reprisals."

80. A adds *in tanta debilitate erat moneta qui* after *adhuc quae.*

81. A reads *xiii libras* for *viginti libras.* "From 1359 on changes in the value of the coins followed each other in a veritable cascade. In 1359 there were sixteen, in 1360 seventeen."—Bridrey, *La Théorie de la monnaie au XIVe siècle,* p. 502.

82. A reads *x solidi* for *duodecim solidi.*

83. See below, n. 93.

84. According to the *Chronique des quatre premiers Valois* (pp. 101–5) this was accomplished by Robert Scot, who had established himself at Blangy. It occurred very shortly after Louis of Harcourt and Le Baudrain de la Heuse had attacked Blangy. Hence it must have been before their capture at Le Favril (see above, n. 75), which, in turn, must have been before the Winchelsea expedition of March 14–15, 1360. A reads *insula Ade lille Adam* for *Insula Adeliae sive Adam.*

85. A adds *et alios* after *illos.*

86. A adds *sicut faciebant diutius nobiles tam maiores quam alii mediocres* after *sustinebant.*

87. This indicates clearly that Jean de Venette is now writing his chronicle contemporaneously with events. Only under such circumstances would comment on the ordinary aspects of the weather appear.

88. A omits *non* before *vidisse.*   89. A adds *iocundum* after *tale.*

90. A adds *regalis vel* after *florenus.*   91. A reads *xiii* for *xx.*

92. Géraud (II, 301, n. 1) remarks that all his MSS read 12, but that the context indicates that 2 is correct. A agrees with the other MSS.

93. *Chronique . . . de Jean II* (I, 256) reads, "The Monday before Palm Sunday, March 23, 1360, there was published at Paris [an ordonnance on] the money, [to the effect] that the silver penny, which had previously been worth 2 Paris shillings should now be worth tuppence, and the gold royal, which had formerly passed for 14 Paris livres, should be worth 32 Paris shillings. And so a measure of good wheat cost 48 Paris livres or thereabouts in this depreciated money." The text of Jean de Venette is somewhat confused as to the figures. Géraud's text reads that the royal florin was to be worth 20 librae, but A reads 13, which is more nearly in accord with the other chronicle, and may have been a misreading of xiii for a badly written xiv. Both Géraud's text and A make the error of writing 12 Paris denarii, when they should have written 2 as the new value for the white denarius, or silver penny. This depreciation of the money by eleven twelfths of its value indicates the chaos in French finances.

1360

1. From the time they left Calais until they arrived at Châtres the English army marched in three columns, each of which was organized as an independent fighting force. They camped separately about a league apart. One column was led by the king, one by the prince, and the third by the duke. *Froissart,* ed. Luce, V, 226.

2. A reads *per* for *versus.*

3. Where Géraud has modern names in italics, A reads *Castas et Monlleheri.*

4. A reads *gallice Cant de leu iuxta Castas.*

5. King Edward set up his headquarters at Chanteloup on Tuesday, March 31, 1360, and remained there a week, until April 7, when he advanced nearer to the city and lodged at Châtillon. "And on this day many [English] appeared before Paris in battle array, but no one came forth from the city."—*Chronique . . . de Jean II,* I, 256–58.

6. See p. 235, n. 18.

7. Like Géraud, A reads *Oly,* but the corrector wrote *Orly* in the margin.

8. A reads *homines* for *omnes,* and omits *patriae.*

9. Good Friday was April 3, 1360.

10. This passage which begins with "While" and ends here is in A but not in Géraud. It reads [*eos impugnari*] *ceperunt qui viriliter se deffendentes et manu ad manum pugnantes dum non pervidebant de futuro Anglici ab altera parte ecclesie murum fregiunt aliis cum eis pugnantibus.*

Et sic eos a parte posteriori ceperunt [*et interfecerunt*]. The words in brackets are in Géraud, which has *fecerunt* instead of *ceperunt*.

11. A adds *tantus* after *enim*.

12. A reads *sub loco illo de Cantulupi* for *sub campo illo,* etc. This does not require the editorial correction suggested by Géraud (II, 304, n. 1), which substitutes *castro* for *campo.*

13. A adds *in adventu Anglicorum* before *cum mulieribus.*

14. A adds *parva* after *alia.*

15. A reads *ad ledendum* for *ad cedendum.*

16. A reads *pagiacis* for *mangonibus.*

17. A omits *descendo;* the translation follows Géraud.

18. A adds *monachorum* after *claustrum.*

19. A adds *quamtotam* before *miserabiliter.*

20. A adds *merito* before *collandabat.*

21. Luce discovered that the captain in this affair was Philippe de Villebon, and that the place had resisted the English for a week. *Froissart,* Vol. V, p. lxx, n. 1.

22. A reads *facientes* for *figentes.*

23. A adds *postea* after *pro ipsis.*

24. A adds *ut alias* before *igni.*

25. In the *Scalacronica* (p. 153), we read, "And as the said king was marching through Beauce, near Turry, that castle chanced to be set accidentally on fire by those within it; wherefore most of them rushed out and threw themselves on the mercy of the said king. The castellan held the keep for two days and then surrendered to the said king, who caused the walls of the said castle to be razed."

26. April 12, 1360.

27. Géraud (II, 307, n. 1) remarks that all his MSS read *nolentes* but that the context requires *volentes.* A reads *volentes.*

28. A adds *Carturientium* after *monasterium.*

29. In the *Scalacronica* (pp. 156–57) we read,

The said king of England took up his quarters before Paris on Wednesday in Easter week [April 8] in the year of grace 1360, in the villages adjacent to the suburb of Saint-Cloud, across the Seine above Paris. He remained there five days, and in departing displaced himself in order of battle before the king of France's son, who was regent of the country and was in the city with a strong armed force. The prince of Wales, eldest son of the said king of England, who commanded the advance guard, and the duke of Lancaster with another column marched close under the faubourgs from sunrise till mid-day and set them on fire. The king's other columns kept a little farther off. A French knight, Pèlerin de Vadencourt, was captured at the city barriers, where his horse, being wounded by an arrow, had thrown him. [Certain] knights of the prince's retinue, newly dubbed that day, concealed themselves among the suburbs when the said columns marched off, and remained there till some came out of the city, then spurred forth and charged them. Richard de Baskerville the younger, an English knight, was thrown to the ground, and, springing to his feet wounded the horses of the Frenchmen with his sword, and defended himself gallantly till he was rescued, with his horse, by his other comrades, who speedily drove back into their fortress the Frenchmen who came out.

The account in *Chronique . . . de Jean II* (I, 259) puts this on April 12, and implies, without stating it, that this was a demonstration covering the withdrawal of the English army. Froissart also has an account of these episodes (ed. Luce V, 230–32).

30. This is a synonym for Monday, and was a form for referring to the days of the week without using their pagan names.

31. For the other contemporary comments on this storm see Delachenal, *Histoire de Charles V,* II, 191–92. "In this same yere, the xiiii day off Aprill . . . Kyng Edward with his Oost lay byfore the Citee off Parys; the which was a ffoule Derke day off myste, and off haylle, and so bytter colde, that syttyng on horse bak men dyed. Wherefore, unto this day yt ys called blak Monday, and wolle be longe tyme here affter."—*Chronicles of London,* p. 13.

32. All texts read *Compendium,* which means Compiègne, but it is quite clear that the English retreating towards the Chartrain would not be anywhere near Compiègne. Can this refer to the episode, which Froissart (ed. Luce, V, 232–34) tells about, of an ambush by English and Gascons, in which the sire de Campremy was captured?

33. At this point Géraud's text (II, 309) has the sentence *Sequitur ergo de pace et ejus tractatu.* A reads *Sequitur de tractatu pacis.* This brief sentence has not been translated.

34. May 14, 1360.

35. This is a reference to the Introit of the Mass, namely, the psalm which is sung as the celebrant enters the church and advances toward the altar. This Sunday is the fourth after Easter, May 3, 1360. The Introit is *Cantate Domino canticum novum; quia mirabilia fecit Dominus; ante conspectum gentium revelavit justitiam suam.* In the King James translation this is Psalm 98:1–2: "O sing unto the Lord a new song; for he hath done marvellous things . . . his righteousness hath he openly shewed in the sight of the heathen."

36. Negotiations, started by papal mediators, had been attempted as early

as April 3, 1360, but were broken off twice. Late in the month, after withdrawing from before Paris, King Edward intimated a willingness to resume discussion. On April 27 a French delegation left for Chartres. It included Jean de Dormans, bishop of Beauvais and chancellor of Normandy, Jean de Melun, count of Tancarville (not yet ransomed from his Poitiers captors), Jean le Maingre (Marshal Bouçicaut), Simon de Bucy, first president of the Parlement of Paris, and nine other clerics, lawyers and citizens. *Chronique . . . de Jean II*, I, 256–58, 264.

37. The English envoys were the duke of Lancaster, the earls of Northampton, Warwick, Stafford, and Salisbury, Sir Walter Manny, Sir John Chandos, Sir Bartholomew Burghersh, Jean de Grailly, Captal de Buch, and a dozen others. (*Ibid.*, p. 265.) They met the French May 1, 1360, at Brétigny.

38. Delachenal advances the theory that the actual agreement was reached May 3, although public announcement was reserved until the seventh. *Chronique . . . de Jean II*, I, 262 and n. 8; *Histoire de Charles V*, II, 198–99. See Petit-Dutaillis and Collier, "La Diplomatie française et le traité de Brétigny, *Le Moyen Age*, X (1897), 1–35.

39. A adds *de Anglia* after *alios*.

40. A reads *et eius filio* for *et ejus consilio*.

41. A reads *universaliter* for *universis*.

42. A adds *Jehsum* after *Domini*, and omits *in Ecclesia* before *Vocem*.

43. The French envoys with six English knights returned to Paris on May 9. *Chronique . . . de Jean II*, I, 314. In indicating the date, Sunday May 10, 1360, Jean de Venette is again referring to the Introit of the Mass, this time the one for the fifth Sunday after Easter: *Vocem jocunditatis annuntiate, et audiatur; annuntiate usque ad extremum terrae, liberavit Dominus populum suum*. In the King James translation this is part of Isaiah 48:20: "With a voice of singing declare ye, tell this, utter it even to the end of the earth; say ye, The Lord hath redeemed his servant Jacob."

44. A reads *beate Marie* for *Virginis gloriosae*. The translation follows neither literally.

45. In this sentence A reads *accendens* and *accendentes* where Géraud has *accessit* and *accesserunt*.

46. A adds *sollemniter* before *alligarentur*.

47. This ceremony is also described in *Chronique . . . de Jean II*, I, 315–16, and *Froissart*, ed. Luce, VI, 19–21.

48. The text reads *Tunc enim audita est illa die per totam civitatem vox jucunditatis et exultatoris laetitiae in tabernaculis justorum et omnium afflictorum*, and Géraud notes this as another allusion to the Introit. Géraud

omits *exultatoris*. But it would also seem to be somewhat confused in Jean de Venette's mind with the passage, *Haec recordatus sum, et effudi in me animam meam: quoniam transibo in locum tabernaculi admirabilis usque ad domum Dei: in voce exultationes et confessionis, sonus epulantio.* In the King James translation this is Psalm 42:4; "When I remember these things, I pour out my soul in me: for I had gone with the multitude, I went with them to the house of God, with the voice of joy and praise, with a multitude that kept holyday."

49. A adds *finaliter* before *alligarentur*.

50. Géraud (II, 312, n. 1) remarks that all his MSS read *Guynosie*. A does the same. D'Achery, the first editor, corrected this to *Guynarum*.

51. The text of the treaty of Brétigny is in *Chronique . . . de Jean II*, I, 267–300; Rymer, *Foedera*, Vol. III, Part 1, pp. 202–9; Cosneau, *Les Grands Traités de la guerre de cent ans*, pp. 33–68. There is an extensive analysis of the treaty in Delachenal, *Histoire de Charles V*, II, 201–7. In addition to the treaty, the earl of Warwick, on May 13, 1360, made an agreement with the city of Paris by which the latter agreed to pay 12,000 florins for the evacuation of Pont-Sainte-Maxence, La Hérelle, La Neuville-en-Hez, Lihus, Farcheville, Itteville, Boissy-le-Sec, Chevreuse, and La Ferté-sous-Jouarre. The people of the countryside around these places were to pay a like sum. This document is published in Luce, *Histoire de Bertrand du Guesclin*, pp. 543–45. For the most recent discussion of the treaty see Chaplais, "Some Documents Regarding the Fulfilment and Interpretation of the Treaty of Bretigny (1361–1369)," in *Camden Miscellany*, XIX, (1952), 1–84.

52. Six florins were worth one pound sterling, so the ransom was equivalent to £500,000. The ordinary revenue in England was about £150,-000 a year. Ramsay, *Genesis of Lancaster*, II, 101; Tout and Broome, "A National Balance Sheet for 1362–63," *Eng. Hist. Rev.*, XXXIX (1924), 404–19. Efforts to translate medieval sums into modern equivalents produce widely variable results; see Delachenal, *Histoire de Charles V*, II, 204, n. 2, where he cites scholarly estimates relative to John's ransom ranging from 250 million francs to 40 million francs, at a time when five francs were worth one American dollar. The latest and most thorough study of the ransom is by Broome, "The Ransom of John II," in *Camden Miscellany*, Vol. XIV, Part 4.

53. A reads *iste* for *ipsae*.

54. The text of this truce is in *Chronique . . . de Jean II*, I, 302–9. Delachenal calls attention to the fact that the original of this document still exists in the Public Record Office, Diplomatic Documents, Exchequer 1493.

55. A adds *debebat et* before *poterat*.

56. Article XII of the treaty stipulated that King John was to be brought to Calais within three weeks after Saint John's day (June 24, 1360).

57. A adds *qui se dicebat comitem de Heu* after *Artesio*. John of Artois was the eldest son of Robert of Artois and Jeanne of Valois. He was born in 1321. Since his mother was half sister of Philip VI, he was a first cousin to King John. The latter released him from prison, where he had been since his father's flight and his mother's arrest in 1334 (see above, p. 151, n. 21). The king made him count of Eu in February, 1351, after the execution of the constable Raoul de Brienne (see above, p. 197, n. 12). Wounded and captured at Poitiers, he was released under the terms of the treaty of Brétigny from obligation to ransom himself, but he became a hostage for King John's ransom. See Moranvillé, "Charles d'Artois," *Bib. de l'Ecole des chartes,* LXVIII (1907), 433–80. It seems probable that Jean de Venette's peculiar phrase that he "called himself count of Eu" is due to the following circumstances. While John of Artois was captive in England the sister of Raoul de Brienne, the former count of Eu, married Louis of Etampes. She claimed the county of Eu as heir to her brother, and the regent Charles dared not refuse her. The wife of John of Artois protested ineffectively against this. When John of Artois returned to France, after the conclusion of the treaty of Brétigny, he attempted by force to repossess himself of the castle of Eu. Not until after King John's return to Paris was the county restored to him. At the earliest this would be about the middle of December, 1360. Presumably Jean de Venette was writing this passage before that restoration. Vacandard, *La Guerre de cent ans dans le comté d'Eu,* pp. 9–10.

58. This seems to refer to an affair which Luce dates May 27, 1360, citing a letter of pardon in Arch. nat. JJ 88, No. 64. The countess of Eu was residing at Péronne. Her husband, coming to visit his wife, with the duke of Orléans and a company of nobles, approached the city. The citizens became alarmed because the duke was reputed to have surrendered many places to the English, so they closed their gates. Fearing that the count would gain access to the city by way of the castle, where the countess was, the citizens surrounded the castle and took possession of it. They then made a sortie and drove away the count and his escort. King John punished them by depriving them of their commune and destroying their belfry. Dournel, *Histoire générale de Péronne,* pp. 108–9. For royal acts of pardon and restoration, see *Ordonnances,* V, 156–64; Delisle, *Mandements . . . de Charles V,* p. 249, No. 493, p. 639, No. 1228.

59. A adds *temporis* after *tunc*.

60. Géraud (II, 314, n. 1) explains that at this point he has taken the

reading from his late MSS. He remarks that his earlier MS reads *diffidaverunt et burgenses quasi extra profiscentes damna rerum et corporum simul perdiderunt.* A also has this reading except that it has *casu* for *quasi* and *intulerunt* for *perdiderunt.*

61. A reads *excubias de nocte et custodias portas sollicitas de die adhibebant.* This makes unnecessary Géraud's suppression of the phrase *de die* (II, 314, n. 2).

62. This was the third of the annual Paris fairs. The first day of the fair was the second Wednesday in June, and it lasted until the eve of Saint John's day (June 10–June 23, 1360). On the opening day the bishop of Paris and the chapter of Notre Dame, carrying a reliquary containing Saint Simeon's arm, marched through the streets to the Champs de Lendit, and the bishop gave a public benediction of the fair. This would be a great public festival. It was also a solemn occasion on which the University purchased a year's supply of parchment and vellum. E. Roussel, "La Bénédiction du Lendit au XIVe siècle," *Annuaire-Bulletin de la Soc. de l'hist. de Paris,* 1897, pp. 68–83, with a contemporary picture; F. d'Ayzac, *Histoire de l'abbaye de Saint Denis en France* (Paris, 1860), I, 414–41; Le Roux de Lincy and Tisserand, *Paris et ses historiens,* p. 230, n. 2.

63. A reads *fuit tentum* for *fuit tunc.*

64. July 8, 1360, two weeks after Saint John's day, King John landed at Calais. *Chronique . . . de Jean II,* I, 319.

65. The first payment of 600,000 florins was due before the end of October, but only two thirds of this could be collected and paid by that date, so King Edward had to relax the treaty terms at this point. Broome, "The Ransom of John II," in *Camden Miscellany,* Vol. XIV, Part 4, pp. vii–viii. The final conclusion of peace between the two kings took place at Calais, Oct. 24, 1360. *Chronique . . . de Jean II,* I, 322.

66. Advent began Sunday, Nov. 29, 1360. King John entered Paris on the third Sunday in Advent, Dec. 13, 1360. *Ibid.,* I, 331.

67. A adds *tamen* after *vocabatur.*

68. "At that time [November, 1360] there were great numbers of English and others in Brie and Champagne, who ravaged all the countryside, killing men and holding them for ransom and doing all the evil they could, of whom some called themselves the Great Company. When these heard that the king of France had been released from prison they left Brie and went into Champagne, where they held many fortresses."—*Ibid.,* I, 327–28. Knighton writes, "At this time was organized a certain band of strong men called *Societas fortunae,* which some called the Great Company. It was recruited from men from different regions, who, now that there was peace

between the two kingdoms, had no livelihood unless they went to work. But they were bold and warlike fellows, accustomed to having good things, and enterprising, who regarded it as their right to live by war, since in time of peace they had nothing."—*Chronicon,* II, 114–15. See also *Froissart,* ed. Luce, VI, 59–65.

69. The Companies took Pont-Saint-Esprit by a night attack, Dec. 28–29, 1360, and remained there blockading Avignon for the next three months. By the end of March, 1361, the pope made a treaty with them by which he absolved them of their crimes and paid them 14,500 florins, and they agreed to go into Italy to war upon the excommunicated Visconti. By another treaty, with certain other companies, made by the constable of France and Marshal Audrehem, money was paid them and they were deflected into Spain. See Denifle, *La Désolation des églises,* II, 389 ff.; Labaude, "L'Occupation du Pont-Saint-Esprit par les grandes compagnies (1360–1361)," *Revue historique de Provence,* I (1901), 79–95, 146–64; Bruguier-Roure, "La Guerre autour du Pont-Saint-Esprit," *Mémoires de l'Académie de Vaucluse,* IX (1890), 96–122, 233–52; Guigue, *Récits de la guerre de cent ans.* The bull of Innocent VI (Jan. 19, 1361) proclaiming a crusade against the companies is in Compayré, *Etudes historiques,* p. 257, No. lxxii. Géraud's text reads *finaliter se ipsos disperserunt vel destruxerunt.* Géraud (II, 316, n. 2) remarks that all his MSS read *despexerunt vel destruxerunt.* A reads *despenxerunt* alone.

70. This is the "Second Plague." According to Ramsay (*Genesis of Lancaster,* I, 444), notices of this visitation "in the writers are scanty; the extent of its ravages must be inferred from indirect sources, such as the lists of men of rank and position who fell victims to it."

1361

1. A reads *maxima* for *magna.*

2. Knighton (*Chronicon,* II, 116) writes, "In this same year (1361) a general mortality called the second plague afflicted the people. Both high and low died, but particularly children and infants. And of our congregation eleven canons died." See also Gray, *Scalacronica,* p. 169.

3. In describing events of 1363 the author of the *Chronique des quatre premiers Valois* (pp. 130–31) writes, "In England there was a very great mortality in which people died very quickly. [This author gave only a sentence to the plague of 1348.] And in this epidemic great numbers died, including a good many of the hostages, namely my lord the count of Saint-Pol, the lord de la Roche, my lord of Préaux whose daughter, heiress to

Préaux, Lord Jean de la Rivière married, and who was married after the death of my lord Jean de la Rivière to my lord Jacques de Bourbon. And most of the hostages from the good towns of France died in this epidemic. And in particular from among the citizens of Paris and of Rouen there died Amaury Filleul and Jean Mustel, who were hostages for the king of France." A diplomatic document of Nov. 15, 1361, names nineteen hostages who died in May or before August. Replacements were demanded. This list includes the count of Saint-Pol and three of the men mentioned above, along with citizens from Paris, Saint-Omer, Amiens, Beauvais, Douai, Troyes, Lyons, Orléans, and Compiegne. Chaplais, "Some Documents Regarding the Fulfilment and Interpretation of the Treaty of Bretigny (1361–1369)," in *Camden Miscellany,* XIX (1952), 11. The documents of 1363 and 1367 in Rymer's *Foedera* (Vol. III, Part 2, pp. 80, 130) presumably refer to Guy VI, count of Saint-Pol, successor to Guy V. The Amiens hostage was Firmin Cocquerel, mentioned in note 94 on page 248.

4. Luce (*Histoire de Bertrand du Guesclin,* p. 477) calls attention to an act of King John, dated June 14, 1362, giving 40,000 florins to the count of Vendôme to pay the ransom he owed to Robert Markaunt (Arch. nat., K 48, No. 23). The latter's name is sufficiently unusual for us to believe that we have glimpses of this adventurer's background in certain documents of 1342 and 1344, in which the bishop of Ely lodges complaints against Robert Markaunt and others for assaulting and robbing his bailiff, poaching in his deer park, maliciously killing his livestock, and attacking his servants. *Calendar of the Patent Rolls, Edward III,* V, 456; VI, 278, 284. Géraud (II, 318, n. 2) identifies him as an esquire from Pykenham in Norfolk. In the invading army of 1359 he was captain of twenty archers. *Report on the Foedera,* Appendix E, p. 40. Géraud (II, 318, n. 3) observes that previous editors put a comma, instead of a full stop, after *elevatus,* seeming to indicate that he became a nobleman by the capture of Vendôme. A agrees with Géraud's reading and begins the next sentence with a capital (*Et tunc*).

5. A adds *praedonum* after *multi modo.*

6. A reads *inhibitum* for *prohibitum.*   7. A reads *isto* for *ipso.*

8. Sir Thomas Gray (*Scalacronica,* p. 169), after describing a storm which would seem to have been in January, 1362, records, "The comet star appeared in this season."

9. "On Saturday, Dec. 12, [1360], sound money was proclaimed in Paris, namely, a new gold franc at 16 Parisian shillings, a royal at 13 shillings 4 pence of Paris, and new fine silver coins at 12 Parisian pence each."— *Chronique . . . de Jean II,* I, 330. "This was a return to sound money and

this time the reform would last."—Bridrey, *La Théorie de la monnaie au XIVe siècle,* p. 505.

1362

1. "On the Wednesday after Easter and on Thursday the next day, April 20 and 21, 1362 (Easter being April 17), the vines were frostbitten throughout France, the Beauvaisis, the Orléanais, the Laonnois, Burgundy, and along the river Marne, to such an extent that there was no wine this year in that region nor in the neighboring regions, so that, in general, you would not find one hogshead of wine to the arpent [about one and a half acres of English measure]. They made more verjuice than usual this year, but the vines grew all to branches. And no man ever saw such a shortage as there was this year."—*Chronique . . . de Jean II,* I, 336.

2. The pope died Sept. 12, 1362. Ten days later twenty cardinals went into conclave. *Ibid.,* I, 337.

3. In the conclave the rival candidates were Cardinal Guy de Boulogne and Cardinal Talleyrand de Périgord, but neither could prevail over the other. The conclave sat, deadlocked, until Oct. 27, 1362, when the cardinals chose the abbot of Saint-Victor, who was then serving as papal legate in Italy. He reached Avignon on Oct. 30 and was consecrated and crowned pope on Nov. 6. *Chronique . . . de Jean II,* I, 337–38; *Froissart,* ed. Luce, Vol. VI, pp. 78–79; p. xxxix, n. 1. In the preceeding year the abbot had been one of the two papal envoys sent with a bull of excommunication against Bernabo Visconti, whom Bernabo had forced to eat the bull in his presence.

4. Sir Thomas Gray (*Scalacronica,* p. 171) writes, "About Michaelmas in the same year of grace, 1362, Pope Innocent died at Avignon; after whose death arose great dissension in the College of Cardinals about the election of a pope. For a long time they could come to no agreement through jealousy, none being willing that any of the others should become pope. At last they chose a black monk, a poor abbot of Saint-Victor near Marseilles, who was so much astonished that he thought that the messengers who brought him the news were making fun of him." According to the author of the *Chronique des quatre premiers Valois* (pp. 133–34), when the conclave was deadlocked, "by the grace of the Holy Spirit, it happened that the cardinal of Boulogne said to the other cardinals, 'We are unable to agree to make one of us cardinals Holy Father. There is a very worthy man who is abbot in Marseilles. He is a strong, competent man. I give my vote for him,' and the other cardinals, with one voice and without disagreement or debate, said, 'So do we all.' And so the pope was chosen."

5. King John had in fact started for Avignon before the death of Pope

Innocent: in August, says *Chronique . . . de Jean II* (I, 337); early in September, according to official documents. He reached Villeneuve-les-Avignon early in November. *Froissart,* ed. Luce, Vol. VI, p. xxxviii, n. 1. Jean de Venette is wrong in his statement that King John wished to marry the queen of Naples himself. The plan was for a marriage between the queen and John's son, Philip, duke of Touraine (later Philip the Bold, duke of Burgundy). Prou, *Etudes sur les relations politiques du pape Urbain V avec les rois de France,* pp. 8–13.

6. Queen Jeanne died of the plague, Sept. 29, 1360. Delachenal, *Histoire de Charles V,* II, 288, n. 3.

7. This statement is obscure in all texts. In Géraud it reads *quondam filiam domini supradicti* and the editor has indicated an omission after the last word. A reads *filii* instead of *filiam* and has no sign of any word omitted. It will be recalled that Jean de Venette has previously shown that he was somewhat confused about this particular Philip.

8. Queen Jeanne of Naples was a first cousin to King John, being daughter to Marie of Valois, sister of King Philip VI. She had been queen since the death of her grandfather, King Robert, in 1343. Her first husband, Andrew of Hungary, was strangled by a band of conspirators in 1345, and the queen was suspected of complicity. Her second husband was her cousin, Louis, count of Tarentum, who died in 1362. (Where Géraud reads *Ludovicum comitem,* A has *Ludovicum comitem de incognitus.* She was to have two more husbands, James, king of Majorca, and Otto of Brunswick, and to die without surviving children.

9. Duke Philip de Rouvre died of the plague at the age of fifteen on Nov. 21, 1361. Petit, *Histoire des ducs de Bourgogne,* IX, 228. This was in the previous year, so again our author has made an error of a year.

10. The succession to Burgundy was more complicated than might appear from Jean de Venette's statement. King John's mother was great-aunt to Philip de Rouvre. (As before [p. 203, n. 9], Jean de Venette erroneously uses the term *matertera* for a paternal relation.) If, however, inheritance was to be determined by the claims of the late duke's great-aunts, Charles of Navarre had a better claim than King John because his grandmother, Marguerite of Burgundy, queen to Louis X, was an older sister of John's mother. Questions of degrees of relationship and of representation and its limitations had to be raised in order to prefer the Valois claim. Lengthy discussion of this will be found in *Mémoires de la Société pour l'histoire du droit et des institutions des anciens pays bourguignons,* Fasc. 3 (1936), containing two articles, Champeaux, "La Succession de Bourgogne à la mort de Philippe de Rouvre," and Gaudemet, "Les Prétentions de Charles

II, roi de Navarre, à la succession de Philippe de Rouvre"; see also Pocquet du Haut-Jussé, "La Succession de Bourgogne en 1361," *Annales de Bourgogne,* X (1938), 54–63. See below, p. 289, n. 21.

11. The dowager countess was Marguerite of France, daughter of Philip de Rouvre's aunt, Jeanne of Burgundy, queen to Philip V. She was a first cousin to Philip de Rouvre, where King John was a first cousin once removed. Jean de Venette is slightly confused. Arras is in the county of Artois. Marguerite received that county and the county of Burgundy (Franche-Comté), along with certain lands in Champagne. For discussion of this inheritance question see Cherest, *L'Archiprêtre,* pp. 137–42.

12. A reads *Britannia* for *Burgundia.*

13. A adds *Aurelianum et* before *Carnotum.*

14. A adds *quam fecerant* after *fortius.*

15. A omits *fortiora seu;* the translation follows Géraud. At the plea of certain citizens and friars the bishop of Paris, on Feb. 17, 1363, authorized the formation of a charitable brotherhood to care for the women and children, refugees from the open countryside into the city since 1360. See Coyecque, *L'Hôtel-Dieu de Paris au moyen âge,* Vol. I, p. 292, No. iii.

16. Jean de Venette has made an error of a year at this point, since the duke died in 1361. The *Scalacronica* (p. 168) says, "Duke Henry of Lancaster died in March in the year of grace 1361, and was buried at Leicester. This Henry was sage, illustrious and valiant, and in his youth was enterprising in honor and arms, becoming a right good Christian before his death." The duke died March 23, 1361. Bateson, *Records of the Borough of Leicester,* II, 124. Since this is before Easter (March 28) it would be, by Jean de Venette's customary reckoning, actually in 1360. Documents of April 6, 1361, deal with the escheat of his possessions. *Report on the Foedera,* Appendix E, pp. 58–59.

17. A royal ordonnance issued at Compiègne, Dec. 5, 1360, prescribed new taxes for paying the king's ransom. These were a sales tax of 5 percent, a 20 percent increase in the price of salt, and a special sales tax of about 8 percent on wines and other beverages. *Ordonnances,* III, 433–39. These were forms of the extraordinary taxes which have already been noted. See above, pp. 44, 113.

18. A reads *exigebant* for *eligebant.*

19. A adds *et capitur* after *debellatur.*

20. This refers to the battle of Launac, Dec. 5, 1362, between Jean I, count of Armagnac, and Gaston Phoebus, count of Foix. The two had been local rivals for a long time, and the succession to Béarn was in dispute between them. The latter was brother-in-law to Charles of Navarre and

represented somewhat the anti-Valois faction among the nobility of the southwest. This meant that Armagnac and the Valois kings tended to draw together. So this battle was another royal reverse, a crushing defeat in which a large number of noble prisoners were taken. Devic and Vaissete, *Histoire générale de Languedoc*, IX, 747; Breuils, "Jean Ier, comte d'Armagnac et le mouvement national dans le Midi au temps du Prince Noir," *Rev. des ques. hist.*, LIX (1896), 44–102; Narbonne, *Gaston Phébus, seigneur du Béarn, 1331–1391*, pp. 88–94.

21. March 30, 1363.

22. A adds *caute facientes* after *manifeste et.*

23. A adds *si potuissent* after *caperent;* this does not appear in the translation.

24. Géraud's text reads *qui erat vidit* and Géraud (II, 323, n. 3) suggests the insertion of *ibi* after *qui*. A reads *qui eos vidit,* which makes this unnecessary.

25. A reads *portaverunt* for *reportaverunt.*

26. A omits *ornamenta.*

27. Luce (*Histoire de Bertrand du Guesclin*, p. 498) in his survey of castles has this passage as his only source for this castle. Géraud inserts *nomine* in his text and gives the name as *Toutnoye*. A lacks the inserted word and spells the name with a *v* instead of an *n*.

28. A adds *cum* before *astucia.*

29. A adds *sociorum* before *statim.*

30. Michael de Brèche, bishop of Le Mans.

1363

1. April 2, 1363.   2. A reads *vias* for *villas.*

3. A adds *et obviamenta* after *remedia.*   4. May 27, 1363.

5. Oct. 18, 1363. According to the *Chronicon Moguntinum* (in *Die Chroniken der deutschen Städte*, XVIII, 167–68), the plague was in Mainz about Michaelmas (Sept. 29, 1363) and lasted in the Rhinelands until the feast of Saint Mark (April 25, 1364), with six thousand victims in Mainz.

6. See above, p. 274, n. 2, the quotation from Knighton. The *Chronicon Angliae Petriburgensis*, p. 171, also notes that this second plague was particularly fatal to children.

7. A omits *ad extremum.*

8. A adds *ut ita loquitur,* and reads *quadrigenta vel quingenta,* where Géraud has *quadraginta vel quinquaginta.*

9. A adds *satis et iuvenum* after *mulierum.*   10. Nov. 22, 1363.

11. At this point there is a marked variation between A and Géraud,

which is important for dating Jean de Venette's work. A lacks the sentence, *Hic dominus Stephanus postea fuit factus cardinalis per sanctae memoriae dominum Urbanum quintum summum pontificum, anno Domini MCCCLXVIII in civitate Montis Flasconis prope Viterbium.* ("Afterwards this lord Stephen was made a cardinal in A.D. 1368 by Pope Urban V of blessed memory in the town of Montfiescone near Viterbo.") The phrase "of blessed memory" could only have been written after the pope's death, Dec. 19, 1370. It seems certain that this sentence was not in Jean de Venette's original text. A was subject to careful correction, and phrases and passages omitted by the copyist were carefully written in the margin with indication of their proper location in the text. There is no correction at this point. But in addition to the corrections A has occasional rubrics, in a contemporary but slightly different hand, noting the subject matter of the text. Under the one indicating the death of Jean de Meulan, bishop of Paris, is the added phrase *Creatione Stephani episcopi finaliter cardinalis.* This creation occurred Sept. 22, 1368, in the same year that Jean de Venette ceased writing. It says nothing of the pope "of blessed memory." This rubric may be regarded as an expression of local pride on the part of the copyist, inasmuch as this was the first bishop of Paris to become a cardinal. Another bit of evidence in support of A as the better text, free of interpolation, and of the theory that Jean de Venette did not mention Bishop Etienne's cardinalate, is the text of the continuator of the chronicle of Richard Lescot (Richard Lescot, *Chronique,* p. 156). This continuation seems to be based on Jean de Venette. It repeats his peculiarities, the tight crossbow strings at Crécy, Grandferré, the motive of King John's Avignon journey, the star seen after Trinity. He too concludes his paragraph at this point with a statement about the death of Jean de Meulan and the succession of Etienne de Paris, which is almost verbatim identical with the Arundel text. There is nothing about becoming a cardinal. Etienne de Paris became bishop Dec. 11, 1363. *Gallia Christiana,* VII, 136.

12. A reads *eodem* for *eo.*   13. Nov. 1, 1363.

14. Luce (*Histoire de Bertrand du Guesclin,* p. 502) was unable to identify this place. He gives no references other than this passage.

15. See above, p. 278, n. 15.

16. Géraud (II, 328, n. 2) remarks that his earlier MS and one of his later ones read *defendendi,* while the other late one reads *offendendi,* the reading which Géraud prefers. A reads *expellendi.*

17. A adds *Parisius* after *urbe.*

18. A adds *qui* after *fabula* and *solet dici* after *lupo.*

19. A adds *dominis vel* before *pastoris.*

20. A adds *et patrarunt* after *saepius*.

21. See Hervieux, *Les Fabulistes latins,* II, 739, for a story similar to this, called "De cane et de lupo et de homine avaro" from *Libellus fabularum Romuli Monacensis.* The moral is very different from Jean de Venette's because the stratagem of the dog and the wolf was necessitated by the stinginess of the dog's master, who refused to feed the dog. I am indebted to Professor Stith Thompson of Indiana University for guidance on this matter.

22. This is Henry V, count of Vaudemont, who has already been mentioned in connection with the defense of Troyes in 1359 (see above, p. 86). He was nephew to the count killed at Crécy (see above, p. 177, n. 68). Géraud's text reads *domino Johanne de Joinville* and Géraud (II, 329, n. 1) points out that this is an error, since the count was named Henry. A omits *Johanne.* In this connection we may note that Henry, sire de Joinville, died before 1367 and was succeeded by his daughter Marguerite, whose husband was Jean de Bourgogne-Comté. Simonnet, *Essai sur l'histoire et la généalogie des sires de Joinville, passim.*

23. Jean I, duke of Lorraine; Robert, duke of Bar. The occasion and motives for this war are obscure. It appears to have lasted from February until August or September, 1363. Delaborde, *Jean de Joinville et les seigneurs de Joinville,* pp. 188–218, 466–67, Nos. 984–89.

24. Arnaud de Cervole, called the Archpriest, was a captain of men-at-arms, who had been in the French king's service since about 1350. He had distinguished himself sufficiently at the siege of Evreux in 1356 (see above, p. 60) to be made captain of the captured city. After Poitiers, where he was captured, he became one of those enterprising captains who carried on semi-independent warfare with considerable success. Chérest, *L'Archiprêtre,* is a definitive work on this personage. For this war in Lorraine, see pp. 221–25.

25. The Archpriest entered the service of Philip the Bold (later duke of Burgundy) in November, 1363, and served under him in suppressing the companies and in the war of the two Burgundies in 1364. Petit, *Ducs de Bourgogne de la maison de Valois; Philippe le Hardi,* Part 1, pp. 63–100; Chérest, *L'Archiprêtre,* pp. 225 ff.

26. A adds *in Neustria* after *Secanam.*

27. Froissart (ed. Luce, V, 215) says that Walter Strael occupied this place, which is near Mantes, in the latter part of 1359. According to his pardon (October, 1368) he "committed and perpetrated many murders, larcenies, robberies, sacrileges, having assaulted towns and fortresses, killed men, women and children, set fires, raped women and violated maids,

burned and destroyed churches, chapels, and monasteries, held men for ransom, ransomed towns and the countryside, and done all other evils, crimes, wrongdoings and delicts which he could."—Secousse, *Recueil*, pp. 295–96. It seems very doubtful if Strael had been at Rolleboise continuously after 1359, because in October, 1363, the English captain John Jowel appeared before the place "and took the castle except a tower into which Madame de Rolleboise with other noble ladies and gentlemen withdrew, where they defended themselves vigorously. But Sir John Jowel agreed to permit the ladies to come out of the tower. And when they did so he put them in a wagon, drew it up to the foot of the tower, and directed his attack on that point. Thus it was impossible for those in the tower to throw down missiles without killing their lady. In that way Sir John Jowel took the donjon of Rolleboise, and then he sent the lady and her companions away."—*Chronique des quatre premiers Valois*, p. 135.

28. "Eight days before Christmas, 1363, there began so severe a frost that there had not been one like it for a hundred years. And on Saint John's day in Christmas week [Dec. 27, 1363] the Seine froze and remained so until the following seventh of February, so that the English who were occupying Rolleboise, forty men-at-arms with their followers, crossed the river on the ice and raided the countryside, pillaging and taking prisoners, and came back over the ice with their booty, without loss, and reentered their stronghold at Rolleboise. And without any rain the ice melted so slowly that no one noticed when it went. And it lasted until the twelfth of March."—*Chronique rouennais*, published at the end of Pierre Cochon, *Chronique normande*, pp. 316–17. This is more explicit than the *Chronique des quatre premiers Valois*, pp. 136–37.

29. *Ibid.*, p. 136; Luce, *Histoire de Bertrand du Guesclin*, p. 410, n. 2; Roncière, *Histoire de la marine française*, I, 519–20.

30. Pierre I de Lusignan, king of Cyprus, had successfully captured Attalia (modern Adalia) on the southern coast of Asia Minor in the summer of 1361. He was now attempting to persuade the Christian rulers in the West to follow up this victory. He reached Avignon March 29, 1363. King John had been there since the previous November. Pope Urban V preached the crusade March 31. King John took the cross and was appointed captain of the crusading army, with Cardinal Talleyrand as papal legate. During the first part of July John returned to Paris (*Froissart*, ed. Luce, Vol. VI, p. xlii, n. 2). The crusaders were to leave for the East by March 1, 1365. Prou, *Etude sur les relations politiques du pape Urbain V avec les rois de France*, pp. 24–29.

31. The travels of the king of Cyprus were more extensive than appears

from Jean de Venette. Instead of accompanying King John, he spent part of the summer in Flanders, Brabant, and the Rhinelands, not reaching Paris until August. From August 13 to September 11, 1363, he was in Normandy, and then visited Brittany before crossing over at Calais to England. He was back in Paris by Christmas. *Froissart,* ed. Luce, VI, 84–93; *Chronique des quatre premiers Valois,* pp. 127–28; Atiya, *The Crusade in the Later Middle Ages,* pp. 330–36.

32. Nov. 30, 1363.

33. We are not very well informed about this meeting of the Estates, which presumably lasted from Dec. 1 to Dec. 5, 1363. Jean de Venette is the only chronicler who mentions it as meeting at Amiens, although the *Chronique des quatre premiers Valois* (p. 130) is probably referring to the same meeting. Thierry, *Recueil des monuments inédits de l'histoire du Tiers Etat,* I, 622; *Ordonnances,* III, 646; Delachenal, *Histoire de Charles V,* II, 349–51.

34. Dec. 21, 1363 (see above, p. 280, n. 14). A adds *apostoli* after *Thome.*

35. This is Jean IV, de Chalon. His father, Jean III, count of Auxerre, having been captured on the eve of the battle of Poitiers, remained a captive for some years and returned from captivity with his reason impaired. His son Jean assumed the administration of the county and was called count, although his father lived until 1366.

36. A adds *ymo tute* after *tuti.*   37. A reads *libere* for *misere.*

38. Under the treaty of Brétigny, as hostages for King John until his ransom was paid, there were to be forty nobles and forty-two burghers, four from Paris and two each from Amiens, Arras, Beauvais, Bourges, Caen, Châlons, Chartres, Compiègne, Douai, Lille, Lyons, Orléans, Reims, Rouen, Saint-Omer, Toulouse, Tournai, Tours, and Troyes (Rymer, *Foedera,* Vol. III, Part 2, p. 92). Chief among these were the four "princes of the fleur des lys," Philip, duke of Orléans, younger brother to King John, the king's two sons, Louis, duke of Anjou, and John, duke of Berry, and Louis II, duke of Bourbon, the dauphin's brother-in-law.

39. This is an error. By special agreement, May 15, 1363, the four Valois princes were permitted to go to Calais until the end of October. This included permission also to leave Calais for four days at a time by special license. This agreement was strengthened by a special oath taken by these hostages whereby they were to be held faithless perjurers among all noblemen everywhere if they failed to conform. Rymer, *Foedera,* Vol. III, Part 2, pp. 76–77; *Froissart,* ed. Kervyn de Lettenhove, VI, 506–8.

40. A adds *sine aliis ab Anglia* before *recessit.*

41. Louis of Anjou is said to have had permission to make a pilgrimage

to Notre-Dame de Boulogne, to have met his wife there, and to have been persuaded by her to accompany her to Guise instead of returning to Calais. On July 9, 1360, Louis had married Marie of Blois, daughter of Charles of Blois, duke of Brittany. "This young princess . . . who had shared with her father the evil days of his captivity in England . . . was, without doubt, the one who caused her husband to decide to break his word by quitting Calais and fleeing with her to Guise. It was also she who caused her father to decide never again to put himself in English hands," as he had agreed to do if he did not pay his ransom in full.—E. Déprez, "La Querelle de Bretagne," *Mémoires de la Soc. d'hist. et d'archéologie de Bretagne,* Vol. VII (1926), Part 1, p. 53. In his discussion of this episode Delachenal demonstrates that it probably occurred about the middle of September. He points out that the Virgin's Nativity is celebrated Sept. 8. *Histoire de Charles V,* II, 346–49. *Froissart,* ed. Luce, Vol. VI, p. xliv, n. 3.

42. A adds *Parisius* after *burgensibus.*

43. This justification before an assembly in Paris is reported only by Jean de Venette, but he would seem to be a first-class source for such an event. Edward III on Nov. 20, 1364, addressed a letter of protest on the duke's flight to the peers of France and the lords of the king's council (Rymer, *Foedera,* Vol. III, Part 2, p. 93), and this gathering may have been in consequence. Is this a topic about which the official and the aristocratic chroniclers might feel that the less said the better? Was this a session of the Parlement of Paris for considering affairs of honor, like the session which considered the controversy between Bertrand du Guesclin and William Felton, Feb. 27, 1364? Luce, *Histoire de Bertrand du Guesclin,* pp. 405–6; Delachenal, *Charles V,* II, 355, n. 3. According to some MSS of Froissart the duke was sent into Normandy and served at the siege of Rollebois. *Froissart,* ed. Kervyn de Lettenhove, VI, 387, 396; *Froissart,* ed. Luce, VI, 290. A reads *fortalitia per patriam indebite occupantes et reponere patriam in pace* for *et fortalitia et patriam redere in pacem.*

44. Debate between John and his advisers on this step took place at Amiens early in December, 1363. The king left Amiens between Dec. 12 and 15, embarked at Boulogne Jan. 3, 1364, and arrived in England the next day. *Froissart,* ed. Luce, Vol. VI, pp. 93–94; p. xlvi, n. 3 and p. xlvii, nn. 2–3.

45. Delachenal (*Histoire de Charles V,* II, 352, n. 4) points out that Charles was not regent but royal lieutenant.

46. At an earlier but unspecified date, probably late in 1356, Pope Innocent VI wrote Emperor Charles asking him to solicit the release from captivity of King John and his nobles in the interest of the crusade then being planned. *Report on the Foedera,* Appendix E, p. 64.

47. A adds *medio yemis* after *stipite*.

48. This "Great Frost" was commented upon very widely, because the ice was so strong and lasted so long, and because it hurt the vines and interfered with outdoor work. The Rhine was frozen from Jan. 5 until March 17, 1364, and even the Rhone was frozen to such an extent that horses and wagons could be driven on the ice. One observer reports frequently crossing the Meuse on the ice, and the freezing of the Seine has already been noted (see above, p. 282, n. 28). In Tournai the chronicler, recording nineteen weeks of ice and snow without a thaw, describes how many of the people, since they could not work any more than on Sunday, amused themselves with making snow men and forts. John of Reading, *Chronica*, p. 160; the monk of Malmesbury, *Eulogium historiarum*, III, 353–54, 385; "Varia chronicum fragmenta," in *Chroniques de Saint-Martial de Limoges*, pp. 199–200; *Magnum chronicum Belgicum*, in Pistorius, *Rerum Germanicarum scriptores*, III, 330; Königshofen, *Chronik*, in *Die Chroniken der deutschen Städte*, IX, 865; *Chronicon Moguntinum*, in *ibid.*, XVIII, 167; Conrad Justinger, *Die Berner-Chronik*, p. 124; *Chronique des Pays-Bas*, in De Smet, ed., *Corpus chronicorum Flandriae*, III, 206. Géraud (II, 344, n. 1) found this sentence difficult and requiring editing. A shows that *Géraud's* MSS lacked the two final words of the sentence. The passage reads *ibidem inferius congelata quod mirum erat superius portabantur*.

49. A reads *fuit postea* for *fuerit postea*.

50. The treaty of Brétigny failed to settle the Breton question. Since the treaty the younger John of Montfort had come of age, and so ceased to be merely a pawn in Edward III's political game. On June 22, 1362, the English king turned over to him that part of Brittany which was still loyal to the Montfort cause. La Borderie, *Histoire de Bretagne*, III, 572. The war between the rivals for Brittany started again in the early months of 1363, with Bertrand du Guesclin as the chief partisan of Charles of Blois. See Luce, *Histoire de Bertrand du Guesclin*, Chap. 12.

1364

1. A reads *Anno domini MCCCLXVIIII inchoando in Paschate quod tunc fuit in vigilia Annunciatonis dominice scilicet VIII^{vo} die Martii versus finem*. This is very different from the Géraud text, and it seems probable that the copyists from whose manuscripts Géraud worked found this example of Jean de Venette's rudeness so difficult to understand that they altered the text considerably. Only once before (1353) in Jean de Venette's life time had Easter come on March 24. With Easter on Sunday, March 24, the octave of Easter is on Sunday, March 31, thus making the end of March

the eve of the Annunciation. Ordinarily the feast of the Annunciation is on March 25, but when this date comes in Holy Week or Easter Week it is celebrated on the Monday following Easter Week. This happens in any year in which Easter comes before April 2, but only when Easter comes on March 24 does this feast coincide with the beginning of the new month.

2. Jean III de Craon had been bishop of Le Mans. He became archbishop in 1355. The citizens of Reims suspected him of favoring the English and of neglecting the fortifications, particularly his castle of Portemars. Varin, *Archives administratives de la ville de Reims,* III, 79 ff.; Delachenal, *Histoire de Charles V,* II, 156.

3. Jean de Venette has made an error of a year. The decree of Parlement on this matter is dated April 8, 1363, which was within the octave of Easter in that year. The controversy went back four years, when the city of Reims was preparing for the renewed warfare which culminated in the English attack. As early as May 5, 1359, Walter of Châtillon, captain of Reims for the regent Charles, ordered the building of a great wall along the edge of the moat of the archbishop's castle, to prevent an enemy gaining access to the city by way of the moat, the city walls being weak on that side. *Inventaire MS des titres de Joursanvault,* cited in Richard Lescot, *Chronique,* p. 142, n. 6; see also *ibid.,* Appendix XV, p. 243. This wall shut off the castle of Portemars from the city. Beginning in 1361 the archbishop made an issue of this in a way to involve the whole question of city government by the citizens. The decree of Parlement upheld the archbishop's complaint about the wall between the castle and the town, and ordered its demolition. On the general matter of jurisdiction, however, the existing autonomy of the citizens was confirmed. There is an order from King John dated July 7, 1363, forbidding the citizens to touch the fortifications, since a renewal of the war was feared. Was this intended to halt or prevent the demolition ordered two months before? Varin, *Archives administratives de la ville de Reims,* III, 204–261; Boussinesq and Laurent, *Histoire de Reims* I, 414.

4. See above, p. 195, n. 17.

5. A reads *ut puta* [*cum rege*] *Arragonie* [*ut dicebatur*] *et aliis baronibus,* etc. Géraud's text lacks the words in brackets; see Géraud, II, 335, n. 1. Charles had gone to Navarre in 1361. For a while he was in alliance with King Peter I of Castile in a war against Aragon. Then on Aug. 25, 1363, he made an alliance with Peter IV of Aragon, primarily against Castile but in a secondary sense against the French king. This was confirmed in a personal interview on Feb. 21, 1364. Brutails, *Documents des archives de la*

Chambre des comptes de Navarre, p. 88, No. 87; Meyer, *Charles II,* pp. 153, 157.

6. Pacy belonged to Pierre de Sacquenville (see p. 122). During the third week of October, 1360, the Bègue de Villaines, a Valois partisan in Normandy, took the place by escalade, with Madame de Sacquenville and her daughters. *Chronique . . . de Jean II,* I, 322.

7. Jean de Venette is in error here. He probably reflects the point of view prevailing in Paris, which may well have been the one put forward officially. The initiative in reopening the war came, in fact, from the dauphin, without any provocation or defiance from Charles of Navarre, and was justified as preventive action anticipating an attack from the latter. Secousse, *Recueil,* pp. 200 ff. As before, at the time of Marcel's activities, the dauphin addressed letters to the French cities presenting his side of the case. About a fortnight (April 24, 1364) after the seizure of Mantes and Meulan, the dauphin appointed Du Guesclin captain-general "to combat the evil purposes of the king of Navarre, our enemy and rebel, and his friends, allies and adherents, many of whom have entered into parts of our duchy of Normandy and have done great damage to our subjects, and are continuing to attack and despoil them, as also are many robbers and malefactors who have occupied and are holding many strongholds there and also in the diocese of Chartres, ransoming the country roundabout and waging all manner of war, to the great grief and loss of our subjects."—Delisle, *Mandements . . . de Charles V,* Nos. 1 and 7. There is a glimpse of unsuccessful approaches made by Charles of Navarre to King Edward late in 1363 in Perroy, "France, England, and Navarre from 1359 to 1364," *Bulletin of the Institute of Historical Research,* XIII (1933-36), 151-54. Géraud (II, 335, n. 2) remarks that all his MSS read *regentis* but that the reading should be *regentem.* A reads *regentem.*

8. Since this is Jean de Venette's first mention of Du Guesclin, and since, at this point, his record is as nearly contemporary as anything we have, it is proper to note the absence of any particular interest or enthusiasm for the future constable. Luce has advanced the view that "the heroic resistance of Rennes [besieged unsuccessfully by the duke of Lancaster from October, 1356, until June, 1357] offered some consolation to our unhappy country, whose cause was bound up with that of Charles of Blois, for the humiliation of Poitiers. This explains the universal favor which was associated with this warlike deed; and Du Guesclin had figured with too much renown in this affair not to share prominently in this popularity. Hitherto his reputation had not extended beyond the confines of Brittany, but the prowess

of our hero at the siege of Rennes spread his fame over all France."—*Histoire de Bertrand du Guesclin,* p. 229. Nothing in Jean de Venette gives any support to this patriotic theory. Although giving considerable attention to Breton affairs, Jean de Venette makes no mention whatever of the heroic defense of Rennes, nor does he show, now or later, any peculiar feeling for Du Guesclin. A, however, copied after 1368, when Jean de Venette had completed his history, shows the copyist to have been a Du Guesclin enthusiast. At this point he capitalized the first three letters of the future constable's name, and wrote all the others larger than the rest of the text. At the next appearance of the name he capitalized all the letters of *Bertrandus,* and for more than half the times when the name appears one or more of the letters are capitalized unusually.

9. A adds *gallicanie* after *Britannie.* The reference is to the French-speaking northern and eastern part of the peninsula, as distinct from the Celtic regions. Du Guesclin came from the neighborhood of Dinan.

10. A reads *accedentes* for *venientes.*

11. Operations by Du Guesclin against the freebooters at Rolleboise (see above, p. 114) began about Easter (March 24, 1364). Attacks on April 5 and 6 were repulsed. At this point Marshal Bouçicaut arrived from the dauphin with orders to seize as quickly as possible all places in the vicinity held for the king of Navarre. Oliver de Mauny set an ambush before the chief gate at Mantes and, when the drawbridge was lowered to permit the exit of a cart, rushed the gate. When Du Guesclin arrived he had it proclaimed that women and children should be unharmed, but by that time the city had already been sacked. The Bretons were notorious for their pillaging. The episode of the defense of the tower belongs, apparently, to the capture of Meulan, not to Mantes. But according to Cuvelier's *Chronique de Bertrand du Guesclin,* I, 135–40, some of the citizens defended themselves in the bell tower of the church, and we observe below that Jean de Venette was interested in this church. Some of the leading partisans of Navarre escaped from Mantes and took refuge in the tower at Meulan. The chief source for this is the *Chronique des quatre premiers Valois* (pp. 137–42). The forces to attack Rolleboise had assembled at Mantes, and the leaders had celebrated Easter in the city, but at that time the citizens refused entry to the soldiers.

12. A adds *inter alios* after *numero.*

13. Durand and Grave, *Chronique de Mantes,* pp. 233–34; Luce, *Histoire de Bertrand du Guesclin,* pp. 593–97. Goods confiscated from some of these were given to Du Guesclin. This beheading of French partisans of Navarre became a regular practice. Bourgeois de Valenciennes, *Récits,* pp. 327–29.

14. A reads *oppugnantes* for *expugnantes*.

15. Meulan was taken three days after Mantes, but the tower there resisted until its foundations had been undermined. It was the men captured here who were taken to Paris and beheaded. *Chronique des quatre premiers Valois,* pp. 141–42.

16. According to the *Chronique normande du XIVe siècle* (pp. 169, 334–35), the dauphin learned that Charles of Navarre was going to renew the war. He informed Du Guesclin. "Bertrand, considering that Mantes and Meulan were two strong places on the Seine, good crossings belonging to the king of Navarre, from which great harm could be done to the king and the regent, sent a large party of men to Mantes and took it, and afterward to Meulan. Then Mouton de Blainville went before Gournay and Neufbourg, where was Queen Blanche, sister of the king of Navarre, and these places surrendered. Then Bellencombre and Longueville surrendered, so there remained no fortresses belonging to the king of Navarre between the Seine and the Somme. They were all in the regent's hands."

17. Notre-Dame de Mantes is a church so similar in design to Notre-Dame de Paris that some have assumed that it had the same architect. We have already had occasion to mention the chapel of Navarre in this church (see above, p. 204, n. 10), which must have been built in Jean de Venette's time. Pictures of this building will be found in Rhein, *Notre Dame de Mantes.*

18. This seems to echo the document of April 24, 1364, published by Secousse, *Recueil,* pp. 200 ff. See above p. 287, n. 7.

19. The end of this sentence, after "great harm," does not appear in A, but it seems more probable that it was carelessly omitted there than that it was interpolated in all the manuscripts used by Géraud.

20. A reads *quare ducem diffidaverat ymo regem Francie patrem ducis erat ista* for *quare diffidaverat regem Franciae et ducem Normanniae regentem ista erat.*

21. This too seems an echo of the document referred to in n. 18, above. On p. 277, n. 10, we noted the question of the Burgundian succession. It became aggravated at this time because on Sept. 6, 1363, King John conferred the duchy upon his youngest son, Philip the Bold. Charles of Navarre claimed that rights of unlimited representation applied, and that the line of the elder sister, his grandmother, prevailed over the line of the younger sister, John's mother. The royal claim was based on the principal of limited representation, viz., a collateral line could be admitted to the inheritance only in one degree, not in two, which meant that a son could represent his mother but a grandson could not represent his grandmother. It would be a mistake,

however, to suppose that this was a matter of legal niceties. The Valois kings were determined to bring Burgundy into royal hands and to exclude the Navarrese claimant. Pocquet du Haut-Jussé, "La Succession de Bourgogne en 1361," *Annales de Bourgogne* X (1938), 54–63. Compare this issue with the ones discussed earlier, p. 151, n. 21.

22. See *Chronique des quatre premiers Valois,* p. 144. Froissart (ed. Luce, VI, 101) tells how Du Guesclin appeared before the gates of Evreux, probably in early April, and was not only refused admission by the justly suspicious citizens, but was driven away with stones from the mangonels.

23. Like all the other MSS, A reads *patre* instead of *fratre*. The translation follows Géraud's correction (II, 338, n. 1).

24. A adds *unde tunc dictus dominus de Enguien venerat transeundo et adducto eo apud Kaynoy prope Valenchenas* after *Kyurnam juxta Valencianas.*

25. A adds *forma judicii* after *sine.*

26. William II, count of Hainaut, had been killed at Staveren in 1345 (see above, p. 168, n. 13), and had been succeeded by his sister Margaret, the wife of Emperor Lewis the Bavarian. She died in 1356, and was succeeded by her oldest son, William III. By September, 1357, he had become violently insane, and his younger brother, Albert of Bavaria, came to Hainaut and was appointed regent March 30, 1358. Jean de Venette has confused Engelbert d'Enghien with his brother Siger d'Enghien. It was the latter who was arrested and beheaded March 21, 1364. Peeters, "Le Comté de Hainaut durant les premières années de la régence du duc Albert de Bavière (1357–1372)" in *Mélanges d'histoire offerts à Charles Moeller,* I, 563–82. According to the Bourgeois of Valenciennes (*Récits,* p. 326), the king of France met Count Louis of Flanders and restrained him from an attack at this time on Albert of Bavaria in revenge for the sire d'Enghien. This may have been on June 27, 1364, when Count Louis did homage at Compiègne. Delisle, *Mandements . . . de Charles V,* No. 38. For earlier studies on this topic see Caffiaux, "Nicole de Dury," in *Mémoires historiques sur l'arrondissement de Valenciennes,* I (1865), 91–219, and the same author's "Commencement de la régence d'Aubert de Bavière (1375-1361)," *ibid.,* II (1868), 225–326, published by the Société d'agriculture, sciences et arts de Valenciennes; also Matthieu, "Histoire de la ville d'Enghien," *Mémoires et publications de la Société des sciences, des arts et des lettres du Hainaut,* 4th series, I (1875), 57–419; II (1876), 148–489. The latest and most scholarly discussion is in Quicke, *Les Pays-Bas.* From these it appears that Siger d'Enghien was arrested at his castle of Baisieux near Quiévrain, although there is disagreement as to the exact date; March 18 according to Matthieu, March 23 ac-

cording to Quicke. Through his mother, Siger d'Enghien was nephew to Walter of Brienne, constable of France, killed at Poitiers (see above, p. 64), and heir to his title of duke of Athens. Engelbert d'Enghien, seigneur de Ramerie and de la Folie, was Siger's youngest brother, but, since he was in Hainaut, the count of Flanders appointed him administrator for Walter, heir to Siger, a minor.

27. The correct date is April 8, 1364. The news reached Paris April 16, Delachenal, *Histoire de Charles V,* II, 362.

28. A reads *digne* for *bonae.*

29. King John's viscera were buried in Saint Paul's cathedral, London. *Chronicon Angliae Petriburgensis,* p. 172.

30. A adds *cum lilius* after *de armis Franciae.*

31. A adds *decenter et sollemniter insignitos* after *simili modo.*

32. On May 5, 1364, Charles V wrote Edward III:

Dearly beloved brother, our cousins the counts of Eu, Tancarville, and other members of the council of our dear lord and father, God rest his soul, who have been in his company in your kingdom, have made report how graciously and with what good cheer you received our dear lord and father again in your kingdom, and of the very good company with which you entertained him while he lived, and of the great diligence you showed for his health and your efforts to cure him in his illness, and of the great pomp you made for his obsequies by gathering together our dear nephews your sons and others of your blood royal, and prelates and other magnates of your kingdom, and by many other arrangements, and of the magnificent procession made for the departure of his remains from London. From these things we are made to understand clearly the great affection you bore toward our lord in his lifetime, and we thank you to the fullest extent of our ability and will always hold ourselves beholden to do anything we can for your honor and pleasure.

—Perroy, "Charles V et le traité de Brétigny," *Le Moyen Age,* XXXVIII (1928), 264–65.

33. Géraud's text reads *quatuor millia torticia,* but A reads *iiii^{xx}.*

34. A adds *instrue lumen seu in capella lignea quod de super corpus in ecclesia Londonensis, comptissime fuerat praeposita* after *sex libris cerae.*

35. A and this translation omit the phrase in Géraud's text, *Et expletis illis nobilibus exequiis funeris,* which might be translated, "And in completion of these obsequies these nobles," etc. A reads *Et conductes* for *conduxerunt.*

36. A adds *ut dicitur* after *lacrimis.*

37. A adds *inclitum* before *corpus.*

38. In 1364 the feast of the Ascension was on Thursday, May 2. The Sun-

day following would be May 5, and the feast of Saint John before the Latin Gate was Monday, May 6. Only when Easter comes as early as March 27 would the feast of the Ascension come before that of Saint John before the Latin Gate. Jean de Venette had experienced only three such early Easters in the past three decades (1353, 1345, 1334). It will be noted that the letter quoted above, p. 291, n. 32 is dated on the funeral day.

39. A reads *devotis missarum et debitis officiis* for *devotis officiis missarum*.

40. May 7, 1364. For another similar account, see *Chronique . . . de Jean II,* I, 342–44.

41. May 19, 1364. Delachenal (*Histoire de Charles V,* III, 64–97) takes occasion to describe in detail a fourteenth-century coronation.

42. This is a repetition of the error on p. 117, above. Since there is no other record nor indication of any such defiance by Charles of Navarre, it seems more probable that this is an item of Valois propaganda advanced in justification of an unprovoked attack upon the Navarrese position in Normandy.

43. A reads *Captan de Beu;* see Géraud, II, 341, n. 1.

44. Géraud's text reads *per aliquas partes maris,* and Géraud (II, 341, n. 2) explains that he takes this from one of his late MS, but that his earlier MS reads *per aiguas partes maris.* A reads *per partes aliquas Normannie.*

45. A reads *partes* for *portas.*

46. For these preparations see Delachenal, *Histoire de Charles V,* III, 33–37.

47. A reads *ad bellandum* for *ad debellandum.* Jean III de Grailly, Captal de Buch, a second cousin to the brothers of Navarre, succeeded Philip of Navarre as lieutenant in Normandy for King Charles of Navarre. Philip died Aug. 29, 1363.

48. This is probably a confused and erroneous report of Du Guesclin's attempts to persuade the Captal de Buch to come down from the strong position on the hill at Cocherel and do battle in a field near the river, or to decide the issue by breaking three lances with Du Guesclin himself. Continuator of the *Chronique de Richard Lescot,* p. 169. No such agreement was made.

49. May 16, 1364.

50. This is a village near Cocherel, where there was a Benedictine monastery.

51. For scholarly discussion of the battle of Cocherel, see Delachenal, *Histoire de Charles V,* III, 38–60; Luce, *Histoire de Bertrand du Guesclin,* Chap. 14; Chérest, *L'Archiprêtre,* pp. 242–53. Oman (*History of the Art of*

War in the Middle Ages, II, 177) points out that this battle shows how the lessons of Crécy and Poitiers had impressed professional captains. The men-at-arms dismounted. The Captal took up a strong defensive position and waited to be attacked. He was defeated because Jowel refused to stand on the defensive, and because he lacked sufficient number of archers to repeat the earlier victories. "It was only in a national levy that these could be found in proper proportion to the other arm."

52. Failing to persuade the Captal to come down from his hill and fight, Du Guesclin started to withdraw from the field after the two armies had faced each other for forty-eight hours. The *Chronique normande du XIVe siècle* (p. 171) says this was because the French had run out of supplies. Other chronicles credit Du Guesclin with the execution of a clever stratagem to entice his opponents into the plain. The attack of the Gascons and Navarrese was, in fact, due to the impetuosity of the Englishman, John Jowel, in spite of the Captal de Buch. *Froissart,* ed. Luce, VI, 122–23. A adds *et aliis suis quos habebant* after *Navarrensibus.*

53. A reads *hoc pedestim [ut in pluribus] non in equis;* Géraud lacks the words in brackets.

54. All accounts agree as to the hard fighting in this battle, and the heavy losses on both sides support this.

55. Baldwin of Lens, sire d'Annequin (near Bethune) was appointed Master of the Arbalasters in 1358. He was also captain of Presles castle in Picardy, and of Saint-Quentin. Sir Bartholomew Burghersh had captured him at Poitiers in 1356, and again took him prisoner in an encounter during the English march to Reims in 1359. *Froissart,* ed. Luce, Vol. VI, p. 211; p. lix, n. 5; *Froissart,* ed. Kervyn de Lettenhove, XX, 93.

56. Louis II, viscount of Beaumont. He had been head of the dauphin's household, and was married to Isabella of Bourbon, a cousin to Charles V's queen.

57. Luce (*Histoire de Bertrand du Guesclin,* p. 446, n. 2, and p. 457, n. 1) shows this to have been Sir Jean de Béthencourt, father of the discoverer of the Canary Islands. Like the other MSS, A reads *Letencuria,* which Luce corrects to read *Betencuria.*

58. A adds *ut iam dixi* after *Gallicorum.*

59. A reads *faciliter* for *finaliter.*

60. A reads *nec poterant faciliter superari* for *per consequens nec superari.*

61. According to the *Chronique des quatre premiers Valois* (p. 146–47), when the Franco-Breton forces were formed for battle, a force of about two hundred Bretons remained mounted with the baggage and the non-combatants. It was this group which made the decisive attack that brought

victory. "All the good prisoners fell to the Bretons, because they came into the fight fresh and unweary, so they made captures very easily."

62. A reads *ascendit, et tunc cito ipse et sui revertentes simul ipos Vascones et alios a tergo invadentes* for *ascendit, et a tergo alios viriliter invadens.*

63. A adds *fortiter* after *nihilominus.*

64. A adds *et aditu reserato* after *sparsis.*

65. John Jowel had been captain of an English company in Normandy, serving independently or under Philip of Navarre since 1357 (*Froissart,* ed. Luce, V, 93). He and James Plantain had been among the captains whom Charles of Navarre brought into Paris in 1358 (*Chronique des quatre premiers Valois,* p. 81). We have seen above how he became captain of Rolleboise (p. 282, n. 27). In this battle he was wounded, but he died a few days later at Pont-de-l'Arche.

66. Jean de Sault, called the Bascon of Mareul. Bascon is a medieval equivalent of the modern word Basque (*Froissart,* ed. Luce, Vol. VI, p. liii, n. 6). He had long been an active partisan of Navarre. At the murder of Charles of Spain it was he who dispatched the victim (*Chronique des quatre premiers Valois,* p. 28). At the defense of Melun he distinguished himself by his boldness and energy. There was a personal feud between him and Du Guesclin (Delachenal, *Histoire de Charles V,* II, 115–19).

67. See above, n. 65.

68. A adds *et erant milites strenui* after *Anglicus.*

69. Pierre de Sacquenville (see above, p. 287, note 6) was one of the most active partisans of Navarre in Normandy. He represented the same anti-Valois localism as did Geoffrey of Harcourt. In the past he had been active in carrying on Anglo-Navarrese negotiations. He too had participated in the murder of Charles of Spain.

70. This execution seems to have been after June 8 and before June 13, 1364. Luce, *Histoire de Bertrand du Guesclin,* p. 455, n. 1, and *Chronique normande du XIVe siècle,* p. 337.

71. A adds *ac alii* after *Navarri.*

72. A adds *quasi satis magna* for *valde magna.*

73. Géraud (II, 344, n. 1) remarks that his early MS reads *quinimo quasi illa societas.* A has this same reading. Géraud suppresses *quasi* as unnecessary.

74. The coronation was May 19, 1364. According to the *Chronique des quatre premiers Valois* (p. 148), news of the victory reached Charles on the previous day. But it was on May 22, at the abbey of Saint Médard at Soissons, that he rewarded the messenger with 500 livres. By May 27 Charles,

at Saint-Denis, had ordered the Captal de Buch, the king's prisoner, to be brought to Paris, and directed that 4,000 livres be paid to Du Guesclin to effect this. *Catalogue analytique des archives de M. le baron de Joursan-vault*, Vol. I, Nos. 33, 34. The Captal surrendered on the field to a Breton squire named Roland Bodin. It was the accepted practice of late medieval warfare that prisoners of distinction, who would have political as well as monetary value, should be turned over to the king, with reasonably gener-ous compensation to their actual captors. Documents on the captivity of the Captal de Buch will be found in Domairon, "Suites de la bataille de Cocherel," *Cabinet historique,* Vol. IV, Part 1 (1858), pp. 67–73; Secousse, *Recueil,* pp. 211–14; Luce, *Histoire de Bertrand du Guesclin,* pp. 600–603.

75. The *Chronique des quatre premiers Valois* (p. 148) tells of the anxiety felt by the royal company on its way to Reims for the coronation. Delachenal (*Histoire de Charles V,* III, 63) has some interesting comments on the decisive character of this battle.

76. There is a detailed and scholarly account of this by S. Luce, "Du Guesclin en Normandie . . . le siège et prise de Valognes," *Rev. des quest. hist.,* LIII (1893), 372–411.

77. A adds *per villagia et* before *per villulas.*

78. A adds *nec secure* before *per itineria.*

79. A adds *velud inimici* before *indifferenter.*

80. A adds *omnes* before *illas.*

81. The word here is *brigantes.* See above, p. 217, n. 35, for discussion of this word.

82. A reads *perpendebantur* for *praetendebantur.*

83. A omits *non* before *intendebat;* the translation follows Géraud.

84. May 27, 1364. Secousse, *Recueil,* pp. 192–95. Although the county had been confiscated from Charles of Navarre in the preceding April, the castle of Longueville was still in the possession of his partisans and re-mained so for a year. When we remember that for fifty years the counts of Longueville had been sons or grandsons of French kings, we can realize that the conferring of the title and territory upon an obscure Breton knight would be a very unusual occurrence.

85. Philip of Navarre died Aug. 29, 1363.

86. A adds *ab hominibus* after *totum.*

87. "Charles, king of France and duke of Normandy, by ordonnance of his council, directed my lord Bertrand du Guesclin, count of Longueville, to clear the Bretons out of the Pays de Caux. And these Bretons crossed the Seine and occupied the abbey of Bec. But afterwards my lord de Friquans took it from the Bretons because they wasted the country so much."—

Chronique des quatre premiers Valois, p. 150. Jean de Venette's statement might be related to the promise made by Du Guesclin, Aug. 22, 1365, to drive the Companies from France, with his county as pledge for his performance. *Froissart,* ed. Luce, Vol. VI, p. lxxx, n. 3.

88. Géraud (II, 347, n. 1) indicates that his MSS read *munierunt et castrum similiter fortificantes,* but he has edited the text by changing *et* to *eam.* A reads *munierunt et similiter castrum ipsum fortificantes.*

89. According to the *Chronique des quatre premiers Valois* (pp. 152–53), siege was laid to Evreux on July 26, 1364. Luce puts this early in July, and indicates that it lasted until October. *Froissart,* Vol. VI, p. lxv, n. 2. See also *Chronique normande du XIVe siècle,* pp. 174–75, 337–38. A reads *ibi verterunt* for *subverterunt.*

90. A reads *addebantur* for *addebant.*

91. May 28, 1364. *Chronique . . . de Jean II,* II, 3–4.

92. In this parenthesis Jean de Venette is going back ten years. The cession of Dauphiné was due to the childlessness and the need of money of the Dauphin Humbert II. Negotiations with Philip VI of France began in 1342. The final treaty was March 30, 1349. By this Humbert, in return for a large money payment, transferred his state to Charles, grandson to Philip VI. When Jean de Venette refers to kinship between Dauphin Humbert and King Philip VI, he is again in error. Humbert was nephew, on his mother's side, to the queen of King Louis X of France. Through his brother and predecessor, Dauphin Guy VIII, he was brother-in-law to the daughter of King Philip V. Philip VI was a first cousin to these two French kings, but was quite unconnected with Humbert. On July 16, 1349, Charles came to Lyons and was invested with the emblems of rule. The next day Humbert became a Dominican friar. He became patriarch in 1351. When the archbishop of Reims died, Feb. 18, 1352, Humbert was appointed in the following month perpetual administrator of the Reims diocese, but he was never actually installed as archbishop. This is an appointment *in commendam,* i.e., "the provisional collation and occupation of an ecclesiastical benefice, [as opposed to *in titulum,* which applies] to regular and unconditional collation of benefices."—*Catholic Encyclopedia.* At the request of King John, Humbert was nominated bishop of Paris, Jan. 25, 1354, but he died at Clermont in Auvergne, May 22, 1355, while on his way to the capital. In general, for this see Guiffrey, *Histoire de la réunion du Dauphiné à la France;* Fournier, *Le Royaume d'Arles et de Vienne,* Chap. 11, section vii; Delachenal, *Histoire de Charles V,* I, Chap. 2.

93. June 11, 1364. The reception at Rouen is described in the *Chronique des quatre premiers Valois,* p. 149.

94. Royal documents show that by June 13, 1364, Pierre de Sacquenville had been executed. *Froissart,* ed. Luce, Vol. VI, p. lx, n. 1. Consequently, it could not have been after the king's return to Paris.

95. A adds *illo opere* after *curando.*

96. A reads *oditus* for *odibilis.*

97. This is Henry Quiéret, second son of the admiral who was killed at Sluys (see p. 154, n. 25). He had been one of those who assisted Charles of Navarre to escape from prison in 1357. Although tonsured, he preferred an active military life, and we have records of his service as captain of Néaufle, one of Charles of Navarre's castles. King John pardoned him in 1360 along with the rest of the partisans of Navarre. Presumably, like Pierre de Sacquenville, he also was taken prisoner at Cocherel. Guy Quiéret, his brother, was also a canon of Amiens cathedral and a councilor to Charles of Navarre. *Syllabus of Rymer's Foedera,* I, 418; Maugis, *Documents inédits concernant la ville et le siège du bailliage d'Amiens,* I, 85; Belleval, *Gauvain Quiéret, seigneur de Dreuil et sa famille,* p. 72. Géraud (II, 348, n. 2) remarks that all the MSS spell the name *Kyriet,* and that D'Achery corrected this to *Kieret,* which enabled Secousse to identify this man. A reads *Kieret.* Delachenal (*Histoire de Charles V,* III, 123, n. 6), following Secousse (*Mémoires,* Part 2, p. 52, n. 3), assumes that Jean de Venette was referring here to Guy Quiéret, because of the fact that the latter was a canon of Amiens. Secousse publishes a document of April 17, 1365 (*Recueil,* p. 221), showing that certain French nobles were guaranteeing Guy's fidelity, and concludes from this that he was pardoned for his adherence to Charles of Navarre. I cannot find anything to warrant Delachenal's assertion that Henry Quiéret was beheaded in 1358. In a document of 1380 (Secousse, *Recueil,* p. 463) there is reference to "the death of the late Henry Quiéret, who was beheaded at Amiens some time ago (*pieça décapité*)," and the document also refers to Jacques de Rue, a partisan of Navarre beheaded in Paris (in 1378). Belleval (*op. cit.*) shows that Henry Quiéret was also a canon of Amiens, and prints an example of his seal bearing that title. He also shows that he was still serving at Néaufle in June 1360. Presumably Jean de Venette's account is correct, and the document in favor of Guy Quiéret indicates a deliberate distinction in the treatment of the two brothers, both partisans of Navarre, one of whom was captured in battle fighting against the king.

98. A omits *saecularium* after *hominum;* the translation follows Géraud.

99. A reads *mota est* for *orta est.*

100. There is a brief summary of this conflict in the article by L. Peeters, "Le Comté de Hainaut durant les premières annés de la régence du duc Albert de Bavière (1357-1372)," in *Mélanges d'histoire offerts à Charles*

Moeller (Louvain and Paris, 1914), pp. 571–73. There were certain territories in dispute between the count of Flanders and the count of Hainaut. Louis de Mâle attempted to use the Enghien trouble in Hainaut as an occasion for advancing his cause, apparently without success. According to Peeters, Valenciennes supported Albert with men and money. As so often happened, the war appears to have been a succession of truces. Peace between Albert and the Enghien family was concluded April 11, 1367, and an alliance between Hainaut and Flanders was agreed upon Sept. 10, 1368. Quicke, *Les Pays-Bas,* has a chapter on "Les Années 1364 à 1366 dans le Pays-Bas: un conflit féodal dans le Hainaut et sa répercussion sur les rapports entre la Flandre et le Hainaut," which covers this subject.

101. A adds *et vastantes* after *flebiliter.*

102. A reads *corporibus* for *uxoribus.*

103. Géraud (II, 349, n. 2) remarks that all his MSS read *Hanoreche,* which earlier editors found unsatisfactory. A reads *Hautreche.*

104. Like the other MSS, A reads *modicum turbabantur.* Géraud (II, 350, n. 1) inserts *non* before *modicum,* but the translation follows A.

105. A reads *aliengenas* for *alias.*

106. A adds *Et sic populus ille in sua libertate sine oppressione suorum remanere voluit dominorum* after *cessabunt.*

107. A adds *Nunc ad alia transeamus.*

108. A omits *guerrae;* the translation follows Géraud.

109. A adds *vulgare* after *proverbum.*

110. A adds *pacis* after *tractatus,* and *quibus cum suis in illis partibus Britannicis* after *habuerunt.*

111. These statements, which are anything but explicit, might apply to the various negotiations after 1360, which resulted in a series of truces; or they might refer to the parleys preceding the battle of Auray, of which Froissart (ed. Luce, VI, 157–62) gives a long, detailed account. See also the *Chronique des quatre premiers Valois,* pp. 159–60.

112. Sept. 29, 1364. Froissart erroneously dates the battle Saturday, Oct. 8. *Froissart,* ed. Luce, Vol. VI, p. lxxi, n. 2. Since he has the longest and most detailed account of the battle, his error has found its way into many secondary accounts.

113. A omits *bellatoris nobilis.*

114. The chief captains in John of Montfort's army were English, Robert Knolles, James Pipe, Sir Hugh Calverly, and others. The real director of the battle was Sir John Chandos. He had been an active participant in the English campaigns of the past twenty-five years, fighting at both Crécy and Poitiers. After 1360 he was rewarded with the barony of Saint-Sauveur-le-

Vicomte in the Cotentin, and was appointed royal lieutenant in France. This was his first independent command.

115. The battle resulted from the siege of Auray by John of Montfort, and the arrival of a relieving army under Charles of Blois. Froissart (ed. Luce, VI, 148–71) has a long story of this affair based, apparently, upon the report of the poursuivant who brought the news to Edward III, and who was promptly promoted to be Windsor herald. See also *Chronique des quatre premiers Valois,* pp. 160–63; *Chronique normande du XIVe siècle,* pp. 175–77, 339; Bourgeois de Valenciennes, *Récits,* pp. 333–40.

116. This refers to Louis de Chalon, called the Green Knight, a prominent figure in the chivalry of the time. Jean de Venette is wrong in reporting him as dead. He was captured, but lived until 1398. In 1379 he succeeded his brother as count of Tonnerre but not as count of Auxerre, because the latter county had been sold to the king and added to the royal domain in 1370.

117. Where Géraud's text reads *septingentorum septuaginta,* A has *vii^c et lxxvii.*

118. This would be Miles de Noyers, son and successor to that count of Joigny who seized the Marché of Meaux in 1358 (see above, p. 223, n. 8), and who was killed at the battle of Brignais, April 12, 1361. In commenting on the Great Company (see above, p. 106), Jean de Venette ignored this battle. *Froissart,* ed. Luce, Vol. VI, p. xxviii, n. 2, citing Petit, *Monographie des sires de Noyers.*

119. Froissart (ed. Luce, VI, 188) states that Du Guesclin was held for a ransom of 100,000 francs, which was paid by the pope, King Charles V, and Henry of Trastamare. Luce (*ibid.,* Vol. VI, p. lxxx, n. 3) refers to documents at the Archives nationales which show that the king contributed 40,000 francs (Aug. 15) and in return Du Guesclin, by an agreement dated Aug. 22, 1365, bound himself to clear France of the Companies, giving his county of Longueville as surety. This agreement was renewed by a document made at Paris Sept. 30, 1365, on the eve of his departure for Spain. For reference to the archives and quotation of some of the significant parts of these documents, see Delachenal, *Histoire de Charles V,* III, 282, n. 4.

120. According to Froissart (ed. Luce, VI, 151–52), she exhorted her husband, as he set out for Auray, not to compromise in any way with her rival. "My lord," she said, "you are going to defend my heritage and yours—for what is mine is yours—which my lord John of Montfort keeps from us and has kept for a long time wrongfully and without right. God and the Breton barons who are here know that I am the rightful heir. So

I urge you not to agree to any arrangement, compromise, or treaty which does not leave the whole duchy in our hands."

121. Since, according to Froissart (ed. Luce, VI, 180), the two elder sons of Charles of Blois, John and Guy, were still prisoners in England, this child would be Henry, the third son. The daughter was Marie of Blois, who had married Louis of Anjou in 1360, and whom we have noted above (p. 283, n. 41) as responsible for her husband's flight from captivity.

122. For Montfort's conquest of Brittany see the Bourgeois of Valenciennes, *Récits*, pp. 340–43; *Froissart,* ed. Luce, VI, 175–78. The latter tells of the surrender of Auray, Jugon, and Dinan in the course of October, and of the siege of Quimper-Corentin, which surrendered Nov. 17, 1364. There is reason to think that the preliminaries of peace were negotiated before the latter place. Jean de Venette's account seems to put these at Nantes. In La Borderie, *Histoire de Bretagne* (IV, 5–9), the section on "La Bretagne après la bataille d'Aurai" makes no mention of Nantes and in other ways sounds very little like Jean de Venette's account, although it is not contradictory.

123. Marshal Bouçicaut was the other royal envoy. Their commission is dated Oct. 25, 1364. In this, the widow was designated as duchess of Brittany. Delachenal, *Histoire de Charles V,* III, 162.

124. The treaty of Guérande, April 12, 1365.

125. Géraud (II, 355, n. 2) changes the *exeunte* of D'Achery's text to *existente;* but A also reads *exeunte.*

126. A adds *huismodi* after *gestis.*

127. A reads *pro tanto qui burgenses consentire volebant* for *quia populares consentire nolebant;* and adds *popularibus ad haec omnino dissentientibus sed contradicentibus fortiter et clamose* after *propter guerras.*

128. A reads *persolvebant* for *solvebant.*

129. A reads *ad eas persolvendas* for *id persolvere.*

130. A adds *et discordiam* after *dissentionem,* and *in civitate* after *guerra.*

131. A very detailed contemporary account of these troubles at Tournai is in *Chronique des Pays-Bas* (in De Smet, ed., *Corpus chronicorum Flandriae,* III, 204–40). Serious rioting began Feb. 2, 1365.

132. The envoys from Tournai returned from Paris with royal letters March 14, 1365. *Ibid.,* III, 216. Summary of these letters recounting the issues in some detail and pardoning the rioting is in Vandenbroeck, *Extraits analytiques des anciens registres des consaux de la ville de Tournai,* I, 295–97.

133. Oudard de Renty was one of the French captains at Cocherel. In July, 1364, his name appears as royal governor for Lille, Douai, and the Tournaisis. He came as governor to the city of Tournai about December (*Chronique des Pays-Bas,* in De Smet, ed., *Corpus chronicorum Flandriae,*

III, 205). Jean de Venette's report of pacification at Tournai appears to be exaggerated. The more violent rioting followed De Renty's arrival, and even after the royal letters of pardon in March, 1365, there was considerable unrest (*ibid.*, III, 217–40). De Renty ceased to be governor in May, 1366 (*ibid.*, III, 235), and in February, 1367, the local government at Tournai was suppressed because there had been so much dissension, and royal officials assumed control (*Ordonnances*, IV, 706–7). May we surmise that Jean de Venette wrote this section shortly after March 14, 1365, when the royal pardons had had a temporarily calming influence?

1365

1. A reads *muliere matrimonio* for *muliere annis*.

2. A reads *alias* for *superius*.

3. April 30, 1365, there is a royal order for paying the sums necessary for the work of destroying Rolleboise, which had recently surrendered by treaty. Jacques le Lieur, captain of Rouen, was commissioned to provide an armed company to protect the workers. We may infer that the work was finished by May 16, 1365. Delisle, *Mandements,* Nos. 213, 221.

4. A adds *per circuitum erat facta* after *in muro* and omits *erat* before it.

5. See n. 8, below.

6. A reads *alias* for *superius*.

7. A reads *rectandis* for *retinendis*.

8. The outcome of the battle of Cocherel made Charles of Navarre more willing to come to terms. Papal mediation had been active since May, 1364. Prou, *Etude sur les relations politiques du pape Urbain V avec les rois de France,* pp. 40–45. It would appear that Jean de Venette must have been writing this section before June, 1365, since later he describes at length the ratification, while here and in the preceding paragraph he shows himself ignorant of the details of the agreement. *Chronique . . . de Jean II,* II, 9, n. 2.

9. A adds *similimis* after *praedonum*.

10. King John conferred the ducal title on Robert I in 1355.

11. About Pentecost (May 31, 1365) the Archpriest was near Metz. Jean de Venette seems to be ignorant of the connection between the Archpriest's movements and the efforts to gather together the Companies for the crusade. See Chérest, *L'Archiprêtre,* Chap. 10, "Rétablissement de la paix en France et en Bourgogne (1364–1365)," and Chap. 11, "Projets de Croisade, l'Archiprêtre à Metz et en Alsace (1365)."

12. The emperor left Prague during the second week in April, 1365. He arrived at Avignon on May 23. For his itinerary, see Delachenal, *Histoire de Charles V,* III, 211–18.

13. An occasion requiring a distinguished French representation was the coronation of Charles IV at Arles, June 4, 1365. There were present King Charles's two brothers, Louis of Anjou and John of Berry, and his brother-in-law, Louis of Bourbon. But the king's ambassadors extraordinary were the archbishop and the chancellor, mentioned here, and Pierre Aycelin de Montagu, bishop of Nevers. Guillaume de Dormans was also chancellor of Dauphiné, and he is presumably functioning in that capacity on this occasion.

14. This shows that Jean de Venette was writing this section shortly after the arrival of Pope Urban's letter of June 9, 1365 (see n. 16, below).

15. A adds *et tam ipsas quam alias similimes societates si vellent consentire absolutionis* after *devastabant*.

16. This seems to be no more than a summary of the following letter from Pope Urban to King Charles V, published in Raynaldus, *Annales ecclesiastici*, VII, 110.

Your Majesty knows that our dear son in Christ Jesus, the very Christian prince, Charles, ever august emperor of the Romans, and king of Bohemia, has lately appeared before the Apostolic See. He has informed us of his interest in peace, in the well-being of Christendom in general and of your kingdom in particular, in the expulsion of the infidels, the propagation of the Catholic faith, and the deliverance of the Holy Land; and he has shown to us his secret plans for the public weal. Our desires being no less ardent than his, we have held many conferences with him, and, in agreement with each other, we have decided that the most pressing matter is the elimination of those hateful Companies, which are devastating your kingdom as well as many other parts of Christendom, by either persuading or forcing them to march against the Turks or other infidels. The emperor is sure that the illustrious King Louis of Hungary, our well-beloved son in God, will furnish throughout the whole extent of his kingdom a free and sure passage for these Companies. Consequently he offers to provide, at his own cost, the things necessary for supplying them from the time when they leave France until they reach Hungary, so that they will not need to forage for themselves. He only demands positive assurances of willingness of the king of Hungary. Consequently we and the emperor have chosen the noble Arnoul, sire d'Audrehem, your marshal, and have sent him to the king of Hungary himself, in order to obtain his definite consent and assurances that he will receive the Companies. If, however, he refuses them passage through his country we have directed that they shall be carried overseas by the ships of the Venetians or of some other maritime power in Italy, although this will be longer and more difficult. To cover the cost of their transportation the emperor generously offers half the revenues of his Bohemian kingdom for three consecutive years. And finally, we are informing Your Majesty of these details in order that, without delay, you can make arrangements with the Companies now in France, so that when Marshal d'Audrehem returns they will be ready to take the road either to

Germany or to Italy, according to whether or not the king of Hungary agrees to receive them. Avignon. June 9, 1365.

As early as May 25, 1363, the pope had been exhorting the Companies to join the crusade, but with little result. Early in the following year the Companies were excommunicated. Prou, *Etude sur les relations politiques du pape Urbain V avec les rois de France,* pp. 31, 37; Denifle, *La Désolation des églises,* II, 443 ff. The Bourgeois of Valenciennes (*Récits,* p. 311), in recording this excommunication, remarked, "but they paid no more attention to it than if they had been pagans or Saracens."

17. June 1, 1365.

18. A adds *aliquantulum* after *caristia.*

19. A reads *extra* for *juxta.*

20. Géraud (II, 362, n. 1) remarks that his text reads *fuit,* but that it should read *tanta fuit.* A has this correct reading.

21. June 24, 1365.

22. A adds *afflictorum* after *solatum.*

23. A adds *Domini praecursoris* after *Baptiste.*

24. A reads *respexerit* for *inspexerit,* and adds *eum* before *ab initio.*

25. A reads *tote;* see Géraud, II, 363, n. 1.

26. A reads *ut transeamus infinitas perturbationes* for *infinitas tribulationes.*

27. A adds *certamina* after *discrimina.*

28. A reads *convertere* for *vertere.*

29. As early as March 6, 1365, a truce had been agreed upon, and it seems probable that terms of peace were formulated at the same time. For this topic see Delachenal, *Histoire de Charles V,* Vol. III, Chap. 6.

30. In the latter part of March 1365 the Captal de Buch went to Navarre to deal directly with King Charles. At the same time the Navarrese envoys also came to report on the terms already agreed upon, presumably in the early part of the month. Delachenal is disposed to regard Jean de Venette's account of the decisive role of Louis of Etampes as exaggerated, but to conclude that the Captal de Buch did exercise a preponderant influence in the agreement. Charles of Navarre ratified the treaty terms on May 4, 1365.

31. As far as we know, the only point at issue involved the failure of Charles of Navarre to seal the ratified treaty with the great seal of Navarre. He sealed with his secret seal, "in the absence of the great seal," and bound himself to seal with the latter before Oct. 1, 1365. The Captal de Buch assumed personal responsibility for accomplishing this last formality.

32. A adds *et boni consilii* after *prudentiae.*

33. A adds *et mansuetus* after *pius.*

34. This is Louis II, of Evreux, on his father's side a second cousin to King John, and on his mother's side a first cousin to King Charles of Navarre. He was a great-grandson of King Philip III.

35. The second Wednesday in June, when the fair opened, was June 11, 1365.

36. It is suggested that this is what attracted Jean de Venette's attention to Count Louis, and led to his crediting the latter with an apparently decisive role, about which all other sources are silent.

37. For a summary of the treaty terms, see Delachenal, *Histoire de Charles V,* III, 190–93. Jean de Venette is accurate as far as he goes. The Burgundian question was to be submitted to papal arbitration.

38. June 20, 1365.

39. A adds *totus* before *populus.*

40. A reads *Male acquisita* [*male finaliter*] *disperguntur.* Géraud lacks the words in brackets. Is this a medieval corruption of Cicero's *Male parta male dilabuntur?*

41. A adds *et quamdiu* before *guerrae.*

42. *Ordonnances,* IV, 555. A synod at Angers in March, 1365, forbade the clergy to wear short garments or shoes called *poulaines* (canon xiii). Mansi, *Sacrorum conciliorum . . . collectio,* XXVI, 432. See also Devic and Vaissete, *Histoire générale de Languedoc,* Vol. X, No. 532, Chap. 14 (see above, p. 158, n. 49). For pictures of *poulaines* see Norris, *Costume and Fashion,* Vol. II, Figs. 564, 633, 634. The style was borrowed from Poland, hence the name. For the same reason these were also called crakows.

43. A omits *mutatus est habitus* before *sperent.*

44. A reads *deo* for *domino.*

1366

1. Easter was April 5, 1366.

2. Peter I succeeded his father, Alfonso XI, king of Castile, in 1350. He was the only offspring of Alfonso's marriage with Maria of Portugal. But King Alfonso had ten bastards by his mistress, and of these Henry of Trastamare was the oldest (born in 1332). Banished from Castile in 1356, he figured as a captain of men-at-arms in southern France. The political situation in Spain grew chiefly from an intermittent war between Castile and Aragon, beginning in 1356, in which the latter was very hard pushed. In mid-fourteenth-century politics Castile tended to be pro-English, and Aragon pro-French. Consequently, both the king of Aragon and the Valois kings in France were favorably disposed towards Henry of Trastamare as a political threat to King Peter of Castile. The latter has become known to history as Peter the Cruel, and there is very little doubt that he was unpopular in many quarters in Castile. It may be questioned, however,

whether he acted more violently than his father or many of his contemporaries. He was certainly the object, and very possibly the victim, of an extensive and hostile propaganda in the 1360s, and his history was written later by his victorious enemies. Not until 1363 did Henry, in alliance with Aragon, openly challenge his half brother's claim to the Castilian throne. The accession of Charles V in France, and the victory of Cocherel followed by peace with Navarre, gave occasion for a more active interest by the French king in the affairs of Spain. This was further stimulated by the problem of the Companies, inasmuch as a Spanish war would serve better than a crusade to attract these troublesome men-at-arms. In July, 1365, the king of France, the pope, and the king of Aragon came to agreement about arranging for an expedition by the Companies against Castile for the following September. Du Guesclin was commissioned to gather the Companies and persuade their captains to undertake this Spanish expedition, just as the Archpriest had done for the proposed crusade by way of Hungary. The papacy took the position that the Companies were on their way to wage holy war against the Moors in Granada. By the end of November, 1365, the Companies were gathering at the Pyrenees, and by Christmas their chiefs were in Barcelona. See Delachenal, *Histoire de Charles V*, III, 247–306; Miret y Sans, "Négociations de Pierre IV d'Aragon avec la cour de France, 1366–1367," *Revue hispanique*, XIII (1905), 76–135; Mirot, "Un Épisode de l'alliance franco-castillane au XIVe siècle: Charles V et l'avènement d'Henri de Trastamare," *Revue des études historiques*, LXXXIV (1918), 54–68.

3. Both here and below Jean de Venette is obviously echoing the Franco-Aragonese-Trastamare propaganda. His phraseology shows that he recognized it for what it was, but that he had no other information.

4. Géraud (II, 369, n. 1) remarks that his earliest MS reads *dictus erat,* which is inadequate, and his later MSS read *dictus Henricus erat,* which is clearly wrong. He indicates that the reading should be *dictus Petrus erat.* A has this last reading.

5. King Peter's wife, referred to here, was Blanche of Bourbon. Through her mother, Isabella of Valois, she was a niece of King Philip VI and a great-granddaughter of Philip III. Her sister was married to Charles V. She had been betrothed to the king of Castile in July, 1352. When she arrived in Spain in the following February the king, having become infatuated with a Spanish lady, delayed the marriage until June 3, 1353. At the nuptial ceremony he displayed marked aversion towards the bride and abandoned her within two days. He soon returned to her, but after two days again departed and never saw her again. In 1354 he declared the marriage null, as having been without his free consent, and proceeded to marry another

Spanish lady, Juana de Castro. Both the pope and the king of France protested at this humiliating and unworthy treatment of a French princess. It seems very possible that the wronged queen became the center for political disaffection among the Castilian nobility. In 1354 she sought asylum in the cathedral at Toledo, appealing for protection to the people and asserting that the king was trying to kill her. The pope excommunicated Peter and laid Castile under an interdict. Peter in 1355 removed Blanche from Toledo to Siguenza, and in 1361 she died. The king was accused of poisoning her, but there is nothing to show this, and death from natural causes is entirely reasonable. Daumet, *Etude sur les relations d'Innocent VI avec D. Pedro Ier;* and his *Etude sur l'alliance de la France et de la Castille,* pp. 23–28.

6. King Peter's treatment of his queen was linked with his alleged favoritism for Jews, and gained wide currency. The fragment of a French chronicle published by Secousse (*Recueil,* p. 642) tells how "there came news that King Peter of Spain, who loved Jews and pagans more than Christians, had put to death the queen, his wife, who was sister to the queen of France; and [Henry of Trastamare, driven from Spain] reported that the king had Jewesses and Saracen women for concubines and abandoned the queen, who was of good life." John of Reading (*Chronica,* p. 172) tells that it was said that because Peter had married a Saracen without consulting his nobles, he incurred the sentence of the pope and was ejected from his kingdom. See also *Chronicon Angliae Petriburgensis,* p. 57, and the Chandos Herald, *Life of the Black Prince,* p. 199. Sir Thomas Gray (*Scalacronica,* pp. 163–64) reports Peter as ruled by Jews, a man who preferred a Jewess as a mistress to his wife, and who offended his nobles by admitting Jews to the Order of the Bend, an order of chivalry established by his father. The Christian knights easily proved their superiority in the field. Similar tales were abroad in Mainz and Avignon. *Chronicon Moguntinum,* in *Die Chroniken der deutschen Städte,* XVIII, 170; Baluze, *Vitae paparum,* I, 311–13; II, 443. Amador de los Ríos, *Historia de los Judíos de España,* II, 209–11, cites this passage from Jean de Venette as illustrative of Henry of Trastamare's propaganda.

7. Of Du Guesclin's men-at-arms the *Chronique . . . de Jean II* (II. 15) says, "they entered into the said city of Burgos and there they killed some Jews and Saracens, but they harmed none of the Christians." The city had opened its gates without offering any resistance.

8. Since 1359 the Jews had been permitted to return to France (*Ordonnances,* III, 351, 468, 603). Luce, "Les Juifs sous Charles V," *Rev. hist.,* VII, 1878), 362–70.

9. Isaiah 33:1.

10. Only at a late hour does King Peter seem to have become aware of

the serious menace offered by the army of the Companies in its invasion of Spain. Early in 1366, when the Companies were gathering in Aragon, he hastened from Seville to Burgos and waited there. The invasion of Castile began in the first part of March. On March 16, 1366, Henry of Trastamare was acclaimed king by his followers. On March 28 Peter fled from Burgos, making for Toledo and later for Seville. Henry made triumphal entry into Burgos April 5, 1365, and was crowned king. By the end of the month he was master of the kingdom. For Peter's flight see *Chronique . . . de Jean II*, II, 23, n. 2.

11. A adds *Eduardum.*

12. Prince Edward had been made duke of Aquitaine July 19, 1362. On June 22, 1362, the English had entered into alliance with Peter of Castile. The plea of relationship seems somewhat strained, since Peter was only a third cousin once removed to Edward. But it is true that the Chandos Herald (*Life of the Black Prince,* pp. 57, 151) does state that Peter's appeal was, among other things, "by reason of lineage," and the prince, in his letter to Henry of Trastamare of April 1, 1367, refers to Peter as a relation and ally (Rymer, *Foedera,* Vol. III, Part 2, p. 132), although we may well believe that this is little more than a phase of the practice among royalty of calling each other "cousin." Negotiations between Edward and Peter started at Bayonne, probably in July, and resulted eventually in a series of agreements dated Sept. 23, 1366.

13. The army crossed the Pyrenees by the pass of Roncesvalles in mid-February, 1367. The Chandos Herald (*Life of the Black Prince,* pp. 70-72, 154-55) describes the march, and Froissart gets his information from this source (ed. Luce, VII, 7-10). It took three days for the army to cross the pass (Monday-Wednesday, Feb. 15-17, 1367). According to Froissart, the marching was difficult on the second day because of the wind and snow, but the Herald seems to put this on the first day.

14. This refers to the combat of Ariñez, March 19, 1367, in which an English force of about four hundred, engaged in foraging and reconnaissance, was surprised and annihilated by a larger Spanish force. Sir William Felton, seneschal of Poitou, was one of Prince Edward's chief counselors and lieutenants in Aquitaine. His brother, Sir Thomas Felton, was seneschal of Aquitaine. Sir William had been very active in King Edward's service for more than thirty years. The Chandos Herald calls him "lion-hearted" (*Life of the Black Prince,* pp. 84-87, 158-59; the editors provide a discussion of the confused accounts of this affair on pp. 210-11). Late in 1363 he had challenged Du Guesclin for dishonorably breaking his word, but the Parlement of Paris, sitting as a court of honor, freed Du Guesclin from the obligation to defend his honor.

15. This refers to a peculiar incident, which was part of the tortuous diplomacy of the king of Navarre. In the wars between Castile and Aragon Navarre attempted to play one king against the other, while seeking always to avoid being too closely bound to any defeated party. This dangerous political game became much more difficult when the arrival of the Companies under Du Guesclin brought a strong military force into the field, and the active intervention of France and England in Spanish politics made the position of Charles of Navarre both more helpless and more dangerous. He attempted to make treaties or agreements with most of the parties to the struggle. The presence of English Companies in his kingdom or on his borders forced him to cooperate with the prince of Wales, and the prospect of success, coupled with promises from King Peter, made such cooperation attractive. But he also had a treaty with Henry of Trastamare. In order to escape being too dangerously involved before the fortunes of war showed who was to be the victor, he resorted to a peculiar stratagem for being absent from the decisive battle. He arranged with Oliver de Mauny, Du Guesclin's cousin, to be "treacherously" captured and held a prisoner, at the time when the armies in Spain were approaching each other. This occurred March 13, 1367 (*Chronique . . . de Jean II,* II, 29). The collusive character of this affair was not long concealed. Delachenal, *Histoire de Charles V,* III, 366–91; the Chandos Herald, *Life of the Black Prince,* pp. 207–9.

16. This refers to the battle of Nájera, April 3, 1367. Two days later the prince wrote the following report on the battle to his wife in Bordeaux:

My dearest and well-beloved spouse. We salute you with our whole heart, desiring etc. And, my dear spouse, as to news, we wish you to be informed that up to April 2 we were lodged in the fields near Najera, and there we had news that the Bastard of Spain with his whole army was lodged two leagues away by the river Najerilla. And the next day, very early, we broke camp to march against him. And we sent scouts ahead to observe the Bastard's position. These reported back that he had drawn up his army for battle in a fine place to await our approach. And at once we set ourselves in battle array to attack him. And by the will and grace of God it came to pass that the said Bastard and all his men were defeated, thanks be to our Lord, and between five and six thousand fighting men were killed, and so many prisoners were taken that at present we do not yet know the names. But among others were captured Don Sancho, the Bastard's brother, the count of Denia, my lord Bertrand du Guesclin, the marshal d'Audrehem, my lord Juan Ramirez, my lord Jean de Neuville, the count Craundon, the Bègue de Villaines, Gomez Carillo [?], the master of Santiago, the master of Saint John, and many captains of castles, whose names have not yet been told us, up to two thousand gentlemen prisoners. And as for the Bastard himself, we do not know at present whether he is a fugitive or dead. And after the battle in the evening we set up our headquarters in the Bastard's own tent, where we were more comfortable than we had been for the preceding four of five days, and we stayed there all the next day. And on Monday, which is the day on which this is being written, we broke camp and set out on the road to Burgos, and we are now well on our way, with God's help. And be assured, dear wife, that we, our brother of Lancaster, and all the important men in our army are in good health, thank God, except Sir John Ferrers, who was badly wounded. Farewell, my dear wife.

—This dispatch has been published and discussed by Déprez, "La Bataille de Najera," *Rev. hist.,* CXXXVI (1921), 37–59; and by Prince, "A Letter of Edward the Black Prince," *Eng. Hist. Rev.,* XLI (1926), 415–18. Froissart (ed. Luce, VII, 32–54) has a long account of the battle, which indicates that the Spanish contingents in Henry's army were the ones first defeated on the field. Froissart borrowed from the Chandos Herald (*Life of the Black Prince,* pp. 92–105, 161–65, 212–15), who was present at the battle. The other eye-witness was Alaya, who was with the Spanish army (*Cronicas de los reyes de España,* ed. E. de Llaguno Amirola [Madrid, 1779–80], I, 451 ff.). A letter of Dec. 27, 1367, relative to Du Guesclin's ransom, is in *Cabinet historique,* Vol. XII, Part 2 (1866), p. 84.

17. A omits *gallicanas* after *istas,* and lacks the words which Géraud (II, 392) puts in brackets and which are omitted in translation. Apparently Jean de Venette was writing this section shortly after news of the battle reached Paris.

1367

1. Easter was April 18, 1367.
2. Pope Urban left Avignon for Montpellier Jan. 9, 1367. On Feb. 14 he consecrated the high altar in the church of the new monastery. He left Montpellier for Avignon March 8. Baluze, *Vitae paparum,* I, 359; II, 512, n. 3. There is a long contemporary account of this visit, written at Montpellier; see Germain, *Histoire de la commune de Montpellier,* II, 267–72. A brief summary of this is in Devic and Vaissete, *Histoire générale de Languedoc,* IX, 785–86.
3. A adds *magnam* after *Roman.*
4. Pope Urban left Avignon April 30, 1367. He arrived at Viterbo June 9. Baluze, *Vitae paparum,* I, 361 ff.; II, 530; for his itinerary see IV, 131 ff.
5. A reads *fuge tutelam cautius* for *citius fugam caute.*
6. A adds *mareschalius suis* after *examinatis.*
7. This uprising in Viterbo was Sept. 5–7, 1367. It is said to have been caused by popular indignation when some cardinals' servants washed their hands at a public fountain. On Sept. 11 two citizens were hanged, and two days later five more were hanged before the house of one of the cardinals. Baluze, *Vitae paparum,* IV, 132. A discussion of this affair, indicating all

the sources, is in Signorelli, *Viterbo nella storia della chiesa*, I, 411–13.

8. Pope Urban reached Rome Oct. 16, 1367. He remained there until April 17, 1370. On Sept. 24 he arrived in Avignon.

9. Dec. 13, 1367.

10. A adds *vel auditum* after *visum fuit*.

11. A omits *tempestate et casu ac ruina*.

12. This was the most important church in Boulogne.

13. A adds *illa nocte* before *ex violento*.

14. The Tournai chronicle has a detailed account of this storm (in De Smet, ed., *Corpus chronicorum Flandriae*, III, 240–41), and it is also mentioned in *Une Chronique valenciennoise inédite*, ed. Delcambre, p. 88. Three other chronicles report violent storms in 1367, but not in December: *Chronicon Moguntinum*, in *Die Chroniken der deutschen Städte*, XVIII, 174; "Chronique rouennaise," in *Chronique normande de Pierre Cochon*, pp. 317–18; and the English *Brut*, ed. F. W. D. Brie (London, 1908), p. 319.

15. Dec. 6, 1367.

16. A adds *de Parisius* after *clientes*.

17. For the story of this affray and the proceedings following it, based on the records in the Archives nationales, see Déprez, *Hugo Aubriot*, pp. 85–94; also Denifle and Chatelain, *Chartularium* III, 171 ff. It may be significant that on April 13, 1368, the commissioners of Parlement ordered those sergeants who had been imprisoned to be liberated, since investigation showed that death had been accidental (Déprez, *op. cit.*, p. 93). When he wrote of this affair Jean de Venette had not heard of this development. May it be argued that this gives some support to the theory that our author stopped writing about the second week in April, 1368? See below, n. 2.

1368

1. These expressions refer to the relationship of the solar year and the lunar months. The scholars at Alexandria, in classical times, observed that 19 solar years embraced almost exactly 235 lunar months. This meant that after 19 years the phases of the moon coincided with the same times in the solar year as they had before. The individual years in this cycle of 19 years were numbered with what were called Golden Numbers, one to nineteen. Jean de Venette is indicating that 1368 is the first year in one of these cycles.

2. Géraud's text reads *duravit ejus apparitio per magnum tempus,* but A stops at *per* and leaves a space. From this it seems certain that Jean de Venette wrote the last section while the comet was still visible, intending to fill in the space with the correct number of days when that should be known. Since he never did this, it follows that this marks the time when he stopped writing his chronicle, possibly the time of his last illness. This date

can be quite accurately computed. Two fourteenth-century observers, Henry of Hesse and John of Legnano, wrote about this comet. The former had studied at the University of Paris prior to February, 1363. In his work *Questio de cometa* the opening line reads, "In the year 1368 a comet was visible from the eve of Palm Sunday until three weeks later," viz., April 1–22, 1368. John of Legnano dated his tract April 20 and said that the comet was still visible. In the face of these two observers the statement in the *Chronicon Moguntinum* (in *Die Chroniken der deutschen Städte*, XVIII, 176) that the comet lasted only until April 16 can be discounted. We may conclude, then, that Jean de Venette stopped writing before April 22, 1368. The notion that he may have died in this year arises from the fact that we have no further knowledge of him, and the fact that by May, 1369, when the chapter general of his order met in Montpellier, he had been succeeded as provincial for France. *Bibliotheca Carmelitana*, I, 63. He had been present at the preceding meeting in 1366 at Montauban (*ibid.*, I, 61). For the explicit statements made by Henry of Hesse and John of Legnano see Thorndike, ed., *Latin Treatises on Comets between 1238 and 1358 A.D.*, pp. 234–35.

3. A adds *et ita fuit in partibus Gallienis* after *contemplati sunt*.

4. This refers to Bartholomew the Englishman's *De proprietatibus rerum* (VIII. xx), based on Bede's *De natura rerum*, cap. xxiv, "De cometis":

Cometa is the name of a star with burning gleams, as Bede saith, and is suddenly created and tokeneth changing of kings, and is token of pestilence, or of war, or winds, or great heat. Sometime it seemeth that such stars, so beset with blazing gleams, move with the moving of the planets, and sometime it seemeth that they are fixed and not movable. And always, as Bede saith, they are seen in a certain part of heaven and do not pass through the different signs of the zodiac as planets do. But they seem to be in the sphere ("circle") called "Milky Way" and "Galaxia," also "Watling Street," and spread their beams toward the north and never toward the west. And therefore they are not seen on the west side, and they are seen only a short space of time, that is seven days. But one was seen eighty days, as Bede telleth. Where of it be that this star called comet cometh and is gendered, whether it be of planets or of stars that are fixed, always it is seen in the firmament in the north side, as they say. Wherefore it follows that the star which was seen at the birth of Christ was not a comet, for it passed out of the east toward the west, and stars called comets do not move so, as John Chrysostom says.

(This quotation is based upon the first English translation of Bartholomew.) Both Henry of Hesse and John of Legnano associated comets with floods and strong winds. Thorndike, *A History of Magic and Experimental Science*, III, 493, 595–96.

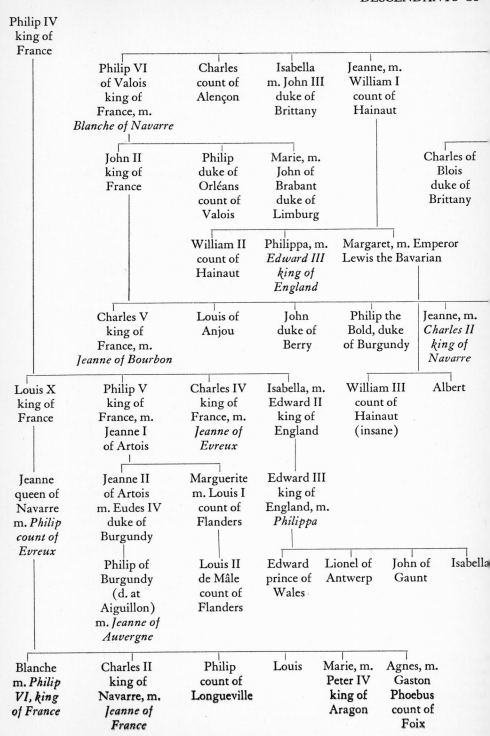

Philip IV
king of
France

Philip VI
of Valois
king of
France, m.
Blanche of Navarre

Charles
count of
Alençon

Isabella
m. John III
duke of
Brittany

Jeanne, m.
William I
count of
Hainaut

John II
king of
France

Philip
duke of
Orléans
count of
Valois

Marie, m.
John of
Brabant
duke of
Limburg

Charles of
Blois
duke of
Brittany

William II
count of
Hainaut

Philippa, m.
*Edward III
king of
England*

Margaret, m. Emperor
Lewis the Bavarian

Charles V
king of
France, m.
Jeanne of Bourbon

Louis of
Anjou

John
duke of
Berry

Philip the
Bold, duke
of Burgundy

Jeanne, m.
*Charles II
king of
Navarre*

Louis X
king of
France

Philip V
king of
France, m.
Jeanne I
of Artois

Charles IV
king of
France, m.
*Jeanne of
Evreux*

Isabella, m.
Edward II
king of
England

William III
count of
Hainaut
(insane)

Albert

Jeanne
queen of
Navarre
m. *Philip
count of
Evreux*

Jeanne II
of Artois
m. Eudes IV
duke of
Burgundy

Marguerite
m. Louis I
count of
Flanders

Edward III
king of
England, m.
Philippa

Philip of
Burgundy
(d. at
Aiguillon)
m. *Jeanne of
Auvergne*

Louis II
de Mâle
count of
Flanders

Edward
prince of
Wales

Lionel of
Antwerp

John of
Gaunt

Isabella

Blanche
m. *Philip
VI, king
of France*

Charles II
king of
Navarre, m.
*Jeanne of
France*

Philip
count of
Longueville

Louis

Marie, m.
Peter IV
king of
Aragon

Agnes, m.
Gaston
Phoebus
count of
Foix

PHILIP III

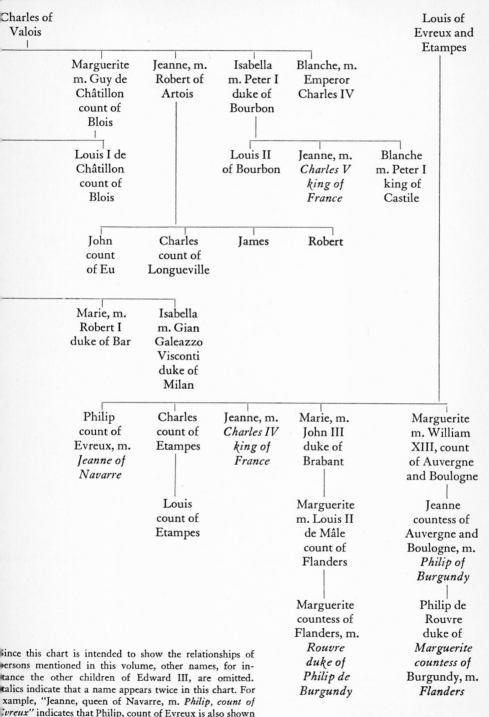

Charles of Valois

Louis of Evreux and Etampes

Marguerite m. Guy de Châtillon count of Blois

Jeanne, m. Robert of Artois

Isabella m. Peter I duke of Bourbon

Blanche, m. Emperor Charles IV

Louis I de Châtillon count of Blois

Louis II of Bourbon

Jeanne, m. *Charles V king of France*

Blanche m. Peter I king of Castile

John count of Eu

Charles count of Longueville

James

Robert

Marie, m. Robert I duke of Bar

Isabella m. Gian Galeazzo Visconti duke of Milan

Philip count of Evreux, m. *Jeanne of Navarre*

Charles count of Etampes

Jeanne, m. *Charles IV king of France*

Marie, m. John III duke of Brabant

Marguerite m. William XIII, count of Auvergne and Boulogne

Louis count of Etampes

Marguerite m. Louis II de Mâle count of Flanders

Jeanne countess of Auvergne and Boulogne, m. *Philip of Burgundy*

Marguerite countess of Flanders, m. *Rouvre duke of Philip de Burgundy*

Philip de Rouvre duke of *Marguerite countess of Burgundy, m. Flanders*

Since this chart is intended to show the relationships of persons mentioned in this volume, other names, for instance the other children of Edward III, are omitted. Italics indicate that a name appears twice in this chart. For example, "Jeanne, queen of Navarre, m. *Philip, count of Evreux*" indicates that Philip, count of Evreux is also shown elsewhere, as the son of Louis of Evreux and Etampes.

Bibliography

Adam Murimuth. Continuatio chronicarum. Ed. by E. M. Thompson. London, 1889. "Rolls Series," No. 93.

Annales Flandriae. Commentarii sive Annales rerum Flandricarum. By Jacob Meyer. Antwerp, 1561.

Amador de los Ríos, J. Historia . . . de los judíos de España. . . . 3 vols. Madrid, 1875–76.

Anonimalle Chronicle; from a Ms. Written at St. Mary's Abbey, York, 1333–1381. Ed. by V. H. Galbraith. Manchester, 1927.

Armitage-Smith, S. John of Gaunt. London, 1905.

Atiya, A. S. The Crusade in the Later Middle Ages. London, 1938.

Baluze, E. Vitae paparum Avenionensium. Ed. by G. Mollat. 4 vols. Paris, 1914–27.

Bateson, Mary. Records of the Borough of Leicester. 4 vols. London, 1899–1923.

Baudot, Jules. Les Princesses Yolande et les ducs de Bar de la famille des Valois. Paris, 1900.

Beaunier, Dom. Recueil historique, chronologique et topographique des archevechez, evêchez, abbayes et prieurez de France. 2 vols. Paris, 1726.

Beaurepaire, Ch. de Robillard de, ed., "Complainte sur la bataille de Poitiers," *Bibliothèque de l'Ecole des chartes,* XII (1851), 257 ff.

Belleval, René de. Gauvain Quiéret, seigneur de Dreuil et sa famille. Paris, 1866.

—— La Grande Guerre. Paris, 1862.

Bellevue, Marquis de, "Monographie de l'église Saint-Armel de Ploërmel," *Association bretonne: Mémoires,* 3d series, XXVIII (1910), 22–43.

Bentley, Richard. A Brief Note upon the Battles of Saintes and Mauron, 1351 and 1352. Guilford, 1918.

Berlière, Dom U., ed. Suppliques d'Innocent VI (1352–1362). Rome, Brussels, and Paris, 1911. "Analecta Vaticano-Belgica," No. 221.

Berthou, P.-A. de, "Essai sur la Chronique de Saint-Brieuc," *Bulletin archéologique de l'Association bretonne: Mémoires,* XIX (1900–1901).

Bertrand de Broussillon, A. La Maison de Laval, 1020–1605. 5 vols. Paris, 1895–1903.

Bertrandy, M. Etude sur les chroniques de Froissart: guerre de Guienne, 1345–1346. Bordeaux, 1870.

Boase, T. S. R. Boniface VIII. London, 1933.

Bock, Friedrich, "Some New Documents Illustrating the Early Years of the Hundred Years War (1353–1356)," *Bulletin of the John Rylands Library,* XV (1931), 60–99.

Böhmer, J. F., ed. Fontes rerum Germanicarum. 4 vols. Stuttgart, 1843–68.

Bonin, M. Analectes historiques, recueil des documents inédits sur l'histoire de la ville d'Evreux. Evreux, 1839.

Bourgeois of Valenciennes, the. *See* Valenciennes.

Boursier, Auguste. Histoire de la ville et châtellenie de Creil. Paris, 1883.

Boussinesq, G., and G. Laurent. Histoire de Reims. 3 vols. Reims, 1934.

Boutruche, Robert, "La Dévastation des campagnes pendant la guerre de cent ans et la reconstruction agricole de la France," in *Mélanges 1945,* Vol. III, *Etudes historiques* (Paris, 1947), pp. 127–63. "Publications de la Faculté des lettres de l'université de Strasbourg," Fasc. 106.

Breuils, A., "Jean Ier, comte d'Armagnac et le mouvement national dans le Midi au temps du Prince Noir," *Revue des questions historiques,* LIX (1896), 44–102.

Breve chronicon clerici anonymi, in J. J. de Smet, ed., Corpus chronicorum Flandriae, III (Brussels, 1856), 5–30.

Bridrey, Emile. La Théorie de la monnaie au XIVe siècle: Nicole Oresme. Paris, 1906.

Brooke, Iris, and James Laver. English Costume from the Fourteenth through the Nineteenth Century. New York, 1937.

Broome, D. M., "The Ransom of John II, King of France, 1360–1370," in *Camden Miscellany,* Vol. XIV, Part 4 (London, 1926), Royal Historical Society, "Camden Third Series," Vol. XXXVII.

Brown, Edward. Fasciculus rerum expetendarum et fugiendarum. 2 vols. London, 1690.

Bruguier-Roure, L., "La Guerre autour du Pont-Saint-Esprit," *Mémoires de l'Académie de Vaucluse,* IX (1890), 96–122; 233–52.

Brutails, Jean Auguste. Documents des archives de la Chambre des comptes de Navarre. Paris, 1890. "Bibliothèque de l'Ecole des hautes études: sciences historiques et philologiques," Fasc. 84.

Bullarium magnum Romanorum. Bullarum, diplomatum et privilegiarum . . . editio locupletior facta . . . cura et studio . . . Aloysii Tomassetti. . . . 25 vols. Turin, 1857–72.

Burne, A. H., "The Battle of Poitiers," *English Historical Review,* LIII (1938), 21–52.

Caffiaux, Henri, "Commencement de la régence d'Aubert de Bavière," *Mémoires historiques sur l'arrondissement de Valenciennes,* II (1868), 225–326.

—— "Nicole de Dury, Maître clerc de la ville de Valenciennes, 1361–1373," *Mémoires historiques sur l'arrondissement de Valenciennes*, I (1865), 91–219.

Calendar of the Patent Rolls . . . Edward III. 16 vols. London, 1891–1916.

Calmette, Joseph. L'Elaboration du monde moderne. Paris, 1934. "Clio, introduction aux études historiques," No. 5.

Calonne, A. de. Histoire d'Amiens. 2 vols. Amiens, 1899–1900.

Campbell, Anna M. The Black Death and Men of Learning. New York, 1931.

Catalogue analytique des archives de M. le baron de Joursanvault. Paris, 1838.

Champeaux, E., "La Succession de Bourgogne à la mort de Philippe de Rouvre," *Mémoires de la Société pour l'histoire du droit et des institutions des anciens pays bourguignons*, Fasc. 3 (1936).

Chandos, the Herald of. Life of the Black Prince by the Herald of Sir John Chandos. Ed. and trans. by M. K. Pope and E. C. Lodge. Oxford, 1910.

Chaplais, Pierre, ed., "Some Documents Regarding the Fulfilment and Interpretation of the Treaty of Bretigny (1361–1369)," *Camden Miscellany*, Vol. XIX (London, 1952), 1–84. Royal Historical Society, "Camden Third Series," Vol. LXXX.

Chérest, A. L'Archiprêtre; épisodes de la guerre de cent ans au XIVe siècle. Paris, 1879.

Chéruel, A. Histoire de Rouen sous la domination anglaise. Rouen, 1840.

Chronica monasterii de Melsa. Ed. by E. A. Bond. 3 vols. London, 1866–68. "Rolls Series," No. 43.

Chronicles of London. Ed. by C. L. Kingsford. Oxford, 1905.

Chronicon Angliae Petriburgensis. Ed. by J. A. Giles. London, 1845.

Chronicon Britannicum, in P. H. Morice, Histoire ecclésiastique et civile de Bretagne, Vol. I (Paris, 1750).

Chronicon Elwacense, in Monumenta Germaniae historica, Scriptores, Vol. X (Hanover, 1852).

Chronicon Moguntinum, in Die Chroniken der deutschen Städte vom 14. bis ins 16. Jahrhundert, Vol. XVIII (Leipzig, 1882).

Chronikalien der Rathsbücher, in Basler Chroniken, ed. by W. Vischer, A. Stern, and A. Bernoulli, Vol. IV (Leipzig, 1890).

Chronique des Pays-Bas, de France, d'Angleterre et de Tournai, in J. J. de Smet, ed., Corpus chronicorum Flandriae, III (Brussels, 1856), 111–570.

Chronique des quatre premiers Valois (1329–1393). Ed. by S. Luce. Paris, 1862.

Chronique des règnes de Jean II et de Charles V. Ed. by R. Delachenal. 4 vols. Paris, 1910–20.

Chronique du bon duc Loys de Bourbon, La. Ed. by A.-M. Chazaud. Paris, 1876.

Chronique du Mont-Saint-Michel. Ed. by S. Luce. 2 vols. Paris, 1879–83.

Chronique normande du XIVe siècle. Ed. by A. and E. Molinier. Paris, 1882.

Chroniques de Saint-Martial de Limoges. Ed. by H. Duplès-Agier. Paris, 1874.

Chronique valenciennoise inédite, Une. Ed. by E. Delcambre. Dijon, 1929.

Chronographia regum Francorum. Ed. by H. Moranvillé. 3 vols. Paris, 1891–97.

Closener, Fritsche. Fritsche Closener's Chronik, ed. by K. Hegel, in Die Chroniken der deutschen Städte vom 14. bis ins 16. Jahrhundert, Vol. VIII (Leipzig, 1870).

Clowes, W. L. The Royal Navy; a History. 7 vols. London, 1897–1903.

Cochon, Pierre. Chronique normande de Pierre Cochon. Ed. by Ch. de Robillard de Beaurepaire. Rouen, 1870.

Compayré, C. Etudes historiques et documents inédits sur l'Albigeois, le Castrais et l'ancien diocèse de Lavaur. Albi, 1841.

"Complainte sur la bataille de Poitiers," ed. by Ch. de Robillard de Beaurepaire, Bibliothèque de l'Ecole des chartes, XII (1851), 257 ff.

Copeland, Jean L., "The Relations between the Secular Clergy and the Mendicant Friars in England during the Century after the Issue of the Bull Super cathedram (1300)," Summaries of Theses, No. clxii, Bulletin of the Institute of Historical Research, XVI (1938–39), 34–35.

Cordey, Jean. Les Comtes de Savoie et les rois de France pendant la guerre de cent ans (1329–1391). Paris, 1911.

Cosneau, E. Les Grands Traités de la guerre de cent ans. Paris, 1889.

Coulton, G. G. The Black Death. New York, n.d.

Coville, A., "Ecrits contemporains sur la peste de 1348 à 1350," in Histoire littéraire de la France, XXXVII (Paris, 1938), 325–90.

—— "Documents sur les Flagellants," in Histoire littéraire de la France, XXXVII (Paris, 1938), 390–411.

—— "Les Etats Généraux de 1332 et 1357," Le Moyen Age, VI (1893), 57–63.

Coyecque, E. L'Hôtel-Dieu de Paris au moyen âge, histoire et documents. 2 vols. Paris, 1891.

Creighton, Charles. A History of Epidemics in Britain. 2 vols. Cambridge, 1891–94.

Cronicques de Normendie (1223–1453), Les. Ed. by A. Hellot. Rouen, 1881.

Cuvelier. Chronique de Bertrand du Guesclin par Cuvelier, trouvère du

XIVe siècle. Ed. by E. Charrière. 2 vols. Paris, 1839. "Collection de documents inédits sur l'histoire de France," 1st series (Histoire politique).

Daumet, G. Calais sous la domination anglaise. Arras, 1902.

—— Etude sur l'alliance de la France et de la Castille aux XIVe et au XVe siècles. Paris, 1898.

—— Etude sur les relations d'Innocent VI avec D. Pedro Ier, roi de Castille au sujet de Blanche de Bourbon. Paris, 1899.

Delaborde, H.-Fr., "Un Arrière Petit-Fils de Saint Louis, Alfonse d'Espagne," in *Mélanges Julien Havet* (Paris, 1895), 411–27.

—— Jean de Joinville et les seigneurs de Joinville suivi d'un catalogue de leurs actes. Paris, 1894.

—— ed. Œuvres de Rigord et de Guillaume le Breton, historiens de Philippe Auguste. 2 vols. Paris, 1882–85.

Delachenal, R., "Deux Prétendues Lettres du régent fils ainé de Jean II au comte de Savoie Amédée VI," *Bibliothèque de l'Ecole des chartes,* LXXII (1911), 271–78.

—— Histoire de Charles V. 5 vols. Paris, 1909–31.

—— Histoire des avocats au Parlement de Paris, 1300–1600. Paris, 1885.

—— "Journal des Etats Généraux réunis à Paris au mois d'Octobre 1356," *Nouvelle Revue historique de droit française et étranger,* XXIV (1900), 415–65.

—— "Premières Négociations de Charles le Mauvais avec les Anglais (1354–1355)," *Bibliothèque de l'Ecole des chartes,* LXI (1900), 1–30.

Delettre, Abbé. Histoire du diocèse de Beauvais depuis son établissement, au 3me siècle jusqu'au 2 septembre, 1792. 3 vols. Beauvais, 1843.

Delgove, J. A., "L'Abbaye du Gard," *Mémoires de la Société des antiquaires de Picardie,* XXII (1868), 117–316.

Delisle, L. Histoire du château et des sires de Saint-Sauveur-le-Vicomte. Valognes, 1867.

—— Mandements et actes divers de Charles V (1364–1380). Paris, 1874.

—— Recherches sur la librairie de Charles V. 2 vols. and album. Paris, 1907.

Delpit, J. Collection générale des documents français qui se trouvent en Angleterre. Paris, 1847.

Delville, A. Histoire du château et des sires de Tancarville. Rouen, 1834.

Denifle, H. La Désolation des églises, monastères et hôpitaux en France pendant la guerre de cent ans. 2 vols. Paris, 1899.

Denifle, H., and E. Chatelain. Chartularium universitatis Parisiensis. 4 vols. Paris, 1889–97.

Déprez, E., "La Bataille de Najera (3 avril 1367); le communiqué du Prince Noir," *Revue historique,* CXXXVI (1921), 37–59.

Déprez, E., "Une Conférence anglo-navarrese en 1358," *Revue historique,* XCIX (1908), 34–39.

—— "La Conférence d'Avignon (1344)," in *Essays in Medieval History Presented to Thomas Frederick Tout,* ed. by A. G. Little and F. M. Powicke (Manchester, 1925).

—— "La Guerre de cent ans à la mort de Benoît XII; l'intervention des cardinaux avant le conclave et du Pape Clément VI avant son couronnement (25 avril–19 mai 1342)," *Revue historique,* LXXXIII (1903), 58–76.

—— Hugo Aubriot praepositus Parisiensis et urbanus praetor (1367–1381). Paris, 1902.

—— "La Mort de Robert d'Artois," *Revue historique,* XCIV (1907), 63–66.

—— Les Préliminaires de la guerre de cent ans; la papauté, la France et l'Angleterre (1328–1342). Paris, 1902.

—— "La Querelle de Bretagne de la captivité de Charles de Blois à la majorité de Jean IV de Montfort (1347–1362)," *Mémoires de la Société d'histoire et d'archéologie de Bretagne,* VII (1926), 25–60.

—— "Une Tentative de réforme du calendrier sous Clément VI; Jean de Murs et la chronique de Jean de Venette," *Mélanges d'archéologie et d'histoire de l'Ecole française de Rome,* XIX (1899), 131–43.

De Smet, J. J., ed. Corpus chronicorum Flandriae. 4 vols. Brussels, 1837–65.

Desnoyers, J. Topographie ecclésiastique de la France. 2 parts. Paris, 1854; 1861–62.

Devic, Cl., and J. Vaissete. Histoire générale de Languedoc. 15 vols. Toulouse, 1872–93.

Deville, A. Tombeaux de la cathédrale de Rouen. Rouen, 1833.

Dodu, G. Les Valois; histoire d'une maison royale (1328–1589). Paris, 1934.

Domairon, L., "Suites de la bataille de Cocherel," *Cabinet historique,* Vol. IV, Part 1 (1858), pp. 67–73.

Douët-d'Arcq, L., "Acte d'accusation contre Robert le Coq, évêque de Laon," *Bibliothèque de l'Ecole des chartes,* II (1840–41), 350–87.

Dournel, J. Histoire générale de Péronne. Péronne, 1879.

Doyen, C. L. Histoire de la ville de Beauvais. 2 vols. Beauvais, 1842.

Dubois, Abbé. Histoire du siège d'Orléans 1428–1429. Ed. by P. Charpentier. Orléans, 1894.

Du Boulay, C. E. Historia Universitatis Parisiensis. 6 vols. Paris, 1665–73.

Du Breul, Jacques. Le Théâtre des antiquitez de Paris. Paris, 1612.

Dubrulle, H. Cambrai à la fin du moyen âge (XIIIe–XVIe siècle). Lille, 1903.

Dufourmantelle, Ch. La Marine militaire au commencement de la guerre de cent ans. Paris, 1878.

Duhem, Pierre. Le Système du monde; histoire des doctrines cosmologiques de Platon à Copernic. 5 vols. Paris, 1913–17.

Dupont, Gustave. Histoire du Cotentin et de ses îles. 4 vols. Caen, 1870–85.

Durand, A., and E. Grave. Chronique de Mantes ou histoire de Mantes depuis le IXe siècle jusqu'à la révolution. Mantes, 1883.

Fallue, L. Histoire politique et religieuse de l'église metropolitaine et du diocèse de Rouen. 4 vols. Rouen, 1850–51.

Farcy, P. de. Abbayes de l'évêché de Bayeux. Laval, 1887.

Félibien, M., and G.-A. Lobineau. Histoire de la ville de Paris. 5 vols. Paris, 1725.

Flammermont, J., "La Jacquerie en Beauvaisis," *Revue historique,* IX (1879), 123–43.

Fortescue, A. The Mass; a Study of the Roman Liturgy. London, 1914.

Fossey, Abbé Jules. Monographe de la cathédrale d'Evreux. Evreux, 1898.

Fournier, P. Le Royaume d'Arles et de Vienne. Paris, 1891.

"Fragments inédits de la chronique de Jean de Noyal." *See* Jean de Noyal.

Francis Beaumont, Brother. Tragicum argumentum. *See* "Un Pamphlet politique."

Froissart. Chroniques de J. Froissart. Ed. by Siméon Luce. 11 vols. in 12. Paris, 1869–99.

—— Œuvres de Froissart. Ed. by Kervyn de Lettenhove. 25 vols. in 26. Brussels, 1867–77.

Funck-Brentano, F. Les Origines de la guerre de cent ans. Philippe le Bel et Flandre. Paris, 1897.

Funk, Arthur L., "Robert le Coq and Etienne Marcel," *Speculum,* XIX (1944), 470–87.

Galbraith, V. H., "The Battle of Poitiers," *English Historical Review,* LIV (1939), 473–75.

—— "Extracts from the *Historia aurea* and a French 'Brut' (1317–47)," *English Historical Review,* XLIII (1928), 203–17.

Gallia Christiana in provincias ecclesiasticas distributa. . . . 16 vols. Paris, 1715–1865.

Garnier, E., "Notice sur Robert de Fiennes, connétable de France (1320–1384)," *Bibliothèque de l'Ecole des chartes,* XIII (1852), 23–52.

Gaudemet, J., "Les Prétentions de Charles II, roi de Navarre, à la succession de Philippe de Rouvre," *Mémoires de la Société pour l'histoire du droit et des institutions des anciens pays bourguignons,* Fasc. 3 (1936).

Geoffrey the Baker. Chronicon Galfridi le Baker de Swinbroke. Ed. by E. M. Thompson. Oxford, 1899.

Géraud, H., ed. Chronique latine de Guillaume de Nangis de 1113 à 1300 avec les continuations de cette chronique de 1300 à 1368. 2 vols. Paris, 1843.

Germain, A. Histoire de la commune de Montpellier depuis ses origines jusqu'à son incorporation définitive à la monarchie française. 3 vols. Montpellier, 1851–53.

Gesta abbatum Trudonensium, in Monumenta Germaniae historica, Scriptores, Vol. X (Hanover, 1852).

Gilles li Muisis. Chronique et annales de Gilles le Muisit, abbé de Saint-Martin de Tournai (1272–1352). Ed. by H. Lemaître. Paris, 1906.

Goldast, M. Monarchia sancti Romani imperii. . . . 3 vols. Frankfort and Hanover, 1611–14.

Grandes Chroniques de France, Les. Ed. by Jules Viard. 9 vols. Paris, 1920–37.
   Volume IX (1937) contains the chronicle of Charles IV le Bel and the chronicle of Philippe VI de Valois.

Gras, P., "Le Registre paroissial de Givry (1334–1357) et la Peste Noire en Bourgogne," *Bibliothèque de l'Ecole des chartes,* C (1939), 295–308.

Gray, Sir Thomas. Scalacronica. Trans. by Sir Henry Maxwell. Edinburgh, 1907.

Guesnon, A., "Documents inédits sur l'invasion anglaise et les Etats au temps de Philippe VI et Jean le Bon," Comité des travaux historiques et scientifiques, *Bulletin historique et philologique,* 1897, pp. 208–59.

Guiffrey, J. J. Histoire de la réunion du Dauphiné à la France. Paris, 1868.

Guigue, G. Récits de la guerre de cent ans: les tard-venus en Lyonnais, Forez et Beaujolais 1356–1369. Lyon, 1886.

Guillaume de Nangis. *See* Géraud.

Guy de Chauliac. La Grande Chirugie de Guy de Chauliac. Ed. by E. Nicaise. Paris, 1890.

Gwynn, Aubrey, "The Black Death in Ireland," *Studies; an Irish Quarterly of Letters Philosophy & Science,* XXIV (1935), 25–42.

—— "The Date of the B-Text of *Piers Plowman,*" *Review of English Studies,* XIX (1943), 1–24.

—— The English Austin Friars in the Time of Wyclif. Oxford, 1940.

—— "Richard FitzRalph, Archbishop of Armagh," *Studies; an Irish Quarterly of Letters Philosophy & Science,* XXII (1933), 389–405; "Richard FitzRalph at Avignon," *ibid.,* pp. 591–607; "Richard FitzRalph, Archbishop of Armagh, Part III," *ibid.,* XXIII (1934), 395–411; "The Black Death in Ireland," *ibid.,* XXIV (1935), 25–42; "Archbishop FitzRalph and George of Hungary," *ibid.,* pp. 558–72; "Richard FitzRalph, Archbishop of Armagh, Part VI," *ibid.,* XXV (1936), 81–96; "Archbishop FitzRalph and the Friars," *ibid.,* XXVI (1937), 50–67.

—— "The Sermon-Diary of Richard FitzRalph, Archbishop of Armagh," in *Proceedings of the Royal Irish Academy*, XLIV (1937), Section C, No. 1, pp. 2–66.

Hammerich, L. L. Beginning of the Strife between Richard Fitzralph and the Mendicants. Copenhagen, 1938.

Hecker, J. F. C. Epidemics of the Middle Ages. Trans. by B. G. Babington. London, 1844.

Heinricus Rebdorfensis, Annales imperatorum et paparum, 1294–1362, in J. F. Böhmer, ed., Fontes rerum Germanicarum, Vol. IV (Stuttgart, 1868).

Heinricus Truchsess von Diessenhoven, Chronicon de Heinricus Truchsess von Diessenhoven, in J. F. Böhmer, ed., Fontes rerum Germanicarum, Vol. IV (Stuttgart, 1868).

Hellot, A. Essai historique sur les Martel de Basqueville et sur Basqueville-en-Caux. Rouen, 1879.

Hendrick, B. J., "Fighting the 'Black Death' in Manchuria," *World's Work*, XXVII (1913–14), 210–22.

Henricus de Hervordia. Chronicon Henrici de Hervordia. Ed. by A. Potthast. Göttingen, 1859.

Hervieux, A. L. Les Fabulistes latins depuis le siècle d'Auguste jusqu'à la fin du moyen âge. 5 vols. Paris, 1893–99.

Honoré-Duvergé, Suzanne, "L'Origine du surnom de Charles le Mauvais," in *Mélanges d'histoire du moyen âge dédiés à la mémoire de Louis Halphen* (Paris, 1951), pp. 345–50.

Hossart, Abbé. Histoire ecclésiastique et profane de Hainaut. 2 vols. Mons, 1792.

Hutton, J. James and Philip van Artevelde. London, 1882.

Isambert, François André. Recueil général des anciennes lois françaises depuis l'an 420 jusqu'à la révolution de 1789. 29 vols. Paris, 1822–33.

Istore et chroniques de Flandres. Ed. by Kervyn de Lettenhove. 2 vols. Brussels, 1879–80.

Jaillot, J. B. M. Recherches critiques, historiques, et topographiques sur la ville de Paris, depuis ses commencemens connus jusqu'à présent; avec le plan de chaque quartier: par le Sr. Jaillot. . . . 8 vols. Paris, 1772–75.

Janvier, A. Les Clabault, famille municipale amienoise. Amiens, 1889.

Jean de Noyal, "Fragments inédits de la chronique de Jean de Noyal," ed. by A. Molinier, *Annuaire-Bulletin de la Société de l'histoire de France*, XX (1883), 246–77.

Jean de Venette, Chronicon ordinis B. V. Mariae de Monte Carmeli, ed. by

Daniel a Virgine Maria, in Speculum Carmelitanum, Vol. I (Antwerp, 1680).

Jean de Venette. *See also* Géraud.

Jean le Bel. Chronique de Jean le Bel. Ed. by J. Viard and E. Déprez. 2 vols. Paris, 1904–5.

Jenkins, H. Papal Efforts for Peace under Benedict XII, 1334–1342. Philadelphia, 1933.

Jessopp, Augustus, "The Black Death in East Anglia," *The Nineteenth Century*, XVI (1884), 915–34; XVII (1885), 599–622.

John of Fordun. Chronicle of the Scottish Nation, trans. by F. J. H. Skene; ed. by Wm. F. Skene, in The Historians of Scotland, Vol. IV (Edinburgh, 1872).

John of Reading. Chronica Johannis de Reading et anonymi Cantuariensis. Ed. by James Tait. Manchester, 1914.

Jourdain, Charles, "L'Université de Paris au temps d'Etienne Marcel," *Revue des questions historiques*, XXIV (1878), 548–66.

Jusselin, M., "Comment la France se préparait à la guerre de cent ans," *Bibliothèque de l'Ecole des chartes*, LXXIII (1912), 209–36.

Jusserand, J. J. Les Sports et jeux d'exercise dans l'ancienne France. Paris, 1901.

Justinger, Conrad. Die Berner-Chronik der Conrad Justinger. Ed. by G. Studer. Bern, 1871.

Kampers, F. Die deutsche Kaiseridee in Prophetie und Sage. Munich, 1896.

—— "Ueber die Prophezeiungen des Johannes de Rupescissa," in *Historisches Jahrbuch*, XV (1894), 796–802.

Knighton, Henry. Chronicon Henrici Knighton. Ed. by J. R. Lumby. 2 vols. London, 1889–95. "Rolls Series," No. 92.

Königshofen, Jacob Twinger von. Chronik des Jacob Twinger von Königshofen, ed. by K. Hegel, in Die Chroniken der deutschen Städte vom 14. bis ins 16. Jahrhundert, Vols. VIII–IX (Leipzig, 1870–71).

Labaude, L.-H. Histoire de Beauvais et de ses institutions communales jusqu'au commencement du XVe siècle. Paris, 1891.

—— "L'Occupation du Pont-Saint-Esprit par les grandes compagnies (1360–1361)," *Revue historique de Provence*, I (1901), 79–95; 146–64.

La Borderie, Arthur de. Histoire de Bretagne. 6 vols. Rennes, 1896–1914.

La Borderie, Arthur de, J. Daniel, R. P. Perquis, and D. Tempier. Monuments originaux de l'histoire de Saint-Yves. Saint-Brieuc, 1887.

Lacabane, J., "De la poudre à canon et de son introduction en France," *Bibliothèque de l'Ecole des chartes*, VI (1844), 28–57.

Lancelot, Antoine, "Mémoires pour servir à l'historie de Robert d'Artois," *Mémoires de littérature tirez des registres de l'Académie royale des inscriptions et belles-lettres,* X (1736), 571–663.

Langlois, E. Table des noms propres de toute nature compris dans les chansons de geste imprimées. Paris, 1904.

La Roncière, Ch. de. Histoire de la marine française. 6 vols. Paris, 1899–1932.

—— "Quatrième Guerre navale entre la France et l'Angleterre (1335–1341)," *Revue maritime,* CXXXVI (1898), 246–300.

La Roque, G.-A. de. Histoire de la maison de Harcourt. 4 vols. Paris, 1672.

Last Age of the Church, The (1356). Ed. by James H. Todd. Dublin, 1840.

Laurent, Henri, "Les Conventions de Saint-Quentin (juin 1347)," *Bulletin de la Commission royale d'histoire,* XCI (1927), 89–180.

Le Batelier d'Aviron. Le Mémorial historique des évêques, ville et comté d'Evreux. Ed. by P. F. Lebeurier. Evreux, 1865.

Lebeuf, Jean. Histoire de la ville et de tout le diocèse de Paris. Ed. by H. Cocheris. 4 vols. Paris, 1863–70.

—— Mémoires concernant l'histoire civile et ecclésiastique d'Auxerre et de son ancien diocèse. Ed. by A. Challe and M. Quantin. 4 vols. Auxerre, 1848–55.

Lecanu, M. Histoire des évêques de Coutances. Coutances, 1839.

Lechler, G. V. John Wiclif and His English Precursors. Trans. by P. Lorimer. 2 vols. London, 1878.

Leroux, A. Recherches critiques sur les relations politiques de la France avec l'Allemagne de 1292 à 1378. Paris, 1882.

Le Roux de Lincy, A., and L. M. Tisserand. Paris et ses historiens aux XIVe et XVe siècles. Paris, 1867.

Levett, A. E., and A. Ballard. The Black Death. Oxford, 1916. "Oxford Studies in Social and Legal History," Vol. V.

Littré, E., "Opuscule relatif à la peste de 1348 composé par un contemporain," *Bibliothèque de l'Ecole des chartes,* II (1841), 201–43.

Loeb, Isidore, "Les Expulsions des Juifs de France au XIVe siècle," in *Jubelschrift zum siebzigsten Geburtstage des Prof. Dr. H. Graetz.* 1 vol. in 2 parts. Breslau, 1887.

Loth, Abbé J. La Cathédrale de Rouen. Rouen, 1879.

Lowe, W. I., "The Considerations Which Induced Edward III to Assume the Title King of France," in American Historical Association, *Annual Report,* I (1900), 535–83.

Lucas, H. S., "The Great European Famine of 1315, 1316, and 1317," *Speculum,* V (1930), 343–77.

Lucas, H. S., The Low Countries and the Hundred Years' War, 1326–1347. Ann Arbor, 1929.

—— "The Sources and Literature on Jacob van Artevelde," *Speculum*, VIII (1933), 125–49.

Luce, Siméon, "Du Guesclin en Normandie . . . le siège et prise de Valognes," *Revue des questions historiques*, LIII (1893), 372–411.

—— La France pendant la guerre de cent ans. Episodes historiques et vie privée aux XIVe et XVe siècles. 1st series. 2d ed. Paris, 1890.

—— Histoire de Bertrand du Guesclin et de son époque . . . la jeunesse de Bertrand (1320–1364). Paris, 1876.

—— Histoire de la Jacquerie, d'après des documents inédits. 2d ed. Paris, 1894.

—— "Les Juifs sous Charles V," *Revue historique*, VII (1878), 363–70.

—— "La Marine normande à la bataille de l'Ecluse," *Bulletin de la Société des antiquaires de Normandie*, XIII (1885). Reprinted in *La France pendant la guerre de cent ans*, 2d series (Paris, 1893).

—— "Négociations des Anglais avec le roi de Navarre pendant la révolution parisienne de 1358," *Mémoires de la Société de l'histoire de Paris et de l'Ile de France*, I (1875), 113–31.

—— "Notice sur Guillaume l'Aloue," *Annuaire-Bulletin de la Société de l'histoire de France*, 1875, pp. 149–56.

Magnum Chronicum Belgicum, in J. Pistorius, Rerum Germanicarum scriptores, III (Ratisbon, 1726), 1–456.

Malmesbury, monk of. Eulogium historiarum [by a Monk of Malmesbury]. Ed. by F. S. Haydon. 3 vols. London, 1858–63. "Rolls Series," No. 9.

Mansi, J. D. Sacrorum conciliorum nova et amplissima collectio. 31 vols. Florence and Venice, 1759–98.

Marie-Joseph, P., "Les Couvents des Grands-Carmes en France pendant la guerre de cent ans et les guerres de religion," *Etudes carmélitaines*, IX (1924).

Matthieu, Ernest, "Histoire de la ville d'Enghien," *Mémoires et publications de la Société des sciences, des arts et des lettres du Hainaut*, 4th series, I (1875), 57–419; II (1876), 148–489.

Maugis, Edouard. Documents inédits concernant la ville et le siège du bailliage d'Amiens. . . . 3 vols. Amiens, 1908, 1914, 1921. Société des antiquaires de Picardie, "Mémoires in-4°," Vols. XVII, XIX, XX.

Mélanges Julien Havet; recueil de travaux d'érudition dédiés à la mémoire de Julien Havet (1853–1893). Paris, 1895.

Mendl, B., and F. Quicke, "Les Relations politiques entre l'empereur et le roi de France de 1355 à 1356," *Revue belge de philologie et d'histoire,* Vol. VIII, Part 1 (1929), pp. 469–512.

Menéndez y Pelayo, M. Historia de los heterodoxos españoles. Ed. by Adolfo Bonilla y San Martín and Miguel Artigas. 7 vols. Madrid, 1911–32.

Meyer, E. Charles II, roi de Navarre, comte d'Evreux. Paris, 1898.

Michon, L.-A. Joseph. Documents inédits sur la grande peste de 1348. Paris, 1860.

Miller, W. The Latins in the Levant. New York, 1908.

Miret y Sans, J., "Négociations de Pierre IV d'Aragon avec la cour de France, 1366–1367," *Revue hispanique,* XIII (1905), 76–135.

Mirot, Léon, "Un Episode de l'alliance franco-castillane au XIVe siècle. Charles V et l'avènement d'Henri de Trastamare," *Revue des études historiques,* LXXXIV (1918), 54–68.

Moisant, J. Le Prince Noir en Aquitaine, 1355–70. Paris, 1894.

Molinier, Auguste. Les Sources de l'histoire de France. Paris, 1901–6. Vol. IV (1904), Les Valois, 1328–1461.

Molinier, Emile, "Documents relatifs aux Calaisiens expulsés par Edouard III," *Cabinet historique,* XXIV (1878), 250–80.

—— Etude sur la vie d'Arnoul d'Audrehem, maréchal de France, 130.–1370. Paris, 1883. Académie des inscriptions et belles-lettres, "Mémoires présentés par divers savants," 2d series, Vol. VI, Part 1.

Mollat, G., "Innocent VI et les tentatives de paix entre la France et l'Angleterre (1353–1355)," *Revue d'histoire ecclésiastique,* X (1909), 729–43.

—— L'Œuvre oratoire de Clément VI," *Archives d'histoire doctrinale et littéraire du moyen âge,* III (1928), 239–74.

—— ed. Vitae paparum Avenionensium. *See* Baluze.

Moranvillé, H., "Charles d'Artois," *Bibliothèque de l'Ecole des chartes,* LXVIII (1907), 433–80.

—— "Guillaume de Breuil et Robert d'Artois," *Bibliothèque de l'Ecole des chartes,* XLVIII (1887), 641–50.

—— "Philippe VI à la bataille de Crécy," *Bibliothèque de l'Ecole des chartes,* L (1889), 295–96.

—— "Le Siège de Reims, 1359–1360," *Bibliothèque de l'Ecole des chartes,* LVI (1895), 90–98.

Morice, P. H. Histoire ecclésiastique et civile de Bretagne. 2 vols. Paris, 1750–56.

—— Mémoires pour servir de preuves à l'histoire ecclésiastique et civile de Bretagne. 3 vols. Paris, 1742–46.

Mortier, R. P. Histoire des maîtres généraux de l'ordre des frères prêcheurs. 8 vols. Paris, 1903–20.

Narbonne, B. Gaston Phébus, seigneur du Béarn, 1331–1391. Paris, 1936.

Nicolas, Sir N. H. A History of the Royal Navy. 2 vols. London, 1847.

Noel, E. B., and J. O. M. Clark. A History of Tennis. 2 vols. Oxford, 1924.

Nohl, J. The Black Death; a Chronicle of the Plague Compiled from Contemporary Sources. Trans. by C. H. Clarke. London, 1926.

Norris, Herbert. Costume and Fashion. 2 vols. New York, 1925–27.

Odier, Jeanne. Jean de Roquetaillade. Thesis, Ecole des chartes. 1925.

Offler, H. S., "England and Germany at the Beginning of the Hundred Years War," *English Historical Review,* LIV (1939), 608–31.

Oman, Sir Charles. History of the Art of War in the Middle Ages. 2d ed. 2 vols. London, 1924.

Ordonnances des roys de France de la troisième race. 21 vols. and index. Paris, 1732–1849.

Oudin, Casimir. Commentarius de scriptoribus ecclesiae antiquis. . . . 3 vols. Leipzig, 1722.

"Pamphlet politique au XIVe siècle, Un," Comité des travaux historiques et scientifiques, *Bulletin historique et philologique,* 1862, pp. 173–77.

Payne-Gallwey, Sir Ralph. The Crossbow, Mediaeval and Modern, Military and Sporting; Its Construction, History and Management. London, 1903.

Peeters, Louis, "Le Comté de Hainaut durant les premières années de la régence du duc Albert de Bavière (1357–1372)," in *Mélanges d'histoire offerts à Charles Moeller* (Louvain and Paris, 1914), Vol. I.

Perrens, F. T. Etienne Marcel et le gouvernement de la bourgeoisie au quatorzième siècle (1356–1358). Paris, 1860.

Perroy, E., "Charles V et le traité de Brétigny," *Le Moyen Age,* XXXVIII (1928), 255–81.

—— "France, England and Navarre from 1359–1364," *Bulletin of the Institute of Historical Research,* XIII (1935–36), 151–54.

—— "Franco-English Relations, 1350–1400," *History,* XXI (1936–37), 148–54.

—— The Hundred Years War. Trans. by W. B. Wells. London, 1951.

Petit, E. Ducs de Bourgogne de la maison de Valois; Philippe le Hardi. Part 1. Paris, 1909.

—— Histoire des ducs de Bourgogne de la race capétienne. 9 vols. Dijon, 1885–1905.

—— Monographie des sires de Noyers. Auxerre, 1874.

—— "Séjours de Jean II (1350–1356)," Comité des travaux historiques et scientifiques, *Bulletin historique et philologique,* 1896, pp. 587–612.

Petit-Dutaillis, Ch., and P. Collier, "La Diplomatie française et le traité de Brétigny," *Le Moyen Age,* X (1897), 1–35.

Petite Chronique françoise de l'an 1270 à l'an 1356, ed. by L. Douët-d'Arcq, in Mélanges de littérature et d'histoire recueillis et publiés par la Société des bibliophiles français, Part 2 (Paris, 1867).

Pirenne, H. Histoire de Belgique. 7 vols. Brussels, 1909–32.

Pistorius, Johann. Rerum Germanicarum scriptores. . . . 3d ed. 3 vols. Ratisbon, 1726.

Piton, Camille. Le Costume civil en France du XIIIe au XIXe siècle. Paris, 1926.

Plaine, Dom. La Guerre de la succession de Bretagne. Nantes, 1886.

Plancher, Dom. Histoire générale et particulière de Bourgogne. 4 vols. Dijon, 1738–81.

Pocquet du Haut-Jussé, B.-A. Les Papes et les ducs de Bretagne. 2 vols. Paris, 1928.

—— "La Succession de Bourgogne en 1361," *Annales de Bourgogne,* X (1938), 54–63.

Poole, R. L., "The Beginning of the Year in the Middle Ages," in *Studies in Chronology and History,* ed. by A. L. Poole (Oxford, 1934).

—— ed. Iohannis Wycliffe De dominio divino; To Which are Added the First Four Books of . . . De pauperie Salvatoris by Richard FitzRalph. . . . London, 1890.

Potter, J. M., "The Development and Significance of the Salic Law of the French," *English Historical Review,* LII (1937), 235–53.

Prentout, Henri, "La Prise de Caen par Edouard III, 1346; étude critique," *Mémoires de l'Académie nationale des sciences, arts et belles-lettres de Caen,* 1904.

Prince, A. E., "A Letter of Edward the Black Prince Describing the Battle of Najera in 1367," *English Historical Review,* XLI (1926), 415–18.

—— "The Strength of English Armies in the Reign of Edward III," *English Historical Review,* XLVI (1931), 352–71.

Prou, Maurice, Etude sur les relations politiques du pape Urbain V avec les rois de France, Jean II et Charles V (1362–1370). Paris, 1887.

Puymaigre, Th. de., "Jean l'Aveugle en France," *Revue des questions historiques,* LII (1892), 391–452.

Quicherat, Jules. Histoire du costume en France depuis les temps les plus reculés jusqu'à la fin du XVIIIe siècle. Paris, 1875.

Quicke, Fritz. Les Pays-Bas à la veille de la période bourguignonne (1356–1384). Brussels, 1948.

Ramsay, Sir J. H. Genesis of Lancaster. 2 vols. Oxford, 1913.

Ramsay, Sir J. H. "The Strength of English Armies in the Middle Ages," *English Historical Review*, XXIX (1914), 221–27.

Raynaldus, Odoricus. Annales ecclesiastici ab anno MCXCVIII ubi desinit cardinalis Baronius. . . . 15 vols. Lucca, 1747–56. These comprise Vols. XX–XXXIV of the whole work begun by Baronius. Ed. with notes by J. D. Mansi and pub. in 38 vols. (1738–59).

Rebouis, H. E. Etude historique et critique sur la peste. Paris, 1888.

Rhein, André. Notre Dame de Mantes. Paris, 1932.

Richard, J. M. Mahaut, comtesse d'Artois et de Bourgogne. Paris, 1887.

Richard Lescot. Chronique de Richard Lescot. Ed. by J. Lemoine. Paris, 1896.

Rigord. Gesta Philippi Augusti, in H. F. Delaborde, ed., Œuvres de Rigord et de Guillaume le Breton, historiens de Philippe Auguste, Vol. I (Paris, 1882).

Robert of Avesbury. De gestis mirabilibus regis Edwardi tertii. Ed. by E. M. Thompson. London, 1889. "Rolls Series," No. 93.

Rodocanachi, E., "Le Premier Jubilé de 1350," in *Etudes et fantaisies historiques* (Paris, 1900), pp. 153–64.

Rusconi, A. J., Assisi. Bergamo, n.d.

Russell, Josiah Cox. British Medieval Population. Albuquerque, 1948.

Rymer, Thomas. Foedera. . . . 3d ed. 10 vols. The Hague, 1739–45.

Sandeman, G. A. C. Calais under English Rule. Oxford, 1908.

Saussaye, C. de la. Annales ecclesiae Aurelianensis. Paris, 1615.

Savage, H. L., "Enguerrand de Coucy VII and the Campaign of Nicopolis," *Speculum*, XIV (1939), 423–42.

Schevill, Ferdinand. History of Florence. New York, 1936.

Secousse, Denis François. Mémoires pour servir à l'histoire de Charles II de Navarre. Paris, 1758.

—— Recueil de pièces servant de preuves aux mémoires sur les troubles excités en France par Charles II dit le Mauvais, roi de Navarre et comte d'Evreux. Paris, 1755.

Shaw, Peter, "The Black Prince," *History*, XXIV (1939–40), 1–15.

Signorelli, G. Viterbo nella storia della chiesa. 2 vols. Viterbo, 1907–8.

Simonnet, J. Essai sur l'histoire et la généalogie des sires de Joinville (1008–1386). Langres, 1875.

Sourdeval, Ch. de, "Les Sires de Retz et le château de Machecoul," *Mémoires de la Société archéologique de Touraine*, II (1843–44), 27–70.

Spicilegium sive collectio veterum aliquot scriptorum qui in Galliae bibliothecis maxime Benedictinorum latuerunt. Ed. by Luc d'Achery. 13 vols. Paris, 1655–77.

Statenrath, M. de, "Etat des fortifications et des enceintes de la ville d'Evreux, à diverses époques de son histoire," *Travaux de la Société d'agriculture de l'Eure,* 1st series, VI (1935), 341–72.

Statutes of the Realm (1235–1713). 11 vols. London, Record Commission, 1810–28.

Stein, Henri, "Comment on luttait autrefois contre les épidemies," *Annuaire-Bulletin de la Société de l'histoire de France,* 1918, pp. 125–50.

Steveni, W. B., "The Ravages of the Black Death in the Fourteenth Century, and Its Re-appearance in the Twentieth Century," *Fortnightly Review,* CI (1914), 154–64.

Sturler, Jean de. Les Relations politiques et les échanges commerciaux entre le duché de Brabant et l'Angleterre au moyen âge. Paris, 1936.

Symon de Phares. Recueil des plus celebres astrologues. Ed. by E. Wickersheimer. Paris, 1929.

Taylor, Rupert. The Political Prophecy in England, New York, 1911.

Templeman, G., "Edward III and the Beginnings of the Hundred Years War," in *Transactions of the Royal Historical Society,* 5th series, II (1952), 69–88.

Theiner, A. Vetera monumenta Hibernorum et Scotorum historia illustrantia (1216–1547). Rome, 1864.

Thierry, Augustin. Recueil des monuments inédits de l'histoire du Tiers Etat. 4 vols. Paris, 1850–70. "Collection de documents inédits sur l'histoire de France," No. 13.

Thompson, E. M., ed. Adae Murimuth continuatio chronicarum. London, 1889. "Rolls Series," No. 93.

Thorndike, Lynn. A History of Magic and Experimental Science. 6 vols. New York, 1923–41.

—— ed. Latin Treatises on Comets between 1238 and 1368 A.D. Chicago, 1950.

Tourneur-Aumont, J., "Conclusion de l'histoire militaire de la bataille de Poitiers (17, 18, 19 septembre 1356)," *Bulletin de la Société des antiquaires de l'Ouest,* 3d series, XI (1936–38), 433–64.

Tout, T. F., and D. M. Broome, "A National Balance Sheet for 1362–3," *English Historical Review,* XXXIX (1924), 404–19.

—— "Some Neglected Fights between Crécy and Poitiers," *English Historical Review,* XX (1905), 726–30.

Tragicum argumentum de miserabili statu regni Francie editum a fratre Francisco de Monte Bellima, ordinis Sancti Benedicti. *See* "Un Pamphlet politique."

Vacandard, J. La Guerre de cent ans dans le comté d'Eu. Eu, 1926.

Valenciennes, the Bourgeois of. Récits d'un bourgeois de Valenciennes (XIVe siècle). Ed. by Kervyn de Lettenhove. Louvain, 1877.

Valois, Noël. Le Conseil du roi au XIVe, XVe et XVIe siècles. . . . Paris, 1888.

—— "Le Gouvernement représentatif en France au XIVe siècle; étude sur la conseil du roi pendant la captivité de Jean le Bon," *Revue des questions historiques*, XXXVII (1885), 63–115.

—— "Notes sur la révolution parisienne de 1356–58; la revanche des frères Braque," *Mémoires de la Société de l'histoire de Paris*, X (1883), 100–126.

Vandenbroeck, H. Extraits analytiques des anciens registres des consaux de la ville de Tournai. 2 vols. Tournai, 1861–63.

Vanderkindere, L. Le Siècle des Artevelde. Brussels, 1879.

Varia chronicorum fragmenta. *See* Chroniques de Saint-Martial de Limoges.

Varin, P. J. Archives administratives de la ville de Reims. 4 vols. Paris, 1843.

Viard, J., "La Campagne de juillet-août 1346 et la bataille de Crécy," *Le Moyen Age*, XXXVI (1926), 1–84.

—— "Itinéraire de Philippe VI de Valois," *Bibliothèque de l'Ecole des chartes*, LXXIV (1913), 74–128; 525–619.

—— Les Journeaux du trésor de Philippe VI de Valois. Paris, 1899.

—— "Lettres d'état enregistrées au Parlement sous le règne de Philippe VI de Valois (1328–1350)," *Annuaire-Bulletin de la Société de l'histoire de France*, XXXIV (1897), 193–267; XXXV (1898), 177–252.

—— "La Messe pour la peste," *Bibliothèque de l'Ecole des chartes*, LXI (1900), 334–38.

—— "Philippe VI de Valois: début du règne (fevrier-juillet 1328)," *Bibliothèque de l'Ecole des chartes*, XCV (1934), 259–83.

—— "Philippe VI de Valois: la succession au trône," *Le Moyen Age*, XXXII (1921), 218–22.

—— "Les Ressources extraordinaires de la royauté sous Philippe VI de Valois," *Revue des questions historiques*, XLIV (1888), 167–218.

—— "Le Siège de Calais, 4 septembre 1346—4 août 1347," *Le Moyen Age*. XXXIX (1929), 129–89.

Villani, Giovanni. Cronica. . . . Ed. by F. G. Dragomanni. 4 vols. Florence, 1844–45.

—— Historie fiorentine, in L. A. Muratori, Rerum Italicarum scriptores, Vols. XIII–XIV (Milan, 1728–29).

Vol. XIV, cols. 9–770, comprises the *Istorie* of Matteo Villani, which continues the work of Giovanni for the years 1348–64.

Viollet, Paul, "Comment les femmes on été exclues, en France, de la succession à la couronne," *Mémoires de l'Académie des inscriptions et belles-lettres,* Vol. XXXIV, Part 2 (1895), pp. 125–78.

—— "Les Etats de Paris en février 1358," *Mémoires de l'Académie des inscriptions et belles-lettres,* Vol. XXXIV, Part 2 (1895), pp. 261–92.

—— Histoire des institutions politiques et administratives de la France. 3 vols. Paris, 1890–1903.

Walsingham, Thomas. Historia Anglicana of Thomas Walsingham. Ed. by H. T. Riley. 2 vols. London, 1863–64. "Rolls Series," No. 28, 1, Parts 1 and 2.

Ward, H. L. D. Catalogue of Romances in the Department of Manuscripts in the British Museum. 2 vols. London, 1883.

Werunsky, E. Geschichte Kaiser Karls IV und seiner Zeit. 3 vols. in 2. Innsbruck, 1880–92.

Wessels, P. G., ed. Acta capitulorum generalium ordinis fratrum B. V. Mariae de Monte Carmelo. Rome, 1912.

—— ed. Bibliotheca Carmelitana. 2 vols. in 1. Rome, 1927.

Westermann, E. J., "Emperor Charles IV and Pope Innocent VI," *University of Colorado Studies,* I (1941), 301–6.

Wilkinson, B., "A Letter to Louis de Mâle, Count of Flanders," *Bulletin of the John Rylands Library,* IX (1925), 177–87.

Winslow, C.-E. A. The Conquest of Epidemic Disease; a Chapter in the History of Ideas. Princeton, 1943.

Workman, H. B. John Wyclif. 2 vols. Oxford, 1926.

Young, Karl. The Drama of the Medieval Church. 2 vols. Oxford, 1933.

Zimmerman, Benedict, ed. Monumenta historica Carmelitana, Lérins, 1907.

Index

Louis II, duke of Bourbon, 302; hostage for King John II, 283

Louis, count of Etampes: role in negotiations for peace between France and Navarre, 134, 303; marriage, 272

Louis I, count of Evreux and Etampes, 194

Louis II of Evreux, 304

Louis I, count of Flanders and Nevers, 44, 178; driven from country, 33, 153; sister, 35

Louis II, count of Flanders, see Louis II de Mâle

Louis, count of Nevers, see Louis I, count of Flanders

Louis II, count of Sançerre, 44, 178

Louis, count of Tarentum, 109, 277

Louis II, viscount of Beaumont, 121, 293

Louis de Chalon, the Green Knight, 299

Louis I de Châtillon, count of Blois, 44, 178

Louis II de Mâle, count of Flanders, 290, 298; ancestry, 47; reluctant betrothal to daughter of Edward III, 47, 184; flight: marriage with Marguerite of Brabant, 48, 184 f.

Louis of Harcourt, 97, 265, 266

Louis of Navarre, 53; kingdom governed by, 60

Luc, John de, Brabançon knight, 210

Maccabees, new, 264

Machaut, Guillaume de, 260

Maillart, Jean, 245

Mainmares, Sir William de ("Maubue"), 58, 59, 203

Malestroit, truce of, 38, 165

Malet, Jean, sire de Graville, 58, 202

Malmesbury, monk of, 214; quoted, 218

Manchuria, plague, 187, 189

Manny, Sir Walter, 270

Mantes, partisans of duke of Normandy in, 117; exposed to great peril, 118; seized by dauphin's men, 120 f., 287; treaty drawn up at, 203; escape of Navarrese from, 288; taken by regent's men, 289; church of Notre-Dame de, 289

Manuscripts of the Chronicle, 20-28; see entries under Arundel manuscript; Chronicle of Jean de Venette

Marcel, Etienne, prévôt, 7, 228; Jean de Venette temporarily a partisan of, 5, 8; killed, 14, 81, 245, 246; took council with citizens of Paris, 67 f.; entreated regent to be merciful to citizens of Paris, 71 f.; council concerning government of Paris, 74; fear of duke of Normandy: plan to turn keys of

Paris over to king of Navarre, 79-80; members of party beheaded, 81; plea for help for people at Dreux, 224; misled the people: charge against duke of Normandy, 224; speech justifying murder of marshals, 225; seizure of royal artillery, 233, 235; letter to regent re complaints of Parisians, 233 ff.; first invitation to Charles of Navarre, 238; released English prisoners, 240

Marcel, Gilles, 245

Marche, Sir Richard de la, 172

Mareul, the Bascon of, see Jean de Sault

Margaret, wife of emperor Lewis, 153, 290; inheritance of Holland and Hainaut passed to, 168

Marguerite of Brabant, marriage with Louis II de Mâle, count of Flanders, 48, 185

Marguerite of Burgundy, 277

Marguerite, countess of Flanders, 222; marriage with Philip de Rouvre, duke of Burgundy, 11, 48, 163, 185

Marguerite of France, countess of Flanders, 278

Marguerite of Valois, countess of Blois, 160

Maria of Portugal, 304

Marie, queen of Aragon, 195

Marie, wife of Robert of Bar, 195

Marie of Blois, 284, 300

Marie of Valois, 277

Markaunt, Robert, 107, 275; cunning, 110; death, 111

Marmot, fur-bearing, subject to epidemic plague, 187

Marriages following plague, 50, 190

Marshals, murder of the, 14, 68, 224, 225

Martel, Guillaume, 97

Mary, daughter of Edward III, 166

Marys, poem on the three, 3

Mass, vision sent during, 31; the five main sections, 147; Introit of the, 269, 270, 271

Matilda of Artois, 151, 152

Maubue, see Mainmares

Mauclerc, term applied to Peter of Dreux, 35, 160

Mauconseil, castle, 87; taken by English, 84

Mauny, Oliver de, 288

Mauron, battle of, 39, 165, 167

Meaux, Geoffroi de, 150

Meaux, town: importance in blockade of Paris, 72, 243; strength of nobles at, increased, 77; misery caused by nobles: destruction of countryside, 78, 243; burned, 78, 243; Marché at, seized, 233; Paris artillery withdrawn to strengthen, 234; fortifi-

168-79 *passim,* 200, 263; revival of title "duke of," 164; struggle of lords for local liberties against Valois kings, 206
Normans, defeated by English, 96, 265
Northampton, earl of, 270; in Brittany, 165, 166
Notre-Dame-des-Champs, burned, 99; English in vicinity, 102
Notre-Dame-du-Pré, monastery of, 41, 172
Noyon, English driven out, castle of Mauconseil destroyed, 87, 256
Nuns, compelled to leave their houses and to enter strongholds, 67

Offémont, d', marshal of France, 39
Order of the Bend, 306
Order of the Star, 167
Oresme, Nicolas, 150
Orléans, duke of, *see* Philip, duke of Orléans
Orléans, English attack upon, 84; establishments belonging to mendicant friars torn down, 95; plundered by Bretons, 107; freebooters at walls of, 110
Orly, fortified church destroyed, 99
Ostensor, see Liber ostensor
Otto of Brunswick, 277
Ourscamp, monastery of, 87
Outlaws, *see* Brigands

Pacy-sur-Eure, 117, 286
Paris, bishop of: appointed cardinal, 146
Paris, fortification, 12, 66, 224; student affray, 19, 20; alarmed by approach of English, 41, 173, 174; earthquake, 57, 201; misfortune added to misfortune, 67; Duke of Normandy's plan to take vengeance on, for murder of his followers, 71, 232; governors entreat Duke to be merciful: league formed by prévôt to involve all citizens, 72; importance of Meaux in blockade of, 72, 243; city gates, 72, 236; supply of bread from Corbeil cut off, 74; Charles of Navarre made captain of men of, 74; removed from office, 75; attitude prevailing in, 74, 238; citizens attacked nobles in fortress of Meaux, 77; overrun by nobles: indiscriminate slaughter, 78; fear of Duke of Normandy: chose Charles of Navarre to defend them, 79; altercation about custody of gates and about proclamations, 80; keepers of gates relieved of their watch, 80; high cost of provisions, 83, 250; blockaded, 83, 88, 97; effect of English occupation upon ringing of church bells, curfew, and matins,

85; blockade raised, 89, 239; church towers fortified in villages around, 99; fortresses around, returned by English, 104; citizens' distrust of nobles, 105; plague of 1363 in, 111 f., 279; people oppressed by friends and enemies, 113; complaint of citizens re soldiers and regent's failure to protect, 233 ff.; artillery withdrawn to strengthen Meaux and Montereau, 234; return of fortresses demanded, 235; prévôt and aldermen ordered to build defenses, 235; citizens ambushed and annihilated by English, 240; citizens killed at Meaux, 243
Paris, Parlement of: session for considering affairs of honor, 284
Paris, University of, 52, 193; sent deputation to Duke of Normandy in interest of peace, 72, 233; students assaulted by sergeants of the guard, 140, 310; supported demand of king of Navarre, 229
Paris militia, massacre of, at Saint-Cloud, 14
Paysan, John, 253
Pearls, prices, 63; restrictions on display of, 214
Peasants, Jean de Venette's unbiased view, 7; defense of Longueil, 12; subjected and despoiled by nobles, 66; miserably slain by knights and nobles, 77; attack upon English at Longueil, 90 ff., 258; defeat of the English, 91 ff., 258, 259; every misery increased, 94; oppressed by friend and foe alike, 95, 113; inability to work land, 98; oppressed and robbed by own lords, 105
Peasant uprising, *see* Jacquerie
Pèlerin de Vadencourt, 268
Penitents, 52, 149, 193 f.
Pepin des Essars, 245
Péronne, taken by John of Artois, 105, 272
Pestilence, *see* Plague
Peter IV, king of Aragon, 195, 286
Peter I, king of Castile, 286, 304; and Henry of Trastamare, disputing possession of Spain, 136, 304–5; alleged favoritism for Jews, 137, 306; propaganda against, 137, 305, 306; treatment of his queen: deposed: enormities reported of, 137, 305; forced to flee, 138, 307; married to Blanche of Bourbon, 305; declared his marriage null; married Juana de Castro: excommunicated, 305-6
Peter of Dreux, duke of Brittany, term applied to, 160, 161
Philip III, king of France, 151, 160
Philip IV, the Fair, king of France: grand-